FRICAN PENAL
YSTEMS

dited by ALAN MILNER

frican Penal Systems is the first book to
xplore the problems of African criminol-
gy. Sixteen distinguished contributors—
ociologists, lawyers, and psychiatrists—
ach an authority on some aspect of
frican penal problems, have collaborated
i this study. It begins with a general
urvey of the penal systems of fourteen
frican countries, variously English,
rench, or Portuguese, or wholly autoch-
ionous. The second section includes six
pecialized contributions on various de-
iled problems in the development and
peration of modern African penal sys-
ems.

In his introduction, Alan Milner de-
cribes the sociological forces responsible
r the increased crime in Africa today
nd examines the possibility of the growth
f a peculiarly African approach to the
olution of its penal problems.

The contents include: "The Congo
emocratic Republic," by Antoine Rub-
ens; "Ethiopia," by Steven Lowenstein;
Ghana," by Robert B. Seidman and
. D. Abaka Eyison; "Kenya, Tanzania
nd Uganda," by James S. Read; "Leso-
io, Botswana and Swaziland," by Robert
. Leslie; "Liberia," by Gerald H. Zarr;
Portuguese Africa," by Fernando O.
ouveia da Veiga; "United Arab Repub-
c," by Ahmad M. Khalifa and Badr El-
in Ali; "Zambia," by William Clifford;
Sentencing Patterns in Nigeria," by Alan
filner; "The East African Experience of
mprisonment," by Ralph E. S. Tanner;
Psychiatry and the Criminal Offender in
frica," by Alan Milner and Tolani Asuni;
Penal Policy and Underdevelopment in
rench Africa," by Jacqueline Costa;
Capital Punishment in South Africa," by
)avid Welsh; and "The Ghana Prison
ystem: An Historical Perspective," by
Robert B. Seidman.

THE EDITOR: Alan Milner is a fellow of
Trinity College, Oxford. From 1963 to
1965, he was Professor and Dean of Law
at Ahmadu Bello University, Zaria,
Nigeria. He is the General Editor of the
African Law Reports.

AFRICAN PENAL SYSTEMS

African Penal Systems

edited by ALAN MILNER

FREDERICK A. PRAEGER, *Publishers*

New York · Washington

BOOKS THAT MATTER

Published in the United States of America in 1969
by Frederick A. Praeger, Inc., Publishers
111 Fourth Avenue, New York, N.Y. 10003

© *1969, in England, by Alan Milner*

Library of Congress Catalog Card Number: 68-19858

Printed in Great Britain

Contents

PART TWO: SPECIAL PROBLEMS

Notes on the Contributors

EDITOR

ALAN MILNER   Fellow of Trinity College, Oxford. Formerly Professor of Law and Dean of the Faculty of Law, Ahmadu Bello University, Zaria, Northern Nigeria.

CONTRIBUTORS

BADR EL-DIN ALI   Assistant Professor of Sociology, Ein Shams University, Cairo, United Arab Republic.

TOLANI ASUNI   Specialist Psychiatrist and Medical Superintendent, Aro Hospital for Nervous Diseases, Abeokuta, Western Nigeria.

WILLIAM CLIFFORD   Senior Adviser, United Nations Asia and Far East Institute for the Prevention of Crime and the Treatment of Offenders, Tokyo, Japan. Formerly Principal, Oppenheimer College of Social Service, Lusaka, Zambia, and Senior Consultant in Social Affairs, United Nations in the Congo.

JACQUELINE COSTA   Assistante, Faculty of Law and Economics, University of Paris, Paris, France.

J. D. ABAKA EYISON   Chief Delinquency Officer, Ministry of Social Welfare and Community Development, Accra, Ghana.

AHMAD M. KHALIFA   Deputy Minister of Social Affairs and Chairman of the Board of Directors, National Center for Social and Criminological Research, Cairo, United Arab Republic.

ROBERT D. LESLIE   Senior Lecturer in Law, University of Botswana, Lesotho and Swaziland, Maseru, Lesotho.

NOTES ON THE CONTRIBUTORS

STEVEN LOWENSTEIN	Instructor in Law, Haile Selassie I University, Addis Ababa, Ethiopia.
JAMES S. READ	Reader in African Law, University of London. Formerly Senior Lecturer in Law, University College, Dar es Salaam, Tanzania.
ANTOINE RUBBENS	Professor of Law, University of Lovanium, Kinshasa, Congo Democratic Republic.
ROBERT B. SEIDMAN	Professor of Law, University of Wisconsin, Madison, Wisconsin, U.S.A. Formerly Special Visiting Research Professor of Law, University of Ghana, Legon, Ghana.
RALPH E. S. TANNER	Chairman, East African Institute of Social Research, Kampala, Uganda.
FERNANDO OLAVO GOUVEIA DA VEIGA	Judge of Portuguese Overseas Provinces, Lisbon, Portugal.
DAVID WELSH	Senior Lecturer in African Studies, University of Cape Town, Cape Town, South Africa.
GERALD H. ZARR	Instructor of Law, Louis Arthur Grimes School of Law, University of Liberia, Monrovia, Liberia.

Abbreviations

ABBREVIATIONS OF LAW REPORTS

A.C.	Law Reports—Appeal Cases
A.D.	Appellate Division of the Supreme Court of South Africa Law Reports
All E.R.	All England Law Reports
All N.L.R.	All Nigeria Law Reports
C.L.R.	Commonwealth Law Reports
C. & P.	Carrington and Payne's Reports
C.P.D.	Cape of Good Hope Provincial Division Law Reports
Cox C.C.	Cox's Criminal Cases
Cr.App.R.	Criminal Appeal Reports
Den.	Denio's New York Reports
E.A.	Eastern Africa Law Reports
E.A.C.A.	Selected Judgments of the East African Court of Appeal
E.A.P.L.R.	East African Protectorate Law Reports
E.D.L.	Eastern Districts Local Division Reports
F. & F.	Foster and Finlason's Reports
F.S.C.	Selected Judgments of the Federal Supreme Court of Nigeria
G.L.R.	Ghana Law Reports
G.W.L.	Griqualand West Local Division Reports
K.B.	Law Reports—King's Bench Division
K.L.R.	Kenya Law Reports
L.L.R.	Liberian Law Reports
N.E.	North Eastern Reporter
N.M.L.R.	Nigerian Monthly Law Reports
N.P.D.	Natal Provincial Division Law Reports
N.R.L.R.	Northern Rhodesia Law Reports
N.(R.)N.L.R.	Northern (Region of) Nigeria Law Reports
N.Y.	New York Reports
N.Y.S.2d.	New York Supplement (Second Series)

O.P.D.	Orange Free State Provincial Division Law Reports
Q.B.	Law Reports—Queen's Bench Division
R. &. N.	Rhodesia and Nyasaland Law Reports
S.A.	South African Law Reports
S.C.	Reports of the Supreme Court of the Cape of Good Hope
S.L.J.R.	Sudan Law Journal and Reports
S.R.	Southern Rhodesia Law Reports
St.Tr.	State Trials
S.W.A.	High Court of South West Africa Reports
T.L.R.	Tanganyika Law Reports
T.L.R.(R.)	Tanganyika Law Reports (Revised)
T.P.D.	Transvaal Provincial Division Law Reports
T.S.	Transvaal Supreme Court Reports
U.L.R.	Uganda Protectorate Law Reports
W.A.C.A.	Selected Judgments in the West African Court of Appeal
W.A.L.R.	West African Law Reports
Wend.	Wendell's New York Reports
W.L.D.	Witwatersrand Local Division Reports

OTHER ABBREVIATIONS

Ag.	Acting
B.L.A.	Bulletin législatif algérien
B.O.	Bulletin Officiel
C.J.	Chief Justice
E.A.L.J.	East African Law Journal
F.C.J.	Federal Chief Justice
JT	Journal des tribunaux
J.O.	Journal Officiel
RO	Recueil officiel des lois fédérales
DP	Recueil périodique et critique Dalloz
S/o	Son of (in E.Afr. case names)

Preface

The more the attention that is focused on the developing countries of the world, the more clearly can be seen the social problems which inevitably accompany development. Much less obvious are the proper solutions to these problems, bedevilled as they are with differential economic and social development, confusing and conflicting legal systems and a wide, frighteningly unexplored range of community structures.

The states of modern Africa share all these problems. All are groping with more or less decisiveness towards their solution. Too often, the appropriate skills to analyse and plan, to project and estimate, are not available. Imagination may be lacking, or money not forthcoming. And in the end, the economic, social, educational and legal structure often remains largely unchanged.

This generalization only too aptly describes the process of penal reappraisal in Africa today. Crime is becoming increasingly common but the social and governmental machinery for coping with it is often neither well-adapted to the task, nor sufficiently developed to measure up to international standards. Decisions are taken and changes made without full and informed consideration of either the consequences or the alternatives; penal developments in foreign countries (usually former colonial powers) are imitated without any examination of the contrasts in vital aspects of the cultures of the two nations; or, worse still, penal measures are made more violent or repressive simply as a means of making life more unpleasant for the political opponents of the government.

Criminology has not yet begun to flourish in Africa and this book is the first small effort to nurture such interest as there is. It is offered with a view to distributing information about experiences in all parts of the continent, so that each country may see the many problems it shares in common with others and derive some benefit from examining their solutions to these same problems.

My foremost and warmest thanks must go to my colleagues who

have contributed to this book. They responded admirably to my original suggestion that they should prepare surveys of their national penal systems, even though to many of them the suggestion must have seemed overly ambitious. That they have been able to construct such comprehensive studies where little existed in the way of prior research and where information could often be obtained only by personal inspection and inquiry, is a tribute to their scholarship and perseverance. That more of them are lawyers than would normally be expected amongst contributors to a survey of this kind is a direct consequence of finding that they were often the best qualified of those available to undertake the work.

Planning a study on a continent-wide basis is never straightforward. It was certainly easy to underestimate the problems of collecting penal information from the nations of Africa, and in the event it is a combination of political, developmental and communications problems which has restricted the scope of this survey.

The political problems have not been slight. Inquiries about matters involving state security in a continent which is in a political turmoil can often be misinterpreted. In South Africa in particular, possible contributors were deterred by the prospect of infringing the rigid provisions of the Prisons Act; the fear was seen to be very real when 1965 brought a crop of prosecutions under the Act, arising out of the publication of purported descriptions of prison conditions. A correspondent in another country was deported after, though not by reason of, his agreeing to contribute. Civil war in another led to a correspondent's abandoning his commission; the holder of high political office in yet another was unable to start work because he was removed from office and contact with him was lost.

Secondly, the very process of development in Africa has affected the availability of material to be included in this survey. Where penal facilities are primitive and trained personnel non-existent, there is obviously little prospect of informed comment coming from within the system. Again, it may be that the rate of change in a country is enough to deny the possibility of a study which can have any lasting validity: as a distinguished lawyer in Senegal explained, its penal system was 'en pleine évolution' and any analysis of existing penal structures 'risquerait d'être périmée rapidement'. In Algeria, to give another example, the extensive disturbances following

xii

the revolution had considerable impact on the penal services, though nothing in comparison with the dramatic action of the country's President in closing fifty-eight of its prisons in 1965.

Thirdly, communication with the contributors has never been easy. At no time have they been gathered together in a single place, or even in a single country. In some cases it proved impossible to establish any contact with potential contributors; in others, contacts once established were lost by failure to answer letters, and promises were made, ultimately to be broken. In the absence of a common language not all my inquiries, requests and suggestions were at first understood, but I am grateful to my friend, Elisabeth Canin, for her help in translation which allowed me to correspond fully and more confidently with my French-speaking colleagues. Chapters 1 and 13 I translated from the original French myself and any errors are my own.

Curiously enough, sudden pressures for information about Africa have also had the effect of restricting the scope of the volume. Dr Stephen Shafer's *International Corrections*, published by the Chandler Publishing Co., San Francisco, in 1967, includes a report on South Africa (which the author was unwilling to reproduce here) and a modified version of Chapter 9 of the present volume. My own study of *The Nigerian Penal System*, to be published by Sweet and Maxwell Ltd. and the African Universities Press, will deal in considerable detail with the penal policies and development of that country. Chapter 10 of the present volume is a limited study drawn from that work.

Work first began on the book in 1963, when I was the Dean of the Faculty of Law of the Ahmadu Bello University, Zaria, Nigeria. On giving up that position in 1965, I was able to continue my own writing and other editorial work during my tenure of a Bicentennial Fellowship at the University of Pennsylvania Law School. I shall always remain grateful to the Dean and faculty of that School for allowing and encouraging me to pursue my African interests during that year.

Of the successive secretaries who have typed many drafts of each chapter, those who have borne most of the burden and who must have my grateful thanks are Beverly Solomon in Philadelphia and Angela Kniveton in Oxford.

ALAN MILNER

Introduction ALAN MILNER

The making of generalizations about Africa is a foolish pastime. From the basic question of the forms of social organization to such matters as economic development, urbanization and industrialization, the level of inter-cultural contact, linguistic forms, monetary forms, religious affiliation and ethnic composition, it is a continent which displays the widest imaginable range of alternatives.

Having said that, let me generalize. One can say with some degree of assurance that little is known about criminality in Africa. Even the volume of criminality cannot be estimated with any accuracy.

The reasons for this lack of information lie in the varying extent to which centralized authority has had an impact upon the administration of each African state. Behaviour which the legal norms of the state designate as criminal will only be recorded as such when there are state officials available to carry out the recording task— and police or administrative services notoriously do not function effectively in many of the more isolated parts of Africa. Even when they do, it may be that the community more easily tolerates breaches of the legal norms than it does the official representatives themselves—often giving rise to a crucial breakdown in reporting even before the recording can begin. This will be particularly true wherever, as we shall later see, the authority of colonial legal patterns has been superimposed upon those of the traditional order, producing areas in which the cultural insensitivity of the law is clearly marked.

In the turbulent political context of twentieth-century Africa, too, the face of crime may take on confusing aspects. It may become confused with the murder, looting and destruction of civil war; with the flourishing or crushing of rebellion; and with the struggle for political independence or relief from discriminatory racial policies. All these factors mean that the level of the recording of crime which can, for example, be achieved in Europe and the United States, imperfect though it may be, cannot be achieved in Africa.

And when the notorious difficulties of census-taking are added to this confusion, the possibility of computing meaningful crime rates with reference to population size disappears completely.

We cannot therefore speak with precision about the quantity of crime in Africa. None the less, all the literature speaks, perhaps inevitably, of African crime being a problem of the developing urban areas. The urban areas are those in which the strength of the police and the concentration of the population will be greatest; hence the greater likelihood of the more consistent recording of a heavier volume of crime. But the size of an urban operation is only one face of the criminal picture; it is the social processes at work in the creation or development of towns and cities which properly form the focus of the study of modern African crime.

Cultural change has long been recognized as a basic factor in the creation of situations of social pathology and the African continent offers the prime illustration of rapid political, social and economic development producing new situations of personal and social stress. The bases of traditional society are being replaced; new values and aspirations, new forms of social organization, new economic and political structures are developing in place of the old. Yet development is differential: traditional forms still co-exist with the new, partially modified forms, with those which are unmodified and with those which have either evolved completely or sprung fully grown out of the heads of the new states. As the twentieth century wears on, the interaction between the different levels of development intensifies, more individuals and communities are caught up in the vast cultural changes taking place, and the stresses increase.

The century so far has seen the greatest population movements recorded in Africa. The new ways of life have brought and are continuing to bring the continent into the international arena. Ports, industrial complexes, cosmopolitan cities, commercial developments and administrative centres are largely creatures of the last hundred, even the last fifty years. Though externally inspired, they have changed the internal face of Africa by stimulating massive population shifts. As trunk roads and railways have opened up each country still further with every passing year, the townward drift of Africans has become more pronounced. There may still be only seven or eight cities with populations of more than half a million,

2

but such has been the change brought about by western contact that now one in every five lives in an urban area.

The incentive to migrate has of course come from this industrial, commercial and administrative development. The continued existence of European-fashioned urban areas and the successful operation of industry and commerce have always depended on the ready availability of African wage labour. Of their capacity to attract it there has never been any doubt. The cash motive is strong: the contrast to the traditional low-level subsistence economy is as striking as any that can be imagined, and the inducement to take part in a relatively thriving cash economy, filled with the status symbols of the European way of life, has often been overpowering.

Migration has therefore taken place in every African country. Usually it has taken the form of the permanent or periodic movement of young men to work in cities, in mining and industrial areas, or on farms. In some cases, a regular connection with home is maintained, as where migrant workers return home with their profits from time to time, or only take on the migrant work for the purpose of saving enough to establish themselves permanently in their home environments. At other times, the young man moves to the town as the advance guard for his wife and children, and they join him at a later stage when he has found a means of livelihood and at least temporary housing for them. Many studies have emphasized that, at least in the early stages of development, the African urban population shows a distinct over-representation of young adult males in its age-sex distribution—the group which, significantly enough, is likely to be the most crime-prone.

The impact of development is thus being felt in the creation of new social patterns in the cities and towns of Africa. The anomic newcomer, the unassimilated village-oriented African transposed into a different context, is one aspect of the problem; the destitute children, looking to the big city for thrills and finding only markets to sleep in, and pilfering and prostitution to keep them fed, are another; the second-generation town-dweller, caught up in a status-conscious, acquisitive culture, with ends in view but no means to reach them, is yet another. These are the personnel of most of the known crime in Africa today. Let us now examine the crime-producing social stresses more closely.

Unemployment, lack of skills to succeed in a competitive economy, existence at or below subsistence level, malnutrition and general ill-health are not the necessary lot of the migrant African, but too often they accurately describe his predicament. Nor are they necessarily associated with criminal behaviour. In the subsistence economy of the African village, all these disabilities are to be found and yet fail to be catastrophic when the bonds of kinship obligation are strong enough to support the individual. The crucial difference lies in the context: the urban philosophy is individualistic and acquisitive, the pressures are for individual achievement and self-maintenance, the kinship obligations become attenuated, and under-achievement and failure predispose to less orthodox ways of succeeding.

Once predisposed, the opportunity for crime can more readily be found in the urban than the rural environment. Wealth is ostentatiously displayed in shops, houses, offices, factories, personal dress and possessions. The economic differential existing between those who have succeeded in the urban environment and those who have not, is not merely a difference—it is a gulf. And in contrast to the egalitarian village, the social and economic caste lines are drawn firmly, albeit not clearly. Upward mobility and its first step of the acquisition of personal possessions can be seen as an avenue open to the African—perhaps even more so following the recent independence of many of the countries—and yet is often frustrated for him by the insistence on qualification and skill as prerequisites of success.

At a much simpler level, it is probably true that the very existence of an urban complex provides more opportunity for law-breaking, as there are many more laws to break than in a less rigidly ordered context. These may be crimes in only an administrative sense—infractions of public health laws, building regulations, market rules, street-trading ordinances—but nonetheless they account for a significant proportion of the total volume of offences. They may, indeed, be criminal laws which strike at the very root of the culture, such as discriminatory pass laws, or laws regulating the employment, residence, education and welfare of Africans in a European-dominated state, or, for example, regulations governing street trading or sleeping in the open, regulating, in fact, the very means of

4

livelihood of whole groups of the population. And if regulations are so framed as to permit conviction without the offender's knowledge that his actions are criminal, it is easy to understand the dilemma of many of those who are unassimilated into the urban context and unfamiliar with its regulated folkways.

It is easier, too, to find in the town a broader range of interests, conflicting patterns of values, deviant individuals and groups, and heterogeneous types of behaviour, which at the worst may confuse and at the best will offer a choice of action to the individual. Sudden exposure to this pattern will often give him for the first time the opportunity for deviance, especially where his previous exposure has been to the largely homogeneous values and life patterns of the traditional culture.

The range of alternatives in social relations is, of course, crucial here. Not only does it offer the opportunity for deviance but the nature of urban relationships themselves effectively influences the intensity of the controls operating upon an individual. The social controls of the village context are believed to be as complete as can be devised in human relationships. The individual's dealings with others in this context will tend to be universalistic—all aspects of his life will affect and come under the scrutiny of those with whom he lives. He will in fact physically live in common residence with many people, connected to them by bonds of kinship and a mutual sense of obligation and support.

Yet the urban context is classically the context in which these life forms cannot exist in this state. The individual becomes more aware of himself as an individual, since the whole orientation of modern commercial and industrial society is in the direction of recognizing and rewarding individual effort and achievement. His relationships will become particularistic as he moves between urban social groups; he lives with one group, takes recreation with another, works with another. The intensity of his relationship with a given group will diminish as his environment expands and the measure of control that any particular group can exercise over him diminishes correspondingly.

The reduction of family control—as compared with the traditional African context—is likely to be the most important. If the young worker has migrated alone, he will be truly on his own to the extent that his life-decisions have to be made by himself. True, he may receive economic support from relatives in the town or from the local unit of his tribal or district association, but he will not have the same universalistic relations with them as he had with his kinsfolk. The urban pressures make it less likely that there will be common, extended-family residence in the town, and the family therefore segments in housing. Economic pressures often make multiple marriage less of a practical proposition and so the number of dependants and the scale of the system of mutual obligations diminish. Seniority, a guiding force in village society, loses its social strength as the experience of the older age-groups becomes no longer relevant to the problems of the younger. Seniority is then challenged as a social value by skills and wage-earning capacity in the urban context. Bridewealth may continue to be paid, senior members of the family group may be advised or even consulted about the choice of marriage partner, but such a choice—just as with the choice of job, place of residence, social and political affiliations—becomes more and more individualistic.

These are the social forces at work, disrupting African communities at the very time that they are being built. What machinery exists for the resolution of these dilemmas and for the protection of the members of these communities? I would like to focus briefly on the criminal laws of Africa and the machinery the African countries have for dealing with criminal offenders.

In the middle of the twentieth century, we are seeing the demise of the multifarious systems of unwritten customary criminal law. They have now been or are being replaced by formal criminal codes or by a gradual legislative, administrative and judicial process by which the jurisdiction of customary tribunals is first limited and then superseded by the jurisdiction of the European-type courts. Several modern constitutions in Africa provide for the voiding of criminal laws which do not define offences precisely and for the non-application of penalties which are not specified in writing.

The demise of customary criminal law has largely meant the abandoning of those offences, procedures and sanctions which were evolved so as to be peculiarly sensitive to the local cultures. In the light of modern conditions, it is clearly right that many of them should have been abandoned: tribally-oriented rules and practices

6

which discriminate against non-members of the tribe, procedures which fail to meet international standards of fairness, and penalties which can be stigmatized as barbaric, have little place in the modern, forward-looking state. It must be remembered too that the cultures to which the customary laws were sensitive are rapidly being modified. The kinds of laws and procedures which are appropriate to resolving disputes in small, universalistic, face-to-face societies at a given economic level are not necessarily appropriate to the government of contemporary, internationally-oriented nations.

Accepting, however, that the customary laws are not in their entirety suitable for application in modern conditions does not answer the question whether they should be applied at all. We are, after all, dealing with conditions of differential development in each African country and there are areas in each one where the traditional culture and its attitudes continue to dominate. There are, moreover, particular areas of the criminal law which are for some reason—religious, moral or otherwise—particularly dependent upon the fabric of the society in which they operate. In one of the codification/unification projects which has concerned itself with customary criminal law, that of Kenya, it has been found that the most appropriate way of dealing with certain customary marriage and family offences has been to incorporate them into the formal penal code following the abolition of all other customary crimes. In the Sudan and Northern Nigeria, the pressures of Moslem majorities lead to the putting into statutory form of certain Islamic law offences, considered to be vital for the preservation of the religion, when other aspects of Islamic criminal law were replaced by common law codes.

By and large, however, the substantive criminal laws in force in Africa bear the clear mark of Africa's European mentors without much attempt at sensitivity to the context. The policy of the Continental European powers to treat their colonies merely as overseas extensions of the mother jurisdiction, resulted in the extension of French, Spanish and Portuguese law to Africa. British Africa has taken first the model of the Indian Penal Code, and later various Colonial Office common-law-based codes, as the groundwork of criminal law. The pattern has only been disturbed in the English-speaking countries of southern Africa, which built upon the pre-existing Roman–Dutch law, and in Sierra Leone, which took the

7

common law of crimes and, in the English fashion, grafted upon it legislation dealing with specific offences.

Although the political developments of the last ten years are unprecedented in Africa, legal development has been slow. The newly-independent countries have continued the criminal laws and penal systems established during their politically dependent periods, and their main aim, unless politically pre-empted as in southern Africa, has been to think out the basis for the unification of their multiple law systems.

That they should have done little or nothing about their ways of dealing with offenders is not particularly surprising. They have been concerned with establishing new political frameworks and overseeing the problems of the distribution of power and the development of the economy. Capital has been scarce and as far as possible has been allocated to development in order of priorities—an order in which penal development or redevelopment figures a long way from the top. Crime, as we have seen, accompanies development and only assumes quantitative importance once development has got well under way. The volume of crime in Africa has not yet reached disturbing proportions and governments have not yet been faced with crises caused by the inadequacy of penal measures.

Nor has national spirit, if it can ever be clearly identified, been mobilized in the direction of providing a peculiarly African orientation to the penal systems of the continent. The structure of the sanctioning machinery has been inherited from the colonial powers and has remained largely as it was before. A stronger argument might have been made fifty years ago for the establishing of forms of sanction which were wholly meaningful in the customary context. At that stage, there were clear signs of an uneasiness in the relationship of the externally-imposed law and the behaviour patterns of the communities. The penalizing of actions which the culture designated as harmless or even meritorious, the limitation of customary punishments, the rigidifying of trial procedures and the introduction of novel forms of sanction, all conspired to emphasize the gulf between rulers and ruled. In more recent times, these have been the very problems which have caused confusion in the giving of new laws to Ethiopia and Northern Nigeria.

But elsewhere the habits of two generations have made the gulf less unbridgeable. The European standards of adjudication and sanctioning have been consciously and consistently put forward as civilized, prestigeful and desirable. The professional and administrative *élites* have been educated within the European frame of reference and their value-patterns have become more closely assimilated with those of the Europeans. And the expansion of African horizons, as we have already seen, has brought quantitatively more familiarity with the attitudes of urbanism and less adherence to traditional laws and ideals.

How far, then, are the penal systems of modern Africa 'appropriate' to Africa? The answers vary. Appropriateness in terms of the effectiveness of individual measures of punishment has seldom been tested, for few African countries have yet produced the trained manpower to carry out proper evaluations. More important, though, is the probability that the spirit of inquiry has not yet extended this far: indeed, many modern European countries are only just at the point of acknowledging that the planning and development of penal facilities should be preceded by trained evaluation. The result is that in so far as there have been any developments at all in the penal practices of modern Africa, they have been based either on clearly *a priori* assumptions or the demands of political expediency.

The new minimum sentence provisions in Tanzania and Ghana extend the familiar security device to fresh areas. Malawi in 1965 reintroduced the age-old European measure of forfeiture as a means, euphemistically speaking, of 'liquidating the indebtedness of those who have dishonoured their civil obligations as a result of treasonable or subversive activities'. Shortly before, it had—one may assume, not after considering sociological evidence—reintroduced public executions; in the same year the Cameroun Republic recorded the public executions of the murderers of foreign missionaries, and 1966 has seen the public hanging of the Government's political opponents in the Congo. The government of Northern Nigeria's remodelling of its penal laws in 1959 involved among other things the statutory enactment of a traditional Moslem lashing penalty and the introduction of new compromise procedures—but parliamentary questioning was directed not so much at their effectiveness as at the possible extension of the law to include public executions and

9

amputations. A contrasting measure of mercy—motivated to no greater degree by criminological considerations—was President Ben Bella's decree closing fifty-eight Algerian prisons in 1965, which effectively reduced the country's institutional facilities by half and resulted in the release of one-sixth of its criminal prisoners.

There is change but there is little progress. Significant advances in the use of probation, innovations in sentencing procedure and evaluation, or the application of more sensitive therapies in correctional work, are lacking. In some cases, to be sure, they are lacking because there has never been any motivation to think that they may be necessary. But mostly it is the familiar tale of lack of resources to apply to the low priority item of penal development.

In occasional sharp relief one can see instances of traditional or colonial sanctioning that would do credit to any modern penal system. Extra-mural labour in Tanganyika, Tunisia, Lesotho and Botswana; rural prison camps with agricultural training in many countries; the reduction or abolition of corporal punishment in the Portuguese colonies and Liberia; the institution of 'productive hard labour' in Ghana or 'educative labour' in Tunisia; the frequent customary use of compensation or restitution as customary sanctions in lieu of punishment; and the compromise procedures of Botswana and the countries which have, now or formerly, adopted the model of the Indian Penal Code.

One hopes that the future will bring an increase in governmental interest in the systematic study of crime, its prevention and correction. Prevention and correction without any doubt are more difficult tasks than the mere study of crime. Correction is more complex and often less practicable than prevention—but this is where our study starts. The following chapters present a record of what exists in the way of African penal facilities and sketches the outline of some of the problems currently being faced. The sharing of experiences will not solve these problems but our hope is that it may stimulate interest and activity in the more systematic inquiry needed to develop the penal systems of Africa.

Part One
Penal Systems in Africa

I
The Congo
Democratic Republic

ANTOINE RUBBENS

I Introduction

No general criminal statistics are available for the Congo after 1959. The day after the country's declaration of independence, the majority of the officials in the administrative service of the courts resigned, together with a large proportion of the colonial judiciary itself. At that time, their Congolese replacements were not ready to take over their work. The 'auxiliary magistrates' appointed immediately were neither qualified nor able to supply meaningful and accurate data. At present the hope is that the progressive build-up of the magistracy with Congolese lawyers—graduates of the local (Kinshasa and Lubumbashi) and overseas universities and diploma-holders from the National Institute of Law and Administration—will soon result in the proper functioning of the administrative services.

II The System of Criminal Law

Side by side with the European criminal laws introduced by the Belgians, customary criminal laws have always existed in the Congo. Their application was always severely restricted by the colonial regime, with the result that at the present time they can only be applied by the customary courts—and their powers have been strictly limited. They are only allowed to impose sentences of imprisonment up to one month and fines up to a maximum of one thousand francs; when the same act is both characterized as criminal by the customary law and punishable under the written law by at least five years' imprisonment, the customary courts cannot take cognizance of it even though the sentence in fact called for would be within their customary powers; the professional courts always take precedence over the customary courts and can even withdraw cases which are pending before the latter and assume jurisdiction over them themselves; and the range of customary penalties has in fact been so reduced that the customary courts can only impose sentences of imprisonment and fine. In consequence, the criminal jurisdiction of the customary courts has dwindled almost to nothing and they are concerned as much with civil matters as with anything else.

The basic provision of the Congolese criminal law is the Penal Code of 1888 as substantially amended (after many partial revisions) in 1940. Although based primarily on the Belgian Penal Code, it was nonetheless devised to take account of the special circumstances of the Congo. It contains a number of provisions which can only be seen as designed to reinforce colonial domination. The infamous *passe-partout* law of 1918[1] (modified many times until it was put into its final form in 1959), for example, unmistakably bears this mark, though it must be added that the penalties it prescribed were not severe. At the same time, other provisions, such as those punishing serious offences against duly constituted authority (articles 136–138) and endangering the security of the State (articles 181–202) follow a pattern similar to that found in even the most liberal western democracies. Many provisions of the Code, on the other hand, were devised to meet peculiarly African social situations. Thus articles 57–62 are aimed at prohibiting recourse to 'superstitious' means of proof (referring particularly to ordeals), the mutilation of dead bodies, and cannibalism, ritualistic or otherwise; article 97 penalizes the misuse of labour; and an ordinance supplementary to the Code punishes the growing of, possession of, and traffic in Indian hemp.

With the change to Republican status, the criminal law has scarce-

16

ly changed. A decree of December 16th, 1963, however, strengthens the state security laws, whilst decrees of November 11th and December 18th, 1964 proscribe certain military offences.

III Judicial Organization

The court structure inherited from the colonial regime has been continued in its existing form, even though it is patently out of date.

(1) The co-existence of a system of professional courts of unlimited jurisdiction with a system of native tribunals only having jurisdiction over Congolese nationals, is hard to reconcile with the structure of the modern Republic. This is especially true when it is remembered that the professional courts take precedence over and control the customary courts.

(2) The territorial boundaries of the various judicial divisions are still determined by the administrative sub-divisions of colonial times, and do not correspond to the boundaries of the provinces which are the present-day political units.

(3) Many senior judicial offices are still held by expatriates, who are either former colonial magistrates or others recruited under overseas technical assistance agreements.

The government has made such provisional arrangements as it has been able to meet the country's immediate needs. First, a decree of January 6th, 1961 transformed the position of auxiliary magistrate, which in colonial times was simply one of a substitute available to be called upon to fill a vacancy, into a permanent full-time appointment. This became necessary upon the extensive withdrawal of the colonial magistracy from the country following independence, with a resulting threat to the effective continuation of the court system. Secondly, an ordinance of October 31st, 1963 was passed in order to cope with the resulting difficulties in judicial administration, giving power to transfer a case from the jurisdiction of a superior court to that of another, when public safety or genuine suspicion of the adequacy of the court demanded it. Previously it had only been possible to do this within the jurisdiction of the same superior court. Thirdly, an ordinance of February 29th, 1964 authorized the creation of courts martial in disturbed areas of the country, with extensive jurisdiction and powers even over civilians. The measure was repealed on the bringing into force of a new military judicial system in December 1964.

All these measures were temporary expedients, and the official statements of the reasons for their introduction scarcely attempted to conceal the fact. With the further changes of power which have taken place in the course of the last two years, little has been achieved in the direction of securing the stability of the judicial system. One may still only express hope for the future rather than speak of substantial present progress; but the hope is for the short-term transfer of judicial power into local hands.

IV The Objectives of the Penal System

It is difficult in a disturbed transitional period to identify any precise official penal policy. In theory, all the classic principles of punishment are recognized as basic elements in the processes of judicial adjudication and penal administration: justly proportional punishment, individualization of sentence, deterrence, the protection of society, and the rehabilitation of offenders and their reintegration in the community. The political difficulties and social disorder which have beset successive governments since independence have, however, had the effect of inevitably compelling greater emphasis to be placed on the generally deterrent and socially protective aspects of penal action. In these circumstances, it is all the more reassuring to

18

see that, despite all the problems, certain principles of social defence have been maintained and that these are, as we shall see,[2] in fields in which the Republic has earned a reputation for progressive thinking.

V General Methods of dealing with Offenders

Penal measures under Congolese law comprise the death penalty, imprisonment (indefinite or for a fixed term), fines (with imprisonment as an additional sanction in default of payment), restriction on place of residence (for a specified period), and prohibition from staying in a particular place or area (for a specified period). Deprivation of civil rights is no longer a practicable penalty, though eligibility for public office depends upon freedom from conviction for infamous crime.

The basic prison legislation of October 15th, 1931 envisages a prison regime which will promote the correction of offenders and at the same time encourage their rehabilitation. Yet despite the considerable energy expended in the final few years before independence, the colonial government was unable to make much progress in the task of developing a constructive approach to corrections. Lack of qualified staff and suitable prison accommodation were the main obstacles; more recently, the dispersal of such qualified staff as there was, and the gross overcrowding of the prisons following the internal disturbances, has prevented further development. The threads of the interrupted programme have only been picked up by the authorities in so far as they have been able to continue experimentally with model prisons: Makala prison at Kinshasa, Kasapa prison at Lubumbashi and Buluo prison at Jadotville. Here, the physical facilities will be adequate, once the number of inmates has been strictly limited.

The conditional release of prisoners who do not constitute a danger to the community is envisaged by article 41 of the Penal Code. In practice, this amounts to the shortening of the sentences of those offenders who have shown good potential by satisfactory behaviour in prison. An ordinance of December 6th, 1962 has notionally improved the system by making provision for supervision after release, though it must be admitted that no high degree of effectiveness will be achieved until properly qualified judicial and welfare officials are available to carry it out.

There is no adequate provision in the Congo for mentally abnormal offenders. Whenever it appears that the responsibility of an accused person has been affected by his mental condition, the court will bear it in mind and impose a lesser sentence. Whenever a mentally abnormal person constitutes a danger to himself or others, administrative procedures exist by which his detention may be ordered without any judicial action being necessary. In certain prisons there are psychiatric sections in which all those who are mentally disordered—whether committed by administrative process or on the order of a court—are kept together and given such minimal treatment as may be available.

VI Young Offenders

A decree of December 6th, 1950 makes available a special procedure for dealing with charges of delinquency against juveniles under eighteen years of age. The decree was brought into force as an experimental measure in 1953 in the Mid-Congo and Lower Congo districts and in the Katangese centres of Elisabethville (now Lubumbashi), Kipushi and Jadotville in 1959. The age of criminal responsibility was reduced to sixteen by legislation of November 10th, 1961.

Whilst one may have some reservations about the ideas underlying these provisions, there can be little doubt that the juvenile courts set up under them have produced extremely satisfactory results. Despite all the changes which have taken place in the judiciary, they have continued to function almost without interruption, though on occasions professional skill has been replaced by simple but remarkable devotion to the cause of the children with which they deal. The juvenile reformatory at Madimba has tirelessly carried out its work and the section of the Kasapa prison given over to young offenders has remained in operation. Actual delinquency has nevertheless continued to increase so rapidly that it is no longer possible to accommodate all the juveniles to whom special attention needs to be given. There is no institution for girls, though the internal disorders of recent years have given rise to an increase in juvenile prostitution and the association of young girls with gangs of criminals.

Even where the juvenile courts have not been set up, the law allows the ordinary courts to send young offenders to the special institutions already mentioned. The overcrowding of the institutions and the disorganization of the transport and escort systems, however, mean that this is in practice very much a dead letter.

VII Capital and Corporal Punishment

Capital punishment has existed under the formal law since the introduction of the Penal Code. It already existed under many of the customary laws, although usually the payment of money compensation by the offender or his family to the victim's family allowed it to be commuted. Today, the death penalty is often commuted to an indeterminate sentence of imprisonment by the exercise of the President's prerogative of mercy. With renewed outbreaks of violence in recent years, the prerogative appears to be exercised less frequently than before, though no statistics are available to confirm or deny this belief.

Corporal punishment has never existed as a judicial penalty under the written law. The sentence of a dozen strokes of the cane was introduced into the customary courts in 1926, but this was reduced to a maximum of eight strokes in 1933 and abolished in 1951. Corporal punishment was for a much longer period of time available for prison offences: in 1906, the prison regulations allowed for disciplinary punishments of from ten to fifty strokes; the maximum was reduced to twelve in 1916, four in 1951 and abolished entirely in 1959.

VIII Conclusion

One cannot discern in the modern operation of the penal system any policy sufficiently definite to form a basis for future development. All the penal measures brought into force in the seven years since independence have been dictated by the needs of the moment and bear the unmistakable signs of temporary expediency.

But the intention of assuring a stable and responsible system of justice appears on all sides. Basic guarantees are now enshrined in the Constitution, and both the government and those working within the judicial system are concerned to maintain and improve upon the institutions created by the colonial regime despite the handicap of lack of adequate resources. The will is there; results will slowly follow.

Footnotes by a Visiting Sociologist*

In the Congo, as in so many newly independent countries south of the Sahara, the existing penal system is a marked survival of the structure established before independence. This is true of laws as well as institutions, and it would be surprising if it were not so. To make over the institutions into some new form, or to express traditional concepts more faithfully, would be both costly and disruptive at this early stage. Moreover, the characteristics of the new regimes are still being evolved and some of the basic principles are only just taking root.

The treatment of offenders in any country eventually expresses some of its society's fundamental values and deeper sentiments as these have become enshrined in the working out of the constitution, be it written or unwritten. Most of the African countries have had little enough time for this steady evolution of the principles and objectives of the treatment of offenders. Nevertheless some have initiated a process of local adaptation of the penal structure inherited from colonial administrations, especially in the integration of customary law and European penal codes.

There are a number of African states, however, which still have to settle to a basic constitution, and amongst these the disruptive events since independence in 1960 have made the Congo Democratic Republic prominent. Since 1960, the Congo has not been accorded either a settled constitution or any adequate period of implementation. Many of its institutions have been carried over from the Belgian administration and these have persisted unmodified in the Congo for longer than perhaps anywhere else in this part of Africa—owing to a great extent, of course, to the difficulty experienced by a succession of governments which have not had adequate time or sufficient security of tenure to give a positive new direction. At the time of writing, General Mobotu has assumed

* At the author's request, his identity has been withheld in order to avoid any embarrassment which his official position might otherwise cause.

power and this may mark the beginning of a new era. Already some fundamental changes have been made in the provincial and central government structures, and the names of the principal towns have been changed. It remains to be seen whether this tendency to revise and reform will eventually extend to the basic penal system.

Professor Rubbens has dealt with the provisions for the treatment of crime. It will be seen that, in practice, imprisonment, fines, probation and the suspended sentence remain the basic features of the system. More is provided by law than can be realized in practice, but this is a problem which the Congo shares with other countries in Africa.

Penal institutions for both juvenile and adult offenders are the responsibility of the Prisons Department of the Ministry of Justice. However, whereas most other government services in the Congo have been deeply affected since independence by transfers of some of the best personnel to promotion posts in other ministries and by the introduction of new or inexperienced staff to fill the vacancies, the Prisons Department has retained a considerable number of people with ten to fifteen years' experience. They are mainly people who were recruited and trained 'on the job' by the Belgians and who have continued to provide the basic skills necessary to this type of work. This continuity, in itself, has conferred an element of personnel stability and career interest.

It does not mean, however, that the service has escaped the debilitating effects of the economic recession. Funds for penal institutions are not easily come by in any country and in the Congo the money available for the maintenance and improvement of the service has often been lacking in recent years. It is not surprising, then, to find that most institutions suffer from inadequate security lighting, from equipment unrepaired, electrical alarm systems which no longer work, and dispensaries lacking essential medicaments. There is usually a severe shortage of transport, a need for more beds, bedding and recreational equipment, and a shortage of materials for the various workshops. This situation of inadequate funds is not unusual to prison services elsewhere in the world which are, by now, used to coming at the end of a country's budgeting. On the other hand it naturally tends to be more serious in the Congo because of the economic collapse: many things really essential for the minimum work are lacking. And the dearth of supplies is by no means peculiar to the Prisons Department. Economic recession and political uncertainty have left many departments short of materials and equipment: it may be true, however, that the penal service has suffered more than most since it is a service which does not readily attract financial help from abroad. Against this, the valuable sense of continuity in personnel may have saved the system from the worst effects of these years of political disruption and official penury and from the paralysing influence of political uncertainty.

The Penal Code provides the country with a series of penal institutions which follow closely the pattern of courts and tribunals. Thus, there is a *Central Prison* wherever a court of first instance is established, i.e. in the main centre of each of the six provinces into which the Congo was divided before 1960. These are now, as before 1960, in Kinshasa (Léopoldville), Mbandaka (Coquilhatville), in Kisangani (Stanleyville), in Bukavu, Luluabourg and Lubumbashi (Elisabethville). *District Prisons* are to be found in the main centre of any district not having a court of first instance. There were 19 of these in 1958, and 20 in 1963—an additional one having been provided in Katanga. In effect, this gives a District Prison to each town and region not already supplied with a Central Prison. At a lower level, one finds 114 *Territorial Prisons* (the same number as in 1958) in those areas or centres without either Central or District Prisons.

In addition, the pre-independence government provided for 82 prison annexes (reduced to 60 by 1963), 18 detention camps (halved by 1963), and 6 re-educational centres for juveniles (4 in 1963). In 1958 there also existed provision for 'itinerant' prisoners for labour on public works, but this idea does not seem to have survived independence.

The prison statistics of the Ministry of Justice show that between 1958 and 1963 there was a considerable reduction in the number of people employed in prison work. Against 3,493 employed in 1958 there were only 1,524 in 1963. Those employed in the Central Prisons had increased from 494 in 1958 to 743 in 1963 but there were substantial reductions elsewhere. District Prison staff fell from 571 to 234 in this period and the Territorial Prisons, which employed 1,286 people in 1958, had only 84 in 1963. It must be remembered, however, that these statistics followed a period when large areas of the country had seceded from central control and the normal procedure for making prison returns had been severely disrupted.

Admissions to prison in 1958 were 205,043 but only 97,388 in 1963. From a daily average population of 24,276 in 1958 there was a fall to only 12,285 in 1963. It is not suggested that crime had decreased during this period, and there is little to explain the fall in population in the penal institutions. It may have been, however, that because of the country's other problems the facilities for imprisonment were reduced and there was recourse to other measures for the disposal of cases. It could mean too that, with the political problems, the police were not arresting quite so many as in earlier years or that they did not have the facilities for their ordinary work, for it should not be overlooked that the police were also suffering a severe shortage of transport and equipment. It is more than likely, however, that returns for certain important areas could not be included.

It is difficult to give precise information as to the real level of crime in the Congo. Even before 1960, documentation on criminal statistics was difficult to find and since independence it has not usually been readily available. The return, however, transmitted by the Belgian Government to the Secretary-General of the United Nations on Non-Self-governing Territories (ST/TRI/B.1957/1.p.2) provides the information for Table 1.

For the benefit of those unacquainted with the terms in this table, both homicide and assaults are classified as either voluntary or involuntary and attract different penalties. Homicide with the intention to kill is known as '*meurtre*' and is punishable with life imprisonment. Where there is evidence of premeditation and planning, it becomes '*assassinat*' and is met with the death sentence in the Penal Code bequeathed by the Belgians to the Congo. Voluntary assaults or woundings (*coups et blessures volontaires*) may be punished with from a week's to six months' imprisonment or a fine. With premeditation this may become anything from one month's to two years' imprisonment and a higher fine; and if illness, incapacity to work, mutilation or disability results, then the sentence may be from two to five years' imprisonment and a higher fine.

The Congo Penal Code, as already explained by Professor Rubbens, also provides penalties for 'superstitious ordeals' and

26

TABLE I. STATISTIQUES DE LA CRIMINALITÉ, 1954–1956

Nombre de condamnations à charge de

Condamnations	Non-Autochtones			Autochtones		
	1954	1955	1956	1954	1955	1956
Assassinats et meurtres	3	6	—	406	414	431
Coups et blessures volontaires	139	218	80	8,584	9,934	8,617
Homicides et blessures involontaires	153	141	101	1,260	1,080	935
Atteintes à la liberté individuelle (Offences against personal freedom)	23	37	8	427	418	410
Vols et extortions (Thefts and cognate offences)	28	36	37	16,052	16,525	16,816
Autres infractions (Other offences)	198	233	204	20,785	21,763	21,192

'barbarous practices', for duelling, kidnapping, illegal detention and for the entering of a domicile without the occupant's permission. Theft without violence or threats carries up to five years' imprisonment and fine (or one or the other); but if there has been violence or threats, the penalty is raised from five to twenty years' imprisonment. Fraud or embezzlement is visited with imprisonment of from three months to five years and a fine; lesser penalties are prescribed for other fraudulent practices. Arson carries a liability to fifteen to twenty years' imprisonment if places of habitation, ships or shops are concerned and there are people present at the time of the fire; otherwise arson and damage have a gradation of lesser penalties. Rape or indecency committed with violence, fraud or threats is punished with six months' to five years' imprisonment, but this is raised from five to twenty years if the victim is under fourteen years of age.

These penalties may seem high but they have to be read against the considerable discretion given to judges to deal more leniently with offenders where there are special circumstances. This cuts the other

27

way as well, and judges can just as easily deal more severely with habitual offenders. Thus a decree of June 25th, 1913, allows a judge to reduce a statutory penalty where there are extenuating circumstances such as the youthfulness of the offender, the influence of custom, superstitious beliefs, provocation or drunkenness, or where there has been spontaneous indemnification of the injured party. And, conversely, a decree of August 8th, 1959, provides for additional penalties and preventive detention for recidivism, considerable discretion again being given to the judge. These two laws give a flexibility to the Congo penal system which allows a number of useful variations to meet individual circumstances.

Other provisions also exist for adapting the penalty to individual circumstances. Thus, where convicted offenders are subjected to one of several penalties depriving them of their liberty, they may be released conditionally after serving a quarter of their sentences but, in any case, not before they have served three months. Those sentenced to life imprisonment must have served at least five years before being considered for conditional release. During such a period of conditional release, an offender can be recalled for committing any further offence or for violating the conditions of his release.

The Code also provides for suspended sentences. The period of suspension is in the court's discretion but it cannot exceed five years. A suspended sentence cannot be ordered, however, if the sentence is one of penal servitude for more than one year, and it is denied to those who have previously served sentences of more than two months' imprisonment.

Whilst it is true that the structure of the Penal Code has not been altered since independence, it should be remembered that successive governments since 1960 have issued decrees to control certain types of behaviour, to increase penalties or to allow for emergency, extra-judicial procedure. A curfew for young people has more than once been imposed on Kinshasa, for example, to control delinquency. The Premier Bourgmestre of the town also created a few years ago a special juveniles squad amongst the police to try to control rising crime. He accompanied this by a number of regulations, e.g. *arrêté* No. 2016/CONT/61 of September 9th, 1961, prohibited juveniles under 16 from going into bars and night clubs. On June 6th, 1962, the age-limit was raised to 18. *Arrêté* No. 1077/CONT/61 of June 5th, 1962, forbids young people under 18 to be on public roads between 8 p.m. and 6 a.m.

To return now to the incidence of crime, the Report on the Administration of the Belgian Congo for 1958 which was presented to the Legislative Chamber in Belgium during the 1959/60 session, provided the following account of judgments in criminal cases:

TABLE 2. JUGEMENTS EN AFFAIRES PENALES, 1958

Type de tribunal	No. des tribunaux	No. des jugements
Territorial	140	6,816
Central	117	34,073
Sectorial	741	93,447
District	554	66,963

In addition there were 168,137 petty offences dealt with by customary tribunals. These included 43,456 matrimonial cases, 37,867 assaults and woundings, 11,482 thefts and breakings (including embezzlement and fraud) and 10,346 cases of threatening, abusing or defamatory language.

We have unfortunately no comparative figures for the years following independence. Just how valuable such a comparison would be, however, may be doubted, since the information above obviously leaves a great deal to be desired.

What seems probable is that crime has greatly increased since 1958. The growth of the main towns would suggest this, unless the Congo has an experience contrary to that of nearly every other country in the world. When one considers the violence and disruption since 1960, the obstacles to efficient police work and steady growth of unemployment, it is difficult to imagine that the Congo can have escaped the tendency for crime to rise as urban development continues. Such a rise is taken for granted by most newspapers and, as we have seen, it has led to special measures being taken to deal with young offenders in towns.

Probation, as this is known in Anglo-Saxon countries, plays little part in the penal system of the Congo. For adults it does not exist at all, for, as Professor Rubbens has pointed out, the ordinance of December 6th, 1962, needs staff for its implementation. For juveniles a form of supervised freedom is provided, but the short-age of social workers to implement it means that it has none of the close supervision and help characteristics which are normally associated with probation. It has some limited effect where, as in Kinshasa or Lubumbashi, a small group of social workers are employed for supervised freedom, but even here lack of transport and other obstacles make it difficult to apply with full effectiveness.

On the other hand, the legal provisions for juvenile offenders are very liberal. By a decree of December 6th, 1950, juveniles under the age of 18 are exempt from all criminal responsibilities. They are relieved of all liability to punishment and the emphasis is placed upon care, supervision and education. The law reserves juvenile cases to the Juvenile Court Judge. But because the law removes juveniles from the rigours of the Penal Code, it extends beyond the offences defined by the code. Indiscipline or misconduct by juveniles which give 'grave discomfort to their parents, tutors, or others responsible for their care' may be brought by such parents or guardians to the notice of the Juvenile Court Judge, who may treat them as he would delinquents. This also applies to juveniles leading disorderly lives, exposing themselves to the influence of prostitutes, to vagabondage or begging, i.e. those demonstrably in need of protection.

The measures at the disposal of the Juvenile Court Judge include releasing the juvenile (who has committed an offence defined by the Penal Code or is in need of protection or control) to the care of his parents or guardians with an injunction that he behaves better or is better supervised in future, or committing him to the care of the State up to the age of 21. State care is exercised by a designated person, society, charitable institution or one of the special re-educational centres organized by the state. If the offence might have been punished by the Penal Code with more than five years' imprisonment had the juvenile been an adult, the committal order may be extended by the judge beyond the age of 21 but not beyond 25. If the offence, however, was one which in the case of an adult would have been punishable by death (e.g. *assassinat*), the committal order may be extended by as long as twenty years after the age of 21. Finally, young people brought before the judge who are not released to their parents or guardians and who are not committed to the care of the state may be placed under the regime of supervised freedom which we have touched upon above. In such cases the judge will designate the persons (of either sex) who will be responsible for the supervision; such persons carry out the supervision under the direction and guidance of the officer of the Ministry of Justice who is charged with juvenile matters. As we have seen, this form of probation, whilst lacking nothing in law, is greatly deficient in practice.

It will be seen that the Congo has a system of social defence which is adequate both in its liberalism and reformative provisions and which bears comparison with that in most countries in Africa. As in most other countries south of the Sahara, however, it is often defeated by geography and by the limited means at the disposal of countries trying to raise their standard of living. The Congo is a vast territory in which it would be impractical to hope to have, for example, a probation system on European lines. Communications are difficult, and although young people living in towns away from their families could in theory be returned to their villages, the organization of escorts and transport creates problems which are almost insurmountable and which presuppose an expenditure far beyond the country's present means. Governments are overwhelmed with work and at the time of writing, although the law seeks to avoid sending young people to prison, there are some 200 young offenders in the Kinshasa Central Prison awaiting disposal. They are segregated from the adults but again the lack of means has prevented the government setting up a separate detention centre for them. The six institutions for the re-education of those juveniles committed to the state for such treatment have been reduced to four since 1960, but it is evident that more are required as soon as the funds and staff are available.

For the same reasons which make country-wide probation impossible, prison after-care or the supervision of those conditionally released is practically non-existent. Some of the prisons, such as Makala in Kinshasa or Jadotville in Katanga, are well-kept and well-run, but others are desperately short of the equipment and facilities they need to provide even a minimum service.

Meanwhile, the small band of devoted workers in this field gives great hopes for the future. In Kinshasa, with the help of volunteers the Juvenile Court Judge has established a small *kibbutz* for the agricultural training and settlement of selected juvenile offenders—

a scheme which has had the personal support of the Head of State himself. This may be expected to continue and be extended. In most of the large prisons the work provided for prisoners, in addition to building, blacksmithing, carpentry, and so on, included imaginative training in art and wood sculpture. The products show a remarkable aptitude on the part of the prisoners themselves.

These few examples will indicate that, with all its problems, the Congo has people with a real interest in the possibilities of penal reform. Indeed, read against the turbulent background of the past six years, the penal work in the Congo, for all its deficiencies and defects and despite, as Professor Rubbens shows, the fact that it has so far been difficult to move into a more imaginative stage of social defence, has shown quite remarkable resilience. This offers great hopes for development when the times and circumstances are more propitious.

NOTES

1. The decree is officially entitled 'A decree to penalize various actions when committed by natives'. The penalties it prescribes are not severe (one to seven days' imprisonment, or a maximum fine of 200 francs, or both) and the kind of actions envisaged are, for instance, the showing of disrespect to a European official, failure to respect established authority or the marks or insignia of such authority, refusal to give information when lawfully requested, the concealing of persons sought by the authorities, and so on.
2. See below, p. 21.

2
Ethiopia

STEVEN LOWENSTEIN

I The Legal Setting

Before the 17th century, the penal law of Ethiopia was primarily a matter of diverse customary practices, although both the Church,[1] concerning moral matters, and an emperor or other more localized kings enforced what might be termed penal sanctions concerning those matters directly affecting their power.[2] No integrated body of penal legislation existed, however, until some time in the 17th century when the *Fetha Nagast* or 'Law of the Kings' was introduced into Ethiopia.

The *Fetha Nagast* is a sophisticated compilation of legal prescriptions concerning both religious and secular matters, written in approximately the 13th century as a guide for a Christian population living within the Moslem society of Egypt.[3] Originally written in Arabic, it incorporated laws drawn from the Old and New Testaments, together with precepts based upon Roman law, the canon law of the Church, and Islamic law, and glosses from the proceedings of the early Councils of Nicaea and Antioch.[4] It was translated in Ethiopia into Ge'ez, the ancient Ethiopic language, and applied throughout the Christian areas of the country by the Church.[5] As is not uncommon in early attempts at criminal legislation, the penal sections of the *Fetha Nagast* tend to blend with the religious aura of the entire work.[6] Nevertheless, the concepts of penal liability set out in the law appear to have been quite advanced for their time.

The *Fetha Nagast*, together with customary law, particularly in non-Christian areas of the Empire, remained the applicable penal law of Ethiopia until November 2nd, 1930.* On that day, the day of

* All dates given in this chapter are presumed to be according to the Gregorian Calendar unless it is stated that they are according to the Ethiopian Calendar.

the coronation of Haile Selassie I, the first modern codified law, the Penal Code of 1930, was promulgated. The new Penal Code, unlike the *Fetha Nagast*, set out precise punishments for specifically defined crimes. Punishment was assessed in relation to title and wealth and the individual personality and motives of the offender. The most rigorous punishments were meted out to offenders of title and wealth, and then ranged down in severity as crimes were attributable to 'lawlessness', 'pride', 'envy', 'treachery', 'revenge', 'intemperance', 'quarrelsomeness', 'carelessness', and 'bullying'. The Penal Code of 1930 was said to have been based upon the *Fetha Nagast*,[7] an assertion quite necessary for its public acceptance at the time, though comparison of the two laws shows considerable disparity, particularly in the Special Part of the Penal Code which specifically prescribed each crime and its penalty. Although the Penal Code was considerably more sophisticated than the earlier *Fetha Nagast*, it remained in many ways vague and formalistic, lacking well-defined general principles and a comprehensive approach to the disposition and treatment of offenders.

It became apparent in the 1940s, after the reconquest of Ethiopia and with the enactment of a number of proclamations in the penal area, that a new and comprehensive penal code to meet the modern needs of developing Ethiopia would have to be drafted. Professor Jean Graven, Dean of the Faculty of Law and President of the Court of Cassation in Geneva, Switzerland, was commissioned to draft such a penal code. Work began in 1954; an *avant-projet* in French was presented by Professor Graven to the Codification Commission composed of both distinguished Ethiopians and foreigners, and after considerable discussion and the moulding of final text, the Code was translated into Amharic and English,[8] and presented to Parliament. The new Code went from Parliament to His Imperial Majesty for approval, was promulgated on July 23rd, 1957 and came into force on May 5th, 1958.

The Penal Code is composed of 820 articles constituting both a Penal Code and Code of Petty Offences. Although the Code draws to a limited extent upon the legal tradition of Ethiopia,[9] it is a modern, advanced law incorporating many of the most recent innovations in continental systems. There is little doubt that its primary source is the Swiss Penal Code of 1937, together with the pre-

1957 Swiss jurisprudence.[10] There are, of course, secondary sources, primarily the French Penal Code of 1810 with respect to general format,[11] the Yugoslav Penal Code of 1951 in relation to military offences, and more generally the Codes of Norway (1902), Italy (1930), Brazil (1940), and Greece (1950).[12]

Apart from notes taken during the discussions of the Codification Commission,[13] there is virtually no legislative history for the Penal Code. The drafter has not made available any *travaux préparatoires* that may exist, nor has he written an *explication de texte*. The records of Parliament are for the most part similarly unavailable. The question arises as to how ambiguous provisions within the new Code should be interpreted. Article 2 provides that interpretation shall be in accordance with the 'spirit', 'legislative intent' and 'purpose' of the Code. Apart from well-accepted tenets of code interpretation and textual analysis, the question remains as to whether Swiss treatises and jurisprudence should be considered, in those instances in which the Swiss provision is clearly the source of the Ethiopian, as the 'quasi-legislative' intent behind the provision. Although the spectrum of opinion runs from the complete adoption of Swiss jurisprudence, if not with binding effect at least with persuasive effect, to total disregard of possible Swiss sources, the writer believes that a sound middle position is possible. Where there is no legislative history or official guidance with respect to the use of Swiss materials, if it appears from the comparison of the relevant provisions that the Swiss Penal Code was clearly the source of the Ethiopian, the meaning attributed to the Swiss provision should be attributed to the Ethiopian provision. In exceptional cases, sound reasons relating to Ethiopian legal development or the specific needs of the country could be given to justify departure from what can be assumed to have been the drafter's (and presumably the legislature's) intent. In a sense, this would create a presumption in favour of pre-1957 Swiss interpretation rebuttable by reasons relating to the changing legal and social needs of Ethiopia. Such a position would make possible some degree of certainty of interpretation and control of possible judicial arbitrariness, and yet at the same time make allowance for differences in the historical and current development of Switzerland and Ethiopia.

An example may be helpful. Article 29 of the Ethiopian Penal

Code concerning 'impossibility' permits a judge to reduce punishment if an offence can be said to have been 'absolutely impossible'. The meaning of the words 'absolutely impossible' is unclear. There is no legislative history on the subject, and rather than allow judges simply to create a meaning for the term, it is suggested that pre-1957 Swiss sources should be consulted if similar language is used in the Swiss Code. The words *'absolument impossible'* appear in the relevant Swiss article;[14] after consulting the Swiss jurisprudence and treatises,[15] one learns that 'absolute' is set off against 'relative' impossibility, with certain types of cases falling within each category. It is maintained that the Swiss interpretation of these words should be adopted unless good reasons exist to the contrary. Now it may be felt in Ethiopia, despite the objective impossibility of an offence, that an individual who attempts to commit an offence, and is prevented by an absolute impossibility of which he had no knowledge, is subjectively quite as dangerous as one who, through better fortune, is able to complete his offence. Further, it may be thought that it is quite necessary, for policies of social defence in Ethiopia, to treat such individuals in the same manner as if they had completed the offence. These reasons would militate for a very narrow interpretation of 'absolute' to limit the use of what amounts to a partial defence of impossibility. Such reasons would offset the presumption in favour of Swiss jurisprudence and allow for flexibility within the rapidly changing legal system.

To a certain extent, the above discussion remains academic in present-day Ethiopia, where the development of the legal system has not kept pace with the promulgation of new codes.[16] There is as yet no organized bar, and although a Faculty of Law was founded in 1963, it was only in 1966 that a class graduated to swell the current small number of approximately twenty university-trained Ethiopian lawyers. There are few legally-educated judges, and a system of reporting court cases is only just beginning. In this setting, it is, of course, difficult to begin to apply a modern, sophisticated, continentally-inspired Penal Code. Many of the concepts embodied in the Code, particularly the general principles governing jurisdiction, attempt, participation, guilt, responsibility and concurrence of offences, are complex and quite difficult for a lay profession to comprehend and use. Other concepts are foreign to Ethiopia. The ideal of rehabilitation which pervades the Code, the provisions concerning the treatment of juveniles, consent to offences, probation, conditional release and numerous Special Part offences are innovations which are not widely understood. Although a beginning is being made in Addis Ababa and several provincial capitals, the Code remains largely unapplied.[17]

The theory behind the Code's enactment was that it should be both a nationally unifying force and a guide for the progressive development of the Ethiopian people. If, however, a code of law is remote from prevailing social values, it may remain to a large extent unapplied and serve to undermine the very values being sought. It is questionable sociologically whether societies grow to adjust themselves to positive law; it would seem that there is little evidence to support such a proposition. The question arises, therefore, as to how the codes may be brought into closer relationship with developing social values. The inception of the new Faculty of Law is important in this respect. Within ten to fifteen years a substantial number of well-qualified lawyers who have been trained in the theory of their own codes and the problems inherent in their application will be produced. These men will staff ministerial legal positions, the courts, a growing bar and the university teaching staff. In addition, legislative committees charged with the redrafting of the codes will have to be constantly at work to keep the codes abreast of a rapidly developing society. Further, a balanced position will evolve with respect to judicial interpretation of the codes. There must be sufficient discretion to allow the law to accommodate to changing ways, particularly as it is a foreign-inspired law, and yet sufficient certainty in the structure to allow for the prediction of legal consequences and the prevention of potential arbitrariness on the part of judges. Through these means it is hoped that the new codes of Ethiopia will, in time, become increasingly related to functioning institutions and responsive to the changing needs of the country.

II The Purposes of Punishment within the Penal System

Until recently, retribution and deterrence seemed to dominate penal philosophy in Ethiopia. The *Fetha Nagast* had already to some extent moved beyond a rudimentary use of the *lex talionis* by partially individualizing punishment to fit the personal guilt of the offender, but had retained a number of rather crude punishments and a large element of retributive theory. The Penal Code of 1930 further individualized punishment by relating it to the subjective factors of intent, motive and personal status, yet there was no expressed interest in the reform of criminals. There was, however, in this earlier Code considerable concern with the welfare of injured parties. Article 18 of the general principles might well be studied by many modern penal legislators:

> If there be a poor man who has no money with which to pay a fine to the court and damages to the injured person on account of abuse, assault or serious injury, the judge shall pay the money to the injured person from the fines which he keeps as a special fund and shall imprison the person who caused the injury and make him work and so cause him to pay the damages and fine. But the Government is under no obligation to pay from any other source than the money from fines which is kept.

Although the earlier emphasis on retribution is beginning to change today, certain strongly retributive institutions remain, the most obvious of which is flogging. Mutilation was discontinued a number of years ago; flogging has, however, been retained by the Penal Code of 1957.[18] The drafter had excluded flogging from his original *avant-projet*, but the Codification Commission and Parliament reintroduced the penalty. The strongest arguments given on its behalf were that it is in harmony with the country's traditions of punishment, that its use is restricted to only very repugnant crimes

40

and that it has a strong deterrent effect.[19] After much debate in Parliament it was finally included within the Code as article 120A[20] and applied only in instances of aggravated theft (article 635 (3)) and aggravated robbery (article 637 (1)). The infliction of flogging is limited to male offenders between the ages of 18 and 50 and may not exceed forty lashes to be carried out under medical supervision; the flogging may be stopped at any time that the doctor considers health to be in jeopardy. After the *coup d'état* attempt in 1961, a decree was passed extending the punishment of flogging to seven other offences which the decree itself categorizes as 'offences which relate to the disturbance of public opinion'.[21] The decree states that the High Court may substitute flogging for the penalty originally provided and that it is to be inflicted in accordance with article 120A, but not to exceed thirty lashes.

Capital punishment has also been retained by the new Penal Code. The Code provided that it shall be executed by hanging and may, in the discretion of the court, be carried out in public to set an example to others (article 116). In the past, tradition and public sentiment in Ethiopia has tended to consider murder a family matter to be disposed of either by conversion into 'blood money' or revenge on the perpetrator, often in the same manner in which he had killed his victim. These feelings were so strong that it has been reported that, even after the enactment of the 1930 Penal Code, a member of the murdered man's family was allowed, in a prescribed place, to pull the trigger which carried out the court's sentence of death.[22] It must be noted, however, that the death sentence may not be inflicted on persons under 18 or of limited responsibility (article 118), and both traditionally and under article 59 of the Revised Constitution of 1955, no sentence of death can be executed without the confirmation of the Emperor. According to the Prison Statistics of 1955 Ethiopian Calendar (1962–63 G.C.), 933 persons were held in prison under sentence of death while only 28 death sentences were executed. Although this may partially be due to inefficiency in obtaining confirmations, the more likely reason is the traditional leniency of the Emperor in the use of his pardon and amnesty powers.[23]

Although retribution and particularly deterrence remain pronounced community values today, the new laws are moving toward more modern and humane disposition of offenders. The Revised Constitution of 1955, among other protection for criminal defendants, provides that 'punishment is personal' and that 'no one shall be subjected to cruel and inhuman punishments' (articles 54 and 57). Although the provisions of the Constitution are not yet fully enforced, the rapidly increasing educational opportunities promise well for more thorough implementation.

The Penal Code of 1957 introduces the concept of rehabilitation into Ethiopia while also retaining deterrence as a basic principle. His Imperial Majesty's Preface to the Code states:

> ... New concepts, not only juridical, but also those contributed by the sciences of sociology, psychology and indeed penology, have been developed and must be taken into consideration in the elaboration of any criminal code which would be inspired by the principles of justice and liberty and by concern for the prevention and suppression of crime, for the welfare and, indeed, the rehabilitation of the individual accused of crime. Punishment cannot be avoided since it acts as a deterrent to crimes; as, indeed, it has been said, 'one who witnesses the punishment of a wrongdoer will become prudent'. It will serve as a lesson to prospective wrongdoers.

Article 1, setting out the object and purpose of the Code, also stresses both rehabilitation and deterrence as the underlying purposes of punishment.

Numerous articles of the Code are designed to implement the new concept of rehabilitation. The judge is given broad discretion in his choice of penalty[24] and is specifically cautioned by article 86 to calculate sentences in the following manner:

> The penalty shall be determined according to the degree of individual guilt, taking into account the dangerous disposition of the offender, his antecedents, motive and purposes, his personal circumstances and his standard of education, as well as the gravity of his offence and the circumstances of its commission.

These criteria are directly related to the rehabilitation of the offender. The Code provides for suspended sentences, probation

42

and conditional release, and states in words that catch much of its new spirit: 'conditional release must be regarded as a means of reform and social reinstatement' (article 206). The Code further sets out specialized penalties for juveniles designed for their reform[25] and provisions for the confinement of irresponsible persons for indefinite duration, although provision is made for judicial review (article 136). Treatment for an indefinite period allows the theory of rehabilitation full play, unlike ordinary fixed penalties which are graded solely on the basis of legislative determination of the seriousness of the crime and emphasize retribution and deterrence. With fixed penalties, a man ready for release before the set number of years must remain confined; one likely to recommit his crime must be released when his number of years expires.

Needless to say, the rehabilitative provisions of the new Penal Code have not yet found wide application in practice. Initial moves are now being made; in 1964, prisoners were given conditional release for the first time, although conflict seems to have arisen between the Ministry of Justice, controlling the courts, and the Ministry of the Interior, controlling the prisons. The division of responsibility for the courts and prisons has caused other problems. Pre-sentence reports prepared for judges by the police remain in court files; the prison administration is only given access to the type of sentence and number of years imposed and not to the full background reports on the offender. Post-sentence classification within the prison system conforms to the sentence passed, and therefore to the crime committed, rather than to the rehabilitative needs of the individual offender. Considerable reorientation of both judicial and penal practice is necessary before the rehabilitative ideals established by the Penal Code of 1957 can be substantially implemented.

III Adult Offenders

The only available statistics concerning the number and type of adult offenders in Ethiopia have been calculated by local police departments and centralized in the Public Prosecution Section of the Ministry of Justice. These figures are incomplete and, more than likely, quite inaccurate, although they are probably reliable enough to reveal broad trends.[26]

In 1954 Ethiopian Calendar (1961–62 G.C.), the last year for which statistics are available, 25,551 convictions are reported, 8,146 of which are attributed to crimes against property and 4,562 to intentional bodily harm. The number of crimes against property is probably greater than indicated, as figures are not given for the reputedly large number of offences against land (articles 649–652). The greatest number of offences were committed in the provinces of Shoa and Harrar, which is to be expected as each has a concentration of urban population.

Statistics are, however, too sparse and unreliable with respect to adult crime to offer more than the most tentative hypothesis as to crime causation. Crimes against property may be partially explained by poverty, unemployment due to rapid urbanization, and the high value traditionally attached to land ownership. A strong concern with honour and status, and volatile, often aggressive, personalities, may be factors partially responsible for the high rate of bodily injury offences. Basic sociological and psychological research in Ethiopia is urgently needed before intelligent planning of crime-prevention and the rehabilitation of offenders can begin.

Under the Penal Code of 1957, there is considerable discretion in the disposition of adult offenders. Each Special Part article which sets out the elements of a specific crime also establishes the discretionary boundaries within which a judge must sentence the convicted offender.[27] Book Two of the General Part provides the broader principles governing punishment and its application.

The Code establishes three basic forms of principal punishment: fine, and simple, or rigorous, imprisonment. The amount of fine is determined by reference to the offender's personal situation and his degree of guilt (article 88). Time may be allowed for payment, but

44

in default a fine may successively be converted into labour, seizure of goods, or imposition of simple imprisonment (articles 91–98). The Code also makes provision for restitution to the injured party within the criminal process (articles 100–101).[28]

Simple imprisonment, which may extend from ten days to three years, is intended for offences of not too serious a nature, as a measure of safety for the public and punishment for the criminal (article 105). The court may, however, substitute compulsory labour for simple imprisonment when it believes it to be conducive to the rehabilitation of the offender (article 106). Rigorous imprisonment, on the other hand, is applicable to offences of a 'very grave nature' and is designed for punishment, rehabilitation, strict confinement, and the special protection of society. Rigorous imprisonment is normally for a period of from one to twenty-five years but may be for life when expressly provided (article 107). An offender may be conditionally released upon probation when he has served two-thirds of his sentence, if both the management of the institution and the court feel that his behaviour has improved and offers grounds for the expectation of continued improvement on release (articles 112, 207).

If the court feels that none of the established penalties will promote the reform of the offender, and if the offence for which he was convicted is punishable with fine, compulsory labour or simple imprisonment, the court may suspend sentence and place the offender on probation (articles 194–195). The period of probation must be between two and five years in length, and in each case provision is to be made for the offender to enter into a bond, and rules for his good conduct are to be laid down (articles 200–203). As yet, facilities for a probation service have not been introduced in Ethiopia, owing primarily to the unfamiliarity of the principle and the dominantly retributive attitude toward punishment that still persists.

In addition to the principal punishments, the court may concurrently apply a secondary penalty, despite the fact that the Special Part offence does not make provision for secondary punishment. These penalties are primarily flogging, reprimand, apology, deprivation of civil, family or professional rights, and dismissal from, or reduction of rank in, the armed forces, the article providing for each secondary penalty and the instances in which it may be imposed (articles 120–127).

45

Further, when the court deems it necessary, it may apply, together with a principal punishment, what is termed a 'general measure'. There are a number of general measures designed for prevention and protection, which include, *inter alia*, recognizance to be of good behaviour, the seizure of dangerous articles, suspension and withdrawal of licences, prohibitions from, or obligations to resort to, certain places, and the supervision and expulsion of aliens (articles 138–160).

The Code provides for special measures with respect to recidivists, irresponsible persons and young persons.[29] Habitual offenders, who show 'ingrained propensity to evil-doing, misbehaviour or incurable laziness or habitually derive livelihood from crime', are to be interned upon commission of a further offence not punishable with more than five years' imprisonment. Internment is to take place in a special institution for an undefined duration of not less than two or more than ten years; any time after two years the court, upon recommendation of the director of the institution, may grant conditional release (articles 128–132). Financial handicaps have prevented the implementation of these provisions, although recidivists are segregated in central prisons where possible.

Irresponsible persons, on the other hand, are to be treated in suitable institutions and, if not dangerous, may be treated as outpatients. Confinement is of an indefinite duration but must be reviewed by the court every two years. When reason for the measure has disappeared, the administrative authority must apply to the court for termination of treatment and the court is to release the individual to the supervision of a charitable organization for at least one year (articles 133–137). Inadequate institutional and psychiatric facilities have as yet prevented wide application of the above provisions.

Offenders who have been incarcerated may, at any time, be granted sovereign pardon or amnesty (article 35 Constitution; articles 239–240, Penal Code). It is traditional for His Majesty, on the anniversary of his coronation and other important holidays, to use these powers liberally. In 1955 Ethiopian Calendar (1962–63 G.C.), prison statistics showed 176 full pardons and 1,442 reductions of sentence.

There are approximately one hundred prisons within Ethiopia, one in each Awradja and a central prison for each Province.[30] In addition, a farm camp has been established at Robi capable of accommodating 450 prisoners. According to the figures of the Ministry of Interior, 15,370 persons were incarcerated in the year 1955 Ethiopian Calendar, an increase of 2,979 over the previous year.[31] There were only 16 persons imprisoned for life, while 2,916 received sentences of rigorous imprisonment for more than five years, and 4,573 simple imprisonment for less than five years. A large number, 6,932, were in prison awaiting trial.

The central prison for Shoa in Addis Ababa is the most advanced prison in the country.[32] Prisoners are classified within three subcategories of rigorous imprisonment and three of simple imprisonment; prisoners awaiting trial, and those imprisoned for life or awaiting execution, are segregated from normal prisoners and do not take part in the programmes of the prison. Rehabilitative planning is minimal, as the Prison Administration receives no background history on prisoners from the judiciary and does not itself attempt to construct it.

Programmes of elementary education, several correspondence courses and limited library facilities are provided for the prison population, 95 per cent of whom are illiterate when they enter prison.[33] A variety of work programmes have been instituted which allow for training in skills, primarily farming, that will be useful in obtaining a job upon release. Unfortunately, prisoners are not paid for their work as earning schemes have not yet been established. Such a scheme is contemplated, however, by a recently drafted Prisons Proclamation, which would divide remuneration for work done into three separate accounts—a current account, a savings account, and an indemnification account.[34]

Lack of funds has kept accommodation in poor condition even in the Addis Ababa prison and has prevented the recruitment and training of adequate staff. Recreational, health and therapeutic facilities are limited and no programme for after-care has been established. Prisoners are reported to be bitter and to feel that their detention is a miscarriage of justice.[35] Provincial prisons have even fewer facilities and for the most part provide only limited opportunities for work. A beginning is being made with these problems as responsible officials are awakening to the need for good prison

47

administration and the importance of careful planning if the principles established in the Penal Code are to be effectively implemented.

IV Young Offenders

As with adult offenders, statements concerning juvenile delinquency in Ethiopia can at best be tentative; there are very few accurate records and no comprehensive studies of the problem.[36] An analysis of the case-history material contained in the files of the Training School and Remand Home of Addis Ababa provides, however, some indication as to trends in juvenile crime.

The more important conclusions that may be drawn from this material are summarized in a recent report to the Ministry of National Community Development.[37] The incidence of juvenile crime is concentrated primarily in a few major cities and, although light, is increasing.[38] The most common offences are petty theft and vagrancy, although the authorities have now decided not to take action with respect to vagrancy except in cases of urgent need.[39] The age-group of 12–16 years constitutes the largest portion of male, juvenile offenders and only 18 per cent of these offenders come from families having both parents. Low income, illiteracy and unemployment are also common factors related to juvenile crime in Ethiopia.

It is not within the scope of this chapter to deal with the causation of such juvenile crime, but a few fruitful areas for investigation might be suggested. The rapid migration to urban areas, especially Addis Ababa, with the consequent dissociation from family and often church, together with the introduction of western educational and economic values, is likely to have caused the considerable confusion of standards to which adolescents are particularly prone. This has led to a breakdown of the traditional authority structure and patterns of social stratification which has increased the possibilities of juvenile crime. The family has been profoundly affected by these changes, and in Ethiopia, where divorce and illegitimacy are widespread,[40] crime by young persons may well have deep psychological significance. Poverty, unemployment and limited educational opportunities may also be substantial causes of juvenile crime, particularly with respect to the high incidence of theft. The fact that juvenile crime is still as low as it is in Ethiopia can be partially attributed to the continued strength of traditional institutions. Research is badly needed to corroborate or refute these tentative hypotheses and to introduce others, so that a sound framework for comprehensive and creative planning of juvenile crime prevention and treatment can begin.

The first law dealing with juveniles in Ethiopia was the Vagrancy and Vagabondage Proclamation of 1947.[41] This Proclamation provided for the detention of persons below the age of 18 years if found wandering abroad without regular employment or lawful residence,[42] but it was repealed by the Penal Code in 1957.

Under the Penal Code, infants who have not attained the age of 9[43] are deemed not to be criminally responsible; offences committed by such infants are to be dealt with by the family, school or guardian concerned (article 52). Children between the ages of 9 and 15 are referred to as 'young persons' and are not subject to the ordinary penalties applicable to adults (article 53). After a determination of guilt, sentence is assessed, taking into account the age, character, degree of mental and moral development of the young person, and the educational value of the measures to be applied (article 54).

The court may use one of the measures from a prescribed list, the most important of which are: admission to a curative institution; supervised education by relatives, guardian, adopting family or charitable institution; reprimand or admission to a corrective institution (articles 161–169). In special circumstances the court may require the payment of a fine, corporal punishment, or even imprisonment if the offence committed is normally punishable with ten or more years' rigorous imprisonment and the offender appears incorrigible (articles 170–173). Measures for treatment or supervised education are terminated only when the medical or supervisory authority thinks it is necessary or when the young offender

49

reaches the age of 18. In the case of young persons sent to correctional institutions, the commitment is for not less than one year and not more than five years; only in exceptional cases may it extend beyond the age of 18 years (article 167). The Code further provides for conditional release (article 167), but lack of an organized probation system has prevented implementation of this provision. The Penal Code also establishes a category of offenders between the ages of 15 and 18, for whom, although ordinary penalties are applicable, the court may, in assessing sentence, take into account special mitigating factors (article 56).

Before 1961, young offenders were taken before ordinary adult courts where the offence committed was believed to be of more importance to the community than the welfare of the child. In 1961, a special tribunal of three High Court judges was constituted to hear juvenile cases under the new Criminal Procedure Code; this court functioned until December 1962, when a special juvenile court was established by order of His Majesty to sit twice a week in Addis Ababa. The Director of Social Defence in the Ministry of National Community Development has been appointed a Woreda Court judge for purposes of hearing cases in the Juvenile Court. In the provinces, young offenders are still tried by adult courts.

The Criminal Procedure Code of 1961 sets out special procedural rules in cases concerning young persons (articles 171–180). These rules provide for an informal hearing in chambers without a charge framed by the public prosecutor unless the offence committed is punishable with rigorous imprisonment exceeding ten years or with death. A complaint is read to the accused and, if admitted, conviction may follow. If not admitted, a hearing is held at which all witnesses are interrogated by the juvenile court judge and may be questioned by the defence, which is conducted by either a lawyer or a guardian. A probation report is prepared by one of two probation officers at present attached to the court, enabling the judge to sentence the offending youth in accordance with the principles established in the Penal Code.[44] As there is as yet no home for girls, they are usually returned to parents or guardians or in exceptional cases committed to prison.[45]

The only institution in Ethiopia concerned with the rehabilitation of juvenile offenders is the Training School and Remand Home established in 1942 in Addis Ababa.[46] Until May 1964 the school was closely connected with the Prison Administration of the Ministry of the Interior, but, in accordance with the growing philosophy of education and rehabilitation, it was in 1964 transferred to the Division of Social Welfare in the Ministry of National Community Development.

The institution provides accommodation for one hundred boys either committed or on remand, whose ages upon admission range from 9 to 18 years.[47] The school is staffed by a superintendent, two probation officers and a number of teachers who provide elementary education. Apart from a little academic training and an even smaller amount of therapy and case-work provided by the probation officers, the lack of trained personnel means that the boys do not receive any regular guidance and counselling. The organization of the school and its planning tend to be loose, equipment and housing relatively poor, and staff inadequate.[48] There has been no official after-care and virtually no follow-up of juvenile offenders. Those who are now responsible for the school, however, are in sympathy with the principles of rehabilitation, and are beginning to make headway. A comprehensive reorganization and development plan for the school has recently been prepared in the Ministry of National Community Development and there is every hope that it will soon be implemented.[49]

The Second Five Year Development Plan for Ethiopia (1963–67) includes a statement in principle that the Empire will undertake 'the rehabilitation of youth so that delinquency and vagrancy among teenagers is controlled and such youths are helped to become useful members of society'.[50] New legislation is now badly needed to realize this ideal. The Social Welfare Division of the Ministry of National Community Development is initiating and co-ordinating efforts in this field and is at present drafting a comprehensive Child Welfare Act. The police force has recently opened a special department dealing with juvenile affairs, and the Municipality of Addis Ababa and such organizations as the Y.M.C.A. and Boy Scouts have begun to form community centres, clubs and other facilities to provide activity and training for youths. Although Ethiopia has been slow in realizing the necessity of preventing juvenile crime and caring for young offenders, it is fortunate in having made a good beginning before the problem has assumed serious proportions.

V Conclusion

The above is a brief outline of the penal system of Ethiopia. Although a good deal more detail could be added with respect to written law, very little is known of the actual day-to-day functioning of the penal system. From what has been seen, however, there is considerable disparity between the principles and ideals set out in the new positive law and their application within the penal system. Both basic research and expanded educational opportunity are very much needed if this gap is to be substantially narrowed. A confident start has been made, and encouragement can be drawn from the growing awareness of the existence of these problems and the desire on the part of many in Ethiopia to work for their eventual solution.

NOTES

1. The Ethiopian Orthodox Church, founded in the 6th century by missionaries from the Church of Alexandria (of which St. Mark is reputed to have been the first Bishop), is the Established Church of the Empire (article 126, Revised Constitution of 1955). At this period of Ethiopian history, the empire was restricted to the central and northern highlands which were almost entirely Christian, but soon developed to include large Moslem and pagan populations. See Perham, *The Government of Ethiopia*, 101 ff. (1948).
2. From the fall of the Aksumite kingdom, Ethiopian history has vacillated between centralized control from a capital city and its ruling emperor, and the constant re-emergence of localized kings and centres of power. The Emperor receives, even today, the Amharic title of *Negusa Nagast*, meaning 'King of Kings'. See 'The Chronicle of the Emperor, Zara Yaqob (1434–1468)', 5 *Ethiopia Observer*, 152 (1961); 'The Chronicle of Ba'eda Maryam (1468–1478), 6 *Ethiopia Observer*, 63 (1962); and more generally, Perham, *op. cit.*, 69 ff., 138 ff.; Pankhurst, *Economic History of Ethiopia*, 119 ff. (1961).

3. The *Fetha Nagast* is reputed by Ethiopian tradition to have been written by 'Three Hundred Sages', that is, the *Selest Meeti*, the 318 Fathers of the Church. See J. Graven, *Le Code Pénal de l'Empire d'Ethiopie*, Introduction (1965).

4. Perham, *op. cit.*, 139.

5. The *Fetha Nagast* is still available only in Ge'ez except for a single translation into Italian published in Naples in 1936 by Ignazio Guidi. An English translation by Abba Paulos Txaduà is at present being prepared under the auspices of the Faculty of Law, Haile Selassie I University.

6. The *Fetha Nagast* is composed of two parts, the first dealing with religious matters, the second with civil. The basically religious nature of the work permeates even the civil sections, as may be seen by the following chapter headings: XLVI—'The Punishment Reserved for One Who Denies the Highest God, Blasphemes Him and Worships Others . . .' and XLVII—'Homicide and Its Corporal and Spiritual Punishment'.

7. The following provisions in the general principles of the Code are quite representative and cite for authority not only the *Fetha Nagast* but the Bible itself:

> 15. Our Lord has said in the Gospel that he who knows much shall be punished much but he who knows little shall be punished little. (*Luke*, xii, 47.)
>
> 16. The Three Hundred, knowing that it is not right to punish according to the extent of the wrong but according to the amount of understanding, have distinguished between a sentence passed on a child, a drunken person, a madman and a forgetful person and the sentence passed on a grown person of full understanding, and accordingly the code is meant to agree with the *Fetha Nagast*. (Cf. *Fet. Nag.*, Pt. 47, p. 303.)

8. Amharic and English are the official languages of the Codes and the *Negarit Gazeta* or law-reporting gazette of Ethiopia. Amharic, however, is the controlling language in case of discrepancy. The original texts of both the Penal and Civil Codes are in French. The difficulties of interpretation and reconciling three linguistic texts can be readily imagined.

9. The legal traditions of Ethiopia that have been retained by the Code are primarily the deterrent and expiative functions of punishment, the death penalty and flogging, a number of Special Part offences and several general principles such as repentance, mistake of law, and aggravating and extenuating circumstances which, although not by any means unfamiliar in Europe, draw also upon Ethiopian tradition; J. Graven, note 3 above, 27 ff.; see also J. Graven, 'Vers un Nouveau Droit Pénal Ethiopien: de la Plus Ancienne à la Plus Récente Législation du Monde', 8 *Revue Internationale de Criminologie et de Police Technique*, 250–89 (1954); J. Graven, 'L'Ethiopie Moderne et la Codification du Nouveau Droit', 72 *Revue Pénal Suisse*, 397–407 (1957).

10. After careful comparison of the General Parts of the Ethiopian and Swiss Penal Codes in French, it is quite clear that the Ethiopian Code is grounded upon the Swiss. Departures are minimal and can usually be traced to the positions of Swiss treatises and jurisprudence. See Zurcher, *Code Pénal Suisse, Exposé des Motifs de l'Avant-projet* (French translation, Gautier, 1908); Logoz, *Commentaire du Code Pénal Suisse* (1942); Thormann and von Overbeck, *Schweizerisches Strafgesetzbuch* (1940); and Hafter, *Lehrbuch des Schweizerischen Strafrechts: Allgemeiner Teil* (1926).

11. The tripartite division of the French Penal Code into offences, misdemeanours and contraventions has been abandoned in the Ethiopian Code for a simpler bipartite division into penal offences and petty offences.

12. P. Graven, *An Introduction to Ethiopian Criminal Law*, 4 (1965). A strong argument has been made by Tedeschi in a book to be published in 1965 that the Italian Penal Code is an important European source.

13. These notes were taken by M. Philippe Graven, the son of the drafter, in French and are as yet unpublished.

14. Article 23, Swiss Penal Code.

15. See Swiss sources in note 10, above, and RO 76 IV 153, JT 1950 74; RO 78 IV 145, JT 1953 105; RO 83 IV 132, JT 1958 2; Waiblinger, *La Tentative, III, Fiches Juridiques Suisses*, No. 1201, Oct. 1957.

16. The Penal Code of 1957 was the first of the modern codes to be promulgated and was followed by a Civil Code (1960) drafted by Prof. R. David of Paris, Commercial (1960) and Maritime (1960) Codes drafted by Prof. J. Escarra, also of Paris (the Commercial Code was completed upon the death of Prof. Escarra by Prof. A. Jauffret of Aix-Marseilles) and a Criminal Procedure Code (1961). A Civil Procedure Code has also been drafted.

17. After numerous visits to the courts, it is apparent that many of the judges in Addis Ababa attempt to apply the Penal Code. However, they tend to restrict their application to more easily comprehended Special Part articles under which defendants are charged.

18. Flogging was also an enumerated punishment in the Penal Code of 1930, but with the proviso in article 3 (pt. 1):

> The sentence of flogging is still in use with a few other governments. Though it is certainly our purpose that the sentence of flogging shall in future be abolished in our country, for the present we have strictly reserved the sentence of flogging, as it has hitherto been administered, for the punishment of those who have committed some great crime which yet does not deserve sentence of death.

19. *Procès-Verbal* of the Codification Commission, April 9th, 1954 G.C., p. 3; Proceedings of the Senate, Hamle 1, 1949 (July 8th, 1957 G.C.), final resolution, Hamle 8, 1949 (July 15th, 1957 G.C.).

20. It is the only article numbered 'A', indicating Parliamentary inclusion.

21. Decree No. 45 of 1961 G.C. Under Article 92 of the Revised Constitution of 1955, decrees having the effect of law may be passed by His Imperial Majesty alone without action by Parliament. Article 92 provides that this is

to be done only in 'cases of emergency that arise when the Chambers are not sitting'. Parliament has the power to approve or disapprove decrees in their next session, but has not so acted on this Decree. It presumably, therefore, retains its force as law.

22. Perham, *op. cit.*, 142 ff.
23. Annual Report of the Prison Department, Ministry of Interior. See p. 46 below with respect to the Emperor's power of pardon and amnesty.
24. See pp. 44–48 and note 27 below.
25. See pp. 49–51 below.
26. Statistics are reported for each of the provinces of Ethiopia except Eritrea, which has been separately administered, under each of twelve specific crimes. Convictions for 'miscellaneous offences' account for more than 30 per cent of all offences committed. Indications of inaccuracy are numerous: only one intentional homicide is reported for Addis Ababa during the year 1954 E.C.; figures are given for 'burglary', which is not a crime set out in the Penal Code; instances of negligent homicide and negligent injuries are reported by the police before a trial has determined the existence of negligence, etc.
27. The following are instances of sentencing provisions within the Special Part, typical of the breadth within the Code:

> Article 383—*Material Forgery*.... is punishable with rigorous imprisonment not exceeding five years or in less serious cases, with simple imprisonment for not less than three months.

> Article 621—*Incest*.... is punishable with simple imprisonment for not less than three months or ... with rigorous imprisonment not exceeding three years. The court may in addition deprive the offender of his family rights.

> Article 636—*Robbery*.... is punishable with rigorous imprisonment not exceeding fifteen years.

The judge is, however, given some guidance in determining sentence within these established boundaries: see article 86, Calculation of Sentence and articles 79–84, Extenuating and Aggravating Circumstances.

28. See also Criminal Procedure Code, articles 154–9.
29. For young persons, see pp. 48–52 below.
30. Eritrea, however, continues to administer its prisons separately.
31. This rise in the number of prisoners may be attributable to more complete reports from provincial prisons in 1955 E.C.
32. Much of the following factual material has been obtained from officials in the Prison Administration, Ministry of the Interior and from my own observations after several visits to the central prison in Addis Ababa. See also Andargatchew Tesfaye, *Corrections in Ethiopia*, 3 *Current Projects in the Prevention, Control and Treatment of Crime and Delinquency*, 7–9 (1963).
33. Ato Chanyaleou Teshome, *Memorandum on the Improvement of Prison Administration*, 1.

34. It is hoped that the Prisons Proclamation will come before Parliament during its current session. Although the proposed proclamation tends to be over-concerned with security, there is at present no law in Ethiopia governing the administration of prisons, and its enactment will effect a number of advances and be helpful in regularizing administration.
35. Ato Chanyaleou Teshome, *op. cit.*, 2.
36. The most complete consideration of juvenile delinquency in Ethiopia has recently been presented by J. Riley, United Nations consultant to the Ministry of National Community Development. Two other short studies have been completed and are contained in the following unpublished reports: Ross, *Juvenile Delinquency in Ethiopia* (1961) and Yeweinsshet Beshah-Woured, *Some of the Causes and Contributing Factors to the Making of Juvenile Delinquents and Prostitutes* (1961); see also Andargatchew Tesfaye, op. cit., 9–11.
37. Riley, *op. cit.*, 8, 23–35.
38. There are no accurate figures as to the extent of juvenile delinquency. Outside Addis Ababa, Asmara and Dire Dawa there seems to be very little juvenile crime, and it is generally dealt with unofficially by the police: see Riley, *op. cit.*, 21–2.
39. The Country Statement of Ethiopia submitted to the Social Defence Meeting in Monrovia in August 1964 states at p. 2 that 'in 78 cases out of 100, boys are committed for petty thefts and vagrancy'. Commitments for vagrancy have declined from 50 per cent to 2 per cent in the last year owing to the newly adopted policy: Riley, *op. cit.*, 9.
40. See Ullendorff, *The Ethiopians: An Introduction to Country and People*, 178 (1960); Lipsky, *Ethiopia: Its People, Its Society, Its Culture*, 80 (1962).
41. Proc. No. 89 of 1947 G.C. The Penal Code of Ethiopia (1930) concerns itself with juveniles only incidentally: see articles 21, 150.
42. Upon the first such offence, a juvenile was to be returned to the custody of his parents: section 8.
43. The French text of the draft of the Penal Code states 'completed nine years': *"Les dispositions du présent code ne sont applicables aux enfants n'ayant pas atteint l'âge de neuf ans révolus."* The same translation error has been made for each age mentioned in the section on young offenders.
44. In 1956 E.C. (1963–4 G.C.), the Juvenile Court judge committed 58·5 per cent of all cases dealt with to the Training School and Remand Home; 13 per cent were placed on probation and 35 per cent were returned to parents or guardians: Riley, *op. cit.*, 20.
45. Ato Andargatchew Tesfaye, the present Juvenile Court judge, states that apart from the lack of an institution for girls, the main problems are poor equipment and as yet a lack of co-operation between provincial police and the Juvenile Court: Interview, December 16th, 1964.
46. Young offenders in the provinces are sent to segregated sections of prisons where such facilities exist.

56

47. In December 1964, the School was accommodating 138 boys, 126 formally committed and 12 on remand: Riley, *op. cit.*, 26.
48. See Riley, *ibid.*, and Singh, *Addis Ababa Home for Juvenile Delinquents* (1959).
49. Riley, *ibid.*, Chap. II.
50. p. 301.

3
Ghana[1]

ROBERT B. SEIDMAN and
J. D. ABAKA EYISON

*Historically, the principal antinomies of the treatment of criminal convicts
are those of general deterrence on the one hand, and special deterrence and reformation on the other. The former measures the punishment of the offender
by the desirability of frightening other potential wrongdoers by his example.
Special deterrence and reformation, on the other hand, limit treatment to that
which is necessary to ensure that the offender will not repeat his crime, the one
by punishment, the other by re-education.*

*In fact, of course, Ghanaian penal legislation, the courts, prisons and
aftercare agencies, as everywhere, speak in a confusion of tongues. We shall
first examine the scope of crime and the nature of the criminals as revealed by
statistical evidence. Then we shall turn to each of the other institutions important in the process of the treatment of offenders, to find the governing
principle in fact used by each.*

I Of Crime and Criminals

Criminal statistics have been faithfully kept in the Gold Coast and
Ghana since at least 1895. The earlier statistics appear most useful,
however, as an index of the development of police activity rather
as an index of crime.[2] The statistics reported here will therefore
include only the more recent ones.[3] They must be viewed against
the radical social, political and economic changes which have swept
over Ghana since 1957, the year of independence.

Economically, this period has been one of dizzying change. A
boom-and-bust cocoa bubble subjected the traditional subsistence

economy, especially in the Ashanti Region, to the eroding forces of the cash nexus; and the steady development of modern trade and industry encouraged by the Government has achieved the same result. Politically, Ghana has in this period thrown off the imperial yoke and embarked upon the exhilarating course of independence, until recently with increasing emphasis upon a socialist perspective —a course into unknown waters, no doubt deeply unsettling at least for those whose patterns of life were interwoven with the agencies of colonial domination. Sociologically, the urban sprawl stretches its tentacles to clasp increasing numbers of Ghanaians. More and more, Ghanaians tend to opt out of the traditional extended family system, an institution arising in the agrarian subsistence sector, but not particularly adapted to the demands of an urban, cash-oriented society. The authority of traditional rule has been undercut by modern secular government. The acquisitive morality of the late colonial era gnawed at the collective solidarity of the traditional village community, an eroding process not yet significantly slowed down.[4]

To replace the older modes of social control, the Government is endeavouring to substitute new devices, purporting to express its socialist objective. Some of these are already operative. The Workers Brigade provides employment for some 12,000 young men in the age-group most prone to crime. The State Farms and industrial enterprises are absorbing a certain amount of unemployment. Better health facilities, welfare services and village amenities contribute to a higher standard of living. The extensive self-help community reconstruction programme strengthens traditional communal solidarity by employing it to achieve secular objectives. Above all, the astronomical increase in educational opportunity now has practically one hundred per cent of Ghanaian school-age children in class.

But these institutional and sociological ameliorations have hardly yet had time to take effect. The criminal statistics here examined therefore reflect a period of maximum social dislocation, before any new institutions of social control have had time to come to operation. It is therefore only to be expected that the incidence of crime generally has increased during the period of 1959–64, as reported in Table 1.[5]

TABLE I. REPORTS TO THE POLICE OF CRIMINAL INCIDENTS (CASES ARISING UNDER THE CRIMINAL CODE[a])

Year	Population[b]	Cases reported	Rate/10,000 population
1959	6,395,000	54,067	84
1960	6,700,000	58,381	87
1961	7,029,000	57,456	82
1962	7,100,000	62,950	89
1963	7,285,000	66,639	91
1964	7,475,000	72,667	97[6]

Source: Supplied by the Ghana Police.

[a] The Criminal Code includes all the traditional crimes, and a number of others usually included among 'statutory offences'. 'Statutory offences' not included in the Code are separately reported.

[b] Population for 1962 drawn from the census; for 1959 and 1961, as set forth in the *Annual Report of the Treatment of Offenders*. Since 1962, the population was estimated at 2·6 per cent per annum increase.

Statutory offences have also increased, from 4,654 in 1959, to 6,922 in 1964. Since these offences are almost all discovered by the police themselves, the rise may be mainly an index of increased police activity, not necessarily of the incidence of such offences.

The pattern of offences in Ghana shows a much greater proportion of crimes against the person than in England. In 1964, of a total of 72,667 reports of crimes and statutory offences, 34 per cent were cases of criminal harm and assault, and 37 per cent were cases of burglary, housebreaking, storebreaking, stealing by means of employment, stealing, and fraud by false pretences. In England the proportion of larcenous crime hovers around 85 per cent. Nonetheless, in Ghana stealing is the most common offence of the young offender.

The incidence of murder and rape is noticeably low and declining, even in the face of a 16 per cent rise in population from 1959 to 1964, as reported in Table 2.

Information about the characteristics of criminals generally is not available statistically in Ghana. The only relevant information is that available from the reports of the Prisons Department. These report the ethnic origin and religion of persons committed to

TABLE 2. HOMICIDAL INCIDENTS AND RAPES REPORTED TO THE POLICE

Year	Murders, attempted murders and manslaughters	Rape, indecent assault etc.
1959	215	835
1960	240	864
1961	195	546
1962	183	469
1963	178	431
1964	174	399

Source: Supplied by the Ghana Police.

prison. It will be noted that the rate of committals of Ashanti have been growing at a rate far greater than those of the other ethnic groups. Significantly, it was the Ashanti who were most affected by the cocoa boom. It is generally believed that the population of Ghana is approximately evenly divided between Christians, pagans and Moslems. The Moslems are largely concentrated in Northern Ghana, the region least affected by the modern trends in the economy; the incidence of crime among them is significantly lower than among Christians or pagans.

Serious crime in Ghana remains largely a male prerogative. Total offences committed by women have grown steadily, from 2,694 committed in 1959, to 6,788 committed in 1964.[7] The great increase in true crime by women has been in assaults: in 1959 there were 524 assaults committed by women; in 1964, 1,392. Stealing is a relatively infrequent offence by women; in 1959 there were 134 cases reported; in 1964, only 266.[8] Statutory offences, on the other hand, increased, from 1,335 in 1959, to 2,968 in 1964.[9]

As a result of the increase in the total number of crimes committed, the proportion of convictions of women has increased, from 8 per cent of the total convictions in 1959, to 14 per cent in 1964.[10] The total number of committals, however, seems to have remained quite constant from 1950–51 to 1962, the last year for which statistics are available, never varying significantly from slightly over 2 per cent of total committals.[11] It would appear that the increased number of convictions of women have been largely for relatively minor offences.

A disproportionate share of the increase in crime is attributable to young adult males. The number of juvenile convictions has remained almost constant: in 1959 there were 735 convictions; in 1964, 853 convictions.[12] In 1948–49, 5,616 adult males of 25–50 years of age were committed; in 1962, 12,217 were committed, a growth of over 200 per cent. By contrast, 1,404 adult males of 20–25 years of age were committed in 1948–49; 7,453 were committed in 1962, a growth of over 500 per cent. The same age-group accordingly increased its share of committals from 17 per cent in 1948–49, to 36 per cent in 1962.[13]

The increase in crime in Ghana has been accompanied by an increase in recidivism. In 1948–49, 33 per cent of all persons committed were second or subsequent offenders; in 1962, 42 per cent were recidivists. There has been an even more striking increase in third offenders; in 1948–49, 15 per cent of committals were of persons who had been committed twice before; in 1962, 21 per cent of committals were of such persons; in absolute numbers, there were 1,176 third offenders committed in 1948–49, and 4,318 in 1962—an increase of fourfold in the number of third offenders.[14]

Several significant conclusions may be drawn from these statistics. (1) The rate of crime has been rising somewhat in Ghana in the recent period. (2) A significantly smaller percentage of these crimes are crimes against property than, say, in England. (3) Homicides and rapes—the two most serious crimes against the person—are relatively infrequent. (4) The rate of incidence of committals has been relatively constant among all ethnic groups save the Ashanti. (5) The rate of crime remains significantly lower among Moslems than among other religious groups. (6) While the incidence of convictions of women has risen sharply, the rate of committals of women apparently has not. (7) Juvenile crime has remained relatively constant. (8) The large growth in crime has been among males in the 20–25-year-old age-group. (10) Recidivism is growing markedly.

II The System of Penal Legislation

To deal with these crimes and criminals, Ghana has a Criminal Code, and a number of other statutes creating criminal offences. The purposes of punishment are nowhere explicitly stated. Every system of criminal law, however, has at least implied objectives, which should determine the purposes of punishment. What are the implicit objectives of the Ghanaian system of penal legislation?

1 THE CRIMINAL CODE, 1960

The Code was adopted originally in 1892, not because it was specifically appropriate to the circumstances of the Colony, but in the interest of imperial uniformity. It was a lineal descendant of Sir James Stephen's Draft Code of 1878, a codification of the common law.[15]

Where there were ambiguities in the case law, Sir James made choices which reflected his views of what the law ought to be.[16] These choices were embodied in a Draft Code for Jamaica which the Colonial Office actually first commissioned as early as 1871, with a view that the Code 'should subsequently be adopted to the circumstances of the other Crown Colonies respectively'.[17] It was never adopted in Jamaica, but it was in St Lucia. When J. T. Hutchinson, then Chief Justice of the Gold Coast, drafted a Criminal Code for the Gold Coast, he wrote that he had 'kept as closely as I could to the St Lucia Code, considering it desirable that there should be as great uniformity as possible in the Codes of the different Colonies'.[18]

In general, the theory of criminal guilt embodied in the Code follows that of the common law. The English judges early adopted deterrence as the objective of the law of crime. But deterrence *per se* is an ambiguous notion: it embodies the contradictory notions of both the general and special varieties.[19] In many cases the quantum of punishment demanded by these two contradictory versions of deterrence is different. General deterrence, consistently applied,

66

demands punishment for the commission of any criminal harm. Special deterrence, on the other hand, demands punishment only when this criminal himself might have been deterred from committing the crime, for unless he was deterrable, his commission of the criminal harm does not identify him as either more dangerous or more deterrable than the average man, and hence not a fit subject for punishment.

The resolution of the contradiction was found in the concept of responsibility, expressed in the *mens rea* doctrine. If an accused was aware of the criminality of his act, and had capacity to conform to the norm, the quantum of punishment required to deter him from crime in the future is the same as that required to deter others similarly situated. The *mens rea* doctrine in its pristine form embodies the principal concession made by the common law to the advocates of special deterrence.

But the doctrine of responsibility, embodied in the notion of *mens rea*, is itself ambiguous. If a person commits a crime when he personally has no *mens rea*, but a reasonable man in his shoes would have had a guilty mind, ought he to be punished? General deterrence urges the affirmative, so that by his example the ordinary man in similar circumstances will be deterred. Special deterrence suggests the contrary, on the ground that if this individual could not have been deterred, punishment for him is pointless.

In resolving this new tension within the notion of responsibility itself, the common law came down mainly on the side of general deterrence by creating the 'modern' notion of 'objective' *mens rea*.[20] Whether a criminal code leans towards general or special deterrence can be discovered by analysis of the extent to which its *mens rea* requirements are more or less 'subjective' than those of the common law. To the extent that they are 'objective', the Code favours general deterrence as its implicit objective; to the extent that they are 'subjective', it inclines towards special deterrence.

The relevance of this analysis to the study of a penal system is obvious. General deterrence and harsh exemplary punishments are natural corollaries. Special deterrence, on the other hand, suggests that the treatment of the offender ought to be primarily directed at ensuring that this criminal will not repeat his crime, and slides easily into notions of reformation.

Deep-seated value-judgments masquerade behind these opposing conceptions of punishment. General deterrence treats the criminal as a means for guaranteeing the good order of society. In the words of Sydney Smith, the editor of the *Edinburgh Review* in the 1830s, 'when a man has been proved to have committed a crime, it is expedient that society should make use of that man for the diminution of crime; he belongs to them for that purpose'.[21] Historically, it has been the position favoured by the privileged classes in the community, for 'common-sense' opinion has always recognized that deterrence works best, if at all, with respect to property crimes. General deterrence has thus been historically the demand of men of property.

Special deterrence, on the other hand, would safeguard the state by treating the individual criminal. It treats the criminal as an end in himself, and not a means. It is obviously favoured, therefore, by those who place human values above property values.

Thus the *mens rea* requirements of the Code imply a statutory imperative as to the principle of punishment. The Criminal Code of 1892 to a surprising degree embodies a subjective *mens rea*, and hence, by necessary inference, it inclines towards the humane objective of special deterrence; the 1960 Code has not changed the critical clauses.

The provisions with respect to punishment in the Criminal Procedure Code, 1960, are more ambiguous. These describe six sorts of punishments: Death, Imprisonment, Detention, Fine, Payment of compensation, and Liability to police supervision.[22] Corporal punishment is notable by its absence. It was remarkably little used in the Gold Coast, being in practice largely confined to juveniles.[23] When the Criminal Code and the Criminal Procedure Code were redrafted and re-enacted in 1960, corporal punishment was apparently dropped (except for in-prison offences), so far as can be discovered, without comment in Parliament.

The Code classifies most crimes as first-degree felonies, second-degree felonies, misdemeanours, and offences.[24] First-degree felonies are subject to a maximum of life imprisonment; second-degree felonies, to a maximum of ten years' imprisonment; misdemeanours, to a maximum of three years;[25] and the various minor offences have specific penalties attached. A court may sentence to a fine in lieu of, or in addition to, imprisonment.[26] Fines are in the discretion of the court (save in the case of the minor offences where a maximum fine is set forth), but 'shall not be excessive'.[27] In default of payment of fine, an offender must go to prison for a period ranging from fourteen days in default of a one-pound fine, to six months in default of payment of a fine in excess of fifty pounds.[28]

In interesting contrast to these punitive and deterrent sanctions are the provisions in respect of discharge, absolute and conditional, and probation. These are available for all crimes, except those for which sentence is fixed by law.[29] A conditional discharge may not subsist for longer than twelve months; the offender, if he commits another offence within the period, is liable to be sentenced for the original crime.[30]

Probation is available when the sentencing court 'is of opinion that, having regard to the youth, character, antecedents, home surroundings, health or mental conditions of the offender, or to the nature of the offence or to any extenuating circumstances in which the offence was committed',[31] it should not order another sort of punishment. The probation order may be not less than six months nor more than three years in duration.[32] It may involve direction to a particular place or even a particular institution, if that be expedient.[33] A probation order for an offender older than 17 years can be made only if he consents.[34]

This barrage of possible punishments and sentences again suggests an ambiguity in respect of the objectives of punishment. The death penalty and life imprisonment—the former still used, the latter available for the wide variety of first-degree felonies—suggest that restraint or general deterrence are the principal aims in view. On the other hand, provisions with respect to fines and relatively short-term imprisonment are ambiguous; they may be directed towards general or special deterrence, depending upon sentencing policy. Finally, the provisions with respect to conditional discharge and for probation obviously suggest that reformation is the objective of such punishments.

2 THE RECENT CRIMINAL LEGISLATION

In the last few years of the Nkrumah regime, a series of criminal statutes were enacted imposing relatively harsh minimum sentences and to some extent seemingly abandoning the principle of responsibility. They reflect contradictions in the value-system inherent in Ghana's drive towards a new economy and social order.

Before 1962, only cocoa smuggling appears to have carried with it a fixed minimum sentence.[35] All other crimes bore only a maximum permissible sentence.[36] The use of a fixed minimum sentence suggests that exemplary deterrence is necessarily the central objective of punishment for that crime. A fixed minimum sentence requires at least that much punishment, whether or not the betterment of the individual convict requires so much.[37]

Since 1960, minimum sentences have been introduced for several offences: for corruption or carelessness with respect to state property,[38] for possessing fire-arms or explosives,[39] for prison officers who permit prisoners to escape or who participate in other violations of prison rules,[40] for violations of certain currency restrictions,[41] and for the illegal exportation of precious stone or metals.[42] In addition, minimum sentences have been imposed in cases of abortion, and of habitual crime.[43] Moreover, the maximum penalties for various larcenous offences have been increased from three years to ten years.[44]

The penalties imposed have been far greater than those previously thought necessary. For example, in the Criminal Code, 1960, it was a misdemeanour, with a *maximum* penalty of three years' imprisonment, for a prison officer to be an accessory to breach of prison discipline.[45] To escape lawful custody (and hence to be an accessory to the escape) was subject to the same penalty.[46] Smuggling illicit tobacco, spirits, or other matter into prison was also a misdemeanour.[47] In 1965 the penalties for these crimes by prison officers were increased to a *minimum* of five years' imprisonment; no maximum was stipulated.[48] A new clause was added, making it a special crime for a prison officer directly or indirectly to aid, encourage 'or in any manner facilitate' the escape of a prisoner, with a minimum sentence of ten years.

In the Currency Act, 1960, there was no provision to limit the importation or exportation of currency. Ghana's economic development demanded that foreign exchange be conserved for development projects. In 1964, accordingly, provisions were introduced to make criminal the import or export of currency without licence.[49] The penalties for violation were a maximum fine of £100, and an additional fine not to exceed the value of the smuggled notes. In 1965, penalties were increased to twenty-five years' minimum, for any quantity of notes smuggled—with no maximum, and without alternative of fine.[50]

The new penalties in the main affect crimes relating to state security and to the development of Ghana's economic system. Heavy minimum sentences, however, have been introduced with respect to two sorts of conventional crimes as well: illegal abortions (increased from second-degree felony, bearing a *maximum* of five years, to a *minimum* of ten years), and habitual crime. The period of detention for habitual criminals was originally five years.[51] It was widened in the Punishment of Habitual Criminals Act, 1963, which made all third offenders previously convicted of at least two felonies or misdemeanours liable to a minimum of ten years at 'productive hard labour' in the discretion of the court. Since it has not yet been possible to implement the 'productive hard labour' provisions, the statute provides, in effect, a minimum ten-year prison sentence for habitual criminals.

The use of the criminal law for the protection of Ghana's new economic and social structure poses a sharp conflict in values. The reasons advanced by the proponents of the new legislation reflect the contradictions inherent in the problem. The proponents of the legislation urged as the values to be protected both the protection of the social order *and* humanism. Mr Kwaku Boateng, for example, in the debate on the Abortion Bill, stated: 'Because of our political and social development, the Party is not going to entertain abortion in this country. The Party is of the view that criminal abortion must carry a heavy penalty.'[52] No more precise reasons were given. In discussing the Public Property (Protection) Bill, 1962, the Minister of Justice said that the Bill was introduced 'to reiterate [Government's] emphasis on the fact that the offences under the Bill constitute an attack on the very foundations of the structure of the State, which, if committed with growing frequency and on a scandalous scale, would gradually diminish and ultimately undermine the moral structure of our civilization'.[53]

Other speakers emphasized the theme of humanism. The Deputy Minister of Education, Mrs Al-Hassan, speaking to the Public

Property (Protection) Bill, 1962, asserted that 'Socialist Ghana is determined to rid herself of the colonialist past and to uphold the moral dignity of the average Ghanaian'.[54] In three of the Bills,[55] the penalty is stipulated as 'productive hard labour', to be served not in a conventional prison, but on a state farm, a state factory, or a co-operative enterprise.[56] Kofi Baako, the Leader of the House, explained the reason for the new penalty with respect to the bill permitting a judge to sentence recidivist thieves to 'productive hard labour': 'We say that a person needs rehabilitation. His punishment should not be just punitive. It should be reformative and so he is out on the farm to farm himself and make a living'.[57]

A few speakers found the resolution of the contradiction in the notion that heavy penalties were important as an educative measure, rather than as a punitive one. Mr Bonsu, the Deputy Minister of Justice, for example, said that 'the reason for the amendment [increasing the penalties for larcenies and abortion] is that we want the people to take a very serious view of those offences'.[58]

With respect to three of the bills, carrying extraordinarily heavy penalties, the primary objective is plainly harsh exemplary deterrence. All of them were introduced in times of great stress, and they reflect the tensions of the period. The death penalty for the possession of fire-arms was enacted during a period in which there was a series of bombings, apparently aimed at the assassination of the President, and actually resulting in many deaths in crowds attending public meetings.[59] The twenty-five-year penalty for diamond smuggling was passed by Parliament at the time of a spectacular (and unsuccessful) prosecution against the illegal exportation of a huge sum in diamonds. The Currency Control Bill, with its twenty-five-year minimum sentence, became law when, because of a disastrous drop in the world price of cocoa, the foreign exchange position of the country seemed extremely precarious. These pressures generated the usual demands for harsh exemplary penalties, without serious consideration of competing humanist values.

As has been the experience elsewhere, the introduction of heavy deterrent sentences in response to emergent pressures has resulted in an erratic pattern of penalties. Cocoa is Ghana's principal foreign exchange earner; cocoa is, so to speak, so much foreign exchange in another form. Yet the illegal exportation of cocoa carries a maximum penalty of only five years; the illegal exportation of Ghanaian currency carries a maximum penalty of twenty-five years.

There seems to have been no empirical study to support the imposition of severe minimum sentences. No reason seems to have been advanced to justify the increase in the sentence for habitual criminals from the five years formerly stipulated to ten years. During the Parliamentary debates, nobody referred to the extensive penological literature questioning the efficacy of deterrence. There was no discussion of alternative means of controlling crime, by increased efforts at detection, by education of the populace, and the like. Instead, in the style of legislators the world over, there was an unexamined, unquestioning faith in general deterrence as the solvent of crime.

The increasing invocation of general deterrence as the penological means of protecting Ghana's economic and social reconstruction has been accompanied by the partial abandonment of the touchstone of responsibility. The crime defined by the Public Property (Protection) and Corrupt Practices (Prevention) Act, 1964, declares a person guilty of an offence if, 'by reason of a careless or dishonest attitude' to the affairs of a state corporation or other organization, he 'so mismanages the affairs thereof as to cause the dissipation of, or grave damage to, public property'.[60] A prison officer who 'directly or indirectly aids, encourages, induces or in any manner facilitates the escape of a person in lawful custody' is liable to a ten-year minimum sentence.[61] A person who illegally exports currency, whether or not his act is 'wilful' or 'knowing', is subject to a twenty-five-year minimum sentence.[62]

The broadest of the new Acts is the State Secrets Act, 1962. It creates an offence in a person who, *inter alia*, 'for any purpose prejudicial to the safety of the Republic' is 'in the neighbourhood' of any prohibited place, or 'obtains, collects, records or publishes, or communicates in whatever manner . . . any sketch, plan . . . article or note that is calculated to be or might be or is intended to be directly or indirectly useful to a foreign power'. It is not necessary to show that the accused person was guilty of any particular act tending to show a purpose prejudicial to the safety or interests of the Republic, but he may be convicted if, 'from the circumstances of the case, or his conduct, or his known character as proved, it appears that his purpose' was one prejudicial to the interests of the Republic. The mere fact that a person has communicated or attempted to communicate with the agent of a foreign power is evidence of a violation of the Act. Unless he proves to the contrary, a person is deemed in communication with the agent of a foreign power if he has visited the address of an agent of a foreign power.

In these statutes the use of heavy minimum sentences, the breadth of the language, and the partial absence of sharply-defined *mens rea* requirements, suggest general deterrence as the principal objective. As a result of this new development, the objectives of Ghanaian penal legislation seem to have become rather complex. In the Criminal Code—i.e. with respect to 'ordinary' crime—the objective remains mainly special deterrence, a humanist objective wholly in accord with the expressed policies of the government. With respect to crimes against state security and the economic order, general deterrence seems the major objective. Whether general deterrence will splash over from the new crimes to swamp the rest of the criminal code remains to be seen.

The invocation of the new system of penology implied by 'productive hard labour' does, however, sound a new strain for the future. It represents an attempt to find a technique of treatment wholly reformatory in objective, and free of the traditional aura of 'punishment' that necessarily engulfs the prisons system. But the courts have developed in the glow of this traditional aura and are by nature conservative. It is to their activities that we now turn.

III Sentencing Practices

The Ghana courts, relying on English education and membership of the English bar, have given an English-orientated content to the criminal law. In general questions of *mens rea* and specific problems of intent, mistake, mental abnormality, provocation and abso-

74

lute liability, they have given the Code a common law interpretation which has forced it in the direction of objective *mens rea* and general deterrence.

The same inclination has been reflected in sentencing practice. The limited invocation of capital punishment in the Code has naturally resulted in a similar slight use of it in sentencing. An increase, however, in the number of persons sent to prison, in the number of persons imprisoned in default of fine, in heavy as well as light sentences, and in the number of remand prisoners, is indicative of the objectives of the court in sentencing.

Capital punishment is little used in Ghana, as Table 3 shows.

TABLE 3. CAPITAL PUNISHMENT: RANDOM YEARS SINCE 1950– 51

Year	Number of persons sentenced to death[a]	Number of persons executed[b]
1950–51	30	13
1953–54	31	9
1954–55	26	17
1959	9	nil
1961	12	5
1962	15	16

Source: Annual Reports of the Treatment of Offenders.

[a] A number of those sentenced to death have their sentences commuted, are released on appeal, or are certified to be insane.

[b] Those executed in any year may include prisoners sentenced in a previous year.

All capital sentences are automatically reviewed by the Executive. The trial judge prepares a memorandum on the case, to which the Chief Justice and the Attorney-General minute their recommendations. The accused may, and usually does, prepare a petition in support of clemency. There is no hearing on the petition. In practice, it would appear that, failing a favourable recommendation by one of the three officials who comment on the case, clemency is rarely exercised. From the reported figures of executions compared with convictions, however, it would appear that clemency is exercised in about half of all cases.

Fines are at the opposite end of the scale; they are the most frequent form of punishment in Ghana. In 1960, for example, out of 30,477 persons convicted of crime, 29 were sentenced to death, 9,036 to imprisonment, and 21,412 'fined, bound over or cautioned'; the vast majority of these were undoubtedly fined.[63]

An increasing number of persons who are fined actually are sent to prison in default of fine. In 1961, 45 per cent of all persons committed to prison went there in default of fine.[64] In 1954–55, only 35 per cent of committals were in default of fine.[65] By contrast, in England in 1954, only about 20 per cent of committals were for that reason.[66]

Probation as a method of treatment in Ghana is confined almost exclusively to juveniles. In 1961, the use of probation for adults and young persons was confined to about 1 case in 700.[67] In England, it was used in 1953 for 10 cases out of 100 for adults, and for young persons, in 26 out of 100 cases.[68]

Prison remains a principal form of punishment. Sentencing policy has seemingly fluctuated wildly. Before 1962, the proportion of convictions ending in committals to prison had been rising relatively steadily. In 1953–54, 36 per cent of all convictions resulted in committals.[69] By 1962, the proportion had risen to 54 per cent.[70] In England by contrast, in 1954, only about 25 per cent of all persons convicted were committed (including committals in default of fine).[71] In actual numbers, 9,890 convicted persons were committed in 1953–54; in 1962, 20,659, or more than twice as many.

The proportion of committals fell off strikingly in 1963, and again in 1964. In 1963, of 46,127 convictions, there were 18,311 committals, or 39 per cent; in 1964, of 48,329 convictions, there were only 15,792 committals, or only 32 per cent.[72] There is no explanation for this remarkable reduction in the total number of committals. It is the impression of the Prisons Department, although at the time of writing without statistical basis, that the trend reversed itself again in 1965, the number and proportion of committals rising sharply.

The sharp decline in the proportion of committals was accompanied, however, by an equally sharp increase in the length of sentences imposed. In 1950–51, 67 per cent of all committals were for less than six months.[73] In 1961, 76 per cent were for the same period.[74] In 1963—the last year for which statistics are available—it was down to 65 per cent.[75] Conversely, the number of long-term sentences increased sharply in 1963. In 1961, of 18,846 convictions, there were 4,461 committals of more than six months.[76] In 1963, of almost the same number of total committals, 18,311, there were 6,394 committals for the longer period,[77] an increase of almost 50 per cent in two years.

Most significant of all, the length of the long-term sentences has grown very sharply in the past few years. In 1962, out of 20,659 convictions, there were 408 in excess of three years,[78] or 2 per cent. In 1963, of 18,311 convictions, there were 723 such committals, or 4 per cent. In 1964, out of only 15,792 committals there were 741 such sentences, or 5 per cent.[79]

Moreover, the number of extremely long sentences grew sharply even in the year from 1963 to 1964. In 1963 the median of sentences of three years and more was three years; in 1964 it was four years. In 1963 there were 87 committals for terms of five years or more; in 1964 there were 208 such committals.[80]

Thus, the sentencing policies of the courts have fluctuated. From independence until 1962, apparently, there was a sharp rise in the proportion of committals, and the prisons were flooded with short-sentence prisoners. Since 1963, following the new legislation with its increased emphasis on deterrent criminal penalties, it would appear that the courts have changed their sentencing policies. The total proportion of committals to convictions has dropped sharply, accompanied by an equally sharp increase in the length of individual sentences.

Although there was a marked decline in the total number of convictions between 1962 and 1963—from 20,659 to 18,311—the shift towards increased sentences implied that the decline in committals was nevertheless accompanied by an increased prison population. Assuming that all sentences in the different categories reported received the maximum sentence in the category (e.g. that all sentences in the three-to-six-months category reported in the statistics were in fact six months' sentences) and that all sentences in excess of three years were four years, the total months of imprisonment to which criminals were sentenced in 1962 was 189,623 months. In 1963, with 10 per cent fewer committals, it amounted to

77

202,305 months. (The assumption on length of sentence is of course arbitrary; but if used consistently, it serves adequately as a basis of comparison.) Thus the reduction in the total number of committals did not alleviate the overcrowding in the prisons; instead, it intensified it.

Remand is not, in theory, a punishment. In fact, however, it is difficult to convince the person remanded of that fact. A sharp increase in the number of remand prisoners suggests that judges too take that attitude. Such a sharp increase is notable in Ghana, as Table 4 indicates.

TABLE 4. REMAND PRISONERS: RANDOM YEARS, 1950–51 TO 1962

Year	Remand prisoners later re- leased	Criminal convicts	Total	Per cent remand prisoners to total
1950–51	5,900	8,353	14,253	41·4%
1953–54	7,366	9,890	17,256	38·1%
1954–55	9,050	10,268	19,318	47·9%
1959	17,586	15,014	32,600	54 %
1962	23,168	20,659	43,827	53·3%

Source: Annual Reports of the Treatment of Offenders.

In 1962, therefore, more prisoners entered the Ghana prisons who were later adjudged not to merit penal treatment, than prisoners who were deemed to merit such a penalty.

The sentencing practices of the courts suggest the absence of any consistent theory of punishment. In the absence of any consistent theory, it is perhaps inevitable that general deterrence or simple retribution should effectively be the primary aims. Fines set so high that the accused cannot pay, a sharp increase in the proportion of convictions resulting in committals, and an equally sudden and sharp decline, wide fluctuations in the proportion of short-term committals and in the length of sentences, the almost complete failure to invoke probation as a method of treatment, and the steady increase in the number and proportion of remand prisoners, all point to this conclusion.

IV Young Offenders

Nevertheless—and, remembering the extent to which Ghanaian penal practices are based on those of England, this is understandable—it is only in the treatment of young offenders that a functional, remedial ideal has been frankly accepted. It is, indeed, precisely on the lines on which England has adopted the ideal that Ghana has chosen to act.

Firstly, the tribunals dealing with boys and girls are the juvenile courts. Their sittings are in private and largely informal. Three magistrates sit together, under a legally qualified chairman who is normally the stipendiary magistrate of the district, and there is provision for one member of every court panel to be a woman. As in the British model, the jurisdiction of juvenile courts does not extend to young adult offenders, who are dealt with by the adult courts. There are eight juvenile courts in the country.

Secondly, although pre-trial or pre-sentence investigation is essential to the success of any functional approach to the treatment of offenders it is not widely used in Ghana. As a result of the chronic shortage of probation officers, the making of reports of investigations has been strictly limited and the courts now tend hardly ever to request them except in juvenile cases: in 1962, for example, 1,272 pre-sentence reports were asked for in juvenile cases, 264 in cases of young adults, and only 71 in adult cases.

Inquiries regarding antecedents are, of course, commonly made by the police, to produce formal background information on the offender. Probation officers' inquiries, however, are undertaken in the context of the officers' casework skills and cover such factors as information about the offender's family and his family relationships, his mental and physical capabilities, his interests and associates, and his attitudes generally, and specifically towards his offence. The officers then give their own assessment of the present life-situation of the offender and conclude by making recommendations for the guidance of the court.

If institutional care is recommended and accepted by the court, the third similarity with the British pattern becomes evident, as the institutional system of Ghana follows in a simplified and much reduced way what is in force in England. A Boys' Home was set up in 1929 at Ada, some seventy miles east of Accra. Run by the Salvation Army—apparently to avoid any identification with the prison system—it provided for the care and training of boys up to the age of 18 years who had been convicted of offences punishable by imprisonment, or who had been neglected or otherwise ill-treated. The inmates received instruction in elementary education and were trained in various trades such as carpentry and shoemaking.

In 1946 the Boys' Home, then stationed in northern Ashanti, was taken over by the Department of Social Welfare, itself a postwar establishment. Now known as the Ministry of Social Welfare and Community Development, it runs four of these homes under the name of industrial schools. Classification is only on elementary lines of sex and age, there being one junior (under 14 years of age) and two senior boys' schools and one for girls. In the last, there is simply the segregation of different age-groups in different dormitories.

There is a single Borstal Institution, situated in Accra and catering for boys of 17 and under 21 years of age. It was established in the early 1940s by the Prisons Department and has been developed after the pattern of English Borstal Institutions.

The training given in the industrial schools and in the Borstal is based upon a mixed programme of trade training and formal education, with emphasis on the former. When an inmate, however, is particularly inclined towards formal education, he is given the opportunity of pursuing his studies either through classes organized internally, or at an ordinary school outside, which he is allowed to attend daily from the institution. In this way, some boys and girls from the industrial schools have either passed the Ghana Middle School Leaving Certificate examination, or succeeded in the general common entrance examination and entered secondary schools or training colleges for teachers. A number from the Borstal are also known to have been pursuing higher technical courses locally or abroad, following their training in the institution.

The main trades taught in the industrial schools are carpentry, masonry and tailoring with farming and cane-work as subsidiary subjects. In the Borstal Institution the programme includes shoemaking, hose-knitting, pottery and training in the driving of farm tractors.

Treatment in the institutions is basically devoted to developing the personality of the inmate. Both an atmosphere conducive to good behaviour and a programme of incentives to honest and industrious life are necessary. For this reason, the internal administration in the industrial schools, for example, is generally based on small units of inmates each under a housemaster and an assistant. Apart from work in the classroom and in the workshop, and apart from such community activities as religious services, singing and some outdoor games, life in the school for each inmate is centred on his particular house unit. The housemaster is the immediate guardian of everybody within the unit, and his duty is to ensure that each inmate learns to live with others and to behave in a way consonant with the principles of the unit. In this way, the inmate is prepared to live acceptably within the broader society outside the school.

The incentives to good behaviour and responsibility in the institutions take the form of awards and promotion to grades of privilege and authority which lead on to parole leave and early discharge. Committals are indeterminate within a maximum of three years, though the maximum may be increased by a subsequent order. An offender so committed may be discharged on licence at any time after six months of detention, in which case he will be under the supervision of an after-care agent for the remainder of the three-year period, with an additional year's supervision required at the expiry of this period.

After-care agents are provided by the Ministry of Social Welfare and Community Development. In the first instance, they provide liaison between the institutions and the homes of the offenders committed. Secondly, they prepare the ground for the offenders' discharge and subsequently guide them through the plans made for their rehabilitation during the supervision on licence. Thereafter, as much intimacy of mutual trust and confidence as possible is maintained between the agent and the discharged offender as a means of following up his progress.

V Conclusion

The principal ethical premise articulated by the Ghana government since independence is that no man shall be treated as a means, but only as an end. How successfully has this premise been implemented thus far in the administration of penal justice?

No spokesman for the government has yet explicitly acknowledged the penological implications of the premise. The government, however, has on occasions expressed humanitarian notions of the treatment of offenders. On the other hand, some recent legislation would seem to raise a question of consistency with the premise. Arguably, there is no inconsistency in the case of heavy minimum deterrent sentences in respect of crimes against the state and economic crimes: a government that is convinced that its social and economic programme is the best guarantee of the attainment of a just and egalitarian society will, almost inevitably, snatch at whatever measure of social control may be found in general deterrence. But there is no evidence that any study has been made that the minima stipulated—some of them extraordinarily long—are really required to achieve the desired deterrent effect; or that the question has been considered, whether general deterrence even in such cases really squares with the premise.

Whatever may be said with respect to crimes against the state and economic crimes can hardly be urged with respect to the severe minima required in cases of abortion and of habitual crime. Whether abortion is really so serious a crime as to merit so stringent a penalty as ten years, even for purposes of deterrence; whether habitual criminals of every sort—even petty thieves—require a ten-year detention; whether such minima are consistent with the government's ethical premise: all these, and a host of similar questions, would appear to require empirical investigation and analysis.

A wide gulf appears to yawn between judicial sentencing practice and the official postulate. The sentences imposed by the courts admit of no systematic analysis; indeed, they suggest that the judges have no clearly defined policy. The inevitable result is that retribution and general deterrence emerge as the objectives attained in practice. A fundamental review of penological policy and judicial sentencing practice seems to be required.

Faced by the physical facts of antiquated prisons, increasing burdens imposed by the rise in committals, antiquated regulations and, above all, universal overcrowding, the Prisons Department appears to be making a reasonable effort to treat the prisoners humanely and, so far as possible, to apply measures directed to the rehabilitation of the criminal. But the appalling overcrowding frustrates both objectives: motivation, no matter how humane, cannot stretch the prisons to twice their size, or produce the open camps and other facilities urgently required.

As a result, the objective of reclaiming the criminal has largely been abandoned. The Ghanaian prisons have, perforce, become inefficient caretaking institutions, in which the prisoners are insufficiently occupied, insufficiently trained, and insufficiently educated to new habits of thought and conduct. The prisoner serves his time and departs, not noticeably better and perhaps the worse for the experience.

What is surprising is that in nearly ten years since independence, during which Ghana has been the one African country pre-eminently to cast aside its colonial trappings in favour of those of nationhood, so little thought should have been given to the problems of attuning Ghanaian law to the social context. The substantive criminal laws remain basically those of the common law, the assumptions of the penal system are British, and the machinery implementing the assumptions is modelled on the British pattern. No systematic review of penal policy has taken place, and little official attempt has been made to articulate the difficulties involved in the application of European norms and policies in the Ghanaian context—or, indeed, to articulate the difficulties of devising new and perhaps more appropriate and effective policies. We earnestly hope that such a review will not be much longer postponed.

NOTES

1. This chapter is concerned with the problem of crime and the treatment of criminal convicts. The treatment of debtor prisoners and of political detainees is not considered. The development of the prison system is dealt with in detail in a later chapter: see p. 429 below.

2. For example, in the middle of the 19th century more prisoners by far were sentenced for theft than for crimes against the person, although in the nature of things the proportion of crimes against the person must have exceeded larcenies. Accusations of crimes against the person were apparently determined without recourse to the English courts.

3. I am especially indebted to the Ghana Police who very kindly brought up to date the existing police statistics on crime for the purposes of this paper, and especially Deputy Commissioner Deku and Inspector Cobbina.

4. See generally Weinberg, 'Juvenile Delinquency in Ghana: A Comparative Analysis of Delinquents and Non-Delinquents', 55 *Journal of Criminal Law, Criminology and Police Science*, 471 (1964); Weinberg, 'Urbanization and Male Delinquency in Ghana', 2 *Journal of Research in Crime and Delinquency*, 85 (1965).

5. In assessing these statistics, it must be noted that the Ghana Police grew in strength throughout the period under review. From 1957 to 1960 alone, it blossomed from 5,866 to 7,366 members, and the rate of growth has not decreased. With the increase in the Force, no doubt there has been an increase in the proportion of offences which have been reported.

6. By contrast, in 1954 there were in England and Wales about 94 reports of *indictable* offences made to the police per 10,000 of population. A substantial proportion of offences arising under the Criminal Code in Ghana would not be indictable in England.

7. Statistics compiled by the Ghana Police.

8. Statistics compiled by the Ghana Police.

9. Statistics compiled by the Ghana Police.

10. Statistics compiled by the Ghana Police.

11. *Annual Reports on the Treatment of Offenders, passim* [hereinafter: *Annual Reports*].

12. Statistics compiled by the Ghana Police.

13. *Annual Reports*, 1948–9, 1962.

14. By contrast, in 1920, of 3,946 committals in the Colony for penal imprisonment, only 482, or 12 per cent, were recidivists; of these, only 81, or 2 per cent, were third offenders: *Blue Book*, 1920. These figures must be viewed with caution, for the police force then was not nearly so extensively organized as it is today.

15. See generally, Read, 'Ghana: The Criminal Code, 1960', 11 *International and Comparative Law Quarterly*, 272 (1962).

16. 1 *Journal of Comparative Legislation*, 147, 177 (1896–7); Stephen, 'A Model Criminal Code for the Colonies', 1 *J. Comp. Leg.* (N.S.) 439 (1899).

17. Circular, February 20th, 1871, ADM 1/691 ['ADM' references are to the National Archives, Accra].

18. Enclosure to Despatch No. 16, January 26th, 1892, Secretary of State to Governor, ADM 1/96.

19. The ambiguity in the concept of deterrence is apparent even in Bentham, the chief ideologue of deterrence: compare Bentham, *Principles of Penal*

Law, Pt. II, Bk. I, c.3 [in *Works*,, 396, 402 (Bowring, ed., 1843)] with *ibid.*, Pt. II, Bk. I, c. 4 (*Works*, 387).

20. Turner, 'The Mental Element in Crimes at Common Law', in Radzinowicz and Turner, eds., *The Modern Approach to Criminal Law*, 198–9, 205 (1945); Hall, *General Principles of Criminal Law*, 2nd ed., 163–70 (1960).

21. Quoted in Radzinowicz and Turner, 'A Study of Punishments: I. Introductory Essay', 21 *Canadian Bar Review*, 97 (1943).

22. Criminal Procedure Code, 1960, s. 294.

23. As early as 1903, out of 3,942 convictions there were only 35 whippings: *Blue Book*, 1903. In 1938–9, out of a total of 29,794 convictions, there were 129 whippings, of which 118 were of juveniles. In the very early period, however, whippings were a usual accompaniment of sentence. For stealing some baulks of wood, one Lartaye in 1858 received, *inter alia*, one dozen lashes: *Civil Record Book I*, June 25th, 1958; another defendant, *inter alia*, 50 lashes for 'having sworn on the head of the Chiefs of Akim and Aquapim': *ibid.*, December 28th, 1858. Acting Governor Bird, in 1859, charged his servant, William Addoe, with being absent from his employment without leave for four days (Addoe claimed he was attending a funeral custom for his sister). He was sentenced to fourteen days' imprisonment and '2 dozen lashes on the spot': *ibid.*, February 22nd, 1859. I can find no statement of the reasons why corporal punishment fell into relative desuetude on the Gold Coast, despite early statements that 'the lash is the only real deterrent': *Blue Book*, 1868.

24. Criminal Procedure Code, 1960, s. 394.

25. s. 296.

26. s. 297(1).

27. s. 297(2).

28. s. 297(3).

29. s. 353(1).

30. *Ibid.*

31. s. 354(1).

32. s. 355(1).

33. s. 355(2).

34. s. 354(3).

35. Criminal Code, 1960, s. 317. Significantly, this is an 'economic' crime.

36. With the exception of murder and treason, which bear the capital penalty.

37. Bentham, *Principles of Penal Law*, Pt. II, Bk. I, c. 6 [in *Works*, Vol. 1, 399–402 (Bowring, ed., 1843)].

38. The Public Property (Protection) and Corrupt Practices (Prevention) Act, 1962.

39. Criminal Code (Amendment) (No. 2) Act, 1962.

40. Criminal Code (Amendment) Act, 1965.

41. The Currency (Amendment) Act, 1965.

42. The Minerals (Control of Smuggling) (Amendment) Act, 1965.

43. The Punishment of Habitual Criminals Act, 1963.

44. The Criminal Code (Amendment) Act, 1962.

45. s. 227.

46. s. 226.

47. s. 228.

48. Criminal Code (Amendment) Act, 1965.

49. The Currency Act, 1964.

50. The Currency (Amendment) Act, 1965.

51. Criminal Code (Amendment) (No. 3) Act, 1962.

52. 30 *Parliamentary Debates,* 135.

53. 27 *Parliamentary Debates,* 169.

54. 27 *Parliamentary Debates,* 172.

55. Criminal Code (Amendment) (No. 3) Act, 1962, (with respect of recidivist thieves), The Public Property (Protection) and Corrupt Practices (Prevention) Act, 1962, and The Punishment of Habitual Criminals Act, 1963.

56. The 'productive hard labour' provisions are not implemented. Persons sentenced under these acts are at present imprisoned.

57. 30 *Parliamentary Debates,* 118.

58. 26 *Parliamentary Debates,* 335; cf. Andreas, 'General Prevention—Illusion or Reality', 43 *Journal of Criminal Law, Criminology and Police Science,* 189 (1952).

59. See 28 *Parliamentary Debates,* 304: 'We are dealing with inhuman monsters who are entirely without scruple and the ordinary attributes of humanity, and for whom the only remedy is complete and absolute extermination'; *ibid.,* 314: 'Recent events—the bomb attack on the Head of State and the second bomb thrown at the masses of this country—justify the measures being taken.' One M.P. said (*ibid.,* 318): 'In the Bible . . . David killed Goliath with a catapult. Since David killed Goliath with a stone it is equally important that catapults be prohibited. If all these fire-arms are prohibited then these mischievous people will certainly turn to such weapons as catapults.' The suggestion was ignored.

60. When questioned in Parliament, the Minister excused the breadth of the language on the ground that of course the Attorney-General would not sanction a prosecution unless there was *mens rea*: 27 *Parliamentary Debates,* 179.

61. Criminal Code (Amendment) Act, 1965.

62. The Currency (Amendment) Act, 1964.

63. *Annual Report,* 1960.

64. *Annual Report,* 1961. This amounted to 25 per cent of all persons convicted. It is the impression of the Prisons Department that the percentage has been increasing since 1962, but statistics are not yet available.

65. *Annual Report,* 1954–5. This amounted to 13 per cent of all persons convicted.

66. Elkin, *The English Penal System,* 41 (1957).

67. *Annual Report,* 1961.

68. Elkin, *op. cit.*, 52.
69. *Annual Report*, 1953-4.
70. *Annual Report*, 1962.
71. Elkin, *op. cit.*, 39.
72. Statistics supplied by the Prisons Department. I am deeply indebted to the Director of Prisons, Mr I. W. Abban, and his Deputy Directors for their whole-hearted co-operation in obtaining information for the preparation of this chapter.

It is interesting that in England in 1954 for a population of 44 million and 106,000 convictions for *indictable* offences, there were 19,600 sentences to imprisonment, and about 5,000 committals in default of fine, or a total of about 24,600 committals. In Ghana in 1964, for a population of about 8 million and 48,329 convictions for *all* offences, there were 15,792 committals (including committals in default of fine).
73. *Annual Report*, 1950-1.
74. *Annual Report*, 1961.
75. Statistics supplied by the Prisons Department.
76. *Annual Report*, 1961.
77. Statistics supplied by the Prisons Department.
78. *Annual Report*, 1962.
79. Statistics supplied by the Prisons Department.
80. Statistics supplied by the Prisons Department.

4
Kenya, Tanzania and Uganda[1]

JAMES S. READ

I Introduction

To the African inhabitants of East Africa, the western type of penal system introduced during the colonial period was essentially alien in character and purpose. Traditional African modes of maintaining law and order were replaced by the unfamiliar apparatus of police, courts and prisons. Many problems resulted and there was a continuous need for the adaptation and development of the penal system, a need intensified by the sweeping economic and social changes which greatly affected the incidence and effects of different forms of punishment. There were those, both African and European, official and non-official, who insisted that the system applied was fundamentally unsuitable. In the era of independent African governments, still comparatively new in East Africa, the basic structure of the penal systems established by colonial rule remains, but the opportunity and the challenge presented by its inadequacies remain as major factors in the field of social progress.

Even before independence, penal policy did not merely imitate the English pattern, but was marked by interesting experiments such as the detention camps of Kenya and the extra-mural penal labour system of Tanganyika. Since independence, Tanganyika has adopted a novel penal instrument in the limited provision for minimum sentences combining imprisonment, corporal punishment and compensation. It is likely that in future years the East African countries, while carefully studying penal developments in western and other foreign countries, will endeavour to evolve their own methods of treating offenders. The strong impulse to assert a genuine independence from foreign control plays a significant part in the formation of national domestic policy. Independent African governments and—more significantly in this context—government departments run by African senior officers, as are the prison services throughout East Africa today, are clearly better able and more inclined to recognize and take account of African feelings and reactions than were the colonial officials (however well-intentioned) of the past. In modern African countries, western influences have been extensive and crucial, but the fundamental structure of society for most people is still essentially of an indigenous pattern. Adapted traditional patterns and laws dominate family life, land tenure and succession—for a predominantly rural population, the most vital areas of law—in most countries. Even in the growing urban areas, where the problems of rapid urbanization are increasingly felt, traditional attitudes and practices will long persist, merging into a new way of urban life which will derive as much from Africa as from the west.

As in many western countries, in East Africa the principal penal reformers are found in the government departments concerned with the treatment of offenders. The main difficulties which they face are those of identifying the nature and scale of the problems facing them, and convincing public opinion and political authorities of the financial and manpower resources which are needed. But in East Africa there is the additional problem of assessing how much of the colonial heritage in this field should be retained, with the knowledge that much of it antedates modern reforms introduced in the United Kingdom. And as East Africa participates in the world-wide movement towards more enlightened, and more effective, penal systems, a fundamental question arises: how far, from this diverse heritage of colonial and traditional concepts, and from the current search for a specifically African response to modern problems, will a distinctively African type of penal system evolve? And how much can it derive from traditional African ideas?

This survey of the current systems and their development is inevitably restricted in extent. The material available for such a study is sadly limited and fragmentary; documentary sources include the annual reports of the relevant government departments, published reports of official inquiries and discussions, and the laws which govern the sentencing and treatment of offenders. An attempt has been made to provide some samples of statistical data, reconstructed from the slender material of official figures published; but the sources are inadequate, and changes made from time to time in the presentation of official reports make it impossible to compile comprehensive tables for more than a few consecutive years. A further problem is that the statistics from different departments sometimes do not coincide. Research in this field has been virtually non-existent until recent years: even sociologists who have worked in the area have commonly ignored the possibilities for research among prisoners. There is, therefore, a total lack of first-hand accounts of the actual impact of the penal system and the first report on the reactions of East African prisoners is the pioneering work of Mr Tanner published in Chapter 11 below.

The present discussion is an outline of the development and present operation of the penal system: impressions of its impact upon individuals must be sought elsewhere.[2]

II The Nature and Incidence of Crime

I THE CRIMINAL LAW AND ITS ADMINISTRATION

The colonial period in East Africa dates effectively from the late 19th century, although of course European contact with the coastal areas was many centuries old at that time and there had been particularly close international contact with Zanzibar. Before the colonial introduction of western legal systems, the laws of East Africa consisted of the customary laws of the different indigenous communities, and the Islamic law which was administered in Zanzibar and in the coastal Moslem societies. Modern colonization led to the rapid introduction of western legal systems.

93

In the Protectorates of Uganda and East Africa (later to be known as Kenya) English criminal law was at first applied, to be replaced at an early date by the Indian Penal Code and the Indian Code of Criminal Procedure, which were also introduced in Zanzibar. In German East Africa the Imperial Criminal Code of Germany was applied, also to be replaced by the Indian Penal Code on the assumption of British jurisdiction under the League of Nations mandate over Tanganyika Territory. In the coastal areas and even in Zanzibar, Islamic laws concerning crime were gradually ousted, though the African communities throughout East Africa retained their customary laws and administered them principally through the 'native', or later 'African' or 'local', courts. The Indian Codes were replaced throughout this area in 1930 (in Zanzibar, 1934) by the Penal Codes and Criminal Procedure Codes which are still in operation and which were intended to reintroduce in codified form the basic principles of criminal law and punishment in force in England.[3]

Until recent years the dual systems of courts have continued in operation throughout East Africa, the High Court and magistrates' (or subordinate) courts applying mainly the introduced law and local legislation to all persons, and the African courts applying mainly the unwritten customary laws and some minor legislation to Africans only. These African courts were constituted as formalized tribunals approximating more or less, depending on the area, to traditional organs of tribal government. In earliest colonial days there was little interference with the tribal courts. Over their procedure and punishments in the East African Protectorate,

> European administrative officers are directed to exercise a reasonable supervision, not unduly interfering with them, unless they should be essentially inhuman or unjust, as for instance, where convictions are obtained by witchcraft or torture, or entail barbarous penalties such as mutilation, cruel corporal punishments, or the enslavement of a condemned person or his relations.[4]

During the colonial period these courts gradually changed in constitution and procedure, increasingly accepting principles of English law and procedure which were introduced partly as funda-

94

mental rules of justice applied by superior judicial or administrative authorities in reviewing African courts' decisions. The distinction between civil and criminal cases, as understood in English jurisprudence, was inculcated by the supervising authorities and there developed in each country a recognized body of modern customary criminal law, which in theory at least was merely a continuation of traditional local customs. Training courses for certain judges of the African courts, in which emphasis was given to the notions of English law, were other means by which western legal principles were advanced. Customary criminal law thus grew into a comparatively sophisticated set of rules capable of application to many of the situations of modern life. Thus, riding a bicycle at night was early held to be a customary criminal offence in Buganda by extension of the ancient custom that it was unlawful to wander abroad at night without a lamp (as evidence of honest intention). The African courts also, of course, acquired jurisdiction to impose penalties for breaches of local by-laws and other minor legislation.

Inasmuch as these courts were constituted under statutory authority, their powers, the orders they could make and the sentences they could pass were also prescribed by statute. Thus, the sanctions in fact imposed for crimes—even those against customary law—were generally of western type, for the penalties which the courts were empowered to apply were defined by legislation in terms of the penalties with which the colonial legislator was most familiar. It was no doubt paradoxical that, although these courts were allowed to judge guilt on the basis of an adapted customary law, it was regarded as part of the civilizing mission of the colonial power to substitute for the traditional penal sanctions those familiar to western nations. The rationale for this policy has been explained thus:

> The demand therefore is not simply for the recognition of indigenous law, but for the application of non-indigenous penal sanctions to infringements of native law which were formerly settled by the payment of compensation. The justification for this demand seems to be that in consequence of the breakdown of the indigenous system there has arisen a need for greater emphasis on the deterrent aspect of justice, and that

for this purpose the mere award of compensation is inadequate.[5]

Fines and imprisonment therefore became standard forms of punishment for offenders who had broken traditional laws. The administrator of the time would probably explain that the recognition of crimes as a distinct category of legal wrongs was not generally found in the customary laws, and that traditional penal sanctions were therefore difficult to identify; and that in some areas some of the traditional sanctions—such as mutilation and severe beatings—were such as could not be tolerated by a western power. Indeed, the survival of such traditional penalties was to produce on occasions a dramatic clash between the old ideas and European principles. In one case, a suspected witch was 'tried' at a large tribal meeting and hanged: forty-four villagers were sentenced to death for murder, though forty-one successfully appealed.[6] A similar situation could arise where the traditional sanction was imposed even by a statutory native tribunal. In 1913 a recognized Kikuyu council (Kiama) tried and condemned certain persons for witchcraft; the sentence was carried out by relatives of the victims, who were forced by the council members to set fire to a hut in which the condemned had been placed. The council members were tried for murder, and it was proved that they were not instructed as to the limits of their authority, that they acted on their chief's advice and that they believed they were justified in exercising their ancient customary jurisdiction. They were convicted of culpable homicide not amounting to murder, having acted in good faith in excess of their powers as public servants, and each was sentenced to one day's imprisonment and a fine.[7]

It will be seen shortly that there were valuable notions in the area of sanctions applied by traditional African legal systems. Provision was made in the colonial legislation for the African courts to award compensation for criminal offences and this was done, often in situations where traditionally it would also have been appropriate. There was, moreover, a residual power to award undefined penalties known to customary law (which were not contrary to fundamental moral principles of the colonial authority) but this avenue appears generally to have been left unexplored in face of the easy and fashionable options of imprisonment, fine and other newly-introduced punishments.[8]

Thus the African courts which dealt with the large majority of minor criminal matters in the colonial period imposed western penal sanctions for breaches of unwritten customary law, which itself increasingly grew to reflect English ideas of criminal law, and by a form of procedure which approximated ever more closely to English law. In 1939, the Attorney-General of Uganda could write of 'the system of native justice' that 'in regard to criminal law in particular, its main principles and concepts are now in close approximation to our system'.[9] In Kenya, indeed, the African courts were at an early stage given a wide jurisdiction to administer certain parts of the statutory criminal laws and this jurisdiction was extended, until in recent years it comprised most of the enacted criminal law. This process did, of course, involve many problems and conflicts, more especially at earlier stages when the same laws were enforced 'according to entirely different rules of procedure and evidence in native tribunals and magistrates' courts respectively'.[10]

Usually, of course, the African courts from an early stage had only restricted powers in regard to sentence. Exceptionally, however, where there had been a highly organized traditional polity, the courts were allowed to retain wider powers; thus, in Buganda, where the Protectorate dated from 1894, the Kabaka's courts retained until 1917 the power to impose the death sentence according to customary law (although such sentences were subject to confirmation by the Protectorate Government); under the Uganda Agreement, 1900, appeal lay from the Kabaka's courts to the High Court where a sentence of more than five years' imprisonment or a fine exceeding £100 was imposed and the Protectorate Government retained a 'right of remonstrance' with the Kabaka in the case of any sentence which seemed 'disproportionate or inconsistent with humane principles'.[11]

The judicial system within which the penal system had developed in East Africa was not destined to continue long after the attainment of independence in the early 1960s. Two policy factors were of vital significance. Firstly, the dual courts systems have been, or are being, replaced by a unified system in each country, to end racial distinctions and confusion in the administration of justice. Secondly, the principle has been accepted that unwritten criminal law is a threat to individual liberty and security, being ill-defined and imprecise. Unwritten customary law was doomed in Uganda and Kenya by constitutional provisions forbidding the punishment of any person for an offence not defined by written law; in Tanganyika, customary criminal law was abolished by the legislation which effected the integration of the courts system.[12] In Kenya, a research project resulted in the recording of those customary criminal offences (such as adultery) which still applied in 1963; in Uganda, the legislature of the Federal State of Buganda enacted a special code of customary criminal law for that state.[13] However, the main result of the recent reforms has been the establishment in each country of a unified system of courts, applying, according to basically unified systems of procedure and evidence, a unified body of criminal law: the penal sanctions available are applicable generally and are of western type, but there are some provisions still which reflect African attitudes. Thus, the lower courts are authorized to promote the settlement of criminal cases by reconciling the parties, and compensation may be awarded to victims of crimes on a scale much wider than that applicable in English law. There are some special enactments regarding the payment of blood-money.[14]

Despite this modern reconstruction, it would be impossible to comprehend the way in which the penal system operates without this examination of its history. But it would be a mistake to assume that in the field of penal law, customary law has been completely eclipsed. There are various ways in which the courts may still be obliged to refer directly to rules of customary law, even when applying the terms of the criminal legislation. When the customary laws remain the dominant source of rules on a wide range of basic matters for the majority of citizens, it would be illogical to suppose that the principles and presumptions of such laws could be ignored in the field of penal law. The adaptation of the penal laws can be considered only in the context of the attitudes and beliefs of the communities as a whole, as reflected to a great extent in their customary laws.

2 THE INCIDENCE OF CRIME

Crime rates in East African countries appear low when compared with those of western countries. Apart from a few particular categories of crimes, such as homicide and cattle-theft, serious crime has only grown to be a regular problem, outside the comparatively few urban areas, in recent years. Yet, as will be seen later, the penal systems have been constantly expanding and are still under severe strain. The overcrowding of prisons in recent years has been largely due to the short-term imprisonment of an increasing number of offenders against tax and local laws. In Kenya and Tanganyika the majority of prisoners are serving short sentences, although in Uganda there is a large proportion of long-term prisoners. In all three countries the majority of prisoners are first offenders, but the recidivists have tended to increase in number steadily.

Table 1 gives statistics of convictions in Kenya from 1955 to 1960 for certain types of offences, showing a rise in offences against property over this period, with substantial increases in offences relating to stock and produce and in forgery. Table 2 shows the increases in serious crime in Uganda over the years 1958–64, especially in offences against property and offences against the person. That the total number of persons convicted by the High Court and subordinate courts actually declined from 14,250 in 1958 to 14,111 in 1964 must be explained by the fact that to some extent there was an increase in the seriousness of crimes being committed.[15]

Table 3 gives figures of convictions in Tanganyika in 1962. It shows that of nearly 34,000 convictions, about two-thirds were for assaults, thefts and burglaries. There were only 196 convictions for homicide and the majority of these resulted in prison sentences for the lesser offence of manslaughter, a very small number indeed being sentenced to death for murder (12). Figures for other forms of serious crimes are low, except for grievous harm (819), receiving stolen property (718) and obtaining by false pretences (558). More than one-third of the total were dealt with by fining.

In Kenya, in 1961, the total number of reported crimes under the Penal Code was 44,470; in 1962, 46,561—an increase of 4·7 per cent.

TABLE I. KENYA: PERSONS CONVICTED OF CERTAIN OFFENCES
BY SUBORDINATE COURTS, 1955–60

	1955	1956	1957	1958	1959	1960
1. Offences against lawful authority	1,102	1,238	1,410	1,563	1,467	1,632
2. Offences injurious to public in general	—	761	1,695	1,115	1,316	1,269
3. Offences against the person	1,533	2,077	2,239	1,922	1,663	1,699
4. Offences relating to property other than stock and produce	6,625	8,783	9,161	8,314	7,999	8,826
5. Offences relating to stock and produce	413	411	733	764	968	1,093
6. Malicious injury to property	295	340	298	354	431	444
7. Forgery, Coining, and counterfeiting	—	253	707	704	639	603

Source: Reports of the Judicial Department.

Notes: The categories of offences are those recognized by the Penal Code:
No. 1 includes offences relating to the public service and the administration of
justice; No. 2 includes sexual offences, nuisances, etc.

TABLE 2 UGANDA: SERIOUS CASES TRIED BY HIGH COURT AND
SUBORDINATE COURTS, 1958–64

	1958	1959	1960	1961	1962	1963	1964
Homicide	231	321	216	224	285	266	401
Rape	21	27	30	30	35	42	26
Unnatural crimes	—	4	3	3	10	—	—
Offences against property with violence to the person	58	73	107	100	484	289	663
Other offences against property	522	652	999	821	2,745	3,672	3,740
Other offences against the person	45	61	84	77	960	1,958	1,970
Miscellaneous offences	30	31	51	57	4,268	5,140	4,133
Totals	907	1,169	1,490	1,312	8,787	11,367	10,933

Source: Reports of the Judiciary.

TABLE 3. TANGANYIKA: CONVICTIONS AND SENTENCES IMPOSED, PENAL CODE OFFENCES, 1962

	Total convictions		Imprisoned		Fined		Probation etc.	
	M	F	M	F	M	F	M	F
Offences against lawful authority	1,002	21	819	18	157	1	26	2
Sexual and other offences against morality	1,350	60	874	9	340	37	121	14
Offences against the person	10,174	870	3,718	112	5,597	669	767	85
Offences against property	16,169	402	11,081	152	3,199	187	1,686	60
Other offences	5,271	421	1,874	61	2,703	297	649	63
Totals	33,966	1,774	18,366	352	11,996	1,191	3,249	224

Source: Judiciary Reports.

The total population of Kenya in 1961 was approximately 6,550,700, giving a rate for reported Penal Code offences of approximately 6,788 per million in that year. In England and Wales in 1960–61, the average number per million inhabitants aged 8 or over of reported offences of larceny alone was 12,631, or nearly double the Kenya rate for all Penal Code crimes. Of course, comparisons with other countries are of little value except as general indications of the comparative incidence of crime: social and economic factors vary so greatly, and so too do police methods and activity. The incidence of particular offences within an overall pattern is not comparable: for example, in England and Wales in 1961 there was a total of 532 known cases of murder, manslaughter and attempts to murder (plus 521 cases of causing death by dangerous driving); in Kenya, in 1961, with a population about one-eighth as large, 341 cases of murder, manslaughter and attempts to murder were reported. Homicide rates are generally higher in East Africa than in England: in Uganda, in 1961, 740 cases of murder and manslaughter were reported.

These figures, and those given in the tables, must be related to the population statistics, which in 1960 were officially estimated as Kenya: 6·5 million; Tanganyika: 9·2 million; Uganda: 6·7 million; and Zanzibar (1958): 299,111.

III The Development of Penal Systems in East Africa

I TRADITIONAL SANCTIONS

As the principal problem already posed involves reference to traditional African ideas of penal sanctions, it is necessary to make some attempt to consider the ways in which offenders were treated in the African communities of East Africa before the new types of penal sanctions were adopted. The attempt is inevitably unsatisfactory because of the dearth of reliable information. The customary laws of East Africa as they existed at the beginning of the colonial period are ill-documented, but some generalizations can be offered, at the risk of distorting the true position in any one area.

The great diversity of political, social and juridical structures in the area resulted in great differences in legal procedures. At one extreme lay the large, highly organized interlacustrine kingdoms such as Buganda, Bunyoro and Ankole, where hereditary rulers governed through centralized administrative hierarchies with sometimes potentially despotic powers. Judicial and legislative authority was formalized, with recognized machinery for law enforcement. At the other end of the political spectrum lay acephalous societies like the Kikuyu where a well-ordered, gerontocratic social system involved an intricate and complex system of clan authorities and age-grades. Here there was no specialized judicial system and a breach of custom might be met by self-help or by community action, involving in an extreme case the collective imposition of a suitable penalty by means of an *ad hoc*, though customary, process.

In the centralized societies, remedies for offences might often take the form of the recovery of compensation. The distinction between civil and criminal matters would be difficult to apply, but usually some point might be reached in particular cases where the need to uphold the law would demand deterrent or retributive action on the part of the ruler or his subordinates. In an acephalous society, where authority resided in the whole community, speaking through a council of elders or other organ, such a situation might be less likely to arise. The incidence of 'penal sanctions', identifiable as such by western standards, would clearly vary between the different communities.

Some general features were, however, common to most traditional societies in East Africa. They knew no prisons. Forms of physical restraint were used, but normally only to detain an offender pending his trial or punishment and even then rarely; certainly detention in itself does not appear to have been regarded as a punishment. In the kingdom of Ankole, a kind of stocks was used on rare occasions to detain offenders, usually pending execution; and an escaped suspect might be brought back from some distant place 'tied with a rope . . . but even that was considered to be too degrading to the accused'.[16] Stocks were used also in Buganda, but prisons were introduced only after the advent of British rule, despite an early reference which suggests otherwise.[17]

What penal sanctions, then, were imposed? From various accounts, several modes of treatment for offenders can be discerned.

Firstly, what was generally sought in legal proceedings for injuries was not so much the punishment of the offender as the compensation of the victim. This is, of course, a principal characteristic of many legal systems at similar stages of development. The scant attention given to the compensating of the victim by the modern criminal laws of East Africa has come to be a source of real dissatisfaction and popular criticism: the victim or his family may feel that no justice has been done, whatever penalty is imposed on the offender, while recompense for the injury is ignored. Junod has shown that this feeling is not restricted to East Africa.[18] In some communities, compensation for certain common injuries was probably in the recent past fixed at a definite rate: Kenyatta records for Kikuyu law that nine sheep or goats had to be paid for adultery or rape, and one hundred sheep or ten cows for homicide, and that this rate did not vary with the wealth or age of the victim, nor with the intention or motive of the killer.[19] This compensation is seen mainly as a balancing payment, to restore the equilibrium of society. The fact that the payment was compensatory rather than penal in intention is reflected in the fact that the family of the offender might be held collectively liable to produce the payment.

Secondly, the payment of a fine or costs to the court or council concerned in settling the case was widely accepted. A young Kamba who persisted in drinking beer without his father's permission could apparently see his prospective inheritance of livestock diminished by fines taken by the family elders.[20]

Corporal punishment of all degrees of severity was known. Death, mutilation, beating and torture were employed as penalties but usually with a very limited application. Death was commonly imposed as a last resort in cases of offenders who had, by the persistence or gravity of their crimes, made themselves dangerous beyond the limits of endurance of their fellows. The machinery of government available to the ruler of a centralized state made it easier to impose this type of penalty, but even in acephalous communities there were occasions when special solemn procedures were adopted, resulting in an execution. In Kikuyu law homicide was normally a matter for compensation, but causing death by poison or witchcraft 'was looked upon as a crime against the whole community, and the penalty was death by burning'. Similarly, theft generally resulted in compensation being paid but an habitual thief was a public danger and was executed.[21] Of the Chiga of Uganda, it is recorded that most breaches of the law were matters only for the small family group, within which most offences would be settled; but

> The only thing that excites community action against one of its members, beyond the limits of the close kin-group directly affected, is a case of witchcraft. . . . A murderer is merely acting as anyone might under similar circumstances: that's human nature. . . . Witchcraft, on the other hand, is a total character

defect, not just a wrong action ... the whole community ...
is menaced ... everyone will join in the mob action of stoning
him or her to death.[22]

The interdependence of individuals in the close-knit societies of
earlier times made ostracism a potent sanction. This might take the
form of social ostracism, perhaps with public ridicule such as attended the pillory in England. Or it might extend to the most
extreme penalty, short of death—banishment, often by a formal
ritual. This was a highly effective penalty:

> The stigma attached to the ostracism was far greater and very
> much worse than that attached to the European form of im-
> prisonment. Many Kikuyu would prefer to go to jail rather
> than to be ostracized. The fear of this was one of the chief
> factors which prevented the people from committing crimes.[23]

Finally, the religious climate of the time made it necessary as
well as convenient to invoke supernatural sanctions in dealing with
many offences. To protect the community from the hostility of
ancestral or other spirits and to expiate the guilty on the one hand
would require remedial religious rites; whereas, on the negative
side, curses of a formal denunciatory kind would also serve as
powerful penal sanctions. Among the Nandi of Kenya, curses
might be uttered by the elders for serious disobedience and unless
formally removed they would prove fatal, spreading also through
the offender to his family and descendants. Less serious matters
could bring down curses from individuals: 'the curse was altogether a most effective sanction, and often merely the threat of it
sufficed to inhibit a crime or to extract a confession of guilt.'[24]

In the Moslem communities of Zanzibar and the coastal area, it
was of course Islamic law which had been applied before British
rule and which for a time continued to apply. The conflict of ideas
which developed was noted by an early administrator:

> According to strict Mahommedan law murder may be atoned
> for, and in cases of mutilation the application of the *lex talionis*,
> which I need scarcely say now no longer obtains in practice,
> may be avoided by the payment of *'diya'* or blood-money with
> the consent of the victim, or, if he has been killed, of his legal
> heirs; and though Eastern Princes have rarely hesitated in

moments of anger to order wholesale executions or massacres, the deliberate infliction in cold blood of a capital sentence, without regard to the prayers of the condemned man or his relatives, is very repugnant to the Mussulman mind.

It may, therefore, sometimes be expedient, if the application of penalties is to correspond to the conceptions of justice prevailing among those whom they are intended to protect or deter, not too rigorously to execute capital sentences even in cases in which one might not hesitate to do so in Europe, should the slightest justification exist for indulgence, but to impose in such instances, in addition to the blood-money required for the satisfaction of the injured party, such terms of imprisonment or penal servitude as may be deemed necessary to satisfy the offended majesty of the law.

Meanwhile, as civilization spreads and European institutions acquire a greater hold upon the country, these primitive individualistic conceptions, which exist among the heathen tribes of the interior, as well as among the coast people, will gradually disappear and give place to views more consonant with our own as to the rights and duties of society as a whole.[25]

These, then, were the sanctions known to the African communities of East Africa at the time when the colonial intrusion brought with it the instruments of western penal policy. It is only too easy to justify the need for new sanctions in the changing circumstances of the area, but it would be a mistake to assume that the sanctions available to traditional authorities before colonization were inadequate or primitive for the societies of the time. They served particularly to promote public satisfaction by the reconciliation of offender and victim, sometimes by a formal process and often after payment of compensation, to remove the danger caused by an intolerable individual and to placate the spirits by expiatory rituals.

2 PENAL SANCTIONS DURING THE COLONIAL PERIOD

There were two stages in the evolution of the penal systems in the colonial period. First there was the introduction of the western ideas and apparatus—legislation, prisons, the training of staff and the gradual replacement of the traditional attitudes in the minds of African court judges and local inhabitants by an understanding of the new processes. The second half of the colonial period was marked by an increasing recognition of the problems which resulted from the large-scale adoption of western methods, by a critical re-appraisal of the system by a series of official inquiries and by the adoption of a number of amendments and innovations designed to improve the functioning and effectiveness of the penal system.

(a) The introduction of western penal methods

The earliest introduction of English criminal law was probably a step backwards rather than forwards, until the administration of justice had been organized on a sound footing. The Protectorate of Uganda was established in 1894, and some notes of cases in the records include some instructive decisions. In 1896, on a charge of stealing a paw-paw worth 50 cowries, the record is that 'The prisoner is convicted of larceny and sentenced to a whipping to be administered by her sister-in-law and guardian.' In another case of the same period, the sentence of the court was a fine on the prosecutor!

It has already been noted that in East Africa the British type of penal system first developed in association with the Indian Penal Code. The latter was, of course, based to some extent upon English law, with many variations; the penalties prescribed were essentially the same as those of 19th-century England. Fines and imprisonment soon became the staple diet of sentencing courts in East Africa. Imprisonment, under the Indian Code, was of three kinds: penal servitude, for Europeans and Americans only (for whom it was the alternative to transportation); rigorous imprisonment (which corresponded to imprisonment with hard labour); and simple imprisonment. Death was an optional punishment for several offences, including murder. Transportation, of course, had been abolished in England half a century before the Indian Code introduced it into East Africa.

Even at an early date the courts were prepared to adapt the penal laws to some extent to meet the situation which they considered to confront them. Thus, in 1903 the High Court of the East Africa

107

Protectorate upheld an order for the 'collective punishment' by fine and imprisonment of five men taken prisoner at a village where stolen cattle had been found, although it added an order, which the lower court had not provided, that on payment of an increased fine the men should be released. The judges noted that collective punishment was appropriate 'where an offence which has clearly been committed by one or more members of that community cannot definitely be brought home to the actual perpetrators'.[26] Statutory authority for such punishments was provided by the Collective Punishment Ordinance, which was used particularly extensively in Kenya during the Mau Mau emergency.[27]

The first prisons in Uganda were established not by the colonial government but by the native government of Buganda, soon after the declaration of the Protectorate in 1894. Two prisons were set up, by the Protestant and Catholic ministers respectively, and when the second minister's post was suppressed under the Uganda Agreement of 1900, the two prisons were merged. The early custodian of one of them has given his name, Njabule, as the popular term for the central Buganda prison down to the present day.[28] Prisons were later established by the colonial government of Uganda, under legislation of 1903, replaced in 1909, but Buganda has continued to maintain a separate prison system to the present time and the other local administrations within Uganda have also been allowed to develop their own prison establishments. There has been for many years, therefore, a dual prison system in Uganda, with numerous problems arising in the attempt to achieve comparable standards of accommodation, staff, diet, training facilities and so on.

In the neighbouring East Africa Protectorate, the earliest years of British rule saw the ancient Fort Jesus at Mombasa soon reorganized as a central prison

on European lines, the prisoners being classified, supplied with regular rations (instead of, as formerly, depending on the charity of their friends or humane strangers), performing regular labour, light or hard, according to the nature of their sentence, and being permitted to earn by good conduct a reduction or mitigation of their punishment.[29]

108

Prisoners sentenced to six months' imprisonment or more in any part of the Protectorate were sent here while those sentenced to less than six months served their sentences in the barracks or forts of the towns where they were convicted, often merely in cells in the government stations. In 1897, Fort Jesus held an average of about 130 convicts at a time; during the year July 1st, 1897–June 30th, 1898, 549 convicts were admitted, including 2 Europeans, 39 Indians and 34 Arabs. The prison was also used for the custody of vagrants, lunatics and paupers, who were accommodated separately from the convicts.[30] Prison Regulations, based on the system of discipline in other British territories, were issued in 1897. The Indian Prisons Act was later applied, until replaced by the local Prisons Ordinance.

In German East Africa, the first prisons were set up to accommodate offenders against the Imperial Criminal Code of 1870. Capital punishment was by decapitation; there were various categories of imprisonment, from 'penal internment' for up to fifteen years to 'confinement' in less arduous conditions for a maximum of five years, and 'detention'. Other penalties authorized were 'loss of civic rights' and 'police supervision'. It is commonly accepted that a characteristic of the German administration was the widespread and frequent use of corporal punishment as a summary punishment. It was not provided for in the Code but was evidently invoked regularly for breaches of other laws, rules and administrative directions. 'Corporal punishment appears to take a prominent part in the enforcement of the laws, for in 1911–12 no less than 5,944 official floggings were administered.'[31] This policy made a deep impression, an impression oddly intensified when it was seen that the British policy which followed was to reverse the process and reduce drastically the application of corporal punishment. English colonial judges in Tanganyika from the first tried to restrict the use of flogging.[32] It is notable that when after independence the wide extension of corporal punishment by the Minimum Sentences Act, 1963, was accomplished, it was the German policy which was cited with approval by many speakers in the Parliamentary debate.[33]

Soon after the British military victory in East Africa and the assumption of British administration, the Indian Penal Code was applied and an ordinance for the management of prisons was enacted in 1921. During the period of British authority which followed, the penal systems developed on lines which generally reflected developments in the United Kingdom, although the administrations and legislatures of the dependent territories were not, of course, able to keep pace with all changes in the English law. Economic depression and war dominated official attention for much of the time.

The present statute laws concerning the penal systems are found in three types of enactment. There is first in each country a Penal Code which defines criminal offences and prescribes the maximum sentences which can be imposed; the Criminal Procedure Codes define the procedure of the courts in trial, sentencing and appeal; and finally a series of special statutes deal with specific forms of treatment, such as prisons, probation, approved schools and so on.

The types of penalty authorized by these laws in East Africa today are familiar to those acquainted with the English penal policy. Capital punishment, imprisonment, fines, corporal punishment, probation, binding over, discharges, special institutions for juveniles—all these are available in each country. Preventive detention in Uganda and corrective training in Kenya are based on the English precedents, but there are some local innovations not paralleled by English methods, notably extra-mural penal employment in Tanganyika and Kenya, detention camps in Kenya and minimum sentences in Tanganyika.

(b) The penal systems under review

The colonial penal systems did not go unquestioned. Many problems were apparent in the adaptation of the systems to African countries which formerly had quite different modes of treatment for deviant behaviour. There was the basic problem for judges and magistrates of how to assess sentences—what factors should be taken into account when social and economic conditions differed so greatly from England? It must be admitted that a satisfactory answer was rarely found to this problem.[34] The impact of imprisonment upon a mainly rural community, to whom it was unfamiliar, was increasingly thought to differ fundamentally from its impact in England. The imposition of fines upon offenders who were only just moving into a cash economy called for the most delicate judg-

110

ment if the prisons were not to be crowded with short-term inmates who defaulted in payment of monetary penalties from sheer necessity. Because of these difficulties, support was forthcoming from African and expatriate sources for the extension of corporal punishment. But this was an argument from despair, abandoning as hopeless the search for more constructive alternatives; and other voices were raised protesting that corporal punishment was already invoked to excess.[35]

On a number of occasions in the colonial history of East Africa, such arguments as these stimulated the appointment of official inquiries by committees or commissions. Thus, in Kenya a special Commission reported in 1923 on the subject of 'Native Punishment'. Colonial policy at the time was to restrict corporal punishment to a few offences, mainly of gross immorality or brutal violence. A number of witnesses before the Commission urged the extension of flogging as an appropriate means of punishment. The Commission thought that this recommendation was made because witnesses realized that imprisonment was an unsuitable form of punishment, but the Commission reported that evidence from African witnesses showed that imprisonment was the most dreaded form of penalty, and that sentences of imprisonment did not inculcate either contempt or liking for prison.

> The arguments advanced in favour of flogging are that it is inexpensive, that it is summary, that the native is a child and should therefore be punished as a child and that it is effective.

The Commission rejected this view:

> . . . it is doubtful if natives can be flogged to a higher morality. It has in the end a brutalizing effect both on the convict, on the magistrate and on the person who inflicts the punishment, and it should in our opinion be confined to juveniles, who might be caned for trivial offences, and to those who commit brutal crimes, who should be flogged.

This was the view of the Chief Justice and one other member of the Commission; but a majority of members, while agreeing that flogging should be restricted, considered that caning should be used as an alternative to imprisonment for many minor offenders, largely to prevent their contamination by hardened criminals in prison. With regard to fines, the Commission emphasized that they should have some relation to the earning capacity of the accused. The very low average level of wages throughout East Africa even to the present day, and the fact that the majority of people have no employment and small earnings from cash crops, must therefore result in fines being imposed at a much lower level than elsewhere, and also in some disparity between different sections of the community because of the large disparities of wealth.

This point recurred in the next examination of penal policy by a Committee of the Legislative Council of Tanganyika. This was appointed in 1931 to consider the question of restricting imprisonment as far as possible so that it might not lose its value through familiarity, and of reducing to a minimum the harmful effects of the association of minor offenders with habitual offenders. The Governor of the time was concerned by the comparatively high number of admissions to prisons, which in 1929 had amounted to approximately 1·5 persons per thousand of the African population. Furthermore, almost one-third of the admissions were of persons on remand who were subsequently acquitted, discharged or given sentences other than imprisonment.[36] The Committee was specifically asked to consider whether the fines imposed were unduly severe, having regard to the capacity of the average person to pay, resulting in an unduly high proportion of sentences of imprisonment in default of payment being carried out.[37]

In its Report, the Committee recommended an increase in the number of judges, to expedite trials, and an increase in the number of police lock-ups to lessen the number of remand prisoners in prison. The Committee found that fines imposed were often beyond the individual's ability to pay, rendering the option of a fine illusory. It was emphasized that when fines were paid, hardship often fell upon the relatives and friends of the convicted person. And one witness at least stressed not merely the general inadequacy but the inappropriateness of fining in general:

In the case of assault, the aggressor, if he is fined, makes a mock of the person he has assaulted, because according to his idea he has not only beaten him but he has paid for him.

The Committee concluded laconically:

> ... in some instances fines have given rise to misunderstanding, bitterness and doubt in the mind of the native, who has a clear idea of the equity of compensation but no comprehension of the reason for a fine other than the belief (still prevalent, although dying) that the money paid in respect of fines goes into the pocket of the magistrate.

It recommended that for first offenders, fines might well be replaced in many cases with cautions or binding over to keep the peace; that strict and full inquiry should be made into the individual's ability to pay before a fine was imposed, and that corporal punishment should be extended, particularly for juveniles.

In its examination of imprisonment, the Committee made a recommendation which was in due course to bear fruit in an important development of the penal system in Tanganyika. First, it assumed that imprisonment would continue for want of any suitable alternative. It recommended that to increase the deterrent effect of prison sentences, imprisonment should be made sufficiently arduous and uncomfortable, which the figures for recidivism were felt to reveal was not then the case. Harder work and less liberal rations were particularly urged as being necessary reforms. The Committee then recommended that, in order to keep first offenders out of prison, a detention camp on the lines of the then existing Kenya camps should be established. It then turned to a recommendation which was to change the nature of punishment for many future offenders. The Penal Labour Ordinance, 1927, of Palestine was cited and quoted, and the government was urged to consider adopting a similar scheme which would enable convicted persons to perform useful public work without being kept in prison. The proposal was in fact accepted and resulted in the extramural penal labour system which is still in operation in Tanganyika.

Finally, the Committee drew attention to the need for care of released prisoners, a particularly difficult problem in the absence of a discharged prisoners' aid society.

Through all these official discussions, the main problem is seen to be the appropriateness of western penal methods in Africa and in particular the value of imprisonment and corporal punishment.

The most searching and influential inquiry into the penal policies of East African governments took place very shortly afterwards, though it was nominally concerned more with criminal procedure than with penal methods. The Bushe 'Committee of Inquiry into the Administration of Justice in Kenya, Uganda and Tanganyika Territory in Criminal Matters' conducted its investigations in 1933.[38] Its membership included a judge from Uganda, the Attorney-General of Kenya, the Secretary for Native Affairs in Tanganyika and, as Chairman, the Legal Adviser to the Secretary of State for the Colonies.

Many witnesses before the Commission complained of the inadequacy of the existing law and penal system and a number of them urged a return to the customary law and traditional sanctions as being more effective. On close scrutiny of these views the Commission concluded:

> ... it appears to us that the material difference between native substantive law and the Penal Code is in respect of punishment. To the native mind what the British regard as crime against the public peace was essentially a private wrong. It might be an offence against the community also, but it was always a tort and usually was punishable as such [sic]. Homicide, we have been told, was frequently punishable with death if the killer was caught by the relatives of the deceased man: if, however, he got to a chief and reported the homicide, the matter was adjusted between the families by the payment of blood-money.

The Commission decided that 'revenge and retribution as methods of punishing criminals must go, and crime must be regarded first and foremost as an offence against the community if the people of these territories are to advance in enlightenment and prosperity'. The conclusion was that,

> save in so far as we later advocate the use of reconciliation and compensation for minor offences and damages for certain more serious offences by way of civil suit before the native courts, the punishments sanctioned by all enlightened systems of jurisprudence are the most suitable for these territories.

114

With regard to imprisonment, the Commission received diametrically opposite views:

> We are told that to 60% of the prison population it is no deterrent; that natives incur no stigma by reason of their having been in prison; that they are well housed, clothed and fed, and that the only irksome feature of imprisonment is the deprivation of beer and tobacco, and enforced silence. . . .

> Such force as there may be in these arguments must apply only to short terms of imprisonment: deprivation of liberty for a long period must be regarded as a severe punishment by all but the comparatively few recidivists who have spent most of their life in prison.

The Commission emphasized that fines should be only for such amounts as the offenders could pay, and referred to the evils which formerly flowed from the then repealed Stock and Produce Theft Ordinance of Kenya, which had imposed a fine of not less than ten times the value of stolen stock on every convicted native.

On the question of corporal punishment, the Commission followed the views, quoted above, of the minority of the Native Punishment Commission, rejecting the proposal that caning and flogging should be made legal as punishments for adults except for the most serious crimes, because they would be damaging to self-respect and tend to brutalize the criminals. 'Any extension of the use of corporal punishment we consider a retrograde step which we must oppose.'

Witnesses before the Commission were unanimous about the value of the provisions in the Codes which enabled the courts to award compensation to persons injured by offenders, in addition to or substitution for any other punishment, and including compensation payable out of fines. But despite the general approval of this power, the Commission recorded that little use appeared to be made of it, and considered that the powers were misunderstood by magistrates. They were, in fact, considerably wider powers than exist in English law and the Commission indicated that they could be particularly effective in view of the fact that the traditional remedy for many offences would have been compensation according to customary law. It was a slight defect, however, that the court had to proceed to conviction in every case before awarding compensation, and could not settle the matter between the parties without trial. The Commission therefore recommended adoption of a provision from the law of Nigeria, which was in fact later introduced into the East African Codes, providing for the court to promote reconciliation, and encourage and facilitate the amicable settlement of various kinds of proceedings. Common assault and private or personal offences not aggravated in degree or amounting to felony, were felt appropriate to be dealt with in this way, and the view was expressed that the approved terms of the settlement might include the payment of compensation.

The Commission also endorsed the recommendation of the Tanganyika Committee on Imprisonment that extra-mural penal labour be introduced for first offenders. This was effected in Tanganyika in 1933. Yet prison population figures continued to rise during the 1930s, perhaps inevitably, as was suggested by Mr (as he then was) Alexander Paterson, the United Kingdom Prison Commissioner, who visited East African prisons in 1939:

A man who builds a prison digs a hole. A hole fills up in time. So long as the prison is there, there is a great risk that imprisonment will almost automatically follow conviction.

The report of this visit gives a vivid picture of East African prisons at this time.[39] Little anxiety existed over security, even when part of the prison wall fell down, for the prisoner 'accepts the prison wall, even when there are gaps in it' and was inclined to stay put. The regime was almost military in atmosphere, with warders armed with unnecessary guns mounting guard and drilling. There was no ill-treatment, brutality or trafficking, and prisoners often may have had an easy time, slowly performing unexacting tasks—the visitor lamented the 'free distribution of amateur gardeners' to the 'houses of the great'! There was no physical training for the prisoners, virtually no mental training and 'only sporadic instances of spiritual training'. The African warder was the heart of the problem: he was nearer to the ideas and values of the prisoner than to those of his European superiors. Clerical and middle ranks were often occupied by Asians:

116

There is a gap between the European intention and the African appreciation of it. This cannot be filled by the interpolation of an Indian clerk who speaks the language of both, but introduces a third mentality, that is alien to both.

The warder, whose job is not a popular one, had a longer, harder day than his prisoners, and was less well fed; most recruits were illiterate, although Uganda had pioneered the appointment of college-trained personnel. Warders' training was still overweighted with squad drill and the use of arms which would virtually never be needed. Paterson made a number of precise recommendations which were generally accepted by the governments, but the intervention of the war led to the postponement of developments.

Four important later investigations of penal policy in East Africa were the Committee on Habitual Offenders in Kenya (1946), the Tanganyika Committee on Corporal Punishment (1952), the McKisack Committee on Juvenile Delinquency in Uganda (1958), and the Conference on Penal Problems in East Africa (1966). The first emphasized particularly the inadequacy of the statistics available for making a complete survey of the problem of recidivism, and examined the efficacy of detention camps, a special development in the Kenya penal system. The Tanganyika Committee was set up as a result of unanimous opposition by the unofficial members of the Legislative Council to the government's proposal to reduce the number of offences for which corporal punishment could be ordered for adults. The colonial policy was to abolish corporal punishment altogether, as in the United Kingdom, for ordinary offences. The Committee reported that public opinion throughout Tanganyika was in favour of retaining corporal punishment as a penal sanction, with some changes in the list of offences for which it might be awarded. Independently of the Committee's findings, strong representations had been made by certain tribal councils, including that of the influential Chagga tribe, against the abolition of corporal punishment.

The McKisack Committee in Uganda[40] recommended the adoption of new rules for the trial and treatment of juvenile offenders; it had received ample evidence of the conditions in Uganda which fostered juvenile delinquency. The Committee recommended also

117

the enactment of new legislation to govern the probation system, but this was not done until the Probation Act, 1962, was passed.

Notable developments more recently in East Africa include the adoption by Kenya of the extra-mural penal employment system modelled on that of Tanganyika, and the enactment in the latter country of the Minimum Sentences Act, 1963, which is of great interest and gave rise to a lively debate, both in and out of Parliament, involving a searching examination of the principles and purposes of the penal system.

These, and other current developments, were reviewed by the Conference on Penal Problems in East Africa, which met at the University College, Dar es Salaam, in January 1966.[41] This brought together for the first time senior representatives of all the government departments and agencies concerned with the treatment of offenders: courts, police, prisons, probation and legal departments, with representatives from the University of East Africa and overseas. It was not the purpose of the gathering to make decisions or recommendations, but this very freedom enabled a most frank exchange of views to take place. There was general agreement on the urgent need for research into the present penal policies of East African governments, and for the consideration of innovations and reforms which might be radical in character; in particular, alternatives to short sentences of imprisonment are needed, and the employment of juveniles and youths on constructive national service was advocated as a means to reduce juvenile delinquency. This discussion may well prove to have been a significant development in the progress of East African countries towards more effective penal systems, especially in stimulating the search for acceptable alternatives to some of the methods inherited from the colonial system.

IV Sentencing Policy in East Africa

In modern times, the courts of East Africa have been so varied in nature that it is far beyond the scope of this discussion to attempt a comprehensive or even a representative examination of sentencing policies in detail. Apart from the distinction between the 'African courts' and the superior and subordinate courts, the African courts themselves were very diverse in character, varying principally according to the diverse traditional political organization of the different communities. The magistrates' courts also differed markedly as between those presided over by full-time judicial officers with legal qualifications and those (the majority) presided over by administrative officers who might only have taken a local administrative officers' law examination but, on the other hand, could justifiably claim a closer knowledge of the local community than the full-time magistrates.

In these circumstances it was a constant problem—mainly felt by High Court judges, or senior administrative officers—to attempt to evolve any measure of uniformity or even consistency in sentencing procedures and policy. The judges of the African courts were, in addition, dealing with sanctions at first unfamiliar to them and often perhaps only partially understood in their wider effects. On the other hand, the refinements of the sentencing process which are now practised in England are modern devices even to English lawyers, and they so often depend upon the availability to the courts of ancillary services of investigation, assessment and report on individual offenders that they would be undreamed-of luxuries to most courts in East Africa. Although medical and probation services have been developed considerably, they are still largely confined to the few major towns and it would be unrealistic to expect that the national economic conditions will, in any near future, permit of the expensive and time-consuming studies which western countries have learnt are necessary for a more just sentencing system.

It is, of course, as in England, a basic assumption that sentencing is a task for the courts. The possibility of sentencing being left to a differently constituted tribunal after a court had determined guilt was considered by the recent Conference on Penal Problems, but it would so markedly increase the cost of criminal justice that it is not a practicable proposal at this stage.

The colonial period, which saw the adoption of English penal methods, saw also the almost slavish imitation of English sentencing practice. On the rare occasions when sentencing was discussed, English precedents were cited with little recognition that East African conditions might require a different approach. An exception was a judgment by an early Chief Justice of Uganda, in holding too severe a sentence of seven years' rigorous imprisonment for stealing a bicycle on a man with four previous convictions:

> The Court of Criminal Appeal in England . . . has frequently said whatever may be the appellant's character, regard must be had to the nature of the offence. . . . In this country I consider that the courts must be governed by the same principle in passing sentence, but the application of the principle requires in my opinion very great modification owing to the circumstances of Uganda. In the first place the native is accustomed to exceedingly severe punishment at the hands of his chiefs, and too sudden a change is inadvisable. Secondly, inprisonment to a native is undoubtedly a very much less severe punishment than it is to a European in England. Thirdly, a lenient system is regarded, as a rule, as a sign of weakness. Fourthly, we have no Borstal system, no reformatories and no provision for preventive detention after the expiration of imprisonment.[42]

East African courts adopted the English rule that an appellate court would not interfere with the sentence of a lower court unless satisfied that the sentence was so severe as to amount to a miscarriage of justice. This was to give rise to difficulties of application because the dominant feature of sentencing policy in the colonial period was the fact that magistrates continually imposed sentences of excessive severity, whether of imprisonment or fine. Indeed, the superior courts and even the law officers of the governments fought a steady campaign to produce a more realistic sentencing policy; although the reasons for such a campaign may often have been empirical rather than philosophical, being related frequently to the overcrowded state of the prisons.

In the end, the most careful examination of sentencing principles came as a result of what the Attorney-General of Kenya stigmatized as the continual abuse by magistrates of their powers of punishment. The Attorney-General had for years advised the Supreme Court that he was unable to support large numbers of sentences which were so severe as to be sometimes, in his own words, 'almost savage'. The judges repeatedly reduced such sentences, but the problem continued until one case was set down for thorough argument in open court. The Attorney-General presented most carefully the case concerning proper principles of sentencing, and the resulting judgment was circulated to all magistrates for their instruction. The case involved a conviction for theft of a goat and kid, valued at three shillings, by a first offender. The magistrate, in imposing sentence of two years' imprisonment with hard labour and a fine of of thirty shillings or three months' imprisonment in default, commented 'that the Nandi tribe are given to stock theft and expressed his view that a heavy punishment was necessary to act as a real deterrent to others'. 'What will the magistrate do in case of the theft of six goats?' asked the Attorney-General laconically, in presenting to the Supreme Court his argument that this sentence was too severe. The Attorney-General cited many English cases and relied upon five principles which the Court of Criminal Appeal in England had enunciated as relevant in sentencing:

> First, the intrinsic value of the subject-matter; secondly, the antecedents of the accused; thirdly, the youth of the accused . . .; fourthly, the conduct of the accused at the trial, particularly in regard to whether he pleaded guilty or not guilty; and fifthly and lastly, the prevalence of the particular crime in question in the neighbourhood.

The Attorney-General went on to suggest 'that two years is just as long in the life of an illiterate African as it is in the life of anyone else . . .'. The Supreme Court reduced the sentence to four months' imprisonment with hard labour, with one month further in default of payment of the fine of thirty shillings, accepting the Attorney-General's statement 'as an exact statement of the guiding principles for the punishment of offences'.[43]

In a later circular to magistrates, the Chief Justice of Kenya urged them to record their reasons for sentences, particularly when passing heavy sentences of imprisonment or substantial fines. In applying the principles stated above, East African courts have indicated that, if any differentiation is made between two co-accused on the ground that one pleaded guilty and the other not guilty, 'any discrimination should be . . . by showing leniency to the one who pleaded guilty, not by being ultra-severe to the one who does not.'[44]

The inquiry made by a court before determining sentence should, of course, be a vital element in the court's decision. Unfortunately, in the normal circumstances of court work in East Africa—certainly in the lower courts which deal with the great bulk of criminal cases—the pressure is such that the magistrate has little time to pursue lengthy inquiries, nor are the investigatory services available which would make it profitable to do so, apart from the small corps of overworked probation officers. Usually the material upon which the sentence is based consists, apart from evidence given in the trial itself, only of a statement by the accused in mitigation and at best a report by the police as to the previous record of the offender. This will reveal previous convictions if they have been traced, but may not touch on many points in favour of the convict.

The courts have rightly insisted that if any new material is tendered as being relevant to sentence, it should be given on oath and be subject to cross-examination. Such statements must not include references to offences with which the accused has not been charged, unless he has agreed to ask that they be taken into consideration,[45] nor should they include assertions incapable of proof —for example, that the accused is 'notorious for profiteering'.[46]

The imposition of fines in East Africa has always given rise to special difficulties: the period when fines were introduced as part of the western legal system was the same period when, for most people, the cash economy was introduced and developed. Many people are still so poor that monetary penalties even of small amounts may relatively be very severe penalties. On the other hand, there are great disparities of wealth and poverty. What principles should the courts adopt? In a leading case, the Supreme Court of Kenya considered the fundamental problem of the appropriateness of a fine where it could apparently easily be paid. An Asian woman was convicted of dangerous driving and the magistrate fixed the sentence as follows:

> The accused is a married woman. I have no doubt that any fine I impose will be paid as to some part or other by her husband or other relations. It should not be able to be said of any convicted person that he or she has been enabled to buy his or her way out of the consequences of the act for which he or she has been convicted. I think the only appropriate deterrent is a short sentence of imprisonment and I therefore sentence the accused to three months' imprisonment.

The Supreme Court allowed the appeal against this sentence, substituting a fine of one thousand shillings or three months' imprisonment in default, and disagreeing with the magistrate's reasoning:

> . . . we consider it irrelevant that any fine that might have been imposed would be paid by the appellant's husband or relations, and, indeed, there was no evidential basis for such a supposition. The determination of the nature of the penalty to be inflicted should depend mainly on the facts and the circumstances of the case . . .[47]

With regard to the poor offender, magistrates in East Africa found it so difficult to find a level for fines, which would prevent the prisons being packed with defaulters genuinely unable to pay, that the superior courts repeatedly urged them to exercise greater care. When an elderly and poor Arab was fined 250 shillings for illegally tapping palm trees, the High Court of Tanganyika reduced the fine to 75 shillings and repeated its advice of four years previously: 'Even a severe penalty must be one which the accused is reasonably likely, when all his circumstances are taken into account, to be able to pay.'[48]

In 1956 the Supreme Court of Kenya issued 'Notes for the Guidance of Magistrates' on the subject of sentencing.[49] These emphasized that imprisonment should be avoided in the case of

first offenders or where the offence was not serious. Before imposing a fine the magistrate should inquire into the means of the accused to pay: a sentence to a fine which the accused cannot pay is
pointless and wrong. Within two months a further circular was
necessary to magistrates in one part of Kenya, because certain
prisons were being 'cluttered up' with convicted persons, mainly
first offenders, sentenced to fines quite beyond their capacity to
pay.[50]

V The Treatment of Adult Offenders

I CAPITAL PUNISHMENT

Death remains the mandatory penalty throughout East Africa for
murder, treason and certain forms of piracy. The English legislation
of 1957 differentiating 'capital' from other types of murder was
specifically rejected by the colonial governments of East Africa on
the advice of their legal advisers. In the early years of colonial rule,
when the Indian Penal Code applied, death was a discretionary
alternative sentence to transportation in cases of murder; later,
imprisonment was substituted for transportation. In Kenya the
death sentence was available as an alternative sentence to imprisonment for rape from 1927 to 1955: it was introduced as a result of six
cases of assault and attempted rape by Africans upon European
women and girls in 1927.[51] In the neighbouring countries this
application of capital punishment was specifically rejected. In
Kenya during the 1952–60 emergency a very large number of
offences were made capital under emergency laws.

The death sentence cannot be passed upon an offender who was
under 18 years of age at the time of the offence: instead, such a

person is detained during pleasure. A woman convicted of a capital offence but found to be pregnant must be sentenced to life imprisonment instead.[52]

The sentence of death is carried out in prison by hanging. During the first decade of this century, in the East Africa Protectorate at least, execution was by police firing squad, the first hangings being in public at Mombasa in 1908; shortly afterwards a public executioner was appointed, but in remote areas police firing squads (apparently with highly inaccurate weapons) were called upon even after this.[53]

The prerogative of mercy vested in the President of each country enables him to grant a pardon, respite or remission of penalty to any convicted person, but it is of particular significance in relation to capital sentences. In Kenya, as in Uganda, there is established by the Constitution an Advisory Committee on the Prerogative of Mercy which must consider all capital sentences and make a recommendation in each case (it may also advise on other sentences). In Kenya the President exercises his prerogative on the advice of the Minister for the time being responsible for justice, who is in turn advised by the Committee (of which he is Chairman) but who must decide in his own judgment what advice to give to the President. In Uganda the Committee advises the President directly.[54] The information available to the committee when it considers a case includes not only the record of the trial and any subsequent appellate proceedings, but also a confidential report by the trial judge and a report by a local administrative officer who will have made inquiries about the condemned person after the trial. Each case is considered upon its individual facts, and thus there has been considerable variation in the proportion of capital sentences actually carried out in different years and countries. This variation is clearly shown in Tables 4 and 5. It is notable, however, that the proportion of capital sentences commuted in Kenya declined considerably during the earliest years of the Mau Mau emergency (1953 and 1954). Yet over the ten-year period 1951-60, for seven years of which the state of emergency was in force, the ratio of executions to commuted sentences in Kenya (Supreme Court sentences only) was approximately 2:1 (a total of 315 executions, 149 sentences commuted); in Tanganyika, in the six years 1947-52, the ratio was approximately 4:3 (178 executions, 134 commuted sentences) but in the six years 1957–62 it was precisely 7:3 (154 executions, 66 commuted sentences).

TABLE 4. KENYA: FINAL POSITION OF PERSONS SENTENCED TO DEATH BY SUPREME COURT, 1951–60

	(1)	(2)	(3)	(4)	(5)	(6)
	Total number dealt with	Acquitted by Court of Appeal	Sentence of imprisonment substituted by Court of Appeal	Otherwise dealt with	Executed	Commuted by Governor
1951	55	6	2	4	19	24
1952	35	2	—	3	20	10
1953	166	60	—	1	91	14
1954	84	5	2	2	56	19
1955	50	1	5	4	23	17
1956	50	1	5	1	30	13
1957	45	3	8	2	15	17
1958	24	—	1	—	10	13
1959	41	1	2	2	22	14
1960	40	—	1	2	29	8

Source: Judicial Department Reports.

Notes: Col. (1) i.e. total number of persons sentenced to death by Supreme Court on whose cases final decisions were made in the year; the figure does not include all sentences passed in each year, for some cases are pending at the end of each year. Sentences of death were also imposed during this period by certain subordinate courts.

Col. (3) i.e. substitution of some other conviction—usually manslaughter.

Col. (4) including 'Found insane', 'Died in prison', 'Retrial ordered', etc.

Although each case is considered on its individual merits, certain questions of general policy have inevitably been raised in the exercise of the prerogative. One was the question of the significance to be attached to an allegation of witchcraft in a particular case: if the condemned man claimed that he had been defending himself against witchcraft in attacking his victim, should this be given weight as an extenuating circumstance, or should it be a reason for exacting the capital penalty as a deterrent to others who might be similarly motivated? This problem received different answers at different times in Tanganyika. In 1932 the Governor, in a despatch to the Secretary of State, referred to the rival views and stated that he accepted the unanimous advice of the Executive Council that 'by exacting the death penalty for murder committed on account of a belief in witchcraft, we will gradually establish the conviction ... that Government so abhors murder that it does not regard even a belief in witchcraft as condoning the offence in any way'. In 1941, however, a later Governor indicated that the 'extreme view' expressed in 1932 was no longer generally accepted and that while each case should be considered independently, some weight should be given to this factor: an honest belief in witchcraft was held to be mitigating circumstance justifying commutation of the death sentence in appropriate cases.[55]

TABLE 5. TANGANYIKA: FINAL POSITION OF PERSONS SEN-TENCED TO DEATH, 1947–52 AND 1957–62

	(1) Total number dealt with	(2) Acquitted or sentence reduced by Court of Appeal	(3) Otherwise dealt with	(4) Executed	(5) Commuted by Governor
1947	86	38	1	22	25
1948	89	10	—	50	29
1949	53	2	1	31	19
1950	48	3	2	22	21
1951	64	12	—	32	20
1952	50	9	—	21	20
1957	26	5	—	17	4
1958	40	10	—	20	10
1959	54	1	—	44	9
1960	52	9	—	29	14
1961	52	2	—	32	18
1962	27	4	—	12	11

Source: Annual Reports.

Notes: Col. (1) i.e. total number of persons sentenced to death on whose cases final decisions were made in the year; the figure does not include all sentences passed in each year, for some cases are pending at the end of each year.

Col. (3) including 'Found insane', 'Died in prison'.

2 IMPRISONMENT

Imprisonment has grown steadily in this century in East Africa as the standard mode of punishment for serious crimes or hardened offenders. Tables 6, 7 and 8 indicate the extent of its growth but do not necessarily reveal a comparable growth in criminality, for a number of factors combine to account for the rise in the prison population.

A Urbanization and other social and economic changes have progressively weakened traditional sanctions, which have been replaced by the new forms of sanctions.

B The courts have frequently imposed excessively severe sentences, whether of imprisonment or of fines with imprisonment only in default; and in a society of poor people, fines occupy a relatively smaller part of the sanctioning machinery and imprisonment a larger area.

C The gradual improvement of the prison services and the expansion of prison buildings, however slowly, stimulated increased reliance upon imprisonment by magistrates; and for much of the early part of the century there were few alternative penalties available.

D The growth of recidivism reflected the inadequacy of imprisonment as a deterrent or reformative influence and contributed to the rising figure.

E Within the overall trends, certain specific short-term factors operated. For example, at times when judicial or police departments were under strain there was increased delay in bringing cases to trial and the population of remand prisoners awaiting trial rose. In periods of political stress during the progress to independence, political offenders were imprisoned and conventional crime also tended to escalate—the outstanding example of this being in Kenya during the emergency, which resulted in fantastic strains upon the prisons service.

F The steady growth in size and efficiency of the police forces, with new areas continually being brought within the range of effective policing, meant that there was a regular increase in the number of crimes reported and investigated which might otherwise never have appeared in the official figures.

TABLE 6. UGANDA: CENTRAL GOVERNMENT PRISONS, AVERAGE DAILY
POPULATION, 1953–62

	1953	1954	1955	1956	1957	1958	1959	1960	1961	1962
Convicted prisoners undergoing sentence	3,074	3,561	3,844	4,383	4,907	5,018	5,817	7,533	8,088	8,239
Remand prisoners, lunatics and debtors	402	511	638	608	671	608	617	592	534	689
Total	3,476	4,072	4,482	4,991	5,578	5,626	6,434	8,125	8,622	8,928

Source: Statistical Abstracts.

TABLE 7. KENYA: PRISON POPULATION, SELECTED YEARS
1931–64

	Total number committed	Convicted prisoners sentenced to imprisonment	Remand [a] and civil prisoners	Daily average population
1931	13,928	6,756	7,172	3,306
1936	12,996	7,193	5,803	2,758
1941	18,126	10,256	7,870	3,771
1946	21,953	11,085	10,868	5,683
1951	32,378	16,673	15,705	9,269
1956	46,749	24,539	22,210	19,320
1961	97,927	28,697	69,230	11,750
1964	71,916	29,112	42,804	11,344

[a] The majority are remand prisoners not subsequently sentenced to imprisonment, but the figure includes lunatics, civil debtors, vagrants, etc.

TABLE 8. TANGANYIKA: PRISON POPULATION, 1951–62

	Total committals to prisons				Daily average prison population
	On conviction	On remand	Civil debtors	Total	
1951	14,961	9,825	17	24,803	6,794·6
1952	16,572	10,832	34	27,438	7,066·1
1953	20,568	12,330	52	32,950	7,873·6

TABLE 8—*continued*

	Total committals to prisons				Daily average prison population
	On conviction	On remand	Civil debtors	Total	
1954	22,695	14,308	51	37,054	9,143·5
1955	21,598	14,667	41	36,306	8,859·6
1956	20,631	14,590	32	35,253	8,158·2
1957	25,484	21,778	50	47,312	8,566·9
1958	31,002	22,543	84	53,629	9,431
1959	33,396	23,693	121	57,210	9,776·1
1960	35,780	23,069	71	58,920	10,218·3
1961	41,852	29,468	105	71,425	11,690·3
1962	37,374	36,426	94	73,894	10,108·3

(N.B. The above figures of prisoners admitted on remand excluded those subsequently sentenced to imprisonment or caning.)

It used to be the form for sentences of imprisonment to be passed with or without hard labour in the discretion of the court. Today the court merely imposes imprisonment, the nature of the labour performed by the prisoner being determined from time to time by prison officials. The criminal laws generally prescribe maximum sentences only, leaving the courts with wide discretion as to the length of sentence—or, indeed, as to whether to impose imprisonment at all. The principal exception today is with regard to those offences included within the Minimum Sentences Act of Tanganyika, which is discussed later in this chapter. Wherever imprisonment may be imposed, a fine may be imposed in addition, or as an alternative to imprisonment. Where several sentences of imprisonment are imposed at the same trial, it is in the discretion of the court whether they shall be served 'consecutively' or 'concurrently': if they are imposed in respect of several offences committed in the same transaction, they will normally be made 'concurrent'.[56]

(a) The prisons

By 1960 the Uganda Prisons Service controlled thirty-three different and specialized institutions (including two Reform Schools). There were eleven District Prisons, six prison farms serving as agricultural training prisons for long-term Star class prisoners or as long-term pre-release open camps, a prison farm for women, an industrial central prison for women, a leper prison, two industrial training prisons for long-term recidivists and long-term Star class prisoners respectively, temporary agricultural prison camps for medium-term Star class prisoners, a central prison for young offenders, a remand prison and a regional allocation prison. The current law governing the prisons is found in the Prison Act, 1958, and Prison Rules of the same year.[57]

Only in Uganda has a dual prisons system developed. Local prisons run by the local government or administration are found in most parts of the country. Originally developed in Buganda, Toro and Ankole, they were introduced into most other districts as a definite central government policy from 1929 onwards. It was the Protectorate Government's long-term aim to take over responsibility for all prisoners sentenced to at least one year's imprisonment but it was never possible to accomplish this. In fact, as Table 9(a) shows, the overwhelming majority of persons sentenced to imprisonment in Uganda serve their sentences in the locally administered prisons. It would appear, too, from the average daily population figures that the sentences served in the local prisons were very much shorter than those served in the central government prison system (Table 9(b)).

TABLE 9(a). UGANDA: NUMBERS OF PERSONS COMMITTED[a] UNDER SENTENCE OF IMPRISONMENT, CENTRAL AND LOCAL GOVERNMENT PRISONS, 1951–58

	Central Government prisons	Local Government prisons
1951	2,933	18,227
1952	3,188	20,850
1953	3,839	20,607
1954	4,313	20,950
1955	4,679	22,848
1956	5,221	28,138
1957	5,623	36,871
1958	6,525	33,547

Source: Statistical Abstract, 1959.

[a] Total committals to each type of prison were considerably higher, including remand prisoners, debtors etc.

TABLE 9(b). UGANDA: PRISON POPULATION FIGURES, CEN-
TRAL AND LOCAL PRISONS, 1958–60

	Uganda Government prisons		Buganda Government prisons		Other local prisons	
	Total committals	Daily average	Total committals	Daily average	Total committals	Daily Average
1958	14,227	5,626	12,601	5,223·3	20,970	3,517·06
1959	16,677	6,434	9,896	2,528	22,453	4,483·19
1960	19,480	8,124	16,563	1,880	21,218	3,163

Source: Prisons Department. Treatment of Offenders Annual Reports.

The most critical stage in the development of penal systems in East Africa came in Kenya during the 'Mau Mau' emergency (1952–60), when very severe strains were imposed upon the custodial system at very short notice. There was a very heavy increase in the number of convicted prisoners admitted—from 16,673 in 1951 to 42,581 in 1953, the highest number in Kenya's history before or since. But in addition, the number of persons admitted to the ordinary detention camps was jolted into a sharp rise—from 18,247 in 1951 to 32,862 in 1953, the difference being that this figure was to continue to rise very sharply (except in 1954) throughout and even beyond the emergency, reaching the dizzy height of 89,687 in 1961. In addition, during the emergency the Prisons Service was responsible for the custody of the very large number of persons detained under emergency powers, which in 1955 reached a total of some 53,000.

A former Commissioner of Prisons in Kenya who returned to investigate the general administration of the system during this period has recorded that this was the most difficult period in the history of the Prisons Service.[58] The extent of the problem is well enough indicated by these figures: in 1951, a prisons staff of 1,143 controlled 99 establishments with an average daily population of 9,269; at the height of the emergency, in 1955, a staff of over 12,000 controlled 176 establishments with a daily average population of 86,634. This astronomical, almost overnight, expansion caused great problems, particularly of recruitment and accommodation.

132

However, in the view of a British Parliamentary Delegation to Kenya in January 1954:

Despite the effort made to keep pace with these new responsibilities—and it has been most commendable and humane—the prisons are still faced with both these problems, of which the training of personnel is undoubtedly the most urgent and intractable. Overcrowding and lack of staff apart, the Prisons Department has discharged its duties well, the treatment of its prisoners is good and in its rehabilitation centres and camps highly constructive work is being attempted.[59]

Although the Prisons Department was responsible for the safe custody of the emergency detainees, their rehabilitation was the concern of the Minister of another department. Of the total of 79,000 detained, about 78,000 had been released by mid-1959. The object of these detentions was rehabilitation, not punishment: the detainees represented a social or political problem, not a penal one. However, in the circumstances it was not possible to segregate emergency detainees entirely from criminal detainees or convicted prisoners, although this was very unfortunate from the point of view of all categories of inmates. The tasks of the Prisons Department in this sphere came to an end in 1959 when responsibility for the remaining emergency detention camps was transferred to a Special Commissioner in the Ministry of African Affairs, following the recommendation of the Fairn Committee on Emergency Detention Camps which had been appointed after the deaths of detainees at the Hola Camp in March 1959.[60] This Committee, while acknowledging the 'gigantic achievement' involved in the measures which had been adopted, reported that the Prisons Department was 'grossly understaffed at the top even in relation to its proper functions' and found that 'generally the morale of the Kenya Prisons Service . . . is at a very low ebb, and immediate and special steps must be taken to restore it'.[61] In particular, the Committee found that the restoration of proper discipline was an immediate necessity, that the standard of entry to the Service should be raised and greater resources provided to ensure its welfare, effective leadership and training. The Committee was shocked to find the living conditions of the prisons staff regularly inferior to those of

the detainees, and was even critical of the training school programme. The government accepted that reforms were needed, but
emphasized the limits of the resources available.

The year 1960 was one of considerable progress in Kenya, particularly in the introduction of modern systems of treatment and
training of prisoners, based upon the Minimum Standard Rules
agreed at the First United Nations Congress on the Prevention of
Crime and the Treatment of Offenders. New legislation to govern
prison administration was drafted, providing for a number of
innovations, including extra-mural penal labour, a progressive
stage system, an earnings scheme, and short-term corrective training. This was enacted as the Prisons Act, 1962, which came into
force in 1963.[62] A working party, which in 1961 considered
measures to relieve continued overcrowding in prisons and detention camps, recommended, *inter alia*, amendment of the poll tax
laws to abolish the lower bracket; this was accomplished and alle-
viated the position to some extent.

In Zanzibar, with its much smaller population and more restricted resources, prison developments have in the past lagged
behind those on the mainland. The responsibility for prisons was
removed from the police in 1951 and transferred to a Superintendent of Prisons. By 1960, the institutions in the system consisted
of the Central Prison, with accommodation for 269 males and
16 females, with separate wards for Europeans, remand prisoners,
civil prisoners, females, juveniles, Asian first offenders, Asian recidivists, African first offenders and African recidivists; four prison
camps, and one prison (for 39 prisoners) and one prison camp on
the island of Pemba.

During the first decade of British administration in Tanganyika,
the steady increase in the prison population gave rise to anxiety.
The Committee on Imprisonment which reported in 1932 made
various recommendations concerning changes. Most notably, it
recommended the substitution of separate cells for the association
wards then most common, a review of dietary scales (said by African
witnesses to be too liberal), and harder work (pointing out that
prisoners worked an eight-hour day but warders one of eleven and
a half hours). The Committee also proposed the introduction of
detention camps on the Kenya pattern. It noted, however, that the

increase in prisoners was partly due to 'closer and more efficient administration, coupled with the enormous increase, during the past ten years, in the number of laws and regulations'.[63]

These recommendations were not entirely acceptable to the government, but the committee deserves a prominent place in the penal history of East Africa for its proposal of the extra-mural labour system which was to keep many convicted offenders out of prisons in Tanganyika.

The shortage of accommodation was increasingly felt with the steady rise in prison population during the late 1940s, and a five-year building programme was initiated in 1948. The aim was to provide accommodation for all long-term first offenders in prison camps. Other categories of prisoners then recognized were recidivists, non-recidivists, remand prisoners and juveniles, females and civil prisoners. The building programme did not keep pace with the rise in prison population; committals to prison continued to rise to unprecedented levels and in 1961 prisons were still 'grossly overcrowded'. The establishments then available included 18 first-class prisons (including one for women, one for lepers and one minimum security prison), 14 second-class prisons for all prisoners except those sentenced to more than three years' imprisonment, 24 third-class prisons for those sentenced to six months or less, 6 road camps, 2 forestry camps and 3 remand prisons. One of the special achievements of the Tanganyika Prisons Service is the Kingolwira Prison Farm, which holds over 1,000 first offenders of both sexes in separate prisons without security walls and comprises a farm of 16,000 acres with a dairy, workshops and other modern facilities.[64]

Total admissions to prisons in Tanganyika rose from 24,803 in 1951 to 73,894 in 1962. Fortunately the rise in the average daily population, from 6,794·6 (1951) to 10,108·3 (1962), was not the the same rate, indicating that an overwhelming proportion of total committals were for short periods. Most disturbing was the increasing number of persons imprisoned on remand and not subsequently sentenced to imprisonment: these numbered 9,825 in 1951 but 36,426 in 1962. Indeed, in 1962, of the total remand prisoner population admitted, 73 per cent were not sentenced to imprisonment on conviction. This was a very heavy burden for the

Prisons Service to carry and indicates clearly how the Service has to cope, in the last resort, with problems created by defects in the judicial or police systems. The problem of remand prisoners, however, is partly attributable to the difficulties which occur in admitting accused persons to bail. In 1963, 49,626 persons were remanded in custody for an average period of 15·6 days each; in 1964 the total number remanded had dropped to 45,118, but owing to an increase in the average time spent in custody on remand (to 26 days), the average daily remand population in prison increased from 1,815·3 in 1963 to 2,092 in 1964. These features are undoubtedly due in part to the fundamental reconstruction of the judicial system in progress at the time, and the shortage of magistrates. From 1963 there has also been an increase in the convicted prison population, due to the effects of the Minimum Sentences Act which resulted in the imposition of longer sentences than many of those convicted would otherwise have received.

The prisons of Tanganyika now include more than seventy establishments in which accommodation is still mainly in association wards. They include prison camps, open prisons, a women's prison and a young offenders' prison.

(b) Prison conditions and administration

The conditions in East African prisons differ widely from those in European countries. Apart from differences in daily life, resulting partly from climatic factors, accommodation is mainly in association wards, not cells. Most prisoners are able to do a normal day's work, being unlocked at daybreak and commencing work after the morning meal. They are not again locked up until after the evening meal, served before sunset, and a period for educational and recreational activities. Overcrowding, sometimes to a severe degree, is as common in East African as in English prisons. The average prisoner in East Africa has much more freedom within the prison campus—and often outside it, on working parties—than his average English counterpart. A much larger proportion of the total prison population in East Africa is engaged upon labour outside the prison walls, often under minimal supervision. The relationship between prisoners and prison staff is much closer in East Africa, as a result of the fact that the two are much closer in their standards of life than would be an English prisoner and prison officer. Even today it is arguable that the warder is worse off than his charges, in material terms, and although he continues to enjoy the life of his immediate family he is, unless he decides to leave the prison service, almost as much a prisoner as the convicts.

(*i*) *Classification of prisoners.* All East African prison systems now classify prisoners on admission, and the different categories are separated as far as possible. Convicted, unconvicted and civil prisoners are segregated; convicts are classified as 'Star' prisoners, 'Ordinary' prisoners or 'Young offenders', Star prisoners normally being the first offenders or those considered suitable for training with first offenders. Further subclassifications are according to age, length of sentence, education, criminal and social history, and nature of offence. The present Commissioner of Prisons in Kenya has described classification as 'perhaps the most important single principle of the penal system'.[65]

(*ii*) *Prison labour.* East African prisons do not normally suffer from the 'work-famine' which restricts hours of employment in English prisons, although there have been temporary difficulties from time to time.[66] The average period of work is eight hours daily, with rests on Saturday afternoons and Sundays. In the conditions of developing tropical countries there is considerable public work available for prisoners, ranging from quarrying or road-building to anti-malarial or anti-tsetse activity. The large and splendid Embakasi Airport at Nairobi was largely built by an army of 3,000 recidivist prisoners. Agriculture is, of course, given a foremost place and the development of prison farms has been a most notable modern development. There can be little doubt that for many, probably a majority of, prisoners in East Africa, adequate opportunities and equipment for cultivation, with advice where needed, provide the most valuable means of employment from the physical, psychological and productive points of view. A former Uganda police officer has given a vivid account of the effects upon prisoners in Uganda of the swift and imaginative creation of a prison farm which within twelve months provided a surplus of food beyond the prisoners' requirements, cleared and ploughed seventy acres of bush, and replaced opportunities for brooding and recrimination by healthy and productive labour.

> The combination of physical endeavour and mental stimulation not only effected an amazing improvement in their health and physique but entirely altered their mental outlook. A measure of self-respect was restored and with it confidence in their ability to take up again, on their release, the threads of community life. . . .[67]

Prison farms have proved to be an important means of agricultural training and experiment. Forestry, and in Tanganyika even viniculture, are extensions of this. Construction, mainly of prison buildings, has been an important type of labour for many years. Within the workshops, tailoring, especially of uniforms for government officers and prisoners, has long been important, but in each country a wide range of prison industries now exists: carpentry and metalwork, mat-making, basket-making, boot-making, spinning and weaving, rope-making and others. For some years Kenya prisons have regularly exhibited products in Nairobi, and in Dar es Salaam in 1965 the first exhibition of prison trades, arts and crafts had a considerable public impact in demonstrating the scope and achievements of prisoners and their instructors. Since 1952 the total revenue from prison industries in Kenya has been well over £100,000 annually. During 1961, a period of difficulty in finding sufficient orders to maintain full employment in the prisons, an Industrial Manager was appointed to the Kenya prisons service, to organize prison industries and control their finances.

An interesting development in Kenya was the creation of a mobile aptitude-testing unit to allocate prisoners to trades, following the report of a committee in 1955 on the employment of convicts. The report stressed the need to test each candidate for training and to ensure that he had adequate time to complete training. The unit set up was so successful that it was later hired out to test candidates for government and private industry.

(*iii*) *Earnings and stage systems.* Earnings schemes now operate throughout the East African prisons. In Uganda and Kenya they are linked to the progressive stage systems: short-term prisoners remain in the first stage; those serving sentences of more than six months spend their first three months in the second stage, and, subject to having committed no offence for a month, proceed to the third stage, at which point they enter the earnings scheme. After fifteen months in the third stage prisoners may proceed to the fourth stage; after eighteen months there they may proceed to the special stage when they are known as 'Honour Prisoners' and enjoy a number of privileges (for example, freedom of movement within the prison without escort, later locking-up time, extra bedding, the receipt of letters without restriction and a small extra remission after two years in the special stage). Rates of pay for each grade are fixed from time to time by the Minister responsible. A prisoner is entitled to spend up to two-thirds of his earnings on tobacco and other small goods in the prison, the balance being credited to him for payment on his release.

(*iv*) *Prison discipline*. Perhaps largely because of the accommodation and work factors already mentioned, which alleviate the boredom and tensions of prison life, discipline in East African prisons is seldom a serious problem. Certainly there is less atmosphere of strain in an African prison than in an English prison. Prison offences are defined in terms of graduated severity with a related gradation of penalties, which may be imposed by prison officers whose jurisdiction varies with their rank. The punishments available include corporal punishment (which can be imposed on a convicted prisoner only, for mutiny or personal violence to a prison officer), loss of remission, solitary confinement for a limited period, penal or reduced diet, or reduction in stage. Until the 1930s corporal punishment was widely applied. The policy of restricting it resulted in an 'amazing metamorphosis' and in 1939 Paterson was able to write:

The reduction in the amount of corporal punishment during the last decade is little short of amazing. From being the most frequent form of punishment, it is now the most infrequent, and during this period the number of assaults on prison officers has tended to fall and not to rise, and the prisoners are better conducted in every way.[68]

Loss of remission has been used as a punishment much more frequently in Tanganyika than in Kenya or Uganda, and this has been a subsidiary factor contributing to the overcrowding which is rather more severe in that country.

(*v*) *Remission*. In modern times East African countries have adopted a standard remission policy. A prisoner may by good conduct and industry earn a remission of one-third of his total sentence after the first month; this remission is credited to him when he is admitted and may be forfeited as a punishment. In Uganda a prisoner may be released on licence before the termination of his sentence. In Tanganyika this system also applied formerly but was abolished when the new rate of remission was adopted in 1958; release on licence had in any case been found difficult to operate.

In Kenya a special system of supervision can be applied to a prisoner on discharge, in connection with the remission system. The Commissioner of Prisons may make a compulsory supervision order on the discharge of any prisoner for whom he considers it desirable or necessary as a rehabilitative measure; he must make such an order in the case of a prisoner who has been sentenced to three years' imprisonment or more and has previously been sentenced to imprisonment on at least two occasions. The supervision order may be operative for any specific period up to one year. If the prisoner commits any offence, or breaks any condition of the order, he may be required to serve the balance of the sentence which he earned as remission, or three months' imprisonment if that is greater.

Kenya also has a parole system enabling prisoners who are serving sentences of four years or more to be released up to three months early on parole.

(*vi*) *After-care*. In the past twenty years East African authorities have grown increasingly aware of the importance of after-care services. In Tanganyika prisoners are given on discharge a gratuity to enable them to meet their immediate needs, and craftsmen are provided with tools. After-care is largely the responsibility of the Probation and Welfare Division, although there formerly existed a Discharged Prisoners' Aid Society and early in 1966 the Commissioner of Prisons called for the formation of a new body which should have the active support of the public as well as the government.[69]

In Kenya the Prisoners' Aid Association is active in addition to the After-Care and Welfare Officers established within the Prisons Service itself. Reception and Discharge Boards exist in every prison. The Uganda Discharged Prisoners' Aid Society, inaugurated in 1960, assists the district committees which were already in existence; trade testing, the provision of tools on release and the construction of a hostel were among its first tasks.

(c) The prisoners

Certain basic general features indicate to some extent the nature of the East African prison community.

A. There is a very high proportion of remand prisoners in all countries, a majority of whom are not subsequently sentenced to imprisonment. Many are imprisoned on remand by mistake, through miscalculation or inefficiency; some are innocent of the offence charged. The serious consequences of the situation have been well summarized by the Commissioner of Prisons, Tanganyika:

> Apart from vindictiveness towards society and contempt towards the machinery employed for detection of the criminal, such humiliating treatment can provoke in the innocent, the problem of preventing contamination of the susceptible by contact with the real criminals is a very real one. The hardships to which such innocent persons are subjected, because of the inadequacy of the existing prevailing systems to prevent them from going to prison, is another saddening aspect. The wastage of public funds in feeding these prisoners and the provision of accommodation and the staff necessary to guard them are other undesirable features. . . .[70]

This is not a new or recent problem in East African prisons, but it has been intensified recently. Thus, of the 97,927 persons received into Kenya prisons in 1961 no less than 52,312 were committed on remand. With 1,136 remaining on remand at the end of the previous year, this gave a total of 53,448 remand prisoners in the year. Of these, only 7,925 were subsequently convicted and sentenced to imprisonment, and 8,051 were sentenced to detention in a detention camp. More than two-thirds—36,303—were discharged from prison custody (1,107 remained on remand at the end of the year, forming 9·51 per cent of the total prison population at that time). The average period of time spent on remand by each prisoner was thirteen days. The daily average of remand prisoners was 1,200 out of a total daily average prison population of 11,750. In 1964, of 71,916 total admissions, 40,696 were remand prisoners of whom 24,198 were subsequently discharged and 12,614 convicted and sentenced to imprisonment or detention.[71]

B. Of the prisoners sentenced to imprisonment, a great number serve short sentences, which for many years have been considered to be of little value. They are too short for remedial measures or deterrent effect, and increase the prisons' administrative problems by rapid turn-over. The Commissioner of Prisons in Tanganyika has described the short-term prisoner as one of his biggest problems:

> The time they are in prison is too short for a proper study of them to be undertaken to discover the causes and reasons for their committing a crime, to teach them discipline and to give them corrective treatment or rehabilitative training. Most of the short-term prisoners, if not all, are first offenders. They have to be vigilantly protected from association with hardened criminals. The difficulties of exercising such strict segregation from hardened criminals is often aggravated by the lack of accommodation and other facilities coupled with their very large number. The question of providing suitable productive labour to these vast numbers is also another serious problem.[72]

In Tanganyika in 1964, 40,111 persons were sentenced to imprisonment, of whom 30,364 were sentenced for six months or less. All of these, of course, were eligible to perform extra-mural penal labour, but only 11,317 were released to do this, mainly because of lack of supervision and local funds. This surely calls for a re-allocation of national resources, for it is considerably more economical to employ offenders on extra-mural labour than to maintain them in prison.

In Uganda the position is somewhat different. There, in each of the years 1958–60, prisoners sentenced to six months or less formed between 33 and 41 per cent of the total number of convicted prisoners admitted; prisoners sentenced to eighteen months' imprisonment or more accounted for between 34 and 38 per cent of the total.

In Kenya the position is about half-way between these others. From 1958 to 1961 prisoners sentenced to six months' imprisonment or less numbered annually between 61 and 65 per cent of the total admissions of convicted prisoners; those sentenced to eighteen months or more numbered only between 6 and 10 per cent of the total admissions, indicating that in Uganda longer sentences were much more frequently imposed.

C. The overwhelming majority of convicted prisoners are aged between 20 and 40 years, with younger and older prisoners accounting on average for no more than a quarter of the total prison population. This figure must, of course, be related to the lower life expectancy of East Africans than compared with that of Europeans; this naturally reduces the proportion of older men in the general community.

D. The recidivist population in East African prisons is low by comparison with England, but is growing steadily.

TABLE 10. UGANDA: RECIDIVISTS IN PRISON POPULATION 1958–62

	Total No. of persons sentenced to imprisonment	No. and percentage of total who had been previously convicted					
		Once		Twice		Thrice or more	
1958	6,525	597	9·1%	266	4·07%	379	5·8%
1959	8,328	958	11·5%	338	4·5%	448	5·3%
1960	9,050	907	10·2%	446	4·9%	558	6·1%
1961	8,068	1,256	15·5%	560	6·9%	736	9·1%
1962	10,179	1,757	17·2%	824	8·1%	1,746	17·1%

Source: 1963 Statistical Abstract.

E. In most countries the proportion of women offenders is very small. In East African countries this feature is even more pronounced than in Europe, and women form a tiny proportion of criminal offenders except in one or two categories, particularly

143

homicide and certain liquor offences. Most are first offenders serving short sentences, but the fact that numbers are small makes the provision of suitable facilities and treatment for women difficult. One interesting disparity emerges from the statistics: whereas in Tanganyika and Uganda the proportion of women in the prison population is consistently below 5 per cent, in Kenya it has not fallen below 10 per cent in recent years. The pattern suggests that this is due in some degree to the part played by women in the 'Mau Mau' emergency, for the highest total of women imprisoned was in 1955 (36 per cent) and after that date there was a steady decline, not merely in numbers but in proportion, until 1962 (12 per cent).

F. For young offenders, Kenya has since 1963 provided a Youth Corrective Training Centre. Offenders aged between 18 and 21 years convicted of any non-capital offence (other than tax offences) may be sentenced by the court to corrective training for a period of four months, provided that they have not previously been sentenced to such training or to imprisonment or detention. Uganda has a central training prison for young offenders with special educational facilities.

G. In Uganda preventive detention may be ordered by a court in the case of certain habitual criminals: this term is defined to mean a person not under 30 years of age who is convicted of an offence punishable with two years' imprisonment or more, who has previously been convicted on at least three occasions, since reaching the age of 16 years, of offences similarly punishable and who was on at least two of such occasions sentenced to imprisonment. The sentence of preventive detention may be for a minimum of five or a maximum of fourteen years; in fact it is seldom imposed and it appears that the system has not been successful in operation.

H. The one category of inmate who is a source of particular difficulty is the mentally ill prisoner. Quite apart from the criminal or suspect, in many parts of East Africa mentally ill patients may be committed to prison pending observation for lack of other specialized hospital facilities. In 1961 the Kenya prisons admitted over a thousand civil lunatics. In Uganda the numbers have been smaller: in 1960, for example, 376. But each case represents a misuse of prison resources and in Uganda it was urged that the situation be improved by the provision of observation wards at hospitals. Even criminal mental patients, however, should not be the responsibility of the prisons, as the Kenya Report for 1961 emphasized. In Tanzania the special institution originally modelled on the English Broadmoor, and formerly within the Prisons Department, is now the responsibility of the Ministry of Health. It accommodates prisoners who become mentally ill during imprisonment, persons who are charged with an offence but cannot be tried because of mental illness, and persons who have been tried and found not guilty by reason of insanity.[73]

(d) Conclusion

There has been much discussion in certain quarters of the efficacy of imprisonment as a penalty in Africa. The growth in prison populations and recidivism is often cited as an illustration of the argument that prisons are not merely alien but inappropriate as instruments of penal policy. The weight of opinion of those who are well qualified to judge is that imprisonment in an African country is a proper form of punishment and in some ways a severe form. Even the apparently relaxed atmosphere of an East African prison conflicts squarely with the sociable and free intercourse of African social life.

> The African hates the idea of going to prison, and having been there hates still more the thought of returning. He may suffer no social stigma; but he suffers very acutely social separation. He would rather be beaten than banished.[74]

> The African convict, clothed conspicuously different from his brethren at large, numbered instead of named and exposed to the ridicule of his fellows by being forced to do work traditionally taboo or normally relegated to women, is keenly conscious of his lot.[75]

On this question, Lord Hailey concluded:

> Doubts have been entertained as to the deterrent value of long sentences of imprisonment which carry no social stigma. The social stigma attached to a term of imprisonment appears in fact to vary inversely with the number of persons committed. When so large a proportion of the African population is sentenced to short terms for 'statutory' offences, as is habitual in

the Union of South Africa, no stigma follows: but when committal to prison is confined to the few who perpetrate serious crime and are severely punished, the convict is likely to be stigmatized as the enemy of society.[76]

The last word may appropriately rest with the present Commissioner of Prisons in Kenya:

> ... A punitive policy based primarily on the incarceration of offenders is now generally considered to be very costly. The process of devising simple, less burdensome and more effective measures is today an important goal. The conventional solution of building more penal institutions and increasing prison staff to cope with the increasing penal population, which, quite apart from any other consideration, drains our countries' financial resources and cannot be allowed to go on indefinitely, should be replaced, where possible, with some other better solution. We should try and aim at treatment of offenders outside institutions, both by greater use of intensive supervised probation as a substitute for prison sentences, and by affording early parole for those offenders who have indicated their readiness to return to society to live within the law.[77]

3 DETENTION CAMPS

Detention camps were introduced into Kenya in 1925 to provide an alternative to imprisonment for the large number of petty offenders for whom other penalties were unsuitable. Originally, some 5,000 prisoners were committed to them annually. Table 11 shows the extent to which the system grew through Kenya's subsequent history, until the recent decline when extra-mural penal employment was introduced as an alternative. The Detention Camps Act provides that an African convicted of an offence for which an adequate punishment would be a fine or imprisonment for not more than six months may instead be sentenced to detention in a detention camp for any period up to six months. To prevent contamination, no one who has been sentenced to imprisonment more than once before may be sentenced to detention. Detainees

146

wear their own clothes in the camps and are required to labour without payment.

In 1930 the average period of detention ordered was thirty days but with a great disparity between different districts, from Eldoret, where the average was nine days, to Malindi where it was thirty-two. Most sentences then were imposed in default of payment of fines and frequently the fine was paid during the detention, resulting in the immediate release of the detainee. In 1930, 8,746 persons were committed to detention and only 68 absconded (21 were recaptured); in 1961, 76,076 persons were committed, 1,141 escaped and 90 were recaptured. The daily average population of detention camps was 573 in 1930, and 11,310·12 in 1961. The official report comments that there were, in 1961, few obstacles to determined escapers: security conditions in the grossly overcrowded camps were poor and supervision of working parties sparse. This was nothing new; in 1933 the Prisons Commissioner had complained to the Chief Justice that magistrates imposed low sentences for escapes. He pointed out that there was practically nothing to prevent escapes: 'In fact, in the circumstances, it seems surprising that half the detention camp population does not simply walk away.'[78]

TABLE 11. KENYA: COMMITTALS OF CONVICTED PRISONERS TO PRISONS AND DETENTION CAMPS, SELECTED YEARS 1944-64

	Committed to prisons	Daily average in prison	Committed to detention camp	Daily average in detention camp
1944	12,803	4,466	15,037	1,593
1945	11,889	4,490	14,167	1,446
1949	15,986	7,749	16,639	2,209
1950	17,956	8,418	18,037	2,535
1954	39,403	27,044	25,970	3,591
1955	30,803	26,053	30,247	4,247
1959	25,297	9,741	67,472	9,933
1960	27,499	10,976	68,314	10,632
1961	28,697	10,085	75,716	11,310
1962	33,843	11,558	74,766	10,682
1963	32,398	13,083	49,905	6,342
1964	29,112	9,959	22,225	2,542

Source: Annual Reports of Prisons Department.

Clearly the detention camps have borne a very large share of the burden of Kenya's penal system; but following the introduction of extra-mural penal employment in 1962, detention camp committals fell to 22,225 in 1964 (the daily average was only 2,541·98). The intention of the Prisons Department was that the new system would lead to the abolition of detention camps entirely.

4 EXTRA-MURAL PENAL LABOUR

Extra-mural penal labour was introduced in Tanganyika in 1933 as an alternative to short sentences of imprisonment for petty offenders. The legislation, in the Prisons Ordinance,[79] was based upon the Penal Labour Ordinance of Palestine, as recommended by the Tanganyika Committee on Imprisonment. Extra-mural employment was adopted by Kenya in 1962.

In Tanganyika a person sentenced to imprisonment for six months or less, or for the non-payment of a fine not exceeding 1,000 shillings, may be released for employment by a government department or local authority on public work unconnected with prisons. He may sleep at home, or in a camp provided near the work where necessary; food while at work is provided. The labour is supervised by government officers and is not paid. The initiative lies with the prisoner himself; he can declare himself willing to undertake such work (providing the court has not debarred him from it expressly). His release also, of course, depends upon the agreement of the administrative officer concerned to provide and supervise the labour. The convict is expected to work for six hours daily for the term of the original sentence, or the balance remaining. If his conduct is unsatisfactory, the officer in charge may return him to prison for the balance of his sentence. In the earlier and later years of the scheme, it has been possible to release convicts directly from the courts. Table 12 shows how very extensively the system has been used and how little the scheme has been abused. Until 1951, failure to attend for labour was a breach of prison discipline, but an amendment of that year made it instead a Penal Code offence punishable by a court. The system has played a vital part in preventing even greater overcrowding in the prisons.

In Kenya, extra-mural penal employment may be ordered by a

court in the case of any man sentenced to imprisonment for six months or less or committed to prison for non-payment of a fine, compensation or costs, or sentenced to detention.[80] Remission of one-third applies to the period of employment. The convict must report to a public officer authorized to administer the scheme, for the details as to the place, nature and time of his work. The new provision came into force on February 1st, 1963, and a good start was made during that year with over 10,000 persons being ordered to perform extra-mural work. But in 1964 there was a falling off, instead of the expected increase: only 7,317 were so ordered. The Prisons Report for the year therefore re-emphasized its value and the economy which would be effected by its proper widespread use.

TABLE 12. TANGANYIKA: EXTRA MURAL PENAL LABOUR, SELECTED YEARS, 1944–62

	Total number of convicts committed to prisons	Released to extra mural labour	Failed to co-operate and returned to prison
1944	10,165	2,435	—
1948	12,350	2,542	—
1954	22,695	4,403	—
1958	31,002	4,877	325
1959	33,396	7,203	333
1960	35,780	7,431	401
1961	41,852	15,569	764
1962	37,374	10,534	—

Source: Annual Reports of Prison Departments.

Notes: Figures of those who failed to co-operate are not available for every year.

The numbers released to extra-mural labour are not all included in the total number committed to prison each year: during 1947–52 and 1959–61 large numbers were released direct from the courts.

5 MINIMUM SENTENCES ACT, 1963, TANGANYIKA

Undoubtedly the most interesting innovation made in the East African penal systems since independence is the Minimum Sentences Act of Tanganyika.[81] This introduced several novel principles of sentencing. While utilizing only the sanctions already

149

available, it changed the application of them so fundamentally as to result, in effect, in a new mode of penal treatment. The Act provides for:

(a) minimum sentences of imprisonment for certain scheduled offences;
(b) the imposition of corporal punishment automatically on persons receiving the minimum sentences, other than women and men over 45 years; this corporal punishment is administered in two instalments, respectively at the commencement and termination of the imprisonment;
(c) the court is obliged to make an order for the payment of compensation by the offender to the victim of the crime whenever the offender acquired property as a result of the offence.

The scheduled offences are mainly offences against property; they are not new offences but were already defined in existing legislation. The minimum sentences vary for different offences: the minimum of two years' imprisonment applies, for example, to burglary, theft of government property or theft by a public servant, robbery, receiving stolen property proved to have been obtained by one of the foregoing offences, and certain types of corruption. For cattle-stealing the minimum is three years, and for various other offences relating to cattle theft the minimum varies from six months to three years. The corporal punishment of twenty-four strokes applies to all the offences.

The courts are left with only a very limited discretion in cases within this Act, which does apply, however, to a very large proportion of the criminal cases tried. Where the accused is a first offender, and the value of the property involved does not exceed one hundred shillings, and there are special circumstances (which the court must record in writing) relating to the offence or the offender, then the court may, instead of the minimum sentence, impose a sentence of either ten strokes of corporal punishment or any term of imprisonment. Even in such a case, therefore, the normal alternatives of probation, fine or discharge cannot be employed. Thus, where a first offender was convicted of corruptly offering a policeman just under one and a half shillings to forbear from arresting him, the High Court, in reducing the minimum sentence imposed by the magistrates, was still obliged to sentence him to imprisonment.

This Act represents the final victory of that undeniably strong body of public opinion which throughout the colonial period called for the extension of corporal punishment, to which the colonial government was strongly opposed.

But its main significance for our present purposes, prescribing as it does the greatly extended use of corporal punishment and a substantial increase in the average length of sentences for a wide range of offences, lies in the severe restriction of the court's discretion and the total exclusion of the many alternative reformative measures which are normally available. The task of the court in sentencing is, of course, much simplified; but it may be seriously questioned whether the emphasis upon imprisonment and corporal punishment will ultimately have the deterrent effect intended. Apart entirely from the inevitable increase in the prison population resulting from the overall increase in the length of sentences, the association of larger numbers of prisoners, an increasing proportion of whom will have been sentenced under this Act, may well increase anti-social feelings and recidivism.

The Act has introduced a prominent ambiguity or dualism in the fundamental purposes of the penal system, which will surely be an increasing burden to those who administer it. The problem has been succinctly noted by the Commissioner of Prisons (although he was not writing with specific reference to this Act):

It is an accepted fact that deterrent punishments can only suppress, at the most, criminal inhibitions and tendencies in the human nature and cannot actually cure them. . . . The psychological set-backs such suppression produces in an individual, and the bitterness against society corporal punishment can invoke in a recipient, can transform an otherwise innocuous transgressor into an anti-social and violent criminal. . . . Such developments in the mental attitudes of a criminal make it difficult, if not impossible, to give any measure of success to the treatment of criminals and their successful rehabilitation.[82]

151

It is difficult to avoid the conclusion that the Tanganyika Government's policy reflects a fundamental dissatisfaction with the existing penal system; yet it also demonstrates that the only change immediately practicable is the reorganization of the application of existing forms of penalties.

6 PROBATION

Probation services exist in each East African country, but they have developed only in recent years and are still limited to the main urban areas. The earliest provision for a modern probation system was made in Kenya in 1943, following the report of a committee which examined the need for such a system.[83] The initiative had come through a despatch to colonial governments from the Secretary of State in London. In Tanganyika, legal and financial provision for a probation service was made in 1948; the service commenced in 1949 as soon as a suitable staff had been found, at first dealing only with juveniles.[84] In Uganda the earliest provision for probation was enacted in 1948, to be replaced by comprehensive legislation in 1962.[85]

Originally set up within the Prison Departments, probation services have now been transferred to the Social Welfare Departments. In Uganda and Kenya there are local Probation Case Committees to advise probation officers and in each country a Central Probation Committee exists. For lack of other social services, probation officers in East Africa are drawn into other social problems and tend to become general social welfare officers. By enabling them to deal with unstable home conditions, this can be an important factor in preventing crime. The tendency for probation officers to become maids of all work was commented upon in 1958 by the McKisack Committee on Juvenile Delinquency in Uganda, which noted the slow growth of the service in its early years owing to lack of adequate funds. The services have also been concerned to develop remand homes and probation hostels and in Tanzania the probation department is also responsible for administering the approved school.

In each country the probation services have regularly recorded a high success rate with their cases.

7 OTHER FORMS OF TREATMENT

East African courts have a wide range of alternative sentences or orders at their disposal in addition to those already discussed. Some of the more significant are now summarized.

(a) Corporal punishment

Apart from its greatly extended application in Tanganyika under the Minimum Sentences Act, corporal punishment is available throughout East Africa as an alternative or additional penalty in a limited number of cases. It may be imposed upon juveniles instead of imprisonment for any offence; upon adult offenders, for only a few offences, such as robbery with violence, rape, defilement and (in Kenya and Tanganyika only) a second conviction of living on immoral earnings; and upon convicted prisoners, for certain serious prison offences. Normally, corporal punishment may not be imposed in instalments, the Minimum Sentences Act making a major exception to this rule. Corporal punishment may not be inflicted on a female or a male over 45 years of age. The form of the punishment is a number of strokes (which number must be specified in the sentence), inflicted with a light cane, the size of which, with the details for carrying out the punishment, is precisely defined by legislation.[86]

(b) Discharge

Discharge may be ordered by a court, either absolutely or conditionally upon the convicted person committing no further offence during a specified period not exceeding one year; in the event of a further offence being committed, sentence may be imposed for the original offence. In Uganda the court may dismiss the charge without proceeding to conviction, or it may convict and caution the offender.[87]

(c) Security for good behaviour

A convicted offender may be discharged subject to a recognizance to keep the peace and be of good behaviour during a specified period (in Uganda not exceeding one year), with or without sureties.

This old provision was in earlier days the nearest approach to a probationary system, and was used mainly where the offender was a juvenile and the court could rely upon his parent to exercise supervision. Today in Tanganyika the provision is in force only in those areas where the probation service does not operate; in Uganda and Kenya it has been found necessary to retain it as an alternative to probation.[88]

(d) Supervision

Police supervision after release from prison may be ordered by courts in Kenya and Tanganyika, when sentencing to imprisonment offenders who have previously been convicted. Supervision orders may be for any specified period up to five years and may include various requirements concerning residence, reporting to the police and the like.[89]

(e) Costs

A convicted offender may be ordered to pay costs to the prosecutor, within a specified maximum; the courts have ruled that this should be done only in exceptional cases for special reasons.[90]

(f) Compensation

East African courts have wider powers than English courts have, to order payment of compensation by the offender to a person who has suffered material loss or personal injury as a result of his crime. The power is, however, rarely invoked, perhaps because it is unfamiliar to the judges and magistrates, who until recent years have been trained in English criminal law only, or because of the heavy pressure of work upon them which reduces the time available for such inquiries after conviction. The legal provisions are not entirely adequate—in Kenya compensation can be awarded only out of a fine imposed, and the courts have properly held that a heavy fine should not be imposed merely to create a compensation fund.[91]

(g) Settlements

An unusual power vested in East African courts is the provision enabling and encouraging them to promote reconciliation in minor criminal cases by promoting amicable settlements which in Kenya and Tanganyika may be upon terms of payment of compensation. The uncertain extent of this provision, adopted from Nigerian law, has limited its application in practice.[92]

VI The Treatment of Juvenile Offenders

It is probably owing to the social cohesion of African societies that juvenile delinquency has not in the past been a major problem; but in the urban areas and especially the principal cities, juvenile crime has grown over the years until it has reached a level causing concern, particularly in Kenya and Uganda. Today each country has specialized facilities for the treatment of juveniles: an approved school and remand home in Tanzania; a Borstal institution, approved schools and remand homes in Kenya; and an approved school, reform schools and a remand home and hostel in Uganda. These institutions are modelled, with appropriate modifications, upon their English equivalents.

I KENYA

Although a Reformatory School had been established in Kenya in 1909,[93] little was done to make it a constructive educational force until it was examined by the Crime Committee in 1932. Following the Committee's report on the unsatisfactory atmosphere of the institution, it was resolved to examine the English Borstals and reformatories with a view to seeing how far they could serve as a model in Kenya. The Juveniles Ordinance, 1934, followed, based on the Children and Young Persons Act of 1933 in England, and this remained in force in Kenya until replaced by the Children and Young Persons Act, 1963, which is the source of

155

current provisions governing juvenile courts, remand homes and approved schools.

The present Borstal institution in Kenya was established under a statute of 1963, but from 1934 a modified Borstal system had been applied in an approved school. In 1964 the Borstal admitted 141 boys, being full to capacity with a daily average of 98·33. The need for a second institution was evident. Orders for Borstal training for three-year periods may be made by a court on 'youthful offenders'—that is, those aged 15 years but under 18 who are convicted of offences punishable with imprisonment.

The first approved school in Kenya was established in 1934 and the second in 1937. They were transferred from the Prisons Department to the probation service in 1955. Today there are five approved schools for boys and one for girls (which, in fact, has little demand for its limited capacity: in 1961 there were no inmates). The boys' schools are specialized, one providing academic education for boys up to 13½ years, one academic and vocational classes for older boys, and one providing vocational training for boys aged 16–18. The 1961 report notes a 'disquieting change' in the type of boy admitted:

> Boys nowadays reject the opportunity of free education and living almost completely and are only anxious to escape and enjoy complete freedom of action. Their attitude to the staff is one of truculence and opposition. Violence is now not infrequently offered to staff. These trends are attributed to the lack of positive treatment of the delinquent in the early stages.

The report cites early case histories of the boys, showing repeated convictions (sometimes as many as twelve), the failure of probation to produce any response and, in the absence of any vacancy in an approved school, the resort to caning as 'virtually the only award'.

Kenya also has a number of remand homes; in 1961 the six homes received 4,974 children aged from 5 years to some over 18 sent in by mistake. There was a 'burning need' for more homes in other areas of the country not then served, where children were still detained in prison in large numbers for lack of other suitable accommodation. Remand home staff was also used as 'almost the only after-care agents' for approved school discharges and to assist in the repatriation of children from the towns.

It is difficult to estimate the success of the training given to juveniles. In 1950 the official report cited an estimate that of the boys discharged from approved schools from 1940 to 1949, 40 per cent had been reconvicted before the end of that period; but in 1952 the official report was more optimistic, estimating that of 463 discharged in the previous six years only 62 proved failures. In 1961 it was stated that the success rate was 65–70 per cent.

Other methods of dealing with juvenile offenders in Kenya include discharge, probation, corporal punishment, fine, compensation or costs ordered against the offender and/or his parent or guardian, imprisonment (only if he is 14 years of age or more); and committal to the care of a fit person or approved society.

2 UGANDA

Although the government recognized the urgent need for institutional treatment for juveniles as early as 1915 and passed a Reformatory Schools Ordinance in 1930, it was not until 1950 that the Ordinance was brought into force and not until 1951 that a school was opened.[94]

Today, youthful male offenders—under 18 years of age—may be sent to a reform school by the court. The system of treatment in the two reforms schools is similar to that of a Borstal institution. There is also a recall centre for boys who have broken conditions after release from a reform school on licence. The approved school accommodates 'care and protection' cases as well as convicted children and is divided into senior and junior schools; the normal ages for admission are from 10 to 16 years, detention being normally for three years or until the age of 16 if that is longer. The McKisack Committee on Juvenile Delinquency made numerous proposals for reform of the legislation governing these institutions, but few of them have as yet been effected.

In Uganda, a 'young offender', that is, one under 16 years, cannot be sentenced to imprisonment by a court. If in a particular case the court considers—for reasons which it must record—that there is no suitable alternative to imprisonment, it must order the detention of the young offender pending an order by the Minister for his continued detention, which may be in a prison only if no other place of custody is suitable.[95] Other methods of dealing with juveniles include probation, corporal punishment (in any case where imprisonment might be imposed), discharge, caution, fine, orders of compensation or costs and binding over to keep the peace.

3 TANZANIA

In Tanganyika an approved school has existed for many years and, long before the union with Zanzibar in 1964, it served also for the reception of juveniles committed from Zanzibar courts. The daily average population of the school grew from 41·2 in 1940 to 167·8 in 1960, and on one occasion had been as high as 216·5 (1954). Admissions have, however, remained well below one hundred annually. In 1958 the school moved to its present site at Malindi on the coast[96] and in 1960 responsibility for it was transferred from the Prisons Department first to the Ministry of Education and later to the Probation and Welfare Division of the Ministry of Community Development. Inmates receive full primary education until the age of 14 years and after that age vocational training is given. An offender under 16 years may be committed to the school until the age of 18 or for any shorter period not less than two years.

The only other institution for the custody of juveniles is the Juvenile Remand Home opened in Dar-es-Salaam in 1961. In other parts of the country it is still sometimes necessary to admit juveniles to prison pending their trials. Since 1957, juveniles have no longer been admitted to prison merely for corporal punishment, which is now administered away from prisons.

Other forms of treatment for juvenile offenders include probation, corporal punishment, discharge, binding over to keep the peace, fine, orders of compensation and costs.

VII Conclusion

This study has shown that East African penal systems include a wide variety of methods of treatment for different classes of offenders. Colonialism, with its introduction of alien principles such as imprisonment, has been the formative influence, although it often ran into difficulties because the purposes of the new system were not understood and the new methods were generally applied with little regard for the principles and practices of traditional African societies. Conflict and misunderstanding arose particularly over the effect of imprisonment and the lack of compensation for the victim of the crime. Today there is a readiness to experiment and to move towards more modern methods of treatment, with a recognition that the existing systems, while they cannot be changed overnight, are in need of considerable adaptation. It remains to be seen how far such reforms may be able to call upon the distinctive features of African legal tradition as well as upon the most modern scientific methods.[97]

NOTES

1. Tanganyika and Zanzibar are in fact dealt with separately throughout, since the union of the two countries does not significantly affect their penal systems.
2. '*Mau Mau*' *Detainee*, by Josiah Mwangi Kariuki (1963), for example, gives a vivid account of experiences in the Emergency Detention Camps of Kenya, 1953–60.
3. It is an express provision in the Codes that they are to be interpreted according to English principles. Kenya: Penal Code, cap. 63, s. 3, and Criminal Procedure Code, cap. 75, s. 261. Uganda: Penal Code, cap. 106, s. 3, and Criminal Procedure Code, cap. 107, s. 250. Tanganyika: Penal Code, cap.16, s. 4, and Criminal Procedure Code, cap. 20, s. 247. Zanzibar: Penal Decree, cap. 13, s. 3.
4. Hardinge, *Report on the Condition and Progress of the East Africa Protectorate from its Establishment to the 20th July, 1897*, Parliamentary Papers, Africa, No. 7, 36 (1897).
5. Phillips, *Report on Native Tribunals*, 265 (1944).
6. R. *v. Komen arap Chelal and 43 others* (1938), 5 E.A.C.A. 150.
7. R. *v. Karoga wa Kithengi and 53 others* (1913), 5 E.A.P.L.R. 50.
8. Phillips, *op. cit.*, 268.

9. Hone, *The Native of Uganda and the Criminal Law*, 6 Uganda Journal 2 (1938).

10. Phillips, *op. cit.*, 259.

11. Article 6.

12. Uganda Constitution, s. 24(8); Kenya Constitution, s. 21(8); Tanganyika Magistrates Courts Act, 1963, s. 66(1).

13. Cotran, *Report on Customary Criminal Offences in Kenya* (1963). The Buganda Customary Offences Law, 1964 (which made imprisonment compulsory for a large number of offences) was held by the High Court to be unenforceable under the Constitution of Uganda in so far as it duplicated areas covered by the Uganda Penal Code.

14. E.g. Restitution of Cattle and Payment of Blood-Money (Procedure) (Karamoja) Regulations, 1965 (Uganda).

15. This is not the sole explanation, because there was in fact a new classification of 'serious crime' introduced into the recording of statistics during this period.

16. Roscoe, *The Banyankole*, 19 (1923).

17. Roscoe, *The Baganda*, 264 (1911); Haydon, *Law and Justice in Buganda*, 296 (1960).

18. Junod, ' African Penal Conceptions and the Emancipation of African States, 1 *Genève-Afrique* (*Acta Africana*), 156–75 (1962).

19. Kenyatta, *Facing Mount Kenya*, chap. ix (1938).

20. Penwill, *Kamba Customary Law*, 98–9 (1951).

21. Kenyatta, *op. cit.*

22. Edel, *The Chiga of Western Uganda*, 114–15 (1957).

23. Kenyatta, *op. cit.*

24. Snell, *Nandi Customary Law*, 86 (1954).

25. Hardinge, *op. cit.*, 37.

26. R. *v. Mianga wa Mwanga and four others* (1903), 1 E.A.P.L.R. 51.

27. Hailey, *An African Survey*, 628 (1956); it is difficult to agree with Lord Hailey that 'the authorization of collective punishment must indeed always be an administrative rather than a judicial proceeding'.

28. Haydon, *op. cit.*

29. Hardinge, *op. cit.*, 37

30. *Ibid.*

31. *A Handbook of German East Africa*, 21 (1916).

32. Alexander, *Tanganyika Memories*, 194 (1936).

33. Tanganyika National Assembly Debates (Hansard), June 11th and 12th, 1963. Extracts from the debates are quoted by Read, 'Minimum Sentences in Tanzania' [1965] *Journal of African Law*, 20–39.

34. See the discussion of sentencing policy, Part IV, below.

35. E.g. Roberts, *Tangled Justice: Some reasons for a change of Policy in Africa* (1937) and by the same author, 'African Natives under the English System of Penal Law', 15 *Journal of Comparative Legislation* (3rd series), 169 (1933).

36. This problem became more acute in later years: see pp. 135–36 below.

37. The same problem was arising in England at the same time: see the *Report of the Departmental Committee on Imprisonment by Courts of Summary Jurisdiction in Default of Payment of Fines and other sums of Money*, Cmd. 4649 (1934).
38. The Report was published in London in 1934 (H.M.S.O., unnumbered). Minutes of Evidence and Memoranda submitted were published as a non-Parliamentary publication, Colonial No. 96.
39. *Report on a Visit to the Prisons of Kenya, Uganda, Tanganyika, Zanzibar, Aden and Somaliland by Alexander Paterson, M.C.* (1939).
40. *Report of the McKisack Committee of Enquiry into the Problem and Treatment of Juvenile Delinquency in Uganda* (1958). See also a Government Memorandum on the Report, Sessional Paper No. 6 of 1958.
41. Read, ed., 'Record of the Conference on Penal Problems in East Africa', 2 *East African Law Journal*, 1–62 (1966).
42. *R. v. Astaliko Ngobi* (1918), 2 U.L.R. 287, *per* Carter, C.J.
43. *R v. Malakwen arap Kogo* (1933), 15 K.L.R. 115–27. For the Attorney-General's views on the severity of sentencing generally, see Enclosure 2 to the Despatch from the Acting Governor of Kenya to the Secretary of State for the Colonies arising out of the *Report* of the Bushe Commission, reprinted as an Annex to the *Report*, at 112.
44. *R. v. Gaudenzio Kihwele and Muhagale Kadefu* (1945), 1 T.L.R. (R.) 81.
45. As in England, the practice has developed in East Africa courts of taking into consideration other offences admitted by the accused, without any statutory authority for this course. At present there is recognition of the practice by legislation in Uganda: Criminal Procedure Code, s. 290.
46. *Mawji Daya v. R.* (1944), 1 T.L.R. (R.) 274.
47. *Sethi v. R.*, [1962] E.A. 523.
48. *Mohamed Juma v. R.* (1942), 1 T.L.R. (R.) 257, citing High Court Circular No. 3 of 1938.
49. Circular to Magistrates No. 13 of 1956; 29 K.L.R. 205.
50. Circular to Magistrates No. 20 of 1956; 29 K.L.R. 213.
51. Foran, *The Kenya Police 1887–1960*, 68 (1962).
52. Uganda: Criminal Procedure Code, ss. 295–6. Kenya: Penal Code, ss. 211–12. Tanganyika: Penal Code, s. 197 proviso (the proviso refers to 'an offence punishable with death' but the section in which it appears is concerned only with the punishment of murder).
53. Foran, *op. cit.*, 29–30.
54. Constitution of Uganda (1967), articles 73–5; Constitution of Kenya (1963, as amended), ss. 88–90. In Tanzania, the prerogative of mercy in respect of persons convicted of offences against the laws of Zanzibar is exercised by the President of Zanzibar: Interim Constitution of Tanzania (1965), s. 22.
55. This paragraph is based upon material in the National Archives of Tanganyika, File 15287.
56. *Fateh Ali Shah Mushhad v. R.* (1939), 1 T.L.R. (R.) 229; *Lucas s/o Mwangela v. R.* (1953), 20 E.A.C.A. 304.

57. Now cap. 313 and Legal Notice 80 of 1958.
58. Heaton, *Report on the General Administration of Prisons and Detention Camps in Kenya* (1956).
59. *Report to the Secretary of State for the Colonies by the Parliamentary Delegation to Kenya, January, 1954*, Cmd. 9081 (1954).
60. *Report of the Committee on Emergency Detention Camps*, Nairobi, 1959.
61. *Ibid.*, para. 82.
62. Now cap. 90. See also Prisons Rules, 1963 (Legal Notice No. 60).
63. Perhaps a pregnant comment on the British Colonial administration, as compared with that of Germany which had preceded it: para. 28.
64. Lord Hailey commented particularly upon Kingolwira in his *African Survey*, 626 (1956).
65. In his *Annual Report on the Prisons Department*, 1964.
66. E.g. in Uganda in 1960 the average number of prisoners in central government prisons set to work daily was 5,424 out of an average daily population of 8,124.
67. Harwich, *Red Dust*, 42 (1961).
68. Paterson, *op. cit.*, para. 21.
69. Rugimbana, 'Various Aspects of the Imprisonment System in East Africa', 2 *East African Law Journal*, 24 (1966).
70. *Ibid.*, at 21.
71. Although there was therefore a decrease in the number of remand prisoners from 1961 to 1964, an increase in the average period spent on remand resulted in an increase in the daily average population of remand prisoners. This was contrasted with the decrease in the average length of sentences of convicted prisoners which resulted in a fall in the average daily population of convicts, although their total number increased:

KENYA: ADMISSIONS TO PRISONS

	1961	1962	1963	1964
Remand prisoners	52,312	49,190	38,878	40,696
Daily average population	1,193	1,200	1,063	1,278
Convicted prisoners	28,697	33,843	32,398	29,112
Daily average population	10,085	11,558	13,083	9,959

Source: Annual Reports, Prisons Department in *Annual Reports on the Treatment of Offenders*.

72. Rugimbana, *op. cit.*, 21–2.
73. In Tanganyika this form of verdict has been substituted for the older form of 'Guilty but insane' which still applies in Uganda and Kenya.
74. Paterson, *op. cit.*, para. 3.
75. Harwich, *op. cit.*, 38.
76. Hailey, *op. cit.*, 625.
77. Saikwa, 'An Approach to Penal Administration in East Africa', 2 *East African Law Journal*, 25 (1966).

78. *Report of the Commissioner of Prisons*, 1932, quoted in Circular to Magistrates No. 8 of 1933, 15 K.L.R. 150. Another Circular of the same year gives a terse comment upon magistrates' knowledge of detention camps:

> I am directed by His Honour the Chief Justice to point out to Magistrates that there exists no accommodation in Detention Camps for females. His Honour is of opinion that until and unless female accommodation is provided in Detention Camps it is obviously undesirable to commit females to them.
>
> (Circular to Magistrates No. 10 of 1933, 15 K.L.R. 152.)

79. s. 87 of the Prisons Ordinance, 1933.
80. s. 68 of the Prisons Act, 1962.
81. Act No. 29 of 1963. For a full discussion of the Act and its background, see Read, *op. cit.*
82. Rugimbana, *op. cit.*, 22. For the views of the Tanganyika Government in introducing this measure, see a speech to prison officers by the Vice-President, the Hon. R. M. Kawawa, extracts from which are contained in the article by Read, *op. cit.* In essence, the Vice-President emphasized that the Government did not like these policies, particularly with regard to corporal punishment, but considered them necessary because in the past, 'when we had a foreign government there was no social stigma in going to prison . . . we have to make people recognize that to commit an offence against the nation, or any of its citizens, is an evil thing which is a disgrace to the man who does it'.
83. *Report of Committee appointed to consider the advisability of introducing a system of probation to the Colony* (1942); Probation of Offenders Ordinance, 1943, now cap. 64.
84. Probation orders may be made for from one to three years: Probation of Offenders Ordinance, cap. 247. (The Probation of Offenders (Local Courts) Ordinance, cap. 361, was repealed by the Magistrates Courts Act, 1963.)
85. Criminal Procedure (Amendment) Ordinance, 1948; now Probation Act, 1962, cap. 109.
86. See, for example, the Corporal Punishment Ordinance, Tanganyika, cap. 17.
87. Criminal Procedure Code, s. 318.
88. Uganda: Criminal Procedure Code, s. 319; Kenya: Penal Code, s. 33.
89. Criminal Procedure Code, ss. 343–5.
90. *Harbans Singh v. R.*, [1958] E.A. 199.
91. *Mehar Singh v. R.*, (1951), 6 U.L.R. 265: *Ahamed Mahamoud v. R.*, [1959] E.A. 1087.
92. Tanganyika Criminal Procedure Code, s. 134; Kenya Criminal Procedure Code, s. 176; Uganda Criminal Procedure Code, s. 177. For the problems which arise in applying this provision, see R. *v. Said Ibrahim*, [1960] E.A. 1058.

93. See Circular to Magistrates No. 1 of 1909; 2 E.A.P.L.R. 169. In the first four years, 59 boys were admitted: Circular No. 2 of 1913; 5 E.A.P.L.R. 220.
94. Approved Schools Act, 1951, now cap. 110; the Reformatory Schools Act is now cap. 111.
95. Criminal Procedure Code, cap. 107, s. 300A.
96. Formerly it had been at Kazima near Tabora.
97. For the plea that African states should retain their own principles rather than follow blindly Western methods in this field see the article by Junod cited at note 18 above, and by the same author, 'Reform of Penal Systems in Africa', 2 *East African Law Journal*, 31–6 (1966).

5
Lesotho, Botswana and Swaziland

ROBERT D. LESLIE

These three countries are grouped together in a single chapter, since, until the independence of the first two in 1966, they were all British territories and share a largely common legal heritage. The chapter was prepared at a time at which negotiations for independence were still in progress and all the references given are therefore to the pre-independence laws of the territories, using their former names of Basutoland, Bechuanaland Protectorate and Swaziland. It is not expected that any of the changes following the granting of independence are likely to alter the substance of what has been written.

I Introduction

Basutoland is a small country of 11,500 square miles completely surrounded by the Republic of South Africa. It is mountainous, most of it lying over 6,000 feet, and internal communications are in general rudimentary. Its natural resources are negligible, with consequently little industrial development, and most of its million inhabitants are engaged in subsistence agriculture, though many men are absent as migrant workers in the mines and on the farms of South Africa. The towns are small, and social services have still to be fully organized to build upon the high literacy rate which has resulted from missionary activity.

Bechuanaland's population is half the size of that of Basutoland, but most of it is concentrated on the better-watered eastern side of the largely arid country. Most of the population is Bantu African but a substantial segment of several thousand is composed of Bushmen and there are some 3,000 Europeans. There has been little

167

industrial or commercial development, except for that connected with the cattle industry, and most men are either engaged in sub-sistence farming or cattle raising, again with periodic migration across the border to work in South Africa.

Swaziland's population is the smallest of the three countries, with Swazis comprising the vast majority of the 290,000 inhabitants, to-gether with about 16,000 Africans of other tribes and some 8,000 Europeans. Over half the land in the country is reserved for occupa-tion by the Swazi, many of them working in subsistence agriculture, and most of the remainder is privately owned by European farmers. In 1962, about half the men of working age were in employment and almost one-third of these worked in South Africa. The country has substantial natural resources and an increasing number may be expected to find employment in local mining, forestry, agriculture and related industries. There are no large towns, Mbabane, the capital, having the largest urban population of approximately 8,500.

The close relationship of these three countries with the forces that have shaped southern Africa has resulted in distinctive marks being left on their legal and judicial systems. In each, the common law is Roman–Dutch but in the field of criminal law this has been substantially modified by English law in Basutoland and Swaziland and, in Bechuanaland, has been totally replaced by an English-style code (based on those of Kenya and Zambia) introduced in 1964. Criminal procedure is based on the English pattern. The customary laws of the indigenous people have, however, been maintained and operate as a parallel system.

The same duality is reflected in the court systems. In each country there is a High Court, from which appeal lies to a common court of appeal and thence to the Judicial Committee of the Privy Council. The lower courts in this hierarchy are the subordinate courts. In the parallel system are the various customary courts—central and local courts (Basutoland), African courts (Bechuanaland) and Swazi courts (Swaziland)—which apply mainly customary civil and criminal law and certain specified legislation. Integration of the court systems where and when possible is recognized as desirable in each country, but the degree to which it is being pursued varies from country to country. Basutoland's training programme for customary court staff and the introduction of the new Penal Code in Bechuanaland in 1964 are both directed towards this end.

II The Offenders and Their Offences

The information about the prevalence of crime in the three countries is meagre and not strictly comparable, but from what is available it seems that the volume of reported crime is not increasing out of proportion to the populations (Table 1).[1]

TABLE I (I). BASUTOLAND: OFFENCES REPORTED TO THE POLICE, 1956–63

Year	No. reported	Estimated population
1956	11,270	641,674
1957	12,359	,,
1958	12,010	,,
1959	10,847	,,
1960	13,166	888,258
1961	15,235	,,
1962	17,726	,,
1963	19,525	1,000,000

The picture is not entirely complete, for the customary courts do not make detailed returns. In 1963, 14,496 criminal cases were heard by the customary courts of Basutoland, 3,611 by the African courts in Bechuanaland and 6,539 by the Swazi courts. Some idea of the breakdown of cases heard in the customary courts of Basutoland and Swaziland can be obtained from the figures recorded as 'otherwise disposed of' in Tables 2 (1) and (3). This category is chiefly composed of accused persons summoned or arrested by the police

169

TABLE I (2). BECHUANALAND: OFFENCES INVESTIGATED, 1958–63

Year	No. investigated	Estimated population
1958	9,928	322,000
1959	9,642	,,
1960	7,588	,,
1961	8,585	,,
1962	9,477	,,
1963	12,667	450,000

TABLE I (3). SWAZILAND: OFFENCES REPORTED TO THE POLICE, 1959–63

Year	No. reported	Estimated population
1959	14,410	265,000
1960	13,898	270,000
1961	14,354	270,000
1962	15,611	280,000
1963	16,501	290,000

and referred for hearing to the customary courts. From these figures, an estimate can fairly accurately be made that the patterns of cases heard in the two court systems are very similar, subject to the proviso that the more serious cases come before the higher courts.

TABLE 2 (I). BASUTOLAND: CONVICTIONS IN THE HIGH COURT AND SUBORDINATE COURTS, 1963

Type of offence	Total No. con- victed	Adults		Juveniles		Otherwise disposed of
		M	F	M	F	
Against person	704	611	44	49	—	5,457
Sex offences	78	59	—	19	—	126
Against property	1,623	1,301	106	212	4	1,681
Against public authority	279	239	25	14	1	79
Other offences	3,116	2,741	312	44	19	1,110
Totals	5,800	4,951	487	338	24	8,453

TABLE 2 (2). BECHUANALAND: CONVICTIONS IN PROCEEDINGS BROUGHT BY POLICE, ALL COURTS, 1963

Type of offence	Total No. convicted	Adults		Juveniles		No. cases heard in African Courts
		M	F	M	F	
Against person	943	802	111	29	1	542
Sex offences	2,044	1,795	95	139	15	1,041
Against property	73	66	5	6	1	24
Against public authority	69	64	3	2	—	10
Other offences	6,512	5,768	696	40	7	1,126
Totals	9,641	8,495	910	216	24	2,743

TABLE 2 (3). SWAZILAND: CONVICTIONS IN THE HIGH COURT AND SUBORDINATE COURTS, 1963

Type of offence	Total No. convicted	Adults		Juveniles		Otherwise disposed of
		M	F	M	F	
Against person	521	451	45	25	—	2,758
Sex offences	48	44	—	4	—	108
Against property	1,276	1,027	102	147	—	1,972
Against public authority	136	127	6	3	—	146
Other offences	4,084	3,560	382	133	9	1,319
Totals	6,065	5,209	535	312	9	6,303

Within the broad categories used in Table 2,[2] there are few offences which stand out. The low level of mechanization results in the unfamiliar picture of traffic offences not heading the list of individual offences in any of the three countries, though in all of them, especially Bechuanaland, breaches of minor regulations account for the majority of reported crime. In each country, the heavy reliance of the economy on animal rearing is accompanied by a high incidence of stock theft—in Basutoland constituting the most common single offence for which convictions were obtained. In Swaziland, the slightly greater prosperity may account for a larger proportion of straightforward theft in the offences against property, though this category as a whole, in fact, accounts for a smaller proportion of the total offences than in the other two countries. This is balanced, however, by a high level of both stock theft and offences against the stock diseases regulations, which probably put the economic development in proper perspective.

The only culturally distinct offence in these countries which has been a source of concern to the authorities is the medicine murder. In Basutoland, where the offence has caused the greatest concern (Bechuanaland having fewer and Swaziland hardly any), records indicate that over 200 such offences have been reported since the beginning of the century, with over a hundred since 1950. The investigation of the problems posed by these murders in Basutoland was the purpose of a commission of inquiry in 1949, to the report of which I am indebted for much of what follows.[3]

It is incorrect to refer to these murders as 'ritual murders' as they have no connection with any religious or magical ritual but are committed for the sole purpose of obtaining from the victim particular portions of his flesh. These portions are now called *diretlo* and are believed to possess special properties which can be transformed into protective medicines (*lenaka*) which are used to advance the political and judicial interests of those for whom they are made. . . .

They are probably due to a recrudescence of the belief in a type of medicine used in the early and middle nineteenth century, but whereas the human flesh (*ditlo*) used in these old *lenaka* came from the bodies of enemies killed in warfare the modern *diretlo* is taken from members of the murderer's own community who are believed to possess specific qualities required for a particular medicine.[4]

The murders follow a regular pattern, they are always premeditated, and they are committed by a group of people for the specific purpose of obtaining *diretlo* which has to be taken from the body of the victim while still alive; if this does not cause his death he is killed and his body is then hidden for a short period after which it is exposed in a manner suggesting an accident.

The victims have been persons of either sex, of any age and

172

drawn from every tribe or group in Basutoland except from the ruling class of chiefs and headmen. The murderers are predominantly members of this class and their followers,[5]

more particularly lesser chiefs and headmen and their followers.[6]

Members of the traditional political hierarchy especially at the lower levels were experiencing a period of considerable change, uncertainty and insecurity, and they, assisted by their followers, turned to *diretlo* to protect their positions and bring about their advancement. Several factors created this insecurity. A principal one was the prevalence of 'placings', a practice under which a chief placed his sons and other close male relatives as junior authorities within his area of jurisdiction, thereby depriving, in most instances, previously existing authorities of all or part of their authority and jurisdiction. Then, certain government 'reforms' aggravated the position by, *inter alia,*

> strengthening the authority and enhancing the status of the greater chiefs at the expense of the lesser chiefs and headmen, firstly by making the position of these lesser authorities subject to government recognition, a recognition which was based on the recommendation of their ward chief, secondly by depriving them of their judicial powers and by making the new judicial system operate on a ward basis, and thirdly by paying fixed salaries to the greater chiefs only and making the remuneration of the lesser chiefs and headmen dependent once more on the recommendation of their ward chief.[7]

Again the struggle for power and changes in the balance of power associated with the disputes over succession to the Paramountcy, which arose on the deaths of Chief Griffith in 1939 and Chief Seeiso in 1940, created uncertainty and insecurity at all levels of the traditional political hierarchy.

Remedies adopted by the government had proved ineffective; more particularly the government's attempts to bring the guilty parties to justice were not, on the whole, successful. Jones says that, of the medicine murders known to the police, prosecution occurred in respect of only 43 per cent and were, as often as not, unsuccessful.[8] Evidence was difficult to obtain, for these murders were often committed by, or for the benefit of, influential people and witnesses would be unwilling to come forward.

> The majority of prominent chiefs and headmen prosecuted for this crime were not enemies of society, but highly respectable members of it.[9]

In addition, the police were unable to give adequate protection to witnesses. Of the attitude of the Basuto in general to these crimes Jones has the following to say:

> The attitude of the Basuto to these murders varies between two extremes: either condemning them and approving the punishment of the murderers, or condoning them and feeling they are more a regrettable necessity than a serious crime. The increase in the number of these murders had led to a swing towards the first view on the part of the common people, the class supplying the victims, while the vigorous prosecution of the murders which followed, particularly the hanging of two principal chiefs, has profoundly shocked the nation and made the ruling class feel that the government has turned against it.[10]

Jones not only made recommendations aimed directly at stamping out these murders, for example, the strengthening of the police by the appointment of local special constables, but he also made recommendations for preventing these crimes by removing their political causes. For instance, he suggested the reorganization of local government on a more decentralized basis, giving greater weight to control from below, since, under the theory of 'indirect rule', the emphasis was rather on control from above. The government took action basically on the lines suggested, but this seems to have had no great influence on the incidence of the crime, although it might well have prevented its further rise. However, its incidence remains alarmingly high and may well increase as a result of the struggle for power and shifts in the balance of power brought about by the development of institutions of democratic government in Basutoland.

It is significant to note that completely different stresses are said to be responsible for the medicine murders of Bechuanaland. In 1964 there were fifteen suspected medicine murders known to the police in that territory. In Bechuanaland these murders are committed to obtain medicine to doctor animals and lands to ensure their fertility and are especially prevalent in times of drought when starvation threatens. The usual victims are old people, mental defectives and children, possibly because they are considered the less useful members of a family unit or society in lean times.

III Adult Offenders

Each of the three penal systems is basically British in form and no penalties peculiar to any of the customary laws may be imposed. As one would expect in small, economically undeveloped countries which have had colonial status for so long, the penal systems are fairly rudimentary and the attitudes which dominate them largely retributive and deterrent. The general lack of organized social welfare services beyond the kin-group level is reflected in the frequently unconstructive approach to penal problems.

I GENERAL

There is common provision, for example, for a criminal court to receive such evidence as it thinks fit before passing sentence, to enable it to select the best method of disposing of the case.[11] Since there are no probation officers or other social welfare officers attached to the courts, however, inquiries into background characteristics cannot be initiated and the courts cannot obtain information about either the suitability of different methods of treatment for a particular offender, or even about the general efficacy of the methods used. Any information which may be given as relevant to sentence is usually provided by the accused himself or by the police, and it is easy to see how such a system simply reinforces the routine 'tariff' method of sentencing.

175

Several non-institutional methods of dealing with offenders do
not, of course, require the presence of social welfare officers.
Cautioning and discharging,[12] binding over to keep the peace[13] and
fines can all be used in minor cases. The High Courts and subordinate courts—though for some reason not the African courts in any
of the countries—also have suspended sentencing powers on con-
victing persons of any offences other than certain specified serious
ones.[14] The court may postpone the passing of sentence for a period
of not more than three years, or may pass sentence and suspend the
whole or any portion of it for such period. But the postponement
and the suspension are conditional. Where the conditions—usually
of good behaviour or freedom from conviction—are not complied
with, the court may pass sentence or bring the suspended sentence
into operation as the case may be. In theory, in the absence of a probation service, this should be the usual substitute for probation; in
practice, probably because the courts feel uncertain about the prospect of release without continuing supervision, the powers are not
much used.

There are two additional and valuable alternatives to short-term
imprisonment which can be utilized by the various courts. First,
courts in all three countries may order offenders who agree to engage in extra-mural labour instead of being imprisoned.[15] The provisions differ somewhat in their details but the same general idea is
followed in each country. The basic provision of Basutoland is that

> an offender who has been sentenced—
> (a) by a Local or Central Court to imprisonment for a term not
> exceeding fourteen days whether without the option of a fine or
> for non-payment of a fine; or
> (b) by any other Court to imprisonment for a term not exceeding
> six months or who has been committed by such Court to prison
> for non-payment of a fine not exceeding one hundred rand;[16] and
> may be in the discretion of such Court and with such offender's
> own consent be employed in work outside a prison. . . .

The offenders live at home, or are supplied with accommodation
if required to work away from home, and are required to perform
what is usually manual labour on projects for the public benefit.
Food is provided for them whilst working and they fall under the

supervision not of prison officers but of whoever is in charge of the extra-mural labour, often a public works official. If they do not work satisfactorily, they may be imprisoned for the remainder of their sentences.

Surprisingly, the information available indicates that only the courts in Basutoland make much use of extra-mural labour, although it is clearly a valuable means of keeping offenders out of prison for short periods. In 1963, Basutoland courts sentenced 578 persons to extra-mural labour; in Swaziland, it was used in only a handful of cases; and the absence of information from Bechuanaland suggests little use there too.

Secondly, there is in Bechuanaland provision for the 'reconciliation' of complainants and defendants in certain criminal cases.[17] In cases involving less serious offences of a personal nature heard in a subordinate court (though the customary courts presumably have the same power under the customary law of criminal procedure), the complainant and the accused may, with the consent of the court and the prosecutor, settle the case without proceeding to a verdict. In so far as this frees the court from the obligation of imposing a penal sanction in cases in which the loss or injury is predominantly caused to a single individual—and which may therefore be more in the nature of a private delict—it is a satisfactory procedure. And even though there were 'prosecutions' and the imposition of penal sanctions for 'crimes' in the pre-colonial customary law, it may be taken for granted that the procedures of that law were much more flexible than those of the modern codes. By allowing the reconciliation procedure a place in the modern law, therefore, an attempt is made (though it is not in fact much used) to encourage the sensitivity of the law to the social context. In this case, the context is the small-scale customary community, in which the preservation of harmonious personal relations and co-operation is paramount, and the infliction of socially disruptive sanctions less vital.

2 IMPRISONMENT

All criminal courts have wide powers to order imprisonment, although, as is usual, the powers of the lower courts are restricted in terms of the length of sentence they may impose.[18] Basutoland follows the South African and Rhodesian pattern in allowing the courts to specify that imprisonment shall be served with or without hard labour,[19] in the case of the High Court and subordinate courts only, or with spare diet or solitary confinement as an added punishment.[20] In the courts of the other two countries, these are not permissible sentences, though spare (or penal) diet and solitary confinement may be ordered administratively for prison offences.[21] Imprisonment may also be ordered in default of payment of a fine[22] and the most recent figures reveal that in fact a substantial proportion of prison receptions are on this ground, in Basutoland the proportion rising as high as 62 per cent and in Swaziland 77 per cent.[23]

These figures underline several characteristics of the countries to which they relate. They indicate presumably the low economic level which makes the satisfaction of minor financial obligations impossible; they point up perhaps the inadequate investigatory facilities of the courts, which in consequence fine too many offenders who have not the means to pay. But they also underline the crucial problem of the courts, which find themselves unable to use the fine extensively to keep the petty offender out of prison, and yet have few dependable alternatives which can accomplish the same end consistently with a policy of deterrence and retribution. As a result, although only about a quarter of each year's sentences are of imprisonment, there is in all three countries a high proportion of first offenders in the receptions into prison, in Basutoland as high as 70 per cent in 1963.[24] Half of these were imprisoned for what the prison authorities termed minor offences, such as breach of the tax laws, minor reserve and police regulations, vagrancy, and so on.[25]

At the other extreme, both because the prison population comprises such a high proportion of first offenders and because the numbers of serious habitual offenders is small, the figures for recidivists in prison are low. Although between about 20 and 30 per cent of all receptions have at least one previous conviction, they do not form an important proportion of the daily population. Basutoland and Swaziland have provision for declaring certain offenders to be 'habitual criminals' and making them liable to detention with hard labour during Her Majesty's pleasure[26] (in Swaziland it is at the pleasure of Her Majesty's Commissioner) but the procedure is seldom used in Swaziland and inquiry reveals that there were only four

178

such prisoners in Basutoland at the end of 1964 out of a total prison population of over 1,500.

The average daily prison population of Basutoland in 1964, the latest year for which data are available, was 1,589.[27] There are ten prisons in the country: a small one at each of the district headquarters accommodating an average of less than a hundred prisoners each,[28] and in Maseru the Central Prison for over 600 men and the Old Prison for somewhat less than a hundred boys and women in separate sections. Classification within the system is rudimentary. Young prisoners and women are all detained in the Maseru Old Prison, except for those in the districts undergoing short-term sentences or awaiting trial. Young prisoners will shortly be moved to the juvenile training centre recently completed in Maseru. The Central Prison takes all adult male prisoners from the Maseru district and long-term prisoners from other districts having no separate facilities for recidivists. In all prisons, male and female, juvenile and adult, and convicted and unconvicted prisoners are segregated. The Bechuanaland prison population of some 600 persons is accommodated in four modern prisons at Gaberones, Francistown, Lobatsi and Ghanzi, and twelve minor prisons.[29] The majority of them are extremely small, in 1963 most of them having a daily population of under thirty, and the largest—Gaberones and Francistown—holding slightly more than 200 each. The smallness of the institutions makes effective segregation difficult but as far as circumstances permit, the same segregation as detailed above for Basutoland is practised, at least in respect of sleeping accommodation. There are, however, no separate institutions for women or juveniles.

At the beginning of 1964 there were eight prisons, nine lock-ups and two prison farms in Swaziland, for a total daily population of nearly 1,200.[30] Only Mbabane Central Prison, with a daily average of convicted prisoners of 308 in 1963, had a population of more than one hundred convicted prisoners, and nine of the institutions accommodated on an average less than twenty convicted prisoners each. Segregation of classes is maintained so far as the limited accommodation permits, but the only concentration of prisoners in a single class is the long-term prisoners who are all housed in the Mbabane Central Prison.

The short sentence is the norm in all three countries. Between 40 and 50 per cent of all prisoners are sentenced to less than three months, thus creating the familiar administrative problem of the tying up of prison staff in supervising a large group of short-term offenders, the length of whose stay is too short to allow of any real change in their basic attitudes and with whom little can be done but guard them carefully to prevent escape.

This position aggravates and is aggravated by the prison labour situation. The state of the economic development of the countries, the type of prisoner most commonly received, the high proportion of short-term prisoners and the general lack of centralization in the prison systems—all in their different ways contribute to weaken the emphasis on constructive training regimes.

For a start, the absence of extensive industrialization in any of the countries means that industrial skills are rare, and not in considerable demand. Training needs to be geared to the life situations of the men who are given the training, and few of those who find themselves in prison for long enough to benefit from training can, in fact, put it to good use. The majority of them, like the population of the country as a whole, are subsistence farmers, who will return to their homes upon discharge with few rehabilitation problems and no employment difficulties.[31] A limited number in the central prisons—Maseru, Gaberones and Mbabane are those with the best developed facilities—obtain training in skilled work such as tailoring, carpentry, shoe-making, mat-making, brick-making and building, and well-behaved long-term prisoners under the Basutoland system have the benefit of an earnings scheme while engaged in this work.[32] The majority of prisoners simply do unskilled manual work, either in the prisons or on outside working parties engaged in the cleaning and maintenance of government buildings and premises, bush-clearing, ditch-digging, road-making and in public utilities work generally. All the smaller prisons simply act as places of custody and no facilities are available for constructive work. It must be emphasized, however, that we are generally dealing here with a prisoner population of low educational level and aspiration. The prison training and welfare systems can often do little more than attempt to restrain the individual prisoner and offer him a brief opportunity to make an inroad into his illiteracy. Elementary school classes are given in English and the main local languages in all the main prisons. Reading matter is always available but the recreational programmes will otherwise only be sporting activities and, in Basutoland, occasional educational talks.

Each of the prison systems has clearly limited its ambitions to the social context and the material available. The material they receive is admittedly poor and unmotivated, and there are few incentives in the outside world to make the prisoners anxious for success. But the prison staffs are trained only in their custodial functions and not in the development of constructive human relationships; job training is unimaginative—some mechanical skills can be an advantage even in a simple community—and little effort is made to improve the skills and understanding of those men who will return to their land and cattle. The wider use of job training as an instrument of rehabilitation must no doubt await the general development of the economy; but it must always be remembered that merely to train a man to do a particular kind of work does not guarantee that he will not get into trouble again. What else can be done with him must, again, be determined by the conditions in his world outside.

3 FINES

All criminal courts may impose fines but maximum amounts are prescribed for the inferior courts.[33] The payment of fines by instalments may be allowed in the discretion of the courts imposing them.[34]

Although fines are commonly used by the courts of all three countries—in 1963, nearly 60 per cent of all convicted offenders being dealt with in this way—it has already been suggested that the fine does not appear to be an effective way of avoiding imprisonment. A sufficiently large number of offenders are unable to pay their fines or meet execution when levied,[35] to make the problem of imprisonment in default a common and disturbing practice. It is possible that, in countries with such low-level economies, the courts should be much more reluctant to impose fines at all and, where they do so, should pay closer attention to the initial question of the offender's means and make greater use of instalment payments.

4 THE DEATH PENALTY

The death penalty may be ordered for persons convicted of murder, treason and, in Basutoland, rape.[36] It is mandatory only where an accused person is found guilty of murder, with no extenuating circumstances reducing his moral guilt. Where there are extenuating circumstances and in the case of the other offences, the penalty is discretionary.[37] Legislation has followed the British pattern in specifically providing that other homicides in special circumstances, such as certain infanticides,[38] killing under provocation[39] and under the terms of suicide pacts,[40] shall not be murder and, consequently, not capital. With these and the other restrictions which have been imposed upon the passing of the sentence—restrictions on sentencing persons under 18 years at the time of the offence,[41] and women found to be pregnant[42]—together with the executive power to commute sentence, the number of persons actually executed is small. The latest figures available to me disclose that in Basutoland forty-three persons were executed in the seven years 1958–64; in Bechuanaland none in the eight years up to the end of 1963, though there have been some since then; and in Swaziland only eight in the period 1957–60 inclusive, six of which were in connection with medicine murder in 1958, while in 1963 there were none at all. In practice, all executions are for murder, and experienced prison officials are unable to say when one last took place for any other offence.

5 CORPORAL PUNISHMENT

Corporal punishment can be ordered for adult male[43] offenders for a wide range of offences, including the more serious ones of aggravated assault, culpable homicide, robbery, bestiality and gross indecency.[44] The maximum number of strokes which may be inflicted is fifteen in Basutoland and Swaziland, where the maximum is only open to the High Court and the first-class subordinate courts, and twelve in Bechuanaland. In all three countries, the subordinate courts' maximum powers are limited according to their grades,[45] with a total denial of the penalty in respect of adults to the customary courts in Basutoland and Swaziland. Sentences of corporal punishment imposed by subordinate courts are subject to automatic review by the High Courts.[46] Similar powers are possessed by the authorities in respect of serious prison offences, with the right of review lying either with the High Court or with the member of the executive responsible for prison affairs. The statistics available indicate that the penalty is disparately used in the three jurisdictions. In Bechuanaland in 1963, for instance, 168 adult males were sentenced to corporal punishment; in Basutoland only seven; and in Swaziland a mere three.[47]

IV Juvenile Offenders

That scarcely any attention has been given to the problem of juvenile offenders reflects in part the adequacy of the customary forces inhibiting delinquency and in part the lack of imagination of the authorities when called upon to cope with a trying and difficult situation.

Basically, the position is that there are almost no special facilities for juveniles in any of the three penal systems. There are no juvenile courts, no probation services and, save in Basutoland, no special juvenile institutions.[48] All the sentences already discussed may be passed on juveniles, subject to the limitation that no one can be imprisoned under 14 years of age,[49] or sentenced to death if under 18 at the time of his offence. The only special provisions for dealing with juveniles other than those discussed below are not in fact used to any significant extent. One is the power of the courts to commit a juvenile to the custody of a suitable person for a specified period:[50] the courts apparently take the view that a probation service is necessary for the proper implementation of this provision, though that was never the intention behind it. The other is the executive power possessed in Swaziland to apprentice a juvenile offender to any useful calling or occupation.[51]

The first special provision applicable to juveniles is basically merely an extension of the power to order corporal punishment. For juveniles it is not limited to any specific offences or any

183

particular class of court but may be ordered in lieu of any other punishment for any offence by any criminal court, provided that in Bechuanaland the offence is punishable by imprisonment. In Bechuanaland, the actual infliction of the punishment is limited by allowing only six strokes; in the other two jurisdictions by requiring 'moderate correction not exceeding fifteen cuts with a light cane'.[52] The courts make extensive use of these powers, no doubt because the alternative methods of disposal of juveniles are inadequate but also because the rigorous treatment of juveniles has strong cultural support. In Basutoland in 1963, 55 per cent (186) of the male juveniles convicted by the High Court and subordinate courts were sentenced to corporal punishment, and the local and central courts sentenced a further 378. Although the number in Bechuanaland in the same year was only 75, this amounted to 35 per cent of the total number sentenced. In Swaziland it accounted for 491 juvenile sentences, and though by reason of the incompleteness of the available statistics it is impossible to say what proportion of juvenile offenders this figure represents, it seems likely that it is as high as 90 per cent of juvenile sentences.[53] The second special provision concerns institutional treatment. The present facilities are rudimentary and are barely differentiated from those for adult imprisonment, especially in the smaller local prisons. At present, the rate of imprisonment of juveniles in Basutoland is higher than that in the other two countries: in 1963, 367 boys under 21, twenty-one of whom were under 16, compared with slightly more than thirty of under 18 years of age in each of the other two. As a result, Basutoland has been forced to establish centralized segregated facilities for the juveniles—a section of the Old Prison at Maseru is set aside—and has been the only one of the three countries to devise a forward-looking training institution.

The new Juvenile Training Centre at Maseru has recently been completed and can house seventy-two boys. A court can order a juvenile male under 18 years to be detained in the Centre for not less than nine months or more than three years. After release, he may be placed under supervision for a further year.[54] The institution is barely in operation and an assessment cannot yet be made of its potential. It is clear, though, that it must at all costs avoid the purely custodial characteristics of the prison system, by employing, at least

184

in part, a staff trained in youth work. It must try to contemplate, too, a much closer liaison between conditions in the institution and life in the community at large than has been achieved in the prison system. If the post-discharge supervision scheme is to work—and this is really part of such liaison—the authorities must be prepared to spend money in building up a social welfare system but even then they will have to face the problems of matching the training to social and economic developments in the community. There are so many opportunities for failure that great determination will be necessary before success is assured.

V Conclusion

An overall view of the penal systems of these three countries reveals, as one would expect from the undeveloped nature of their economies, that they are somewhat backward. The emphasis is still on punishment, and little is done to reform or rehabilitate the offender. This is especially true in respect of juveniles, Basutoland alone having a special institution for their training, and that of very recent origin. There is, as mentioned before, no probation system in any of these countries. The lack of other means of dealing with juvenile offenders and the continued vitality of traditional approaches mean that corporal punishment is much used in respect of male juveniles. In contrast, it is rarely used as a punishment for adult males, save in Bechuanaland.

Not all the unsatisfactory features of the systems can be blamed solely on the lack of finance available to develop them. For instance, it has been noted that an alarmingly high proportion of prisoners are in jail because they have been unable to pay fines for offences such as failing to pay tax. Apart from the undesirability of imprisoning first offenders convicted of minor offences, this creates practical difficulties. No doubt this situation is to some extent the result of the lack of suitable alternative means of dealing with offenders of this type, but a greater use of the alternatives available such as extra-mural labour and suspended sentences would go some way towards the solution of this problem. Perhaps the hope for future development lies in the fact that I have found among those responsible in these countries for the operation of the penal systems a growing awareness of the defects in the systems and a desire to overcome them.

NOTES

1. *Sources:* Annual Reports of the three territories; Annual Reports of the Commissioners of Police of the three territories.
2. *Sources:* Annual Reports of the Commissioners of Police of the three territories, 1963.
3. Jones, *Basutoland Medicine Murder*, Cmd. 8209 (1951).
4. *Ibid.*, paras. 57–8.
5. *Ibid.*, paras. 60–1.
6. *Ibid.*, para. 119.
7. *Ibid.*, para. 181.
8. *Ibid.*, para. 190.
9. *Ibid.*, para. 170.
10. *Ibid.*, para. 170.
11. Basutoland: Criminal Procedure and Evidence Proclamation, 1938 (hereafter 'C.P.E.'), s. 289 (2); Local and Central Courts (Practice and Procedure) Rules, 1961, r. 89 (j). Bechuanaland: C.P.E., s. 289 (2). Swaziland: C.P.E., s. 289 (2). In the latter two cases, the C.P.E. can be applied only by the High Court and Subordinate Courts and there is no equivalent provision for the African and Swazi Courts. They nonetheless appear to exercise inherent rights to call for information.
12. Basutoland: C.P.E., s. 313; Bechuanaland: C.P.E., s. 312; Swaziland: C.P.E., s. 312.
13. Basutoland: C.P.E., s. 305 (High Court and Subordinate Courts only); Bechuanaland: C.P.E., s. 304 (3); Penal Code, s. 34 (High Court and Subordinate Courts only); Swaziland: C.P.E., s. 304 (High Court and Subordinate Courts only).
14. Basutoland: C.P.E., ss. 308–11 and Third Schedule; Bechuanaland: C.P.E., ss. 307–10; Swaziland: C.P.E., ss. 307–10.
15. Basutoland: Prisons Proclamation, 1957, s. 23; Bechuanaland: Prisons Law, 1964, s. 62; Swaziland: Prisons Proclamation, 1964, s. 60.
16. The Bechuanaland limits are 6 months and R200: Prisons Law, s. 62. Those of Swaziland are 6 months and R100: Prisons Proclamation, s. 60.
17. C.P.E., s. 318 A.
18. Basutoland: Subordinate Courts Proclamation, 1938, ss. 62 and 65; Native Courts Proclamation, cap. 6, s. 11—Local Courts 3 months, Central Courts

12 months; Bechuanaland: Subordinate Courts Proclamation, cap. 5, ss. 71–71A; African Courts Proclamation, 1961, s. 14; Swaziland: Subordinate Courts Proclamation, cap. 20, ss. 71, 74; Swazi Courts Proclamation, cap. 21, s. 11—ordinary Swazi Courts 12 months, Court of Appeal 2 years.

19. C.P.E., s. 291 (a) (2) (a); Native Courts Proclamation, s. 11; Subordinate Courts Proclamation, s. 62.

20. C.P.E., ss. 291 (2) (a) and 296 (2), (3).

21. Bechuanaland: Prisons Law, ss. 59, 61, 72–4; Swaziland: C.P.E., s. 290 (2) (a); Prisons Proclamation, s. 40.

22. Basutoland: C.P.E., s. 298; Native Courts Proclamation, s. 11; Local and Central Courts (Practice and Procedure) Rules, 1961, s. 98; Bechuanaland: C.P.E., s. 297; Penal Code, ss. 28 (3), 30; Swaziland: C.P.E. s. 297; Swazi Courts Proclamation, s. 11.

23. Basutoland: *Prison Service Annual Report 1963*, 17; Bechuanaland: *Annual Report on the Treatment of Offenders 1963*; Swaziland: *Annual Report of the Prisons Department 1963*, 9.

24. In Swaziland it was 58 per cent in 1963. The Bechuanaland figure of 83 per cent for 1963 is for offenders who had not previously been in prison.

25. *Prison Service Annual Report 1963*, 10.

26. Basutoland: C.P.E., s. 297; Swaziland: C.P.E., ss. 296 and 326. The comparable Bechuanaland provision (C.P.E., s. 296) was repealed in 1964.

27. *Prison Service Annual Report 1964*, 7. The description of the Basutoland system is based largely on the Annual Reports and information kindly supplied by the Director of the Prison Service.

28. Berea (116), Leribe (210), Butha Buthe (81), Mokhotlong (106), Qachasnek (84·4), Quthing (98·9), Mohales Hoek (91·6) and Mafeteng (141·3).

29. *Bechuanaland Protectorate, Report for the Year 1963*, 80. The description of the Bechuanaland system is based largely on the *Annual Reports of the Treatment of Offenders*.

30. *Annul Report of the Prisons Department 1963*. The description of the Swaziland system is based largely on the Annual Reports.

31. There are in consequence no officially organized after-care services but the obligations of the authorities are confined to returning the men to their home or place of conviction, whichever is nearer. For some, the need of assistance is real: Bechuanaland reports that urban workers, such as clerks, often find re-employment very difficult and the prison authorities then try to find work for them.

32. Under the Basutoland system, deserving long-term prisoners who have received trade training are on discharge given tools to enable them to earn a living at their trades.

33. Basutoland: C.P.E., s. 291 (c); Native Courts Proclamation, s. 7; Bechuanaland: Penal Code, s. 30; Subordinate Courts Proclamation, s. 71; African Courts Proclamation, s. 12; Swaziland: C.P.E., s. 290 (2) (c); Swazi Courts Proclamation, s. 11.

34. Basutoland: *ibid.*, s. 309; s. 11; Local and Central Courts (Practice and Procedure) Rules, s. 96; Bechuanaland: C.P.E., s. 308; African Courts Proclamation, s. 16 (1); Swaziland: *ibid.*, s. 308; s. 14.

35. Fines are recovered by a process similar to civil execution. Basutoland: C.P.E., s. 299; Local and Central Courts (Practice and Procedure) Rules, r. 99; Bechuanaland: *ibid.*, s. 298; s. 16 (4); Swaziland: C.P.E. s. 297 (2).

36. Basutoland: C.P.E., s. 291 (1); Bechuanaland: Penal Code, ss. 37, 38, 202; Swaziland: C.P.E., s. 290 (1).

37. Basutoland: *ibid.*, s. 291 (1), third proviso; Bechuanaland: *ibid.*, s. 203; Swaziland: *ibid.*, s. 286 (1), third proviso.

38. Basutoland: *ibid.*, s. 291, first proviso; Bechuanaland: *ibid.*, s. 208; Swaziland: *ibid.*, s. 290 (1), first proviso.

39. Basutoland: Criminal Law (Homicide Amendment) Proclamation, 1959, ss. 3–4; Bechuanaland: *ibid.*, ss. 205–6; Swaziland: Criminal Law (Homicide Amendment) Proclamation, 1959, ss. 3–4.

40. Basutoland: *ibid.*, s. 5; Bechuanaland: *ibid.*, s. 207; Swaziland: *ibid.*, s. 5.

41. Basutoland: C.P.E., s. 291 (1), second proviso; Bechuanaland: Penal Code, s. 27 (2); Swaziland: C.P.E., s. 290 (1), second proviso. The accused is detained at Her Majesty's pleasure (Basutoland), or at the pleasure of Her Majesty's Commissioner (Bechuanaland and Swaziland).

42. Basutoland: *ibid.*, s. 293; Bechuanaland: *ibid.*, s. 27 (3); C.P.E., s. 292; Swaziland: *ibid.*, s. 292. The woman is sentenced to imprisonment instead: in Basutoland, somewhat ambiguously, with hard labour; in Bechuanaland, for life or for any lesser period.

43. No woman may suffer the penalty at all. Basutoland: C.P.E., s. 303; Subordinate Courts Proclamation, s. 62 (4); Bechuanaland: *ibid.*; Swaziland: C.P.E., s. 302; Subordinate Courts Proclamation, s. 71 (4).

44. Basutoland: *ibid.*, ss. 291 (2) (e), 301–4; Bechuanaland: *ibid.*, s. 29; s. 300; Swaziland: *ibid.*, ss. 290 (2) (e), 300–3; Subordinate Courts Proclamation, ss. 71, 81. An upper age-limit of 40 years is imposed for liability to the penalty in Bechuanaland: Penal Code, s. 29 (3). The special provisions for the corporal punishment of juveniles are considered in Part IV below.

45. Third-class Subordinate Courts: nil; second class: eight strokes with cane; first-class: fifteen strokes with cane; Basutoland Subordinate Courts Proclamation, s. 62; Swaziland Subordinate Courts Proclamation, s. 71 (1); Bechuanaland Subordinate Courts Proclamation, s. 71.

46. Basutoland: *ibid.*, ss. 67, 72; Bechuanaland: Subordinate Courts Proclamation, s. 77; Swaziland: *ibid.*, ss. 76, 81.

47. Basutoland: *Prison Service Annual Report 1963*, Appendix II; Bechuanaland: *Annual Report of the Commissioner of the Bechuanaland Protectorate Police 1963*, Appendix F; Swaziland: *Annual Report of the Prisons Department 1963*, Appendix E.

48. Provision exists in Basutoland and Swaziland for the transfer of juvenile offenders to institutions in South Africa but the system is not used. Basutoland: Prisons Proclamation, 1957, ss. 33–6 and First Schedule; Agreement

under Prisons and Reformatories Act (Amendment) Act, 1920, s. 14 (S. Africa) between the Governments of Basutoland and South Africa, November 16th, 1920; Swaziland: Juvenile Offenders' Removal and Apprenticeship Ordinance, cap. 98; Reformatories Proclamation, cap. 97.

49. Basutoland: C.P.E., s. 291 (2), proviso; Bechuanaland: Penal Code, s. 28 (1); Swaziland: C.P.E., s. 290 (2), proviso.

50. Basutoland: *ibid.*, s. 300; Bechuanaland: C.P.E., s. 299; Swaziland: *ibid.*, s. 299.

51. Juvenile Offenders' Removal and Apprenticeship Ordinance, cap. 98.

52. Basutoland: C.P.E., s. 302. In Basutoland only the High Court may order for juveniles the type of whipping inflicted on adults. Bechuanaland: Penal Code, s. 29. Swaziland: C.P.E., s. 301.

53. Basutoland: *Prison Service Annual Report 1963*, Appendix II; *Annual Report of the Commissioner of Police 1963*, Appendix II; Bechuanaland: *Annual Report of the Commissioner of the Bechuanaland Protectorate Police 1963*, Appendix F; Swaziland: *Annual Report of the Prisons Department 1963*, Appendix E.

54. Prison Proclamation, ss. 7, 9.

6
Liberia

GERALD H. ZARR

I Introduction

The present pattern of criminality in Liberia is only meaningful when considered in the context of the rapid economic growth which the country has experienced in recent years and which may be expected to continue in the future. It has been estimated that for the years 1954–60 the rate of growth of no African country exceeded that of Liberia on a *per capita* basis. Under the impact of such growth, the face of the country has vastly changed. Monrovia, once a small West African trading port, has trebled in population within the past fifteen years and has developed into a centre for commerce and light industry. In the interior of the country, large iron ore and other mining complexes have been established, drawing their labourers from all parts of the country and all segments of the population.

Not all the changes have been for the better. The large increase in the population of Monrovia has exerted considerable strain upon the facilities and services of the city, particularly in the spheres of housing, labour, health and education. In the interior a 'boom town' atmosphere pervades many of the camps which have sprung up in the shadow of the new mining complexes, and these camps attract juveniles and young adults, as well as hardened criminals and misfits. The migration has been indirectly aided by the government's Unification Policy, which has sought to create an integrated society of all Liberians by subordinating tribal loyalty to national allegiance.

Although the long-range benefits of economic growth are evident, the social change and dislocations in behaviour patterns resulting from it have created immediate problems.

193

The first is the familiar weakening of the well-integrated extended family system and the diminution of tribal authority which have followed the migration from the villages. The effectiveness of tribe and family as agents of social control has always depended upon the cohesiveness of the particular unit. In the urban areas, this cohesiveness increasingly gives way to individualism and the vacuum created by the decline in family and tribal authority has only been filled by the impersonal sanctions of the law.

The second problem is the breakdown of the pattern of collective security which is inherent in tribal life. Traditionally, each individual in need has the right to make demands upon his extended family and tribe, and when able is similarly obliged to provide aid and support for others. A migrant villager who finds this familiar form of security denied to him at a time of need may resort to crime as the most obvious alternative.

The growth of materialism among Liberia's tribal people is likewise conducive to anti-social behaviour. The newcomer to the urban areas is exposed for the first time in his life to commercial establishments with large stocks of goods and to individuals with substantial material possessions. The pressures on him to acquire goods are not matched with legitimate opportunities for doing so. Resort to crime—perhaps made less discreditable by the communal doctrine of tribal society under which the disadvantaged are allowed to share in the property of the more affluent—is the frequent result. Charitably described as 'roguery' by most Liberians, this behaviour is nonetheless punishable under the criminal law as larceny, burglary or housebreaking, as the case may be. Larceny accounts for 30 per cent of all offences committed in Liberia, and burglary and housebreaking considered together account for a further 13 per cent.

These foregoing factors have contributed to the recent increase of crime in Liberia. Records of the Liberian National Police show that 1,501 offenders were arrested during the first three months of 1965, compared with 1,097 and 994 offenders arrested during the same months of 1964 and 1963 respectively.[1] Furthermore, there is evidence of an increase in the number of crimes committed against the person in Liberia. Although criminality in Liberia generally takes the form of property crimes, it is significant that of the 1,501 offenders arrested during the first three months of 1965, 235 were charged with common or aggravated assault—17 per cent of the total. During the same period substantial numbers of individuals were arrested for affray,[2] breach of the peace,[3] and robbery.[4]

Murder has generally been considered not to be a quantitatively important crime in Liberia. Formerly the majority of accused murderers in any given year were motorists who had been involved in fatal car accidents. The practice is initially to charge such motorists with murder, subject to reduction of charge upon a subsequent hearing before a magistrate. However, there is now some evidence that murder is on the increase. The country has recently been plagued with a string of unsolved murders which have received considerable public attention.[5] Secondly, statistics show that an excessively large percentage of those incarcerated in Monrovia Central Prison have been charged with or convicted of murder. Of the 352 prisoners detained there in April 1965, 55 were so charged or convicted—over 16 per cent of the total. In May 1965 a team of experts was commissioned by President Tubman to draft a comprehensive plan for the prevention of crime in Monrovia and other parts of the country. That its work involves the investigation of crime in parts of the country other than Monrovia serves to accentuate another important development in the pattern of Liberian crime.

Historically, Liberia's crime problem has been a Monrovia problem. Seventy-five per cent of all criminal cases come to court in Monrovia and its environs each year. But in recent years there has been a pronounced increase in crime in the interior counties—particularly in the vicinity of the giant mining complexes. This trend may be expected to continue and accelerate as the interior is progressively developed.

II The Criminal Law

Throughout most of its history, Liberia has had a dual legal system which has reflected the different origins of its inhabitants. The American settlers of the country were subject to the jurisdiction of the constitutional and statutory courts which were established in the five littoral counties and administered the common and statutory law of the Republic. For the tribal peoples, tribal courts in the Hinterland and County Area administered the customary law of twenty-eight different Liberian tribes.

The present criminal court system, following the government's Unification Policy, tries to avoid this dualism. Exclusive criminal jurisdiction is now vested in the stipendiary magistrates, justices of the peace,[6] circuit courts[7] and the Supreme Court.[8] The concurrent criminal jurisdiction of the tribal courts was abolished in 1963[9] but it is likely that the chiefs will continue to exercise jurisdiction in minor criminal cases for a few years until the legislation can be strictly enforced. Even before the 1963 amendment, however, it appears to have been the practice for all important felony cases to have been transferred to the circuit courts.[10]

The one procedural device which is peculiar to the tribal courts is that of trial by ordeal. Legislation authorizes

> Ordeals which are of a minor nature and which do not endanger the life of the individual. . . .
>
> A person desiring to practise as an ordeal doctor shall undergo tests to be given by the Department of the Interior to establish the applicant's competence and skill. On passing such tests, the applicant will receive from the Department a certificate which will authorize him to perform ordeal trials and will entitle him to the fees to be assessed by the authority granting the ordeal.[11]

All ordeals are commonly referred to as 'trial by sasswood', but the actual use of the poisonous bark of the sasswood tree has been declared illegal in a long line of Supreme Court decisions and finally by statute.[12]

The substantive criminal law too has undergone changes. The American common law of crimes was received into Liberia by the provision of the Constitution of 1820.[13] Subsequent modification resulted in the introduction of English common law in 1859 but the criminal law has been entirely statutory since 1914, the Criminal Code of which year forms the basis of the modern Penal Law.[14] Likewise, the form of the penal system has not changed considerably. The prisons in the country have for some years been controlled directly or indirectly by the government, and the prisons legislation applies to them all.[15] Corporal punishments ordered by the tribal courts have always been subject to confirmation by governmental officials[16] and only fines imposed directly for breach of local custom would be paid to the Tribal Treasury instead of the Board of Revenues.[17]

III The Objectives of the Penal System

As with many countries at a similar stage of development, Liberia is finding it hard to develop a firm penal policy. Retributive punishment still dominates the practice of sentencing and the operation of the penal system. Yet there are gestures towards a policy which would promote the individual readjustment of offenders. In 1949, for example, a probation system covering first offenders was introduced,[18] but as it has not yet been fully implemented, many convicted criminals are still sentenced to imprisonment even though their offences are relatively minor.

But the prison system itself is undergoing changes in its orientation. The preamble to special legislation enacted in 1953 authorizing the construction of a new prison building in Monrovia stated that the 'object of society in providing for the punishment of crime

197

is not only for its protection but primarily to provide for the reconstitution of the character of the offending member if possible'.[19] Similar statements have been made by government officials from time to time,[20] and the change in attitude has even extended as far as renaming the Department of Justice's Division of Prisons the Division of Rehabilitation. Beyond this official articulation of the objective, however, actual practice does not go. The modern prison system envisages nothing by way of educative or therapeutic programmes for prisoners, no workshops for teaching skills or crafts, or facilities for aiding discharged prisoners.

IV The Prison System

For good or bad, the prison system is at the core of the penal facilities of the country. At the present time, it comprises nine central prisons—one for each of the nine counties—and ten small jails which serve as temporary detention centres for offenders awaiting trial. By far the largest institution is Monrovia Central Prison with a population ranging from 350 to 400 prisoners—more than the total capacity of all other institutions in the system. It may be estimated that the aggregate capacity of the other central prisons in the system varies from 175 to 225, and that the jails do not confine in excess of 125 prisoners. The total capacity of the prison system is thus in the order of 650–750 prisoners.

As indicated above, a major step towards the modernization of the prison system was taken in 1953 with the enactment of legislation authorizing the expenditure of $500,000, principally for the construction of a new building in the Monrovia Central Prison compound. The preamble to this legislation stated:

Present prison facilities have been found not only inadequate but wholly unsuited to modern methods of prison administra-

198

tion, the ultimate purpose of punishment of offenders against the law, and the humane methods generally accepted and adopted by civilized communities and peoples in such instance. It has therefore become necessary for the Government to plan and provide better prison facilities than exist in the Republic today.[21]

The construction authorized by this legislation was completed in 1962, but the building was not formally opened until 1965—during the administration of Attorney-General Pierre and on the initiative of the Hon. Augustus Roberts, Assistant Attorney-General for Rehabilitation.

The facilities of this building contrast sharply with those available at other Liberian penal institutions, and also with those of the older buildings of Monrovia Central Prison itself. It contains forty-eight large, well-ventilated rooms, each of which can accommodate five prisoners, making the total capacity 240 prisoners. A modern dining-room, kitchen, lounge and medical dispensary are provided, and there are also separate toilet and bathing facilities for men and women. The selection and preparation of prison food are under the supervision of a full-time dietician. A doctor and psychiatrist are in attendance.

The other jails and prisons of Liberia vary considerably in their physical condition from each other, but have officially been described as being in a deplorable state of disrepair.[22] Conditions are particularly bad in the jails. Many of these are small huts containing two or three narrow cubicles. It is for this reason that the Division of Rehabilitation recently instituted the policy of using them only as temporary detention centres for newly-arrested prisoners. After a short period of confinement each prisoner is sent to the central prison situated in the county in which his alleged offence was committed.

In none of the penal institutions other than Monrovia Central Prison is there central preparation and distribution of food to prisoners. At present, prisoners are given their ration of food and do their cooking in small groups. This has recently come under official criticism, as being both uneconomical and inefficient,[23] and it is expected that the practice will be abandoned shortly.

Apart from the jails which are used only as detention centres, there are no specialized institutions for different types of offenders. For example, each central prison may contain prisoners of both sexes and all degrees of criminality. The Monrovia Central Prison contains accused and convicted misdemeanants, those charged with petty offences, and accused and convicted felons. However, this prison does have an internal classification system. The new building is used for those who are charged with or convicted of crime punishable by imprisonment for three months or more; all others are incarcerated in the old wing. In the new building there is also a separate cell-block for women and separate facilities for juveniles. No other institution has an internal classification system, though the system is at present under study by the Division of Rehabilitation.

Classification apart, the major problem facing the prison system is how it can be transformed into the rehabilitative complex which the government believes it should be. In an elementary sense, it already has its rehabilitative components—its medical facilities (including the single psychiatrist available in Monrovia) and facilities for religious instruction. But there are as yet no educational or therapeutic programmes in existence and no means of promoting the resettlement of the discharged prisoner in the community.[24]

Even the vital field of prison industry remains to be properly organized. There are as yet no prison workshops and no agricultural projects sponsored by the prison system to help to provide part of its own maintenance. That all convicted prisoners, except those under sentence of death, must work, is a basic rule.[25] It was implemented at least until 1961 by assigning prisoners to work for private employers at the rate of twenty-five cents each per day but the practice has since been discontinued.[26] The expense of providing guards for prisoners exceeded the receipts from their labour; workers in the community were deprived of the opportunity of employment; and the practice was highly disturbing to discipline. At the present time, prisoners are only assigned to work on governmental projects as such projects become available.

Recent recommendations for the reorganization of the system envisage far-reaching changes. It is suggested that the nine central prisons should be used only for convicts serving sentences of less than one year. A new prison would then be constructed on a central site which would be used for all prisoners serving sentences of one year or more. It is felt that such an institution could more readily be used as a rehabilitation centre than the present congested and insecure[27] prison site in Monrovia. A workshop would be built at the new prison where inmates could learn and engage in various trades according to their aptitudes. Moreover, at a rural site prisoners would be able to work on agricultural projects to provide food both for their own use and for sale.

At the same time, plans are under way to establish standards of prison staff selection and training. The present simple custodial regime makes little demand on staff ability but, with a more positive rehabilitative effort in view, selected warders from each county will be sent abroad for training, so that they may be in a better position to implement the new policies.

V Alternative Methods of dealing with Offenders

I PROBATION

It has already been mentioned that provision has been made in Liberia for a probation system for first offenders since 1949. Although the statutory authority is there, however, no probation officers have so far been appointed. In the few cases in which an adult[28] offender has been put on probation, the functions of the probation officer have been assumed by the police, who can be expected to do no more than keep the probationer under occasional surveillance.

The basic provisions of the probation law are as follows. Any court exercising criminal jurisdiction may upon application made or *sua sponte* suspend the execution of a judgment due to be entered against a first offender and place him on probation if his crime is not punishable by death. The criteria which the court is expected to consider, in deciding whether to grant probation, are the character, antecedents, age, health and mental condition of the defendant, the nature of the offence, the existence of any extenuating circumstances, and the interest of the community. If the court decides that probation is justified, a probation order is issued which states the terms and conditions under which probation is granted. Then it becomes the duty of probation officers to determine that the probationer is complying with the order and to assist in his reformation.

2 FINE

Imposition of a fine is another method of dealing with offenders which the Liberian judge may utilize as an alternative to imprisonment in cases of minor crime. Under Liberian law a felony is defined as a crime punishable by imprisonment without the option of a fine, whereas in the case of misdemeanours and petty offences the imposition of a fine is optional.[29]

If a person is sentenced to pay a fine but is unable to do so, he will be imprisoned for such a period as will liquidate the fine at the rate of twelve dollars per month.[30]

3 PSYCHIATRIC TREATMENT

Treatment is available to offenders under certain circumstances. Under the Penal Law an otherwise criminal act done by an insane person is not a crime, nor can an insane person be tried, sentenced or punished.[31] In the event that a defendant raises the defence of insanity, he will be examined by a government-appointed psychiatrist who submits a report of his findings to the Department of Justice. If found sane, he will stand trial at which the issue of insanity may be presented for judicial determination. If found insane, he will undergo further psychiatric treatment at a rehabilitation centre or in a separate cell in prison until such time as he is fit to stand trial. At the trial, if defendant is able to establish that he committed the offence while insane, he will be exculpated.

4 ILLEGAL IMPRISONMENT

One method of dealing with offenders which has come under re-
current attack in the Annual Reports of the Department of Justice
has been the practice of justices of the peace ordering the imprisonment of individuals 'for further examination' which in many cases
has never materialized. In a recent Report the practice was criticized
in the following words:

> Justices of the Peace have shown an increasing tendency to im-
> prison persons arbitrarily and needlessly, and then forget about
> them. It is not uncommon for about ten persons to be impris-
> oned by one Justice of the Peace within a few hours. As a re-
> sult, the cells of the [Monrovia] Prison Compound are crowded
> beyond their intended capacity. A common ground for im-
> prisonment among the Justices of the Peace is 'for further ex-
> amination', and in very few instances are there any examina-
> tions.[32]

Although the government is committed to eliminating these illegal imprisonments and considerable progress has been made in
this respect lately, there still may be found cases where individuals
have undergone prolonged periods of prison detention without
trial. Of the forty-five prisoners incarcerated in Monrovia Central
Prison in May 1965 on charges of murder, nearly half had been in
detention for periods of two to six years and I encountered three individuals who had each been incarcerated for more than ten years.

It is true that many of these individuals have indirectly contributed to the length of their detention by not insisting on their right
to be released. Under Liberian law a defendant who has not been in-
dicted within two successive terms of the grand jury is entitled to be
discharged from custody upon application made to the circuit
court.[33] None of these prisoners had made such application, but
then again few were financially able to retain counsel or sufficiently
educated or knowledgeable in the law to be in a position personally
to enforce their rights. Although a defence counsel is appointed in
each county and is charged with defending those who are financially
unable to retain counsel, it is impossible, in the more populous

counties, for one man adequately to represent all those who require legal aid.

VI Young Offenders [34]

At a United Nations conference held in Monrovia during August 1964 on the subject of the development of national programmes for the prevention of juvenile delinquency, the Hon. Augustus P. Horton, Director of the Liberia National Youth Organization, described in the following words the difficulty in determining with exactitude the extent of juvenile delinquency in Liberia:

> The lack of pertinent documentation, the absence of a reliable reporting and/or recording system, and the common notion in this country by certain officials in authority that juvenile delinquency is non-existent in Liberia have made it difficult, if not impossible, to describe accurately the extent to which this country is faced with the problem. . . . This, nevertheless, does not deprive us of the knowledge that, especially in Monrovia, this country has a a delinquency problem to the extent that it demands immediate attempts both by government and private organizations to make child welfare more positive than negative.

Other experts have similarly concluded that a juvenile delinquency problem of serious proportions exists and continues to grow in Liberia. In 1961 a special consultant to the Department of Justice estimated on the basis of projected population statistics that between 4 and 6 per cent of the youthful male population of Monrovia was dealt with annually by the police and courts. He further concluded that 20–30 per cent of the youthful male population of Monrovia were dealt with by the police and courts during the eight years from ages 13 to 21.

For the same reasons that Mr Horton indicated that it was difficult to determine the extent of juvenile delinquency in Liberia, it is likewise difficult to determine the prevalence of other juvenile disorders. Those juveniles whose conduct is of an overtly criminal nature comprise, of course, only one segment of the problem youth of Liberia. In addition, there is a class of juveniles, generally under 15 years of age, who have not committed criminal acts as such, but whose conduct is potentially delinquent. These are boys who continually run away from home, loiter in the streets at night, beg for alms and street-trade. These may be referred to as children in need of care and protection. The third type of problem youth is characteristically an unprotected child who may graduate from mildly into seriously anti-social behaviour which may fall within the ambit of crime. This is the marginal child. His usual offences in Liberia are defacing property, letting air out of car tyres and overturning groceries and wares.

Further, the Liberian youth problem is at present a Monrovia problem. At the present time, 90 per cent of the cases involving juveniles which are handled by the police arise in Monrovia and its environs. Yet the typical juvenile migrant to Monrovia is not a delinquent. He is a young boy who with parental consent leaves his village in a rural area in order to further his education or pursue a trade in Monrovia. Arrangements are made for him to live with a relative or friend. After some time relations with the relative or friend may deteriorate, or perhaps the job is lost or the education forgotten. Whatever the reason, the boy then leaves his abode and goes into the streets to live. At this point he begins his descent into marginal activity and delinquency.

Lastly, crimes against the person are minor among Liberian juvenile delinquents. The offences which are most common are petty larceny, burglary, housebreaking and malicious mischief.

Official concern over juvenile delinquency resulted in the enactment of legislation in 1959 authorizing the President in his discretion to establish a juvenile court system in Liberia.[35] Under this law a juvenile court would be set up in each county with power to decide all cases involving offenders under 19 years of age, with a view towards securing the best interests of the juvenile and the protection of the state. Once a juvenile was adjudged delinquent, he would be placed under the supervision and guidance of a probation officer attached to the court. The probation officer would see that the delinquent attended school regularly, learned some useful trade or profession and was adequately maintained. Periodic reports would be made to the court covering the delinquents under each probation officer's authority. These provisions have thus far not been implemented, even though more recent recommendations have been made that they should be put into effect without delay.[36] Even if a juvenile court system were to be established, however, there would remain the substantial problem of what remedial treatment should be applied to delinquents. At the present time, any juvenile charged with crime, and many potentially delinquent loiterers, beggars and street traders, will be handled by the juvenile division of the national police. If he has not committed any offence, he will usually be released into the custody of his parent or guardian, although he may be detained overnight at police headquarters or in prison and may be subjected to minor physical punishments. If he receives an institutional sentence, it will be served in prison—in Monrovia in a separate wing of the new prison building. There are no official training institutions for juveniles, although as long ago as 1944 legislation was passed which authorized the establishment of such a school[37] and more recently the Department of Justice has recommended that two juvenile detention homes, one each for boys and girls, be constructed.[38] Outside Monrovia, there are no institutions other than the ordinary prisons to which juveniles are normally committed.[39]

There are at the moment, however, two institutions in Liberia which are dedicated to the care and betterment of Liberian youth and which may in future play a more active role in the treatment of delinquents.

The first is a private institution, known as Boys' Town, which was established with government support for juvenile males in need of care and protection. It accommodates fifty-five privately-committed boys between the ages of 10 and 18. The popularity of the institution is attested to by the fact that many homeless boys present themselves for commitment. Boys' Town has a school with grades from one to six, an advanced farm project and a workshop. Religious and moral training forms a central part of the institution's

206

activities. Since security measures are non-existent, some boys abscond though most runaways voluntarily return after a short while. There is no formal programme of after-care for boys who have been discharged at 18 but the director and staff make informal attempts to keep in touch with their alumni.

The other institution is the Youth Camp of the Liberia National Youth Organization. The Youth Organization was created in 1962 as an agency of government within the Office of the President of Liberia and is charged with the responsibility of dealing with all Liberian youth between the ages of 14 and 20 for the promotion of morality, patriotism and social and civil consciousness.

Although the Youth Organization is not constituted to deal with delinquents as such, since 1965 it has sought to provide training at its camp for delinquents turned over by the police and for other children privately committed. The Youth Camp has dormitories for boys and girls and maintains an agricultural project and workshop. The Youth Organization through its director, the Hon. Augustus Horton, has also been instrumental in the attempt to obtain legislation directly related to the problems of wayward youth. The proposed legislation makes provision for the creation of a Youth Welfare Division which would be charged with such duties as formulating programmes for community development and for the treatment, rehabilitation and after-care of juvenile offenders.

VII Capital and Corporal Punishment

Although the statutory penalty for murder in Liberia is death by hanging,[40] there has not been an execution since 1954. The reason is to be found in the fact that by law each death warrant must be signed by the chief executive,[41] and for the past eleven years

President Tubman as a matter of conscience has refused to sign any such warrant. Thus in practice a convicted murderer now serves a life sentence even though no formal action has been taken to commute his sentence.

Of course, the complete abolition of capital punishment lies only through legislative action. Short of this step, any future chief executive will legally be in a position to re-institute the practice of President Tubman's predecessors. Moreover, there now appears some likelihood that capital punishment may be utilized in the more immediate future. As a result of the widespread public concern over the pronounced increase of crimes of violence, some suggestion has been made in the newspapers and other media that capital punishment be used. At a recent press conference, President Tubman indicated his continued unwillingness to sign death warrants, but suggested as a possible solution that the Chief Justice of the Supreme Court be given that function. This proposal has received considerable attention.[42]

It is only in recent years that corporal punishment has ceased to be generally used both as a legal sanction and a means of enforcing prison discipline. Now there are but two vestiges of corporal punishment retained in the law. One is that in cases of petty larceny the offender receives as part of his punishment 'not exceeding fifteen lashes on the bare back'.[43] The other is in connection with a violation of prison rules, where the prisoner may be subjected to fifteen lashes or be kept in solitary confinement.

VIII Conclusion

It is clear that penal policy is not static in Liberia today. In the area of the administration of criminal justice, progress is evident in the disestablishment of the tribal courts with their confused procedure and repetitive appeals and the consequent establishment of a unitary court system for the country. In the area of penological thought, progress is shown in the recent emphasis that has been placed upon rehabilitation as the central goal of penal policy. In the area of juvenile delinquency, progress is manifest in the work of the Liberia National Youth Organization and in the operation of Boys' Town. In the area of prison policy, progress is shown by the construction and operation of a new prison building which serves as a model for the entire system. In the general area of sanctions, too, progress is evident in the recent abandonment of corporal punishment except in a few instances.

Developments have taken place so precipitately, however, that the legislature has in some instances enacted reforms more quickly than the government can implement the legislation. Examples of legislation which as yet have not been fully implemented are the Juvenile Court Act, the Probation Law and the Act authorizing the establishment of a school for delinquents. Nonetheless, the legislature must be called upon in future to enact other needed reforms, such as legislation creating the Youth Welfare Division, and it can only be hoped that implementation will soon follow. Yet there exists today less cause for optimism than perhaps existed ten years ago. For the simple fact is that crime and delinquency have also been making much progress in recent years. Extreme social change and dislocations of population—those undesirable by-products of economic development—have produced in Liberia an ever-increasing rate of crime and delinquency. Accordingly, the need for enlightened action for the prevention and control of delinquency and crime is greater than ever. It is to be hoped that this challenge will be met.

NOTES

1. Although records are not available, I am informed by competent authorities that the percentage of increase in crime was almost as great in the period from 1960 to 1962 as it was from 1963 to 1965.
2. 8 per cent.
3. 12 per cent.
4. 2·6 per cent.
5. 'The wave of violence which is sweeping Liberia today is one which must stir the conscience of every Liberian who values human life and is dedicated

to the rule of law. Besides, in years gone by, one murder a year was all that we could stomach. But today, a dozen murders in the last two months are really taking matters out of hand. Formerly, it was the trucks, cars and taxis which slaughtered us and thus dwindled our already poor numbers. Today it seems a number of secret societies have sprung up requiring human sacrifice. Violence is thus illegally licensed. This, in an enlightened and progressive society, is intolerable' (*Liberian Star*, June 9th, 1965).

6. The jurisdiction of stipendiary magistrates and justices of the peace is specified in the Judiciary Law, ss. 550–7 (Liberian Code of Laws, 1956, abbreviated in this chapter as L.C.L.) A magistrate but not a justice of the peace must be a qualified lawyer: *ibid.*, s. 94.

7. Appointees to these courts are qualified lawyers (*ibid.*, s. 32) who exercise both original and appellate jurisdiction (*ibid.*, ss. 510, 511, 556 (d) and 557 (d)).

8. The Court can hear appeals from circuit courts (*ibid.*, s. 501) but in recent years the numbers of criminal appeals have declined from 48 in 1960 to 16 in 1964.

9. 1962–3 Acts of the Legislature, 128.

10. See, e.g. *Sartu v. Liberia*, 11 L.L.R. 400 (1954).

11. Aborigines Law, s. 422 (L.C.L.).

12. *Jedah v. Horace*, 2 L.L.R. 265 (1916); *Posum v. Pardee*, 4 L.L.R. 299 (1935); *Peehn v. Liberia*, 5 L.L.R. 192 (1936); *Koffah v. Liberia*, 6 L.L.R. 336 (1939); *Tenteah v. Liberia*, 7 L.L.R. 63 (1940); see now Aborigines Law, s. 422 (L.C.L.).

13. Article VI, as quoted in Huberich, *The Political and Legislative History of Liberia*, ii, 1263 (1947).

14. Title 27, L.C.L.

15. See now Criminal Procedure Law, s. 700 (L.C.L.).

16. Aborigines Law, s. 145 (L.C.L.).

17. *Ibid.*, s. 147.

18. 1949–50 Acts of the Legislature, 16. The Law is codified in the Criminal Procedure Law, ss. 330–4 (L.C.L.).

19. L.C.L., vol. ii, 624–5.

20. E.g. 'The primary aim of any prison system, in accordance with modern thinking, is based not upon punishment but upon rehabilitation of the prisoners. Under the new system, prisoners will be taught handicrafts, arts, agriculture and various trades. They will be permitted to attend school on the compound and learn to engage in wholesome recreational activities. In short, we intend to prepare the prisoner to take his place in society again and contribute thereto upon his release.' *1962 Annual Report of the Attorney-General of Liberia*, 26.

21. An Act Approving the Nine Year Program for the Economic Development of Liberia, L.C.L., vol. ii, 623.

22. *1963 Annual Report of the Attorney-General of Liberia*, 24.

23. *1964 Annual Report of the Attorney-General of Liberia*, 28.

24. The associated measure of parole, i.e. conditional discharge from prison, is at present being studied by the Department of Justice. Only routine remission of sentences for special industry and good conduct (Criminal Procedure Law, s. 748 (L.C.L.)) and Presidential commutation and pardon (Constitution, Art. III, section 1st; Criminal Procedure Law, s. 422 (L.C.L.)) are now practised.

25. Criminal Procedure Law, s. 733 (L.C.L.). Prisoners awaiting trial are not obliged to work but may do so if they volunteer.

26. The practice was originally expressly sanctioned by the Attorney-General: see *Opinions of the Attorney-General of Liberia*, i, 168 (1924). Although the government was paid for the labour, the prisoners themselves received—and still receive—no pay.

27. The Report of the Superintendent of the Monrovia Central Prison for the quarter ending March 31st, 1965 stresses the fact that there is an urgent need for a new concrete fence around the prison. Although statistics of escapes are not available, it is apparent that all the prisons face a major security problem; cf. *1963 Report of the Attorney-General of Liberia*, 24.

28. Juvenile offenders and probation are discussed in Part VI, below.

29. Criminal Procedure Law, s. 5 (L.C.L.).

30. Penal Law, s. 42 (L.C.L.).

31. Section 14.

32. *1963 Annual Report of the Attorney-General of Liberia*, 4; see also *1964 Annual Report*, 27.

33. Criminal Procedure Law, s. 203 (L.C.L.).

34. For a more detailed discussion of this subject, see Zarr, *Juvenile Delinquency and Liberian Law*, 1 *Liberian Law Journal*, 201 (1965).

35. Judiciary Law, ss. 170–81 (Supp. 1959).

36. See, e.g., *1961 Annual Report of the Attorney-General of Liberia*, 33, which also recommended that a qualified lawyer be sent to the United States for training as a judge of the juvenile court and that others be sent for training as probation officers.

37. Codified in the Education Law, s. 36 (L.C.L.).

38. *1961 Annual Report of the Attorney-General of Liberia*, 33.

39. The former practice of parents committing wayward children to prison without court action for as long as the parents wished has been abolished only in recent years.

40. Penal Law, s. 232 (L.C.L.).

41. Criminal Procedure Law, s. 326 (L.C.L.).

42. 'By Legal Enactment and by practice, the Chief Executive is authorized to approve or disapprove a death sentence by any Court of Law. He could do this by signing a death warrant. There is no constitutional compulsion in this matter, hence it becomes one of personal conscience. It has been suggested that the Chief Justice should be made responsible for the signing of death warrants. The reason given is that as head of the Judiciary branch of government he is competent to follow the legal process in the conviction

of a man for murder. This reason, though novel, is quite logical. Further, there is no constitutional provision as to who should or should not sign a death warrant' (*Liberian Star*, June 9th, 1965).

43. Penal Law, s. 297 (L.C.L.).

7
Portuguese Africa

FERNANDO O. GOUVEIA DA VEIGA

1 Introduction

The fundamental principle of the penal law of Portuguese Africa is that it is basically the same as that in force in the rest of the national territory wherever in the world it happens to be. From as long ago as the 14th century onwards, however, it has never been the government's policy to insist on the rigid application of legal principles irrespective of the cultural background. The earliest instructions to the Crown's viceroys, governors and captains always recommended that the principles of Christian charity should be applied in their contact with the peoples of the various territories. Ultimately, when decrees of 1869 and 1880 formally extended the Civil and Penal Codes to the overseas territories, provision was specifically made for the respecting of local usages and customs in the application of the law.

This is facilitated by the provisions of article 84 of the Penal Code relating to sentencing. It is laid down in general terms that before passing sentence the judge should 'take into account the seriousness of the offence, its results, the degree of deceit or of guilt, the motives of the offender and his personality'. The courts are therefore given a complete mandate to examine the cultural background against which the offence was committed and to impose a balanced penalty which gives some consideration to the special cultural pressures to which the offender was subjected, whilst at the same time aiming at his complete readjustment in the larger culture of which he forms a part.

It was as an aspect of the same policy that, for many years after the assumption of power over overseas territories, it was commonplace for Portuguese magistrates to sit with local assessors in criminal trials. The assessors were recruited from amongst local tribal elders or chiefs, and their role was that of explaining to the magistrates in detail the usages and customs of each region. By taking these into account, the courts found it possible to strike an acceptable balance between the Portuguese law and the local customary law, by being able both to moderate some of the excessive penalties prescribed by the latter and to produce a more sympathetic application of the former. The principal significance of this policy today is that the spirit of much of the Portuguese law has been assimilated with the local customs and traditions; violently repressive measures are no longer tolerated and many kinds of offence, especially, for example, those bound up with fetishist practices, have become much less common.

The moral basis of the criminal law is nonetheless firmly insisted upon. The ideological framework used by the draftsmen was clearly articulated in the preliminary report on the Penal Code, and is worthy of being set out in full:

When an offence disturbs the moral order of society, this disturbance is always temporary, since the application of the law inevitably leads to the re-establishment of the order and peace disturbed by the offence. The damage to the citizen who has been the victim of the offence may in some cases be irreparable or permanent; and the same may be true of the material damage to society. But the penalty imposed by law is not designed to be the counterpart of these sorts of damage, which are either totally irreparable or only reparable by means other than penal ones.

The penalty is only the counterpart of the damage caused to the moral order of society, and such damage is always reparable and transitory. The logical consequence therefore is that, first, the penalty should not be permanent or irrevocable, for then it would no longer be the counterpart of the damage caused to society, but would exceed the amount of reparation to society; and, secondly, the damage caused to the individual's own nature by the imposition of the penalty should be proportionate to the damage caused to the moral order of society by the offence.

II The Penal Legislation

According to the terms of article 124 of the Portuguese Political Constitution,

> penalties and security measures shall be prescribed for the purpose of protecting society and achieving as far as possible a social readjustment of the offender.

It is this articulated emphasis on the constructive role of the criminal law that has resulted in the absence in Portuguese legislation of some measures commonly found in other European countries or their dependencies. Corporal punishment, for example, has not existed for several centuries; and the death penalty was abolished in 1867, the abolition being extended to all Portuguese provinces in Asia, Africa and Oceania by a decree of 1870 and thereafter entrenched in the Constitution.

The Penal Code provides for three general groups of penalties: major penalties, correctional penalties and special penalties for civil servants. A further selection of security measures have as their object the prevention of future delinquency through the improvement of the offender's character or at least the elimination of forces or opportunities which may predispose him to delinquency.

I PENALTIES

The major penalties basically take the form of varying lengths of imprisonment, between a minimum of two years and a maximum of twenty-four. The deprivation of political rights for fifteen or twenty years is also envisaged. Correctional penalties may also involve imprisonment, for a minimum of three days or a maximum of two years, and otherwise will include the temporary deprivation of political rights, fine, banishment or reprimand. The special penalties applicable to civil servants all concern their professional activities and involve discharge, suspension or reprimand.

217

2 SECURITY MEASURES

Security measures will be either measures which require the offender to be deprived of his liberty, or those which take effect without his detention. He may be placed in a criminal mental institution, a clinic for drug addicts, a labour camp or agricultural colony; or he may be given supervised freedom (i.e. probation), required to give security for good conduct, prohibited from carrying on a particular profession, or, if an alien, expelled from the national territory.

Various other measures, more within the administrative than the judicial province, serve the same ends but are not strictly security measures. These so-called police measures may take four forms: (a) the closing down of houses of prostitution, bars and premises where games of chance are illegally played; (b) the seizing of arms and explosives and of pornographic, subversive or other clandestine publications; (c) the repatriation of persons displaced from their place of residence, or whose conduct or mode of life are suspicious; (d) special police supervision of offenders on probation or persons who have previously been convicted of security offences.

To return, however, to supervised freedom—a measure having the greatest social and economic significance. The first Washington Penal Congress having expressed the opinion that progressive treatment should, wherever possible, involve the use of supervised conditional freedom (probation), and the London Congress of 1872 having passed a resolution to the same effect, Portuguese legislation introduced the system of conditional freedom in 1893. The system applies and has always applied to the entire Portuguese territory.

Both forms of the measure, the suspended sentence and the system of conditional freedom, were introduced. Article 88 of the Penal Code lays down that a magistrate, having considered the degree of the offender's guilt, his moral conduct and the circumstances in which the offence was committed, may order the suspension of the penalty if the offender has not previously been sentenced to imprisonment. Only sentences of imprisonment and fines may be suspended; the suspension is to be for not less than two years and not more than five; and the fulfilment of certain conditions by the offender may be required.

218

If the period of the suspension expires without the offender committing another offence for which he is convicted, and if he fulfils the conditions imposed, the sentence originally passed will be considered null and void. If, on the other hand, the offender is convicted of another offence during the period of suspension, he has to serve both the sentence attributable to the original offence and that which is passed for the further offence. This is not done, however, by the straightforward addition of the two sentences; at the time the second sentence is passed, the judge takes the first sentence into consideration and passes a combined sentence for both offences.

Probation differs, of course, in that the sentence is not suspended but is in itself a sentence of supervised freedom. It may be ordered in lieu of or in addition to any other sentence where the offence is punishable with at least six months' imprisonment, and, unlike the suspended sentence, it is applicable both to first offenders and to recidivists. In the case of first offenders, the court will normally pass a suspended sentence anyway, or even substitute a fine for the imprisonment which it has the power to impose. In the latter circumstances, the fine would be made proportionate to the offender's income, within the prescribed limits of from ten to one hundred escudos per day, with a firm limitation being put on the number of days over which the fine can be extended.

Probation may be ordered for an initial period of between two and five years, and, if the offender's progress is not satisfactory during this time, may be extended by successive periods of two years up to a maximum of ten years. Conditions may be imposed upon the probationer, either singly or cumulatively, requiring him, for example, to offer reparation for the damage caused by the offence, to refrain from carrying on certain specified businesses, to live in or leave certain specified areas or places, to avoid the company of suspicious characters or persons notorious for their bad behaviour, and so on. Where appropriate, that is where the necessary personnel are available, he is obliged to accept the supervision of an appointed authority or of a person specifically appointed as his supervisor.

A form of probation which is the equivalent of supervised parole may also be required. Where a single sentence is passed the offender cannot be released on probation until he has served at least half the sentence, or the minimum period prescribed by the security measures applying to him, and can give an assurance of being willing and able to lead an honest life. Where consecutive sentences are passed, there can be no release on probation until the offender is serving the last of those sentences, and has completed the minimum period required by the security measures.

III Classification of Offenders

Since criminology is unable to offer any uniform classification of offenders, the Portuguese penal legislation has adopted the common international pattern of grouping offenders 'chiefly from the standpoint of juridical treatment, i.e. according to the different legal measures which can be ordered in respect of each group'.

The main criminological interest lies in four categories of offenders who are subject to special regimes and treatments.

First, habitual offenders, whatever the basis of their recidivism, are by article 67 of the Penal Code liable to suffer either major or correctional imprisonment. Once the sentence has been passed, it may be ordered to be extended for successive periods of three years until the offender proves himself capable of leading an honest life, or has at least ceased to be a danger to the community.

Secondly, offenders who, though not legally irresponsible, are nonetheless dangerous to the community as the result of mental illness, may be placed in a special asylum prison 'and the sentence of correctional or major imprisonment which has been passed on them may be extended for successive periods of three years until the mental condition which causes them to be a danger to the community no longer exists'.

Thirdly, mentally irresponsible persons, who commit crimes which make them liable to imprisonment for more than six months and who constitute a danger to the community, may be detained in criminal lunatic asylums and are only released when the court has ascertained that they no longer constitute a danger.

Lastly, certain sorts of offenders are liable to the security measures already referred to in Part II, above. A large and ill-defined category of asocial offenders is recognized, comprising such persons as vagrants, beggars, those living wholly or partly on the earnings of prostitution, persons who habitually practise unnatural vices, prostitutes, those responsible for the moral corruption of minors or those who habitually engage in procuring women for purposes of prostitution. All are liable to detention in work camps or agricultural colonies, or in appropriate circumstances to non-institutional treatment. Habitual drunkards or drug addicts, who also form a group liable to security measures, may on the completion of their sentences be detained in either special institutions, prison asylums, work camps or agricultural colonies for a period varying between six months and three years, renewable for successive periods of three years.

IV The Prison System

The general prison legislation calls for the provisions of some prisons, committal to which will be dependent upon the length and nature of the sentences passed, and others which are designed to deal with special groups of offenders. In the latter category are to be found, for example, prisons offering special educational facilities, hospital prisons, asylum prisons, prisons for habitual offenders and so on.

Although the legislation is common to the entire Portuguese national territory, this is not to say that the same facilities exist everywhere. Prisons are built in accordance with demand and available financial resources, though planning, building and the recruitment and training of personnel necessarily take time. It was in acknowledgment of the special circumstances existing in the overseas provinces, however, that in 1954 provision was made for a simplified and culturally-orientated system of institutions. Two types of prisons were set up: those that were simply detention institutions, and those that offered a special environment, classified as penal colonies, correctional colonies or correctional farms.

Pursuing the general policy of attempting the readjustment of the offenders to community standards, the emphasis in the prison system has been placed on work as the medium through which this is to be achieved. The penal colonies are based on a requirement of predominantly agricultural labour in conditions of partial freedom —a system which proves much more effective than labour under security conditions with too rigorous supervision. Indeed, so much store is set by this pattern that the law itself provides that

> prison life will be so orientated as to foster a habit of working in co-operation with others. There shall be no cellular confinement, except for a period not exceeding one month at the beginning of the period of detention, for the purpose of studying the offender.

Stress is continually laid on the moral and social necessity of producing hard-working citizens. In the preliminary report which preceded the legislation we read:

> Idleness is harmful to honest living; work has always been a school of virtue, and is therefore an instrument of reformation. But this is not the only reason for requiring it: one must also consider the need for creating the conditions necessary for a prisoner's reassimilation into society when he is released, an objective which will be difficult to achieve if he has been idle too long.

Schooling is therefore provided, to teach both reading and writing to illiterate prisoners; elementary education is offered with a view to improving their moral and cultural standards. In the penal colonies offenders are re-trained to carry on their previous occupations more effectively, or are given new skills to encourage them to take up new employment on their discharge. Earnings schemes are operated both as a stimulus to the prisoners, and as a means of

achieving some measure of social justice. The earnings are fully credited to the prisoner in the first place; part of them is deducted by
the state to pay for his upkeep; part is paid to the victim of the offence as compensation; and part is set aside for the prisoner himself.
A certain proportion of this is held in reserve and given to the prisoner on discharge with a view to helping him to meet his immediate needs, and to creating or maintaining habits of economy in the
management of his capital.

V Young Offenders

The constructive philosophy underlying the measures applying to
juveniles is set out fully in the preliminary report to Order-in-
Council no. 38,386 of August 8th, 1951:

> The State's organization for dealing with juveniles is entrusted
> with the re-education of those in whom the lack of care has al-
> ready brought about a tendency to vice or a deterioration of
> character—in short, in whose personalities the danger of crimi-
> nality is already apparent. It is much more difficult to re-educate
> than to educate, to re-make than to make for the first time. . . .
> The facilities for dealing with juveniles represent the final
> attempt [at re-education] and are therefore the final hope. They
> should be given every chance of success.

The State is concerned with all sorts of juveniles in trouble—
those who are in moral danger, or who do not have adequate means
of support, those who pose disciplinary problems and those who
actually commit criminal acts. The criminal law is directly concerned only with the latter, but, consistent with the energetic approach to the problem already described, the solution that it has
tried to adopt is uniformly one which aims at the constructive treatment and full social rehabilitation of the offender.

The major dividing line is drawn by the criminal law at 16 years of age. Beyond that age and until he is 21, the juvenile is still not brought within the scope of the ordinary law. He is dealt with in an ordinary court, but the method of adjudication is not so much to take account of the seriousness of the offence, as to estimate its symptomatic significance. The committing of the offence, the manner of its commission and all the other surrounding circumstances must be used to make an assessment of the educational or re-educational measures necessary. Nonetheless, there is still the possibility that stringent measures may be applied to the child. School-prisons are available to those in this age-group who, it is felt, can benefit from this kind of regime.

Below the age of 16, a juvenile cannot be found criminally responsible. He is within the jurisdiction of the juvenile court, which does not pass criminal sentences as such, but orders measures of a welfare, educational or re-adjustive nature. These will normally be the use of probation, reprimands, fines (up to 200 escudos), placing offenders with foster families or in public or private educational institutions. Brusquer measures, however—up to fifteen days' detention in the police cells of the juvenile court, six months in a welfare institution, or up to six years in a reformatory—are all possible.

Below the age of 9, a juvenile offender is always regarded as being in moral danger, and is liable to educative measures only. Between 9 and 13, all the measures described in the last paragraph may be applied and, for the 13–16-year-old age-group there are three additional possibilities in cases where a major penalty could be applied to an adult: (a) up to one year's detention in a correctional colony, (b) up to one year's detention of this sort but renewable in a correctional colony or reformatory after the expiry of the one year, and (c) detention in a correctional colony for up to five years in the first instance or until the offender comes of age, whichever occurs first.

In all cases legislation provides for parallel measures to be taken affecting the offender's social environment. If he has a family, inquiries are made as to whether they cannot or do not know how to provide guidance for him; in such cases, the state provides moral and economic support for the family itself. Alternatively, there may be intervention in the environment by withdrawing parental authority over the child and requiring its supervision by welfare or educational authorities.

224

8
The United Arab Republic

AHMAD M. KHALIFA and
BADR EL-DIN ALI

I Introduction

No systematic study has ever been undertaken of the incidence and trends of criminal activity in the United Arab Republic. Certain rough conclusions may nonetheless be drawn from the Annual Judicial Statistics of the Ministry of Justice. It is evident, for example, that the total number of offences reported annually is rising steadily, with the most marked increases taking place in the number of felonies. Little can be said with certainty about urban and rural crime patterns, except that it appears that offences against property are more common in rural areas. The two most dramatic forms of crime in recent years, towards which a great deal of public attention has been directed, are murder for vengeance and drug addiction—both of which in the setting of the United Arab Republic are the product of sub-cultural values which offer a complete rationalization for the occurrence of these offences.

From the statistical data available, something can be said with a little more certainty about the characteristics of the offenders. The most common type appearing is the offender who has had three or more previous convictions, is within the 20–30 age-range, is unmarried, an unskilled labourer and has committed an offence against property, usually the felony of theft.

II Non-institutional Measures of Punishment

Since 1940, probation has been used as a measure applicable to juveniles (under the name of 'social supervision') but it has never been applied to adults. Corporal punishment does not figure at all in the contemporary penal code, though it still has some significance in military law. This being the case, the only sentences for adults of which special mention need be made are fines and capital punishment.

Fines are the commonest penalty imposed in the United Arab Republic, being used in about 90 per cent of all cases proceeding to conviction. Typically, they are imposed for contraventions of traffic and local regulations, less commonly for misdemeanours and only rarely for felonies. Article 510 of the Law of Criminal Procedure authorizes the judge in suitable cases to allow an offender to pay a fine in instalments, provided that the period does not exceed nine months. All fines are collected by using the procedures normally applicable to civil debts, or may be satisfied by the serving of imprisonment in lieu, at the rate of one day's detention for each ten piastres. In the case of contraventions, imprisonment shall not exceed seven days for the fine and seven days for the costs or other sums due to the State; in the case of felonies and misdemeanours, the maximum terms are of three months in each of these two respects.

The present Penal Code, influenced by the modern reformative approach, has restricted capital punishment to a relatively small number of cases. In the last four years there has been some informal pressure to secure the complete abolition of the death penalty but there have not as yet been any signs of an official move in this direction. At the present time, therefore, premeditated murder, poisoning, murder accompanying the commission of a felony, arson or the use of explosives causing death, giving false evidence in a criminal trial resulting in the execution of the accused, or suborning such evidence, treason and other felonies endangering the safety of the state all remain capital crimes.

228

The actual number of death sentences imposed has steadily increased during the last decade, rising from nine cases in 1954 to thirty-one in 1963. It is still true, however, that the courts commonly make use of life imprisonment instead of the death penalty wherever they are at liberty to do so. And even apart from this consideration, the actual carrying out of the death sentence is made less certain because multiple confirmation by the Supreme Court, the Mufti (the religious rector) and the President of the Republic is needed. Whether there is any deterrent or other identifiable social value in capital punishment has never been the subject of inquiry or report in the United Arab Republic.

III The Correctional Institutions

According to the annual reports of the Prisons Department, the total number of convicts in prison increased regularly to a peak of 57,070 in 1962, since when it has fallen to 46,117 in 1963 and 39,692 in 1964.

I THE INSTITUTIONS

Act No. 396 of 1956, organizing the Prisons Department, envisages four types of prisons in the United Arab Republic:

(a) Penitentiaries, where all terms of imprisonment with hard labour are served. Life imprisonment and terms of imprisonment with hard labour can only be ordered on conviction for felony. Only adults can be ordered to serve hard labour sentences and in practice they are not imposed on women, or on men over 60.

(b) General prisons, where sentences of ordinary imprisonment of three months or more are served, and where prisoners awaiting trial are detained. Separate facilities are available in each prison for these two classes.

(c) Local prisons usually deal with prisoners sentenced to imprisonment for less than three months and with those sentenced to imprisonment in default of payment of fines.

(d) Special prisons may be established for certain specific categories of prisoner. Three developments in this area deserve particular mention.

Firstly, there is as yet no special classification or reception centre for prisoners. New prisoners are simply isolated as far as possible within the local prisons for ten days, while they receive medical examinations and are fitted into the simple classification scheme. Present plans are, however, to adopt the principle of the complete segregation of convicted prisoners and prisoners awaiting trial into separate institutions. The process of change has been begun by dividing the Cairo prison into two independent units, each with distinct personnel and administration, and allocated to one or other of the two classes of prisoner referred to.

Secondly, the Middle East Seminar on the Prevention of Crime and the Treatment of Offenders, held in Cairo in 1953, recommended that, where the establishment of open prisons was not practicable, an attempt should be made to reduce security in some institutions, particularly where outdoor work was possible. Consequently, the Guiza prison near Cairo was selected for transformation into a medium security prison in 1954. After two years' experimentation, a more suitable site was found at El Marg, also near Cairo, where the premises of a juvenile training school have been converted to accommodate adult offenders in medium security conditions. The site includes a farm and the prisoners engage in agricultural and rural industrial work with minimal official supervision.

Thirdly, in 1956 a training school at Kanater was converted to form the first separate prison for women in the country. Formerly, it was the practice that women prisoners were accommodated in special annexes to the ordinary men's prisons. Now, all women prisoners from the Cairo area are channelled into this prison; special facilities are available for women with young children, who are allowed to keep the infants within the prison and to care for them, but away from the atmosphere and restrictions associated with the normal running of such an institution. Special medical and social work services are available to the group.

2 SHORT-TERM IMPRISONMENT

The number of short-term sentences has continued to rise steadily since 1954 and gives cause for some concern. A recent survey showed that the largest groups of offenders serving sentences of six months or less were those guilty of petty theft or attempted theft, begging and vagrancy, fraudulent misappropriation of property, and the breach of police supervision orders. The trend of opinion in the United Arab Republic in recent years, following the recommendations of both national and international conferences, is in the direction of disapproving of these measures.

It is recognized that short-term sentences seldom achieve the penal objectives which are now commonly accepted as desirable. The prisoner's stay in prison is too short to devise any constructive programme of treatment; his habits of work are disrupted and his family liaison disturbed; he is normally confined in a small local prison with few facilities, little work and inadequate supervision and discipline.

The present alternatives to short terms of imprisonment cannot be clearly indicated. It has already been mentioned that probation is not yet available as a measure for adult offenders. The measures which are available under the existing legal system, however, are sufficiently varied to be capable of dealing with a large proportion of the offenders who are at the moment sentenced to imprisonment; it merely remains for fuller use to be made of them.

(a) In the case of an offence, the Parquet (which is charged with the duty of investigation and prosecution) may withdraw proceedings if it is of the opinion that the offence is not grave or that it is not essential in the public interest that the prosecution be continued (Law of Criminal Procedure, article 209).

(b) In all cases of felony and misdemeanour, the court may, if it thinks fit, suspend the execution of the sentence of imprisonment or fine for a period not exceeding one year. The guiding consideration is that the court must feel that, in the light of the character and antecedents of the convicted person and the circumstances of the offence, he is unlikely to commit a further offence. The suspension is withdrawn wherever the offender is convicted of another offence and sentenced to a term of imprisonment exceeding one month, within a period of three years of the passing of the original sentence (Penal Code, articles 55–59).

(c) Persons sentenced to simple imprisonment for any period not exceeding three months are entitled to request that they serve the sentence by engaging in extra-mural labour for the prescribed time (Penal Code, article 18 (2)).

(d) Any offender who is liable to imprisonment in default of paying a fine, may request the Parquet to allow him instead to perform six hours' daily work on behalf of a government department or a municipal council in the town where he lives, for a period equal to that for which he is liable to imprisonment.

3 TREATMENT FACILITIES

A special branch of the prison service concerned exclusively with social welfare was started in 1952. Every prison in the country now has one social worker, though this, of course, is hardly adequate to meet the need for social services in the larger prisons. A social investigation of each prisoner is carried out to shed light on his circumstances and to provide the basis for planning any guidance that may be needed. Counselling is then undertaken by the social workers themselves, since there are at the moment no psychological or psychiatric services available to the prisons.

In addition to these conscious attempts to change prisoners' attitudes, the remainder of the efforts of the Prisons Department are directed towards providing motivation for the prisoners. One or more Moslem preachers are appointed to every prison to encourage spiritual care for those prisoners (the great majority) who are of this persuasion. Special arrangements are made for visits by Christian or Jewish ministers where appropriate. In every prison a team of qualified teachers gives literacy instruction to prisoners under 45 years of age and elementary educational courses to other groups. Small libraries are available and special facilities are provided for interested students to obtain needed books and references and to participate in the examinations of schools and universities. In recent years successful experiments have been carried out in allowing basic teaching to be done by qualified prisoners and in giving facilities for correspondence studies.

At the same time as it began its social welfare services, the Prisons Administration started a positive programme for the improvement of the physical conditions in prison. Beds have gradually replaced sleeping mats; prisoners' uniforms and other clothes have been standardized and improved to ensure minimum standards of dignity and cleanliness; a greater variety of food, with more attention paid to nutritional requirements, is now served; small prison shops have been set up; electric lighting has been installed in all rooms; dining, bathing and hairdressing facilities improved.

4 VOCATIONAL TRAINING

Prison labour in the United Arab Republic has traditionally been organized with a view to producing goods needed by the Prisons Administration and thereby making the prisons self-sufficient. In the last ten years, however, the major development in this sphere has been the expansion of training facilities, not to meet a changing official demand for products, but to provide more effective and useful training for the prisoners themselves. Article 206 of the basic prisons legislation provides that every prisoner sentenced to more than one year's detention or imprisonment with labour shall be assigned to a trade or craft within the prison, selected according to his position in life and health, so as to provide him with a potential means of earning his living after his discharge from prison. Prisoners serving one year or less cannot be assigned to vocational training but must perform the ordinary labour necessary for the maintenance of the institution.

In fact, however, the vocational training facilities, particularly in the industrial sector, are very limited. These facilities are not, of course, widely available in the outside community but as the general industrial facilities develop the plans devised some years ago for broader industrial training in the prisons are slowly being implemented. The main work being carried out, therefore, ranges from leather work, shoe-making, carpentry and weaving to the almost exclusively agricultural work of rural prisons: land reclamation and cultivation, animal husbandry, poultry-raising and blacksmithing. A relatively small group of prisoners are engaged upon training as fitters, riveters and builders, and some years ago a further small number began work in a plastics workshop set up in Alexandria Prison by a local company as one of its branches. The prisoners were paid wages at industrial rates and given the opportunity of employment in the company following their discharge. In the prison system as a whole, prisoners are paid for their work, though not at rates comparable to those prevailing in the outside community. Part of this income may be spent in the prison shops on items for the prisoners' own comfort, and part is accumulated and either sent to assist their families or given to them on discharge.

5 INMATE SOCIETY

No systematic study has been made of the forces operating within the prison communities of the United Arab Republic but some general observations may be made.

The values of the inmate society normally develop gradually and tend to be more accepted and less resisted by urban than by rural prisoners. The relationship between the prisoners and the prison staff is characterized by varying degrees of fear and suspicion on the part of the prisoners and by caution and mistrust on the part of the staff. The assimilation of the prisoners into their society is nonetheless achieved gradually and more or less automatically through imitation, suggestion, repetition, compliance with administrative regulations (for fear of punishment) and with the values of the inmate community (for fear of isolation or discrimination). The influence of outside contacts is sporadic and is normally confined to that of relatives and friends, though in the case of organized crime—which is minimal in the United Arab Republic and confined almost exclusively to drug-trafficking—persistent and strong outside influences have been found to operate.

The individual response to imprisonment obviously varies considerably but a majority of prisoners appear to accept prison life without resistance, aggression or resentment. It may be true that changes in attitude and behaviour following upon imprisonment are in fact for the better, though this is a subject which has not been documented or even investigated. There are no data on which to base an opinion as to the proportion of discharged prisoners who become adjusted to the outside world; no statement can even be made about the rate of recidivism, since accurate statistics are not available.

6 AFTER-CARE OF DISCHARGED PRISONERS

A 1957 decree of the Ministry of Social Affairs underlined the need for assisting released prisoners. Assistance now takes the form of the arranging of vocational and commercial projects jointly by the Ministry's representatives and the private associations involved in welfare work of this sort.

The Cairo Association for the After-Care of Prisoners, founded in October 1954, was the first of these private associations and is still the largest and most active. Associations of a similar nature have been registered in several other cities but they either have fairly limited functions or have only recently started operation.

IV Perspectives

The salient features of the contemporary correctional system of the United Arab Republic appear most clearly through a study of the two major developments of the last decade: the Prisons Law of 1956 and the establishment of the Higher Advisory Council for Prisons in the same year. The former lays down basic rules requiring the fair and humane treatment of prisoners, gradual preparation for release, payment for prison work and the abolition of corporal punishment; the latter is concerned to study, plan and improve reformative policies, training of prison personnel, the protection of prisoners, prison security and physical conditions, and penal legislation.

The promising innovations of the last ten years arise mainly from these two developments. A training centre for prison personnel has been set up; a Records and Statistics Department has been created in the Prisons Administration; the first medium security prison and the first women's prison have been opened, and separate facilities for Cairo prisoners awaiting trial have been provided; after-care for discharged prisoners has been put on an organized basis; and the cloak of secrecy has been lifted from the prison system by allowing visits by journalists, scholars, students, foreign experts and members of international and domestic welfare agencies.

The main problems identified by the Prisons Administration and now being further examined are the overcrowding of prisons, the poor organization of prison labour, the lack of open or semi-open correctional institutions and of any significant alternatives to short-term imprisonment, and the deficiency of specialized personnel for the prison treatment programmes. Three basic projects are being initiated: firstly, the establishing of new and adequate reception centres, separate prisons for offenders awaiting trial and a well-equipped central hospital within the prison medical service; secondly, a broad scheme for industrializing the prisons and extending vocational training facilities; and thirdly, the recruitment of more highly qualified personnel capable of specializing in the techniques needed for the effective operation of a modern correctional service.

9
Zambia

WILLIAM CLIFFORD

I Crime and Criminals

A report on crime in Northern Rhodesia in 1960[1] showed that criminal convictions in the country had increased about threefold over the previous thirty years, at a time when the total population of all races had grown by less than 70 per cent. In the same period serious crime had doubled. The report also showed changes in the racial distribution of crime. In 1931, one in every seventy-five Europeans and one in every 807 Africans was convicted of a Penal Code offence. In 1953, the rate was one in every 144 Europeans and one in every 298 Africans. By 1958, it had become one in every 194 Europeans and one in every 271 Africans. Although doubt may be cast on the accuracy of these proportions as a result of the varying accuracy of the census figures, the rise in crime over the years has been mainly a rise in crimes by Africans—a difference which the report shows to be more readily attributable to social circumstances than to any other factor.

In 1962, the Police Report showed the following number of convictions for crime:

TABLE I. TOTAL NUMBER OF CONVICTIONS, 1962

	Penal Code offences	Other offences	Total
Africans	12,155	40,561	52,716
Europeans	555	4,379	4,934
Asians	5	279	284
Coloureds	65	223	288
Totals	12,780	45,442	58,222

The Penal Code offenders were, of course, those convicted of the more serious offences. In this same year there were nearly 2,000 juvenile offenders, most of whom were convicted of Penal Code offences. They were distributed as follows: 1,888 Africans, 91 Europeans, 3 Other Races.

Thus, juveniles (i.e. between 8 and 19 years of age) constituted about one-sixth of all the Penal Code offenders. This, in a population about 50 per cent of which has been estimated to be under 21 years of age, is by no means alarming, but it should be noted that juvenile crime has increased tenfold since 1939 and most of the offences committed by juveniles are those for which adults might be imprisoned. This has been borne out by a recent study of juvenile delinquency completed by the present writer for the United Nations.

In Zambia, as elsewhere in the world, women seem to commit far less crime than men. Persons convicted are only divided in the Police Reports by sex in the account given of the punishment awarded. The 1960 Report on Crime in Northern Rhodesia, to which reference has already been made, gave the following analysis for those imprisoned and fined:

TABLE 2. MALES, FEMALES AND JUVENILES IMPRISONED AND FINED, 1955–58

	Males		Females		Juveniles	
Year	Imprisoned	Fined	Imprisoned	Fined	Imprisoned	Fined
1955	5,804	42,675	61	3,853	234	326
1956	6,990	42,208	215	4,091	152	275
1957	6,543	45,614	159	4,000	128	478
1958	6,553	52,353	74	3,829	210	202

Most of the women who were imprisoned had committed simple larcenies and most of the fines imposed on women were for breaches of municipal or Township Ordinances, i.e. for breaches of minor regulations. A considerable number had been fined for brewing beer illegally. The brewing of beer is, of course, a traditionally female occupation and in the towns it is associated with the adulteration of bottled beer and the running of 'shebeens' for drinking and prostitution.

Studies of the patterns of crime in Zambia suggest that, for most practical purposes, they follow those common in the more developed countries. Over the years, crimes against the person have declined and crimes against property have increased. Moreover, here as elsewhere, crime is a distinctly urban phenomenon, the crime rates varying with the size of the town and its rate of development. More important in the case of young offenders is that it appears that tribal differences—often so productive of violent crime in the traditional context—have become less important than the influences of urban life, and that the mixing of tribes in these areas, though devastating for family life, is not so much so as the increase in mobility, the pressures enforcing a nuclear family pattern, and the frustration of unfulfilled ambitions that is created by a limited education and the great temptations of urban living.[2]

II The Development of the Penal System

The treatment of offenders in Zambia has followed a pattern of development similar to that in most of the former British territories in Africa.

Prior to colonization, the indigenous Central African tribes enforced their own customary laws through their own courts. As has been commonly seen in Africa, no clear lines were drawn between criminal and civil misbehaviour but the basic conceptions tended to follow the lines of division between public and private injury. Where the safety of the community was involved, as in cases involving witches or persistent offenders, death or exile was the usual penalty. In other circumstances, the law was dominated by the idea of compensation to counterbalance loss and restore amity in the local residential group. Prisons were unknown and even murder, assault and property damage could be redressed by compensation and only provoked penal sanctions when their effects threatened the stability of the community as a whole.

The settlement of the territory by the British South Africa Company at the end of the 19th century brought English law and courts, with qualified magistrates in the towns and the usual English penal sanctions of the time. In 1924, the company handed over the administration to the British government, a Governor was appointed and Northern Rhodesia became a colonial territory with laws and sanctions modelled upon those in England. Prisons were erected, but for another twenty years there was no separate prison service. Instead, the local prisons were administered by the provincial administrators and their 'district messengers' who served as policemen, foremen and warders besides having many other duties of an administrative nature. Later as a separate police force was established, central prisons were erected for long-term prisoners or for those who could not be conveniently dealt with in the smaller and less commodious local prisons. In 1935, when the first report on the prisons in Northern Rhodesia was issued, four of the six central prisons had police officers serving as Superintendents of Prisons. The other two central prisons and the twenty-nine local prisons were administered by District Commissioners.

In 1938, Mr T. C. Flynn, Secretary to the Southern Rhodesia Department of Justice and Director of Prisons for Southern Rhodesia, was invited to visit and report upon the prison system in Northern Rhodesia. At that time he found male and female offenders, male and female certified mental patients and juveniles in the same prisons with inadequate facilities for classification and segregation. Amongst other things, he recommended a prison service distinct and separate from the police; but it was 1942 before an independent Commissioner of Prisons was appointed and 1947 before the separation of police and prisons was complete.

In 1964, Northern Rhodesia inherited its share of the penal system of the dismantled Federation of Rhodesia and Nyasaland. This inheritance was really a form of re-possession, for in 1953 Northern Rhodesia had ceded its prisons to the then newly created Federation. The prison service which had been handed over to the Federation in 1953 had been one which followed closely the pattern of prison administration in the United Kingdom, although it had lacked many of the latest and more imaginative reformative innovations of the post-war years and it was without an adequately trained staff. It had been, as we have seen, an independent service for only six years when the Federation took over. When Northern Rhodesia again became responsible for its prisons in 1964, there had been no fundamental changes. A reformatory which Northern Rhodesia had set up before Federation had been developed on Borstal lines at Katambora, and two new prisons had replaced older central prisons at Ndola and Broken Hill. But trained staff was still lacking and many of the buildings were received in 1964 much as they had been handed over in 1953. There were one or two 'open' work camps for prisoners but the emphasis was on security rather than on reformative measures.

There were parts of the penal system, however, which never became Federal. For example, the courts and the police had remained a territorial responsibility and each country of the Federation had retained and developed its own social welfare services. In Northern Rhodesia, these social welfare services included a probation system —established with trained officers in 1954—with the Director of Social Welfare gazetted as the Principal Probation Officer. The Federal Constitution also recognized that the territories were responsible for their own approved schools. In fact, Northern Rhodesia did not have an approved school of its own until 1961 and for many years before this it had made use of the approved schools and reformatories in Southern Rhodesia and South Africa—especially for European and Coloured offenders who did not appear before the courts in large enough numbers to justify special institutions. South African reformatories had been used for African boys at a time when there were fewer delinquents and Northern Rhodesia had no reformatory of its own.

There were legal provisions both in the South African and Northern Rhodesian statutes which allowed for this transfer of offenders to the country which had better facilities. This seemed reasonable when the country had so few offenders of different types that special institutions were difficult to justify and it was cheaper to pay for the sending of individuals to countries with large institutions of the type required. The use of South African institutions, however, declined with the rise of crime locally, with the setting up of the Federation in 1953 and with the gradual development of local facilities. Northern Rhodesia steadily moved to a position where it could provide for its own offenders but even today the accommodation and trained staff to provide for adequate classification and for the variety of treatments is admittedly far behind the need.

It is clear that the profound changes in the prison service have had a detrimental effect both on the staff and on planning generally. Moving from the provincial administration to the police, then in 1947 to a separate service, becoming Federal in 1953 and territorial again in 1964, the prison service has found little time for the development of a settled pattern of administration. The inevitable changes of staff and the changes in the responsible authorities have made prison policy all the more difficult to carry into effect.

III The Modern Penal System

The Penal Code is the basic law which all courts—even the native courts—administer in dealing with criminal offences. It sets out the powers available for imposing the various penal sanctions, reserving the more serious for the higher courts. In preparation for independence, the dual court system—the High Court and magistrates' courts on the one hand and the native courts on the other—was integrated so that no court deals any longer exclusively with people of a particular race or ethnic origin.

Section 24 of the Penal Code reads as follows:

The following punishments may be inflicted by a court: (1) Death; (2) Imprisonment; (3) Corporal Punishment; (4) Fine; (5) Forfeiture; (6) Payment of Compensation; (7) Finding security to keep the peace and be of good behaviour or to come up for judgment; (8) Deportation; (9) Any other punishment provided by this Code or by any other law.

The application of the various penal measures to offenders in Zambia in 1962 is shown by Table 3:

TABLE 3. PUNISHMENTS AWARDED BY ZAMBIA COURTS IN 1962

Punishment	Males	Females	Juveniles
Death	40	—	—
Imprisonment	6,949	96	431
Caning	183	—	1,150
Fine	45,001	3,278	386
Totals	52,173	3,374	1,967

There were also 896 persons who were dealt with otherwise, i.e. by absolute or conditional discharges or probation. Any discrepancy between these figures and those already given from the Police Report for 1962 is accounted for by the fact that some people were given composite sentences.

I THE DEATH PENALTY

The death sentences were for murders and of course a number of these may have been commuted later; the details are not available.

2 IMPRISONMENT

The committals to prison have not changed much over the years. In 1935, for example, 7,168 persons were committed; in 1947, 7,732; and in 1953, 9,512. These figures include committals for debt which are not included in Table 3, so that the total figures for 1962 are probably higher than that given in Table 3.

With the change in prison administration annual reports have not been published since 1953. The figures for the years 1947–53 show, however, that a great many of those sentenced to imprisonment were sentenced to periods of three months or less. Thus in 1947, 66 per cent of all committals were for less than three months; in 1950, 65 per cent were committed for less than three months; in 1953, about 57 per cent. If those sentenced to between three and six months were included, the percentage would be higher. The disadvantages of the short prison sentence have been shown by a number

245

of writers in this field. The risk of contamination is more serious in Zambia where there are limited facilities for segregation, and of course the short term allows no time for constructive training and rehabilitation. We are not surprised to find, therefore, that over these years the recidivist rate, as calculated by previous convictions on admission to prison, rose from 11·5 per cent in 1947 to 18·28 per cent in 1953.

There can be little doubt that the prison system is in need of considerable extension and improvement to meet modern standards. Firstly, classification and segregation facilities are inadequate in all but the two modern prisons at Ndola and Broken Hill. The undesirable practice of imprisoning mental patients has been discontinued since the building of a mental hospital in Lusaka in 1961, but there still remains the problem of the lack of facilities for juveniles awaiting trial or disposal, and for women prisoners. When women have to be imprisoned or detained, special *ad hoc* arrangements are made to keep them segregated from male prisoners. The numbers, however, are not substantial.

Secondly, there is a need for adequately equipped workshops with greater facilities for vocational training. The small local prisons are of limited value for reformative training, and thought could be given to their discontinuance as communications improve and the movement of prisoners to central prisons can be easier accomplished. At present, however, even the central prisons have only limited facilities: much of the work done is of a routine agricultural nature, though tailoring, carpentry and shoe-repairing are taught. It seems likely that the open work-camp idea developed under the Federal Prison Service will be extended in the years ahead. Academic facilities are minimal: there is limited provision for the arranging of educational classes and to this end each prison tries to develop a small library.

Thirdly, there is an urgent need for the recruitment and training of prison staff. An experienced Commissioner of Prisons has recently been recruited from the United Kingdom and he is extending training facilities beyond the low-level in-service training schemes formerly found to be unsatisfactory. Provision needs to be made in particular for the appointment of officers with special responsibility for individual prisoners.

3 CORPORAL PUNISHMENT

Corporal punishment means caning, and its application is carefully restricted in the later sections of the Code. Anyone under 21 who has committed an offence for which he would be liable to a sentence of three months or more may be caned either instead of or in addition to the sentence of imprisonment. Caning may also be awarded for burglary, housebreaking or theft and for certain scheduled offences which include rape, indecent assaults on females, boys or mental patients, procuration, wounding, grievous bodily harm, robbery and being found armed with intent to commit a felony. The law stipulates that caning may be awarded in such cases, 'where it is expedient in the interests of the community'. It may also be used in cases concerned with the misconduct of prisoners, in the jurisdiction of the native courts, for the care and protection of juveniles or to prevent cruelty to animals. But the Penal Code restricts corporal punishment to twelve strokes of the cane if the offender is under 19 years of age and to twenty-four in any other case. Furthermore, a female cannot be caned and no caning takes place except in the presence of a medical officer. Nor can caning be given in instalments— it has to be inflicted on the one occasion.

Corporal punishment appears to have declined in significance as a method of disposition available to the courts but comparative statistics are unfortunately not available. As long ago as 1933, the Commission of Inquiry into the Administration of Justice in Kenya, Uganda and Tanganyika Territories in Criminal Matters reported (at paragraph 178 of the Report):

We are unable to subscribe to the view that caning and flogging should be made legal as a punishment for adults, whether generally or for natives only, for any but the most serious crimes. Such a form of punishment must be damaging to self-respect, particularly to those Africans who have advanced to a certain stage of civilization and may even tend to brutalize its victims. Any extension of the use of corporal punishment we consider a retrograde step which we must oppose.[3]

The *Magistrates' Handbook*, for general distribution among the magistracy, contained similar injunctions and pointed out the limitations which were imposed on the practice in England:

> The corporal punishment of adults by judicial whipping (i.e. lashes with 'the cat') was in English practice (before its total abolition by Parliament) reserved for one crime—robbery with violence. Even then it was awarded only when the violence amounted to brutality, when it was considered justifiable on the principle that the punishment should fit the crime. If a whipping is ordered here it must be justifiable by reference to the same principle. . . .[4]

4 FINES AND COMPENSATION

It will be seen from Table 3 that fines predominated, nearly 85 per cent of all offenders having been fined. This is a significant rise, related no doubt to the larger numbers of both young and old who are now earning wages. In relatively few cases, however, was the fine imposed on the parents of young offenders, and compensation seems to have been awarded but sparingly. Usually compensation is awarded in addition to a penalty and for that reason it is not shown in our tables. From cases studied, however, it is clear that magistrates' courts make far less use of compensation than the native courts. With the latter, of course, compensation is the traditional way of dealing with offences and the satisfaction of the victim is as important as the punishment of the offender.

In a study of seven urban native courts in 1959[5] the writer found that compensation was awarded in the great majority of cases—usually in addition to some other penalty. Even so, the native courts seemed to favour imprisonment and awarded imprisonment or the option of a fine or imprisonment in 67 per cent of the 4,000 cases they dealt with in the period under review. They were sparing, however, in their use of caning and had recourse to it in less than 2 per cent of their sentences. Fines were exacted in 30 per cent of the cases dealt with by the urban native courts.

IV Juvenile Offenders

Juvenile delinquency in Zambia, like its adult counterpart, is an urban phenomenon. As families move into the towns, their ability to exercise close control over the activities of their members diminishes. The pressures of a homogeneous community, of common family residence, and of traditional respect for age and authority, are dissipated. The accumulation of material wealth in the towns serves to attract to them large numbers of unskilled workers and their dependants who are unable to enter into effective competition for employment and a share in this material wealth. A recent census estimates that about 40 per cent of Zambians under the age of 21 have never been to school, and large numbers have to leave school for lack of places before they complete even a primary education. On the other hand, it is clear that lack of educational facilities is not by itself a factor which significantly produces delinquent behaviour: truancy from school is found to be a feature of many young delinquents' lives.

In a working paper prepared by the Northern Rhodesia Government for the C.C.T.A. Conference on the Treatment of Offenders (Juvenile Delinquents) held at Kampala in 1956, the treatment of a group of 719 juveniles dealt with by the police was given as in Table 4, where it is compared with the 1962 figures:

TABLE 4. TREATMENT OF JUVENILE OFFENDERS, 1956 AND 1962

Treatment	1956 %	1962 %
Imprisoned	11	28
Sent to Reformatory	7	4·4
Caned	71	51
Fined	5	9·4
Bound Over, Warned, Probation	5	7

There appears to have been a rise in the use of probation for juveniles over these years from less than 2 per cent in 1956 to about 6 per cent in 1962. The fall in sentences of caning is marked, but it will be

249

seen that over one-half of all the young offenders before the courts are caned—presumably, as we have seen, to avoid having to send them to prison, especially in those rural areas which as yet do not have the full benefit of a probation service. The figures suggest that full attention has not been paid to the policy enunciated in the *Magistrates' Handbook* in 1951:

> It is specially desirable that offenders who are not over the age of 18 should be kept out of prison. Where a caution or binding over will not suffice, and if the juvenile accused has no earnings out of which to pay even a moderate fine . . . it is better that the juvenile should be caned than that he should be sent to prison; and unless he gives notice of appeal the caning can be carried out at once and the matter finished.

There is but one reformatory, situated at Katambora, on the banks of the Zambesi River, about thirty miles from Livingstone. Here the dormitories are small huts built around a central compound and accommodating four to six boys each. This institution was opened in 1950 but has had difficulty developing because of the lack of accommodation and training facilities and the difficulty of obtaining trained staff. Yet despite these difficulties there has been remarkable improvement over the years and a Borstal-type administration has been established, with housemasters and a house system. There is also a grade system for the boys, who are employed in woodwork, basket-making, weaving, building, tailoring and agricultural work. There is a primary and intermediate educational programme for all boys, and recreational facilities include boxing, football, basketball, athletics, gymnastics and Scouting. In 1962, 49 pupils were said to have passed their intermediate examination, and senior Scouts had been taken on outings to places of interest such as the Victoria Falls and the Livingstone Museum.

In a special report provided for this inquiry, the Superintendent wrote:

> The main object of our educational programme is to bring the illiterate type up to the stage when he can read and write his own language and have sufficient knowledge of English to compete for employment. Classes are organized from Sub A

up to Standard IV for the brighter types and by the use of qualified warders as teachers each juvenile now receives at least 25 hours of schooling per week.

Again, the country has only one approved school. This was gazetted in 1960 and received its first committals in 1961. It was then in rented quarters which had previously been occupied by a school for the blind and were not very suitable for approved school work. In 1963, the approved school was moved to Mazabuka, about 80 miles south of Lusaka, on the line-of-rail. Here there was more agricultural land and the accommodation was built to meet the need as far as funds allowed. Two large dormitories were erected and housing provided for the staff. The funds available were limited, however, and at the time of writing the dining-room is a tent and the kitchen is in the open air. Approximately fifty boys are at the school and for the time being this is the limit of its accommodation. There are no special workshops and recreational facilities are limited.

Here again there is a house system and a regular educational programme, the teachers for which are seconded from the Ministry of Education. The school itself comes under the Director of Social Welfare and operates within the Ministry of Housing and Social Development. The Report of the Director of School Welfare for the year 1962 gave the following account of the work:

During the year the daily average population of the school was forty pupils and the maximum in training at any one time was forty-six. Formal education to Standard IV level was provided but (because the buildings were not very suitable for the vocational and handicraft training of pupils and because the site is also unsuitable for agricultural pursuits) only limited facilities for other training were available. Residential employment is not popular with social workers and during the year the training programme at the school suffered from frequent changes in personnel.

The remaining institutional facilities for juveniles are remand homes in Ndola and Lusaka and a temporary 'place of safety' in each area, which normally consists of a small house in one of the urban locations.

The use of probation, though not formally limited to juvenile offenders, is in effect considered as more appropriate to their needs than to those of adults. The report of the Director of Social Welfare for 1962 showed 322 persons placed on probation and indicated that in the current case-loads of probation officers there were only nineteen adults. This means that not only was an infinitesimal percentage of adult offenders placed on probation but that the service is being used for only about 6 per cent of the total number of juveniles—a very limited use even in the urban areas where the officers are available.

Legal provision was made for probation as early as 1933 but a regular system of full-time officers did not come into being until 1954, when an officer was recruited from the United Kingdom to initiate and develop the service. Since then probation offices have been opened in every large town. One of the main limiting factors, however, is distance: officers cannot operate effectively beyond thirty miles from their base and vast areas of the country therefore remain uncovered. If a probationer moves more than thirty miles from a town, or returns to his home village beyond this distance, for all practical purposes official supervision ends.

Yet in the years since 1954, the records show that eight out of every ten placed on probation do not get into trouble again during the period of supervision. No precise information is available about the period following supervision but the impression in the field is that the rate of unsatisfactory cases increases by about 100 per cent, giving a total of four unsatisfactory outcomes in every ten cases. Although we have had no comparative evaluations of the effectiveness of short prison sentences or caning in Zambia, if experience elsewhere is a guide it seems very likely that they are far less effective than probation for most cases of confirmed delinquency.

The transition from colonial to independent status has had the advantage of the continuation of the comprehensive conception of social welfare administration which formerly prevailed.[6] There is no compartmentalization of welfare services but all are gathered together in the same organization. The Director of Social Welfare is the Principal Probation Officer and also the Commissioner for Juvenile Welfare. Similarly, all probation officers are Juveniles Inspectors. In this role the service is responsible for the protection of children and for the care of those without family supervision or beyond control. There are foster homes and children's houses run by the service, and missions throughout the country are subsidized to take in children whose mothers have died in or shortly after childbirth and who might die if a wet nurse was not locally available or the necessary baby foods could not be provided. Usually such children are returned to relatives as soon as they are able to take ordinary food.

This widespread child-care service enables the Director to deal with a great many cases of pre-delinquency before the child commits an offence for which he might be prosecuted. It is a valuable preventive of crime which has proved its worth over the years. Similarly, in the absence of an adequate country-wide system for the after-care and licensing of offenders, the probation officers provide an institutional after-care service wherever they are able to do so. Unfortunately, it is limited to the towns along the line-of-rail and to the larger urban centres elsewhere, with the result that many boys are released from the reformatory or approved school who do not have the supervision and guidance they need. There is a voluntary Prisoners' Aid Society for both adult and juvenile offenders but the amount of resettlement work which can be done by its single social worker is obviously very restricted.

V The Future of the Penal System

The multiple objectives of the modern penal system are no easier to achieve in Zambia than anywhere else. Outmoded facilities and attitudes are to be found existing side by side with a more modern will to use penal sanctions as constructive forces. Although positive efforts are handicapped by the limit on funds available for many of the changes which are necessary, it should be noted that the reformatory, the approved school and the probation system are all developments of the last fifteen years. All are characteristic of the wish to reform; and there are now signs that even the prison service is moving in the same direction and beginning to introduce more effective training and classification.

The cornerstone of all such measures is, of course, efficient selection at all stages of the penal process. It is disturbing that the courts, which are so prone to cane and imprison, should show such reluctance to use the facilities already available for pre-trial or pre-sentence investigations. The records for 1962 show that only about 400 investigations were made, whilst the total number of sentences passed was nearly 60,000. Although it is conceded that the social welfare services available for conducting investigations are limited,[7] it is suggested that there is ample scope for their greater use by the courts. The need for trained personnel is now being tackled by the Oppenheimer College of Social Service in Lusaka, which began the training of professional social workers in 1961 and graduated its first class in 1964 after a three-year diploma course.

But if the existing structure of penal and remedial institutions is to be made more effective, it is obvious that considerable extension of the facilities will be necessary. It is meaningless to speak of the better selection of individuals for treatment if there cannot be effective classification on entry into the institutional setting. With respect to juveniles in particular, there is ample reason to believe that two remand homes, one approved school and a reformatory are not sufficient to meet the increase in offenders. They cater, of course, for all types and age-groups. No one type—sexual deviant, epileptic, subnormal, persistent or first offender—or age-group is sufficiently large at present to justify separate facilities in an underdeveloped country, where funds are limited and the emphasis is on economic development. Yet if the present single institutions are called upon to cope with even greater numbers, with no increase in staff to ensure some individual attention, the problems of management are sure to become considerable.

From all points of view, the extension of the probation service appears both desirable and likely to be advantageous, not only in providing for the more extensive supervision of probationers but in offering an effective after-care and licensing service to the various institutions. With trained staff coming forward only slowly, however, it might be wise at this stage to consider the appointment of village headmen, chiefs and teachers as *ad hoc* probation officers. It was, after all, through responsible volunteers that probation and after-care was extended in England and the United States and today many French-speaking countries in Africa use teams of volunteers, each under a trained *assistant social*, to operate a similar system. Many potential probationers in Zambia live in towns other than those in which they are convicted, or in completely rural areas.[8] It would be a valuable link between the modern and traditional if the respect owed to traditional authorities could be utilized to provide effective supervision in the areas into which the modern probation services will find difficulty (especially in terms of expense and distance) in penetrating.

To keep strictly within the framework of the present penal system, one may refer to the possibilities which seem to be available for fining more regularly the parents of young offenders and for imposing in nearly all cases an order for the compensation of the victim. These are ways in which Africans have traditionally dealt with offenders; they would be understood, and provision is already made for them in the law. Provision might be made in future for a system of extra-mural labour, such as is in force in some other African states, which would ensure that those who did not have the means to pay the compensation could work in their own time to earn money to do so. Again, this would have cultural foundations in the customary community and would have the added appeal of being an economic measure.

VI Conclusion

The fact that a number of the present Zambian Ministers have spent time in prisons as a result of their political activities has made them aware of the need for a better penal system. In a speech to the Prisoners' Aid Society in 1963, Dr Kaunda, then the Minister of Local Government and Social Welfare, referred to himself as an ex-prisoner and called for more creative work in the prisons and an improvement of after-care facilities. On the other hand, the problems of crime and its treatment are not widely understood in the country, and in the last analysis it is a question of priorities when the estimates for the Budget are being prepared. The facilities required are costly and it may only be possible to achieve them piecemeal.

The country's approach to the problem of crime is in line with the best traditions. Reform is the aim and, as we have shown, the provision made over the past fifteen years or so amply bears this out. But good intentions do not disguise the fact that at present there is no more than the basis for future development. A great many services which would be regarded as normal in developed countries do not yet exist here.

It is clear too that it will not be sufficient for Zambia to borrow ideas from other countries. True, its problem of crime seems to approximate to the problem in developed countries but here there are opportunities for adapting treatment to traditional values and social controls. These customary ideals and procedures have not disappeared by any means and extra-mural labour, a variety of open work-camps, the organization of a market for the products of prison labour, a wider use of home leave, the extension of informal education, and the more effective application of compensation would all be traditionally understood ways in which Africans could be brought back into the society against which they have offended.

There is need for imagination and adaptation; and this brings us back again to the need for adequate training programmes for those who will have to deal with the offenders of the future. Both institutional and non-institutional services call for people who are flexible and open-minded, prepared to adopt useful approaches from other countries and ready to improvise within the present limitations. They must be innovators, studying ways in which the country can get the best not only by borrowing ideas but by grafting methods from traditional modes of living.

In conclusion, it should be noted that, though the philosophy for the treatment of offenders has been imported, along with the penal measures, from England, there has been little attempt yet to educate public opinion on the treatment of criminals. This again is a task for the future. If enlightened methods are to be widely understood and supported by the people, there will have to be greater opportunity for public discussion and a greater participation of the public in the measures intended to reform offenders and give them a fresh start in life.

NOTES

1. Clifford, *Crime in Northern Rhodesia*, Rhodes–Livingstone Communication No. 16 (1960).
2. Clifford, *Profiles in Crime* (1964).
3. Quoted with approval in Northern Rhodesia by Law, C.J. in R. *v. Audreyi Chongo and Others*, (1940) 2 N.R.L.R. 93.
4. The quotation is from the 1951 edition.
5. Clifford, *Criminal Cases in the Urban Native Courts* (1960).
6. In Northern Rhodesia, as in several other former British territories, the general social welfare facilities in fact developed out of the probation service. This service was first offered as the magistrates' courts became increasingly aware that they were unable to deal with the broader problems of juvenile delinquency; from the earliest days the probation officers provided such after-care services as they could in addition to their ordinary supervisory duties; and as it became obvious that delinquency was closely interwoven with under-privilege and neglect, child-care and public relief services emerged.
7. In so far as medical and psychiatric diagnostic facilities are needed in criminal cases, they are provided in the Government hospitals. But with overcrowding and understaffing—there are two psychiatrists in the single mental hospital—it is not easy to provide special attention in such cases.
8. For this reason, among others, conditions of residence are not very often inserted in probation orders. Generally speaking, the condition required is that the probationer reside in a remand home or 'place of safety' in a town where he can be adequately supervised.

Part Two
Special Problems

10
Sentencing Patterns in Nigeria*

ALAN MILNER

* This chapter forms part of a larger study of *The Nigerian Penal System*, to be published by Sweet and Maxwell Ltd.

I Introduction

Since the establishing of British rule in Nigeria at the beginning of
the 20th century, two types of criminal law—the indigenous and the
introduced—have been enforced to a greater or lesser extent. Today, all tribunals apply only the statutory criminal laws and it is
the objective of this chapter to examine this application in a functional way by studying the variant sentencing practices of the courts
of the country—the High Courts, the magistrates' courts and the
native or customary courts. The purpose will be to see if there are
any significant differences in these sentencing practices and, if there
are, to examine how far they may be attributed to differences in the
nature of the courts and in their cultural affiliations.

The differences which may prove to be crucial arise from the
duality of law systems generated by colonial rule. The British recognized the existence of local criminal laws and implemented a
policy of allowing them to be applied through the medium of the
traditional courts. At the same time, they introduced first the common law of crimes and then a criminal code successively into Northern Nigeria and finally Southern Nigeria, together with a colonial
magistracy and judiciary to apply them. And from the very beginning of British rule it was made clear to the local rulers that their
customary penal structures would be brought under the close scrutiny of the administration.[1] Some customary penalties were therefore specifically abolished by statute. Prohibitions on mutilation
and torture appeared at once,[2] trials by ordeal and their built-in penalties were made illegal,[3] and slavery, which had been a customary
way of getting rid of persistent offenders, was finally legislated
away after being the subject of treaties and ordinances since the

1830s.[4] The remaining penalties were made subject to the requirement that they should not be repugnant to 'natural justice and humanity',[5] a requirement which was to continue until they were completely abolished. In practice, this meant that the prisons which had so horrified Lord Lugard[6] came under administrative supervision at once, though conditions in local prisons remain a cause of concern to the present day. Death sentences passed by native courts had to be carried out in a humane way, though at various times in the history of customary laws hanging, beheading, stoning, drowning, burying alive and killing by the identical means used by the murderer, had been allowed.[7] The more bizarre methods had apparently fallen into disuse before 1900 and beheading with a sword —approved by Maliki law and practised in the northern emirates— was the only one to persist as an alternative to hanging. Even this noticeably diminished in popularity before its abolition in 1936.[8] The humanity of the various forms of corporal punishment was apparently not questioned until 1933, but restrictions introduced in that year limited the weapons to rattan canes and single-tailed whips of prescribed dimensions.[9]

From the beginning, limits were placed, too, on the native courts' powers to impose humane punishment by specifying their powers of sentence either by statute[10] or in the warrants establishing the courts.[11] In fact, it was only in the north that complete criminal jurisdiction was ever conferred on the native courts, the great majority of serious offences in the south falling within the exclusive jurisdiction of the British courts. The power of the central administration to authorize the native courts to apply Nigerian ordinances[12] was not extensively used and was intended merely to supplement their jurisdiction in matters of a local and customary nature.

Unfortunately, when the power to try statutory offences was first conferred, no specific statement was made about the relationship between statutory offences and customary offences and punishments. In due course a native court at Bukuru (Plateau Province) passed a customary sentence of corporal punishment, ostensibly for an offence under a revenue ordinance but more correctly for the customary offence of open defiance of the local authority.[13] The revenue ordinance itself made no mention of such a penalty and this fact, coupled with the government's concern with limiting corporal punishment at that time, led to a review of the punishment powers of native courts. The stage was set for what is now one of the most notorious incidents in recent Nigerian legal history.

The Criminal Code was amended in 1933, with the intention of restricting the native courts' powers to award punishments.[14] Executive instructions were issued both about the use of corporal punishment, specifying the occasions on which it could be ordered for actions criminal under both customary law and statute, and about the general relationship of the two types of offences.[15] Somewhat remarkably, the latter made the specific point that although native courts could continue to deal with offenders under customary law, they should sentence in accordance with the provisions of the Criminal Code where the action was also a statutory offence. I say remarkably because, although these instructions precisely met the needs of the Bukuru case, their general impact on the administration of Islamic law in Northern Nigeria would have been disastrously inconsistent with the rest of the government's northern policy. They would have curtailed without any prior consultation the powers of the Islamic courts in homicide cases and made an entire Hausa–Arabic speaking legal system subject to the Criminal Code rules which the judges neither understood, nor sympathized with, nor had copies of.

In practice, the instructions were never enforced in such a way as to limit the homicide powers of the northern native courts. But in 1947 the obscure way in which the 1933 amendment had been made gave rise to the wholly unexpected decision of the West African Court of Appeal in *Tsofo Gubba v. Gwandu Native Authority*.[16] The court held that the amendment in 1933 had the effect, not of limiting punishments to those specified in legislation, but rather of requiring that actions which were offences under both customary law and statute should actually be *tried* under the statute. The details of the controversy which followed in the next ten years are of little penal significance.[17] The power of the native courts to use customary penalties for customary law offences was reconferred at once[18] but in 1951 the original 1933 instructions were reproduced in legislation providing that the punishment of an action under customary law should never exceed that possible under statute for the same action.[19] This stayed the same after regionalization,[20] though in

265

practice there were still real difficulties, particularly in the north, in making the restriction workable.

The preparation for independence in 1960 brought general agreement between the governments that customary criminal laws and penalties should be abolished. Northern and Western Nigeria both acted in 1959—Northern Nigeria by specifically invalidating them[21] and Western Nigeria by withdrawing customary criminal jurisdiction from the customary courts.[22] The new Constitution duly made liability to conviction and sentence for a criminal offence depend on the existence of a defined crime and a written penalty.[23] Any conviction or sentence according to customary law will now be invalid, though there is evidence that the customary laws retain their vitality in some areas despite the prohibition.[24] Such customary laws as remain have been incorporated into the legislation, most notably the offences of adultery, insults to the modesty of women and drinking[25] and the Islamic *hadd* punishments[26] incorporated into the Penal Code of Northern Nigeria. Extensive powers remain, however, to reproduce customary criminal laws in the form of local regulations.[27]

The government of independent Nigeria found itself, therefore, on October 1st, 1960, with a single system of criminal law in force in each part of the Federation. In the southern Regions and Lagos, it was the original Criminal Code, as supplemented by local legislation and regulations; in Northern Nigeria it was the new Penal Code and local legislation and regulations. In all parts of the country, the criminal laws were to be applied by the native or customary courts and by the High Courts and magistrates' courts alike. In the North, where the native courts had completely concurrent jurisdiction with the British-type courts, courses of instruction in the new criminal law and procedure were begun at once for native court personnel. In the South, progress had already been made in appointing professionally qualified presidents to the higher-grade customary courts and this policy was continued.

II Sentencing Policies

Since all courts apply the same laws and penalties, subject to the variations between Regions, there can no longer be any differences in policy based on the conflicting ideologies of the law-givers. That there can nonetheless be differences in policy based on the conflicting ideologies of the *judges*, is abundantly plain. Were the gravity of an offence to be the sole consideration of the sentencing judge, which it is not, there would be variations in the making of such an estimate. There are differences between the views of judges which are attributable to the varying weight they give to the elements of deterrence, retribution and social adjustment which make up a criminal sentence. And no doubt other disparities between sentencing decisions can only be explained in terms of the moral, social and economic attitudes of the individual judges. Research studies in England and the United States have focused upon both the disparities[28] and the attitudes which may give rise to them[29] and have all stressed the theme of the lack of objectivity in the sentencing process.

Certain kinds of variations can be shown in the study of Nigerian sentencing. In a series of 1,571 cases (1,335 sentences) tried in four Northern magistrates' courts in 1962, for example, the use of imprisonment varies between 45 per cent of the sentences at Makurdi and 18 per cent at Ilorin. The Ilorin court disposed of only 15 per cent of its cases of imprisonment by sentences of three months or less, whereas in Jos 40 per cent of the sentences of imprisonment were of this duration. And whereas only 24 per cent of all the sentences in Jos were fines, in Ilorin they accounted for 74 per cent. Makurdi apart, there was nothing to indicate any major difference in the types of case dealt with.[30]

In the sphere of native court activity in the same Region, the returns of the courts of the same grade show no narrower a range of methods of disposing of cases. In the thirty Grade A Limited courts in 1962–63, the percentage of sentences represented by imprisonment ranged from a median of 28 per cent to the extremes of 64 per cent in the court of the Chief Alkali of Adamawa and 8 per cent in that of the Chief Alkali of Bauchi. And while the latter court's rate of fining (88 per cent) was far in excess of the median of 68 per cent, the opposite end of the scale fell as low as 20 per cent in the court of the Chief Alkali of Kano. The unfortunate defendant before the Emir of Fika would take little comfort from the fact that 58 per cent of the sentences of imprisonment in that court were for over a year; he would much rather have been before the Chief Alkali of Argungu, of whose prison sentences only 7 per cent were of this length and 72 per cent for three months or less.

If it is possible to generalize about the basic attitudes displayed in the application of the British-type criminal law by the introduced courts, one may say that they are repressive and oriented towards deterrence. Rehabilitation and social adjustment are honoured by the inclusion of probation and discharge provisions in the laws but not implemented in practice by reason of both disinclination and, in the case of probation, lack of facilities. Given the condition of the prison system, sentences of imprisonment are punitive, protective and deterrent and not imposed with any intention of bringing about individual betterment.

The prevailing ethos of any given system of customary law depends very much upon the nature of the community in which it is enforced. It is probably true to say that the rigid application of Islamic law, such as was found in the most northerly provinces of the country, was accompanied by an authoritarian attitude towards sanctions which closely resembled that of those responsible for applying the British-type law. At the same time, the smaller and less politically organized communities of the Bauchi Plateau and of Eastern Nigeria appear to have adopted attitudes which were often entirely socially adjustive—that is, they were less concerned with the application by strict rote of penal sanctions in a given situation and more with using techniques of compromise and settlement aimed at preserving the unity and cohesiveness of the small community.[31] The sanctions of the Yoruba kingdoms might be said to have fallen in between these two extremes, with manifestations on the one hand of the authoritarian rule associated with strong central government and on the other with the more permissive and adjustive attitudes found in the homogeneous Yoruba towns and villages.

It is important to remember, though, that even before the abolition of customary criminal law, the application of customary penalties had been considerably restricted both by legislation and administrative action. The *forms* of punishment became largely the same in both the customary court and the professional court spheres. More basic, however, were the customary *attitudes* towards punishment. There is evidence that British administrative pressure was brought to bear at an early stage with a view to assimilating customary with British attitudes. At the very beginning of the century, Lugard was advising his political officers that

the form of the punishment inflicted . . . must be that which is most deterrent and most likely to suppress crime. Native courts must be instructed that the restitution of stolen property, or of an abducted person is not of itself a sufficient penalty. . . .

and added elsewhere that 'a punishment should always be added to restitution'.[32] Yet, in 1953, Mr Justice Brooke was still able to note that compensation was more often used in resolving criminal disputes in native courts than in professional courts,[33] apparently dismissing as unrealistic

the anxiety . . . at one time expressed lest the difficulty of securing respect for European systems of justice might be increased by the apparent unsuitability of European ideas of penology to African conditions.[34]

III The Statistical Data

In any jurisdiction, given relatively stable social conditions, patterns of both crime and sentencing will be established which will not fluctuate much overall. That is to say, the community will normally demonstrate a given, built-in crime potential and the mixture of retributivistic, deterrent, reformative and other sentencing objectives will produce a fairly consistent distribution of sentences between the available methods of different severity.

It is unfortunate that the reporting and compilation of sentencing data in Nigeria has not yet reached a high enough measure of detail and comprehensiveness to be of much use to the criminologist. The statistics published by the Federal Office of Statistics follow the pattern established over half a century ago in the Statistical Blue Book and are designed rather to supply for administrative purposes a limited range of information as part of the overall picture of social and economic activity in the country than to present data suitable for serious research purposes. A range of offences is listed and the total number of sentences imposed for each is specified under the four headings of death, imprisonment,[35] fine and binding over. No indication is given of the amount of fines; and 'binding over' is apparently meant to include probation and discharges. Recent years have unfortunately brought further incompleteness[36] and inaccuracy,[37] while in due course the Office will no doubt note the fact that a Penal Code was introduced into Northern Nigeria in 1960 which does not use the same classification of offences as the Criminal Code it superseded.

Except in Northern Nigeria, where the native courts exercise a criminal jurisdiction almost fully co-extensive with the High Court and magistrates' courts, customary tribunals have ordinarily had limited criminal powers. Any comparison of patterns of sentencing in the higher courts and the native courts must therefore be restricted to data from Northern Nigeria. The Northern Ministry of Justice has kindly made available returns of sentences collected from the more than 750 native courts in the Region in 1962 and 1963. As far as possible it has supplied deficiencies and checked doubtful returns, with the result that an estimated 95 per cent of the cases tried in over 90 per cent of the courts are covered by the statistics. The returns are full in some respects: they detail the lengths of sentences of imprisonment passed and include information on fines, imprisonment in default of payment of fine, corporal punishment and offences compounded. They do not give any breakdown of offences according to type, cover probation, discharges, compensation and restitution, or indicate sex and age differences among the offenders.

270

The crucial question about them, however, remains their accuracy, for they are prepared by local court officials who will often have only limited administrative skills and virtually no direct supervision. Whether they fully understand the significance of the forms on which they make the returns, or whether the forms are accurately completed, must always remain open to doubt. All that can be claimed is that the obvious errors have been investigated and corrected.

On the basis of such information as is available for recent years, certain rough conclusions about judicial attitudes may be drawn.[38]

IV The High Courts and Magistrates' Courts

I ADULT OFFENDERS

In each Nigerian jurisdiction, these courts exercise between them the full range of sentencing powers. Comparison of the available data shows the substantial similarities which exist in the overall use of different methods of disposal in the different parts of the country (Table 1).

The similarities exist despite two qualifying factors. First, the range of cases dealt with in the Northern High Court and magistrates' courts probably differed from that in the other Regions. The native courts in that Region may be expected to have dealt with a large number of petty offences and breaches of local regulations which would be dealt with by magistrates' courts in the other Regions. The reduction in fining in the Northern High Court and magistrates' courts which would be expected to follow this division of jurisdiction, however, is not clearly indicated.

Secondly, the data cover the period in which the basic criminal

TABLE 1. DISPOSAL OF CASES BY HIGH COURTS AND MAGIS-
TRATES' COURTS, 1958–63. ADULT OFFENDERS

			% sentenced to		
Jurisdiction	Period	No. sentences	Imprison-ment	Fine	Binding over
E. Nigeria	1958–63	136,401	42	50	7
N. Nigeria	1958–63	26,786	45	47	4
W. Nigeria	1958–60	37,533	33	59	4
M.-W. Nigeria	1963	4,034	40	47	9
		204,754	39	51	6

law administered by the High Court and magistrates' courts in
Northern Nigeria changed from the old Criminal Code to the new
Penal Code. From the study of data for the individual years from
1958 to 1963, no change in the sentencing patterns of the courts
appears to have accompanied this innovation.

TABLE 2. DISPOSAL OF CASES BY HIGH COURTS AND MAGIS-
TRATES' COURTS, 1958–63. ADULT OFFENDERS. OFFENCES
AGAINST PERSON (EXCLUDING MURDER)

			% sentenced to			
Jurisdiction	Period	No. sentences	Imprison-ment	Fine	Binding over	Corporal punishment
E. Nigeria	1958–63	32,204	42	49	8	—
N. Nigeria	1958–63	2,459	52	35	9	3
W. Nigeria	1958–60	7,101	30	54	11	4
M.-W. Nigeria.	1963	1,091	37	46	13	4
		42,855	45	49	9	9

The most distinctive feature of the patterns illustrated in Table 1
is the relatively lower rate of imprisonment in the Western courts
and their slightly more frequent use of fining. This is maintained
consistently throughout the analysis of specific types of offences
given in the following three tables. In Table 2, which shows the

relatively even balance in the use of imprisonment and fines as sentences for offences against the person, the West shows a preponderance of fines even though its proportion of assaults—offences for which fines are most commonly used—is no higher than that in the other Regions. It is, in fact, some 20 per cent lower than the East's proportion of assaults as 97 per cent of its total offences against the person. The similarity in the figures for bindings over suggests that there is a general agreement that a simple binding over or conditional discharge can be fruitfully used in cases of less serious assault.

TABLE 3. DISPOSAL OF CASES BY HIGH COURTS AND MAGIS-TRATES' COURTS, 1958–63. ADULT OFFENDERS. STEALING AND ALLIED OFFENCES

			% sentenced to			
Jurisdiction	Period	No. sentences	Imprison-ment	Fine	Binding over	Corporal punishment
E. Nigeria	1958–63	28,203	84	14	3	—
N. Nigeria	1958–63	6,692	78	16	2	4
W. Nigeria	1958–60	5,036	67	23	2	8
M.-W. Nigeria	1963	674	78	12	3	5
		40,605	80	15	3	2

In Table 3, the Western Nigeria figure for fines is still somewhat higher than in the other Regions, even though there is a substantial shift in the overall distribution of penalties. Imprisonment is heavily used for stealing and associated offences, presumably on the basis that these are the offences which have caused so much concern in recent years and so are dealt with severely with the intention of deterring, whilst fines of any substantial amount cannot be imposed because of the low economic level of the accused. This is in direct contrast to the situation in Table 2, where fines for assault would not normally be substantial, and to that in Table 4, where it seems likely that the courts may be fining more regularly because the accused have obtained some direct financial advantage from their offences. The courts are always clearly reluctant to allow offenders to hold on to any such benefits, and heavy fines, either alone or together with other penalties, would be a means of both removing

273

any accrued benefit from a fraudulent course of action and demonstrating the unprofitable character of the behaviour.[39]

TABLE 4. DISPOSAL OF CASES BY HIGH COURTS AND MAGISTRATES' COURTS, 1958–63. ADULT OFFENDERS. OFFENCES INVOLVING FRAUD

Jurisdiction	Period	No. sentences	% sentenced to			
			Imprison-ment	Fine	Binding over	Corporal punishment
E. Nigeria	1958–63	6,534	76	20	3	—
N. Nigeria	1958–63	2,649	68	31	2	3
W. Nigeria	1958–60	3,419	49	47	2	2
M.-W. Nigeria	1963	221	62	31	4	2
		12,823	67	29	2	1

The distinctive patterns of Western Nigeria are hard to explain. They may reflect an economic difference: the West is a prosperous Region and the greater availability of money may lead to the courts' greater willingness to impose monetary penalties, bearing in mind that it is a cardinal principle of sentencing that fines should only be imposed on offenders who have the means to meet them. The contrast could certainly be drawn with the less prosperous North and is probably less supportable but still valid with reference to the East and Mid-West. Again, it may reflect the greater sensitivity of the Western bench to penal problems within their cultural setting. During the period under review, the entire bench became indigenous and, though they would necessarily view criminal responsibility through the confusing mists of English legal training, it may be that their cultural affinity with Western Nigeria and their more marked closeness to Yoruba life would make them more aware of the limitations of penal sanctions in small group situations. But this is all surmise.

Outside the field of fining, there is no distinctive Western Nigerian pattern. The patterns of imprisonment—in terms of length of sentence—are given in Table 5. They show, despite concern which has been expressed for many years over the volume of short-term sentences, the continued heavy reliance on sentences of less than six months, though less so in Eastern Nigeria than elsewhere.

TABLE 5. SENTENCES OF IMPRISONMENT BY HIGH COURTS AND MAGISTRATES' COURTS, 1958–63. LENGTH OF IMPRISONMENT

% imprisoned for

Jurisdiction	Period	No. sentences	Less than 3 months	3 months and less than 6	6 months and less than 12	1 year and less than 3	3 years and more
E. Nigeria	1958–63	57,043	29	18	31	17	4
N. Nigeria	1958–63	12,813	42	21	24	9	4
W. Nigeria	1958–63	19,700	43	17	28	9	2
M.-W. Nigeria	1963	2,787	44	18	21	12	5
		92,343	34	23	26	14	3

It would be revealing to compare the sentencing practices of the English and English-trained judges in Nigeria with those of the judges in England, to see how far the assumptions lying behind sentencing have survived the transplanting of the law and legal education. Comparison is made difficult, however, by the vast number of traffic offences—nearly 90 per cent of the total volume of cases—handled by the English magistrates' courts, by the division of the English statistics into those for indictable and those for non-indictable offences, and by the existence of a large non-professional element in the body of English magistrates. In 1963, magistrates sentenced to imprisonment 23 per cent of the male offenders over 17 whom they convicted of indictable crimes and the higher courts 73 per cent. Magistrates imprisoned in 1 per cent of non-indictable cases. All courts fined 46 per cent of those convicted of indictable offences, and magistrates 95 per cent of those not convicted on indictment.[40] The data available on the length of imprisonment passed by the English courts closely resembles that given for Nigerian courts in Table 5.[41]

The data available about sentences of imprisonment[42] on female offenders in Nigeria adds little to the overall picture. The length of imprisonment for women in the Eastern and Western Regions follows the same patterns as in Table 5, though the numbers involved are of course much smaller than for men.[43] The substantial difference appears in the North, where between 1958 and 1963 only forty-three women were imprisoned on the order of magistrates' courts. The explanation for this is probably to be found partly in the social structure of most northern communities, which assigns a completely domestic role to women and so reduces delinquent opportunities, and partly in the administrative relationship between the Federal and native authority police forces. Magistrates' courts deal almost exclusively with cases brought by the Nigeria Police; since this force's investigations are limited to complex cases and those arising in townships, the bulk of offences committed by women—stealing, minor assaults, offences involving prostitution, etc.—will be dealt with by the native authority police and brought before native courts.

TABLE 6. DISPOSAL OF CASES BY HIGH COURTS AND MAGISTRATES' COURTS, 1958–63. JUVENILE OFFENDERS

			% sentenced to			
Jurisdiction	Period covered	No. sentences	Detention	Fine	Binding over	Corporal punishment
E. Nigeria	1958–63	7,054	1	11	6	79
N. Nigeria	1958–63	1,602	8	9	23	57
W. Nigeria	1958–60	1,292	1	31	14	52
M.-W. Nigeria	1963	659	10	14	7	18
		10,607	3	17	9	69

The feature which stands out in respect of juvenile cases is the considerable use of corporal punishment. In Eastern Nigeria it overshadows all other methods of disposing of cases, perhaps reflecting the feeling which in 1955 led the Eastern legislature to prohibit the whipping of adults and limit corporal punishment to juveniles. It is clear that in many of Nigeria's ethnic groups, the highly aggressive punishment of children is commonplace and that the judicial belief in the value of beating children therefore has extensive cultural support.

It is not easy to explain the disparities among the remaining figures. A feature associated with the stronger emphasis on institutional treatment in the North may be that no magistrate's court there sits as a juvenile court. In the East, West and Mid-West, the presence of lay members on such courts may have the effect of curbing the inclinations of the professional chairmen to use detention; in the North, the magistrate is left unchecked by lay members. It may be significant, too, that in the period under review, the Northern magistracy was almost wholly expatriate—a factor which has perhaps had an inevitable impact on sentencing practices. That the percentage of detentions is not outstandingly high in any Region can be accounted for by the small number of approved schools and the resulting limitations on their possible intake.

The differences in the numbers 'bound over'—this category including the making of probation orders—probably reflects the extent of the development of the probation services in the Regions. The Northern service began to develop following the Probation of Offenders Law in 1957 and the period under review here marked the initial period of the expansion of the service under the supervision of overseas technical aid advisers. In the West, a start was made a little earlier but until 1960 the shortage of trained officers was being constantly felt. Probation in Eastern Nigeria was minimal until into the 1960s, the endeavours of the Regional social welfare service being confined to Calabar alone.

V Professional and Customary Courts

For reasons which have already been explained, it is only possible to make a meaningful comparison between the attitudes of the two types of courts in Northern Nigeria.

An initial comparison can be made by reference to Tables 1 and 7. The average rate of imprisoning in the native court system is significantly lower than that of the professional courts. The highest native courts rates, which even then do not approach the professional court average level, are to be found in the Grade A and A Limited courts. These courts try the more serious offences within the native court system but, just as significantly, are all Moslem-controlled courts mainly concentrated in the north of the Region. It may be suggested that it is the authoritarian Islamic tradition and the cultural familiarity with the objectives and practices of imprisonment which predispose these courts to using this method of disposal. The most noticeable difference in the patterns of imprisoning beyond this is that the native courts, consistent with their less frequent use of imprisonment, impose it most often for short periods. Over half the sentences are for three months or less, and it is again only in the higher grades that the more even distribution of terms is to be found.

The rate of fining in the native courts is substantially higher than in the professional courts, and it may be that in fact they try a greater number of petty offences for which fines would normally be imposed. Fining is one of the most familiar forms of punitive but non-institutional sentence and is clearly consistent with some of the objectives of customary sentencing. It is unfortunate that there are not available full data concerning other measures in the same area—compounding, compensating and making restitution. The impression from personal observation is, however, that compounding in the professional courts is never as freely practised as in the 8 per cent of native court cases, and that the observations of Brooke on compensation practices in 1953 are still largely true today.

VI The Native Courts of Northern Nigeria

These courts handle over 95 per cent of all the litigation in the Region and about the same proportion of all the criminal cases. They number over 750, though a large number of the Grade D courts have only civil jurisdiction, or criminal jurisdiction only over marriage offences.[44] All the courts having criminal jurisdiction apply the Penal Code of 1959 as the basic criminal law, together with other legislation which they are specifically given power to apply.

I THE GRADATION OF THE COURTS

The courts are graded according to the extent of their sentencing powers, with the most complete powers (including capital) being exercised by the Grade A courts—that is, the emirs' courts which traditionally have had such jurisdiction—the Grade A Limited courts having unlimited imprisoning and fining powers, and the subordinate grades of B, C and D being limited in terms of the length of imprisonment and the amount of the fine they can impose.[45] The higher courts therefore hear more serious cases and, all other considerations apart, this must be expected to find reflection in the overall patterns of sentencing.

Details of 206,483 cases heard in 1962 and 1963 are given in Tables 7.1 and 7.2. Not all the information available in the original returns is set out here but only that which assists in clarifying the overall picture of judicial activity.[46] The higher the court, the more serious the offence, and therefore the higher the proportion of sentences of imprisonment and of longer sentences of imprisonment. Correspondingly, there are fewer opportunities for fining and probably for compounding offences.[47] The lower the grade of court, the more petty offences it will hear and so the fine will be a more frequent penalty. Imprisonment, when it is imposed at all, is usually short-term and the court's jurisdiction to imprison becomes more limited the lower down the scale it is.[48]

TABLE 7.1. DISPOSAL OF CASES BY NATIVE COURTS, NORTHERN
NIGERIA, 1962–63. COMPARISON BY GRADE OF COURT

Grade	No. cases	% compounded	No. sentences	% sentenced to Fine	% sentenced to Imprisonment
A & A Ltd.	15,425	1	12,514	67	29
B	120,685	7	91,050	64	28
C	52,858	8	40,978	69	22
D	17,515	16	13,612	74	11
	206,483	8	156,154	67	25

TABLE 7.2. SENTENCES OF IMPRISONMENT BY NATIVE COURTS,
NORTHERN NIGERIA, 1962–63. COMPARISON BY LENGTH AND
GRADE OF COURT

Grade	No. sentences	% imprisoned for 3 months or less	More than 3 months and less than 12	12 months and more
A & A Ltd.	3,638	35	31	33
B	25,494	58	28	13
C	9,015	49	24	26
D	1,497	64	35	
	39,644	54	27	18

Comparisons between the grades of court, however, are likely to conceal substantial differences of approach to sentencing problems between courts of the same grade. One of the most revealing intra-grade studies would probably be that of urban and rural sentencing patterns, but it is not possible to carry out such a study from the available data.[49] What is possible is the examination of patterns established in Moslem and non-Moslem courts and in different general areas of the Region.

2 MOSLEM AND NON-MOSLEM PATTERNS

If the characteristics of Moslem and non-Moslem attitudes already discussed are based on valid generalizations, the Moslem-controlled courts may be expected to treat criminals in a more authoritarian way than the non-Moslem, while the latter will favour more regular peaceable and consensual settlement of disputes (compounding) and make greater use of non-immobilizing penalties.

The Moslem-controlled courts of Northern Nigeria can be clearly identified as those of the traditional rulers and their judges (*alkalai*). It is less easy to identify those which are not Moslem-controlled. Many multiple-member courts will include both Moslems and non-Moslems; others will have no Moslem members at all but serve the interests of small non-Moslem communities in Moslem-dominated areas. Overall differences in the following review of their sentencing patterns may therefore tend to be concealed by the inclusion of some strongly Moslem-influenced courts in the category of non-Moslem.

TABLE 8. DISPOSAL OF CASES BY NATIVE COURTS, NORTHERN NIGERIA, 1962–63. COMPARISON BY NATURE OF COURT

Type of court	No. cases	% com-pounded	No. sen-tences	Fines	Imprison-ment	3 months or less	More than 3 months and less than 12	12 months and more
						% sentenced to	% imprisoned for	
Moslem	137,050	7	105,607	65	29	55	28	14
Non-Moslem	69,433	9	52,547	70	20	51	34	13
	206,483	8	158,154	67	25	54	27	18

As Table 8 shows, the simple differentiation of Moslem and non-Moslem courts reveals no substantial variations. The variations are concealed within the gradation of the courts within these two categories and their intra-Regional distribution. Tables 9.1 and 9.2 show the significance of the gradation factor. There are only slight but consistent differences between the patterns at the Grades B and C levels. At the Grade B level, there are marginally lower percentages of imprisonment and a higher percentage of fines imposed by the non-Moslem courts, but these insignificant differences in one direction are counterbalanced by an unexpectedly higher proportion of long-term imprisonments in those courts. At the Grade C level, the principal differences seem to be a greater use of fining and compounding by the non-Moslem courts and a less frequent use of imprisonment, though the percentages of long and short sentences are the same. The same pattern appears at the Grade D level with an even greater disparity between the proportions of cases compounded.

TABLE 9.1. DISPOSAL OF CASES BY NATIVE COURTS, NORTHERN NIGERIA, 1962–63. COMPARISON BY NATURE AND GRADE OF COURT

Grade of court[a]	Nature of court	No. cases	% compounded	No. sentences	% sentenced to	
					Fine	Imprisonment
B	Moslem	84,376	8	63,423	63	30
	Non-Moslem	36,309	4	27,627	65	22
C	Moslem	36,515	6	29,072	69	25
	Non-Moslem	16,343	13	11,906	78	17
D	Moslem	734	4	598	68	25
	Non-Moslem	16,781	16	13,014	74	18
		191,058	8	145,640	67	25

[a] No comparison is possible in Grades A and A Limited as there are no non-Moslem courts in these grades.

TABLE 9.2. SENTENCES OF IMPRISONMENT BY NATIVE COURTS, NORTHERN NIGERIA, 1962–63. COMPARISON BY LENGTH AND NATURE AND GRADE OF COURT

Grade of court[a]	Nature of court	No. sentences	% imprisoned for		
			3 months or less	More than 3 months and less than 12	12 months and more
B	Moslem	19,027	62	26	11
	Non-Moslem	6,078	47	35	16
C	Moslem	7,268	50	35	14
	Non-Moslem	2,024	50	36	14
D	Moslem	150	84	15	—
	Non-Moslem	2,343	63	35	—
		36,890	59	28	12

[a] See note to Table 9.1.

3 INTRA-REGIONAL VARIATIONS

The patterns can be probed further by comparison of the returns from different parts of the Region. Three main zones can be delineated:

(1) North-Northern Nigeria is predominantly Moslem and comprises the provinces of Sokoto, Katsina, Kano and Bornu. Adherence to the Islamic religion and its distinctive cultural ideas is traditional and rigid.

(2) Mid-Northern Nigeria includes the provinces of Niger, Zaria, Plateau, Bauchi, Adamawa and Sardauna. The rigid patterns seen in the North zone penetrate into this zone but there are vast areas inhabited by pagan peoples who are unaffected by either Islamic or western civilization.

TABLE 10.1. DISPOSAL OF CASES BY MOSLEM NATIVE COURTS, NORTHERN NIGERIA, 1962–63. COMPARISON BY GRADE OF COURT AND ZONE

					% sentenced to	
Grade of court	Zone	No. cases	% compounded	No. sentences	Fine	Imprisonment
A and A Ltd.	North	9,147	—	7,295	61	31
	Mid	6,278	—	5,219	74	22
	South	a	a	a	a	a
B	North	47,055	6	35,287	61	33
	Mid	35,557	12	26,543	65	28
	South	1,764	1	1,593	91	7
C	North	27,165	7	21,238	66	27
	Mid	6,811	2	5,670	78	18
	South	2,539	6	2,164	72	19
D	North	306	—	226	53	39
	Mid	111	8	92	76	21
	South	317	7	280	77	15
		137,050	7	105,607	65	29

a Numbers negligible.

283

(3) South-Northern Nigeria, represented by Ilorin, Kabba and Benue, marks the southern limits of the Fulani emirates. It has, however, been exposed to the influences of Christianity and European culture and education and, except for parts of Benue, the unaffected pagan element has been substantially reduced.

The Moslem courts of all grades in the North zone show the predicted tendencies (Tables 10.1 and 10.2). The percentage of cases dealt with by imprisonment in these courts never falls below 27 per cent, whereas this is the highest proportion reached by any of the Moslem courts in the other zones. In the South zone, the level of imprisonment drops sharply, suggesting that the cultural patterns are still influenced more by the well-developed customary legal ideas of the Yoruba and their associated tribal groups than by those of the Moslem culture of the North.[50] On the other hand, the

TABLE 10.2. SENTENCES OF IMPRISONMENT BY MOSLEM NATIVE COURTS, NORTHERN NIGERIA, 1962–63. COMPARISON BY LENGTH, GRADE OF COURT AND ZONE

			% imprisoned for		
Grade of court	Zone	No. sentences	3 months or less	More than 3 months or less than 12	12 months and more
A and A Ltd.	North	2,261	35	31	33
	Mid	1,148	35	33	31
	South	a	a	a	a
B	North	11,645	66	23	10
	Mid	7,432	56	31	12
	South	112	32	43	24
C	North	5,734	50	34	15
	Mid	1,021	55	37	7
	South	411	35	40	24
D	North	a	a	a	a
	Mid	a	a	a	a
	South	a	a	a	a
		29,764	55	28	14

a Numbers negligible.

Moslem courts in the South zone on the whole prefer to use longer sentences of imprisonment, the percentage of sentences longer than three months being considerably greater than for shorter periods in both the Grade B and C courts. It may be that these figures do not reliably indicate any attitude, as in both grades the number of cases involved is relatively small. The most that can be suggested with confidence is that these courts are reluctant to use imprisonment at all but that they do so as a last resort where no other punishment can be devised or the community can be protected in no other way.

The contrast offered by the non-Moslem courts at all levels is well-marked (Tables 11.1 and 11.2). Imprisonment is less frequently used and, except for the South zone, long-term imprisonment is considerably restricted. Fining remains at a high level throughout. By far the most distinctive feature is the exceptionally high rate of compounding in the Grade C and D courts of the Mid zone. It originates in the isolated and mainly pagan areas of Sardauna, Plateau and southern Zaria Provinces. If the data are accurate, they provide

TABLE 11.1. DISPOSAL OF CASES BY NON-MOSLEM NATIVE COURTS, NORTHERN NIGERIA, 1962–63. COMPARISON BY GRADE OF COURT AND ZONE

					% sentenced to	
Grade of court[a]	Zone	No. cases	% compounded	No. sentences	Fine	Imprisonment
B	North	4,239	4	3,692	61	16
	Mid	6,573	9	5,693	67	26
	South	25,497	3	18,242	65	22
C	North	1,201	3	942	67	26
	Mid	11,931	17	8,120	82	14
	South	3,211	3	2,844	70	21
D	North	229	—	60	b	b
	Mid	10,189	25	7,451	75	18
	South	6,363	3	5,503	74	18
		69,433	9	52,547	70	20

[a] No comparison is possible in Grades A and A Limited as there are no non-Moslem courts in these grades.

[b] Numbers negligible.

excellent support for the proposition that the tendency of some customary laws to encourage the settlement of cases, and not to be concerned with authoritarian repression, has survived the change in the structure of adjudication—customary law to Penal Code—unaffected.[51]

TABLE 11.2. SENTENCES OF IMPRISONMENT BY NON-MOSLEM NATIVE COURTS, NORTHERN NIGERIA, 1962–63. COMPARISON BY LENGTH, GRADE OF COURT AND ZONE

Grade of court[a]	Zone	No. sentences	% imprisoned for		
			3 months or less	More than 3 months and less than 12	12 months and more
B	North	591	84	8	7
	Mid	148	50	44	5
	South	4,013	41	32	26
C	North	245	44	33	21
	Mid	1,137	54	35	10
	South	397	42	39	18
D	North	b	b	b	b
	Mid	1,341	68	31	—
	South	991	56	42	—
		8,863	51	34	13

[a] For footnotes see Table 11.1.

VII Conclusion

Individual sentencing attitudes are not, of course, clearly revealed by bare figures. The various methods of disposing of offenders can each reflect more than one judicial attitude and it is not possible to identify any particular one from the figures alone. Both retributive

286

and deterrent approaches may be concealed in the data for imprisonment and fines; and some judges may use both of these methods with socially adjustive purposes in mind. Of the data given in this chapter, only those for binding over and compounding properly reflect an unalloyed adjustive philosophy, and it is only unfortunate that information is not available about probation and compensation practices to round out this picture.

By quantifying that which is available, however, it has proved possible to relate judicial sentencing practices, superficially at least, to the cultures of which the sentencers are part. English judges and English-trained Nigerian judges no more form a consistent and homogeneous group than do all the customary and native court judges. But their sentencing practices bear the distinctive mark of the English legal attitudes in which they were all trained. Without doing too much injustice to the Islamic tradition in Northern Nigeria, it may be said that similar cultural attitudes to those of the English lawyers appear there too. And in the non-Moslem native courts there is a distinct suggestion that sentencing practices remain influenced by the nature of the organization of the local communities and the values formerly expressed in their customary laws.

It is especially important to see how cultural legal attitudes can survive a change in the structure of adjudication. This chapter is not designed to answer the many doubts that have been expressed about the ability of the Northern native courts to handle the conceptualization of the new criminal law introduced by the Penal Code. Nor can statistics say whether individual courts or groups of courts are unjustifiably severe or lenient, or whether appropriate methods have been used for particular offenders. But it can be demonstrated that at the level at which the suitability of law for a culture can be seen in practical terms, the Northern reforms of 1959 and 1960 have not suppressed customary attitudes. It is still possible, within the broad framework of disposal adopted by the Codes, for adjudication to be sensitive to the ideas of the culture— and this, slight though it may be, is some measure of the success of the reforms.

NOTES

1. See, e.g., the terms imposed by Lugard on Kano and Sokoto: *Annual Colonial Reports, Northern Nigeria, 1900–1911*, 92–3, 164.
2. Native Courts Proclamation, 1900, s. 9 (N.N.). The limitation does not appear in Southern Nigeria until 1914: Native Courts Ordinance, 1914, s. 9 (S.N.).
3. Ordeal, Witchcraft and Juju Proclamation, 1903 (S.N.), 1908 (N.N.).
4. It was first the subject of treaties with local coastal rulers and was then regulated on a broader basis by the Slave-dealing Ordinance, 1874 (Gold Coast Colony), the Emancipation Ordinance, 1874 (Gold Coast Colony), the Slavery Proclamation, 1901 (N.N.), the Slave-dealing Proclamation, 1901 (S.N.) and the Slavery Abolition Ordinance, 1916.
5. See footnote 2 above; in the south there was at first an additional requirement that punishments in default of payment of fines should be 'not repugnant to natural justice or to the principles of the law of England': Native Courts Proclamation, 1901, s. 27 (S.N.).
6. His account of the gruesome prison conditions he found in Kano is given in *Annual Colonial Reports, Northern Nigeria, 1900–1911*, 83–9: 'A small doorway, 2 ft., 6 in. × 1 ft., 6 in. gives access to it. . . . The interior . . . wall was pierced with holes at its base through which the legs of those sentenced to death were thrust up to the thigh, and they were left to be trodden on by the mass of the other prisoners till they died of thirst and starvation. . . . Recently, as many as 200 have been sentenced at one time. As the superficial ground area was only 238 square feet, there was not, of course, even standing room. Victims were crushed to death every night and their corpses were hauled out in the morning. . . .'
7. See, e.g., beheading—Talbot, *The Peoples of Southern Nigeria*, vol. III, 634, 635, 637 (1926) (of the Yoruba and Edo-speaking groups); stoning—Ruxton, *Maliki Law*, 331 (1916); Al Qayrawani, *La Risala*, transl. Bercher, 5th ed., 253, 355 (1960); drowning—Hassan and Ahuaibu Na'ibi, *A Chronicle of Aduja*, transl. Heath, 10 (1962); burying alive—Bradbury, *The Benin Kingdom and the Edo-Speaking Peoples of South-Western Nigeria*, 119 (1957); *Annual Colonial Reports, Northern Nigeria, 1900–1911*, 71 (an isolated incident in Zaria); Meek, *Law and Authority in a Nigerian Tribe*, 216 (1937) (of the Ibo).
8. Lugard had specifically approved beheading and drowning as humane. *Political Memoranda, 1913–1918*, Memo. VIII, para. 34. The information about beheading is taken from *Returns of Capital Sentences, Northern Provinces*, S.N.P. 17/2, Nos. 1169, 1170, 2 vols., National Archives, Kaduna; The public hangman is first mentioned in connection with native court death sentences in 1938: see *Northern Provinces Office Guide*, 35, para. 14, n. (ii) (1932), amendment of January 1938.
9. Flogging was abolished for statutory offences (Criminal Code (Amendment) Ordinance, 1933, s. 4) and the Native Courts (Corporal Punishment)

Regulations, 1933, specified the details of the punishment allowed. The whip (of the *bulala* type) was retained for punishments in Moslem courts, the cane specified for use in other native courts. Despite immediate local and administrative protests that the cane was more brutal than methods previously used, no further change was made at that time: see *Corporal Punishment in Nigeria*, S.N.P. 17/2, No. 3049, 200–42, National Archives, Kaduna.

10. E.g. Native Courts Proclamation, 1901, ss. 14, 16 (S.N.), setting out the limits of the jurisdiction of 'Native councils' and 'minor courts'.

11. Native Courts Proclamation, 1900, s. 8 (N.N.), continued for the whole country by the Native Courts Ordinance, 1914, s. 10.

12. Native Courts Proclamation, 1901, s. 18 (S.N.); Native Courts Ordinance, 1914, s. 12.

13. *Reports of the Native Courts (Northern Provinces) Commission of Inquiry*, para. 553 (1952).

14. Criminal Code (Amendment) Ordinance, 1933, s. 2.

15. On September 9th, 1933, the Governor issued a draft of the new corporal punishment regulations and required them to be enforced by executive action until they were formally approved. His general instructions were issued at the same time. A further memorandum explaining the new situation with regard to corporal punishment was issued in December 1934: see *Corporal Punishment in Nigeria*, at 110–13, 215–18. By 1936, the administration apparently believed that for native courts to order whipping for a customary offence, when the Code did not specify it for such an offence, was contrary to natural justice: see *ibid.*, at 300.

16. (1947), 12 W.A.C.A. 141.

17. Their legal significance is dealt with in detail and with appropriate criticism in the *Report of the Native Courts (Northern Provinces) Commission of Inquiry*, paras. 460–85 (1952); Gower, *Nigerian Statutes and Customary Law*, *1 Nigerian Law Journal*, 73, 74–80 (1964), and with varying historical interpretations by Brown, C.J., in *Fagoji v. Kano Native Authority*, 1957 N.R.N.L.R. 57, 58–59; Jibowu, Ag. F.C.J., in *Jalo Tsamiya v. Bauchi Native Authority*, 1957 N.R.N.L.R. 73, 75–82, and Foster Sutton, F.C.J., in *Maizabo v. Sokoto Native Authority*, 1957 N.R.N.L.R. 133, 135–9.

18. Native Courts Ordinance, 1948, s. 3.

19. Native Courts (Amendment) Ordinance, 1951, s. 10A.

20. See Customary Courts Law, 1956, s. 24 (E.N.); Customary Courts Law, 1959 Laws, cap. 31, s. 21 (W.N.); Native Courts Law, 1956, s. 22 (N.N.).

21. Penal Code Law, 1959, s. 2 (3).

22. Customary Courts (Amendment) Law, 1959, s. 9.

23. Constitution of the Federation, 1960, s. 21 (10), re-enacted in the 1963 Constitution, s. 22 (9).

24. *Aoko v. Fagbemi*, (1961) 1 All N.L.R. 400. Cf. a similar conviction based on adultery, reported in the *Daily Times*, February 22nd, 1965, which had successfully negotiated both Grade A and B customary courts in Ibadan before

being quashed by the High Court. For further illustrations, see Okonkwo and Naish, *Criminal Law in Nigeria*, 12 (1964).

25. Penal Code Law, 1959, ss. 387–8, 400, 403.

26. *Ibid.*, s. 68 (2).

27. E.g. under the Native Authority Law, 1954, s. 43 (9) (N.N.). The powers under s. 48 of this law to make a declaration of customary law presumably cannot be used to declare a customary offence in view of the provisions of the Penal Code: see, e.g., the Native Authority (Idoma and Borgu Native Marriage Law and Custom) Orders, 1959 and 1961, paras. (2) (polyandry), (3) (knowingly marrying within prohibited degrees) and (18) (inducing desertion by wife).

28. Hood, *Sentencing in Magistrates' Courts* (1962); Glueck, *The Sentencing Problem*, 20 *Federal Probation* 15 (1956), and studies cited there.

29. See esp. Green, *Judicial Attitudes in Sentencing*, chap. 1 (1961), and studies cited there.

30. Throughout this period, outbreaks of rioting and assault, which were confined to Benue Province, were dealt with by the Makurdi court. I am grateful to the Hon. Chief Justice of Northern Nigeria for allowing these inquiries to be made and to my research assistants Niyi Oshe and Paul Anyebe for collecting the data.

31. I have dealt with this judicial attitude more fully in 'The Sanctions of Customary Criminal Law: A Study in Social Control', 1 *Nigerian Law Journal*, 173 (1965). What promise to be classic analyses of the attitude are to be found in Gluckman, *The Judicial Process among the Barotse of Northern Rhodesia*, 20–1 (1955) and *The Ideas in Barotse Jurisprudence*, esp. chap. 1 (1965).

32. *Political Memoranda, 1913–1918*, Memo VIII, para. 54; Memo III, para. 23.

33. *Native Courts Commissions of Inquiry, 1947–1952, Appendix and Summary of Recommendations*, 105–6 (1953).

34. *Ibid.*, 106.

35. Tables headed 'Persons in prison during the year' are misleading: the figures in fact give the details of sentences of imprisonment passed during the year.

36. No returns have been published (or apparently collected) for Lagos since regionalization, or for Western Nigeria since 1960.

37. E.g. sentences of corporal punishment passed by native courts in the North were apparently added in error into the figures for magistrates' courts in 1960 and 1962, increasing the totals from 87 and 93 to 3,673 and 3,806 respectively: see *Annual Abstract of Statistics*, 1963, Table 127. The 1964 *Annual Abstract* credits the Northern magistrates' courts with the power to apply the death penalty: see Table 16.11.

38. Since the number of cases dealt with in each of the following tables is so large, and the proportions of cases dealt with either 100 per cent or only as low as 95 per cent of those arising, the level of statistical significance is, of course, too high for the meaningful application of approved tests of signi-

ficance. I am grateful to Mr D. Akman, of the University of Pennsylvania Center of Criminological Research, for helpful discussion of the statistical implications of my data and suggestions for improving the form of the tables.

39. This view is admittedly impressionistic and assumes the practice of imposing substantial fines for this range of offences. Whether they are in fact substantial is not disclosed in the published data.

40. *Criminal Statistics, England & Wales, 1963,* Cmnd. 2525, chaps. 6–8 (1964).

41. Hall Williams, 'The Use the Courts Make of Prison', in Halmos, ed., *Sociological Studies in the British Penal Services,* (Soc. Rev. Monograph No. 9), 49 (1965).

42. No information is available about other sentences on women offenders.

43. The annual averages from available data are 586 (E. Nigeria, 1958–63), 453 (W. Nigeria, 1958–60), 7 (N. Nigeria, 1958–63), 85 (M.-W. Nigeria, 1963).

44. See Native Courts (Jurisdiction and Powers) Notice, 1962 (N.N.) as amended.

45. The jurisdictional limits are set in the Native Courts Law, 1963 Laws, cap. 78, s. 17 (1) and First Schedule.

46. Four specific types of information are not dealt with: (1) sentences of death —these normally amount to less than twenty a year and are exclusively within the jurisdiction of the Grade A courts; (2) imprisonments in default of fine; (3) corporal punishment—this is consistently used but seldom reaches more than 2 per cent of the sentences in any grade or type of court; (4) acquittals. The *haddi* lashing, specifically permitted for Moslem offenders in certain cases, is only of importance in the orthodox areas of the far North and is not regularly used further south. It is, however, included in the estimated 2 per cent given in (3) above.

47. Twenty-five out of twenty-eight compoundable offences are triable in all the courts from Grade D native court and Grade III magistrates' court upwards: since they are cognizable by the lower native courts they will, therefore, seldom reach the higher.

48. The maximum imprisonments available to each grade of court are: Grade A and A Limited—no maximum; Grade B—3 years; Grade C—18 months; Grade D—9 months; Native Courts Law, First Schedule, Part 1.

49. Census data are notoriously unreliable and thus raise the basic hurdle of the impossibility of identifying urban areas by reference to population size. Moreover, comparison would only be possible at the lower levels of courts: the higher grade courts are entirely urban, though their jurisdiction necessarily extends over large rural areas.

50. Cf. Anderson, 'Conflict of Laws in Northern Nigeria', 8 *International and Comparative Law Quarterly,* 442 (1959), who noted the low rate of *diya* (blood money) paid by Yoruba Moslems when compared with the more orthodox areas of Northern Nigeria; in *Islamic Law in Africa,* 197 (1954), Anderson noted the frequent ignoring of the 'obligatory' Moslem penalty for drinking, among the Moslem Yoruba. Examination of the native court returns

for 1962–3 confirms that the *haddi* lashing was rarely invoked for any offence in the Yoruba areas.

51. These are the courts about which, by reason of their isolation, low-level administrative skills and irregular supervision, some doubts have arisen in relation to the accuracy of data supplied and, at a judicial level, to the precision with which the new Codes are applied. Yet even if, as has been suggested to me, the range of compoundings reported is swollen by the courts' misunderstanding of the limited range of offences which can be compounded, the proposition in the text is not weakened. It may even be strengthened; for a court to allow the illegal compounding of offences shows its complete devotion to the principle.

11
The East African Experience of Imprisonment

RALPH E. S. TANNER

I Introduction

Africans convicted of criminal offences have been confined in government prisons, controlled by Prison Departments by means of rules and orders based largely on English penal precedents,[1] since the earliest days of colonial rule.

It has sometimes been thought that the passivity of African convicts in prison and the lack of tension with which they move in and out of prison, is due to the fact that prison represents a marked improvement on anything that they might experience in their own way of life and that therefore they like prison and regard it as an hotel. Consequently, prisons do not penalize or reform, but only confine willing prisoners. The English lawyer remarks, 'It means nothing to them. It's a hotel. Good food, plenty of sleep and not too much hard work. No wonder crime increases.' It is therefore intended to examine their experience of imprisonment to test this stereotype.

Detailed observations were carried out in one East African prison and prisoners were given the opportunity of expressing their opinions freely or in answer to specific questions. The quotations which appear in this chapter are from essays written by English-speaking convicts—which are given without correction in the form in which they were originally expressed—or from vernacular essays translated by the author. In addition, the author had the benefit of administrative experience in seven other East African prisons and became widely conversant with the views of convicts, social workers and magistrates.

The prison examined in detail held an average of 900 convicts in conditions of medium security. It was intended to be a first offenders' prison but during the year in which the study was undertaken it also held a proportion of recidivists awaiting transfer to other prisons. Of the prisoners, 87 per cent were Africans; the balance non-Africans. The largest single group of offenders were those convicted of theft (20 per cent); violence against the person accounted for 12·6 per cent; drunkenness 11 per cent; burglary 10·6 per cent.[2]

The physical environment was reasonably comfortable. In construction, the prison had an administrative block around the gate and the prison area beyond, in which the cell blocks and work sheds were in a half-circle round a wide asphalt and grass-patched courtyard in which a few trees were growing. The overall impression was one of spaciousness, with large open spaces between the buildings and in the centre, and white perimeter walls which did not menace or give any appearance of height.

Most of the convicts lived in cell dormitories with lavatories attached, rather than in small cells. This, combined with bars instead of walls or doors in many places, meant that there was little privacy. There were a few unpleasant smells, usually confined only to the small cells, which contained a lavatory bucket for night use.

Noise in the cell blocks were noticeable: loud talking and shouting with its echoes, the clatter of food utensils and the clanging of doors. No convict complained about this noise nor of the physical proximity of others all the time. The prison gave the appearance of cleanness and brightness; only the alcoves for seeing visitors, with their shade and glass partitions, were depressing.

The weather is uniform with only mild variations between hot and cool seasons, and appears to have no influence on the incidents involving the breaking of prison rules recorded for the prison over several years.

The physical environment within the prison could not be related to the home conditions of any of the convicts. In terms of water to hand, food in quantity and at regular times, healthy conditions and the availability of medical help, and even in material possessions, the majority of convicts were undoubtedly better off in prison than they would have been in their own homes.

II The Psychological Environment

The convicts in general regarded prison conditions as unpleasant but not hard. Recidivists often compared it unfavourably to the old days when work was harder and staff attitudes and conduct, although harsher, were in their opinion both standard and predictable. A number commented that each of the senior staff had his own separate rules which he tried to administer, particularly concerning the attitude to adopt when making a request, when to wear tunics and when to talk. Such minor variations seemed to take on high importance, so much so that they considered it difficult to conform to a pattern of behaviour acceptable to authority as a whole.

> In fact in prison we have no converted people. Although some are not wholly converted their margin between the obedient and the disobedient is very small. No matter how they try to be obedient and error-proof, nature would never allow them to be so due to unworkable rules of the prison department. They are very coward people. Polite in manners who have suffered shocks of life. A family type; always talks about romance.

Every convict stated that the worst thing about prison was the plain fact of the deprivation of liberty regardless of whether the prison was hard or comfortable. They were prevented from enjoying everything which they held to be good in life. Every convict interviewed expressed the opinion, both for himself and other convicts with whom he was associated, that, no matter how poor the material conditions outside, no one would seek imprisonment for food and shelter. They stressed that the community life round their homes under any conditions provided satisfactions which prison could never replace. They did not like prison, except possibly for a small number of multiple recidivists for small offences who appeared to regard prisons as the only constant dependable factor in their very uncertain lives. The warm climate limits the needs of vagrants, who do not need to seek shelter on this account alone.

Prison life is one of the worst lives one can lead. Anybody in prison is always behind the time outside. In prison one is unable to do anything he wants because life is too routine. One is forced to sleep even if he does not want. It is not bad to keep discipline but in prison it is too exaggerated.

Many convicts commented on the traumatic effect of the first experience of prison, but it was obvious that this stunning shock wore off after a very short period, possibly not lasting as long as a week. This, of course, was confined to first offenders and may, in fact, have worn off through the experience of being on remand before and during the trial long before the man is sentenced.

He is convicted, sentenced and sent to where many other unlucky people like him have landed and vaved their worried and live a care free life. They fell at home while the new adminission is full of fear and worried thinking the next few days will look like. On first arrival the others tell the unhappy new admission is not to worry two years is nothing. Here we are always happy despite lack of some luxuries. In course of two days his worries and fear are almost wiped away.

Nevertheless, this familiarity with the continuance of imprisonment did not diminish the pain of this loss of liberty—it was there all the time. The convict adapted very quickly to the idea of imprisonment so that the general tenor of the prison was a passive, if not willing, acceptance of the conditions, anxiety being identifiable with prisoners who had received more than primary education. Unpleasant though it was in prison, it was not a situation which provoked resentment either in theory or practice.

Few appeared anxious about their families, as they were assumed to be looked after by their relatives and, at the same time, the prison welfare services did what they could to organize relief for those in serious difficulties. A parallel was drawn between a prison sentence and a period of migrant labour away from home; the man did not appear to make any special arrangements or to feel that he ought to make any. Those who did worry could not have it relieved by letters since they were predominantly illiterate and letters would not in any case be an easy medium for the relief of such tension. The permitted visits also could not help in most cases, since the prison was near to few homes and even fewer of the families could afford the fare to come. Special arrangements are made for family visits to long-term prisoners, who have not been visited for long periods. No prisoner took his full entitlement of letters and visits.[3]

The convicts were thus emotionally involved in the outside world but not apparently in relation to a limited number of persons with definite roles, as would be the case in a society composed of nuclear families; they longed to be free, but were not subject to the tensions related to a particular woman or child.

III Social and Personal Equilibrium

For the vast majority of the convicts a state of personal and social equilibrium in relation to the demands of prison life was very soon reached. It is probably true that only the convict with some education may suffer a character deterioration. The majority find adaptation comparatively easy because of the normal subordination of personality in outside life to the group requirements of the family, lineage, clan and tribe. There was an easy familiarity in their response to the demands of routine which they interpreted as orders.

Possibly the educated convict of post-primary standard is able to fend off deterioration by preserving his superiority, helping others in their writing of letters and petitions, and keeping himself noticeably neater than the average convict. The prison authorities tend to have a stereotype of the convict as a stupid and bovine man. The convicts were aware of this and the intelligent, though not necessarily educated, ones accepted the implications of this stereotype, and manipulated authority from within this characterization. This often provided these men with the mental stimulus and material rewards which enabled them to pass their sentences in comparative ease. The stereotype of dullness and passivity was more a surface judgment on the mass rather than on the individual, whom the authorities, under existing bureaucratic conditions, have little opportunity of getting to know or understanding.

The equilibrium was replaced by some anxiety during the period immediately before release, particularly among the educated, who appeared to get worried about their status after release rather than about the difficulty of finding employment.

> Everytime I think of going to the big offices looking for a job a big lump of anger strangles in my throat because the only greetings I will receive will be universal 'have you ever been convicted'. I will find all my friends holding big responsible positions; hence they will take me for a spoilt man who can be good enough to dust their shoes. I choose to be a hermit for some time. Will all my friends trust me anymore.

Within the prison there were few extreme personality problems. Their small numbers make it possible for administrative rather than medical action to mitigate situations which otherwise might become serious. The aggressive psychopath can be given useless supervisory work to do which relieves his tensions; the homosexual aggressor can be moved from cell block to cell block so that his activities cause less disturbance, and the deeply introverted convict can be left to sit in the sun where he irritates no one. In medical terms, the seriously ill were looked after, even if the psychotic were ignored.

The convicts did not suffer from a deprivation of goods and services, since their major loss was of choice only. The standard of the prison's material services was above that of the home life of the majority, and indeed, in many cases, they readily admitted that this was so. The prison earning scheme, which allowed convicts at work to earn up to twenty cents (East African)[4] per day and to spend up to two-thirds of this money on tobacco, food and other small luxuries, has meant that goods were available in the prison in both satisfying and stimulating quantities for men who normally had little material wealth.

> Some don't want to go home. They say that in prison I get everything given to me by the authorities like blankets, food,

and even a monthly salary to buy sugar and cigarettes. So that I won't lose remission or get my salary cut, whatever I am told by the warders or senior officers I must follow.

The limited availability of goods was also eased by the relative simplicity of smuggling and the fact that even rubbish-accumulation can supply some of their needs for status by possession and for exchange; every search produced bottles, tins, rags, string, small articles of tin and wood manufactured within the prison, tinder sets and paper, with which a large part of the trading within the prison was carried on from day to day.

Within their passive acceptance of imprisonment their complaints concerned the monotony of the diet and the latrine facilities in the small cells, though they admitted that the latter was balanced by the satisfaction of privacy. The majority, in fact, gave confinement as their main complaint. The authorities assumed that the convicts had only material needs and that these were satisfied, while the convicts made few references of their own volition to these so-called material satisfactions.

Few commented on the loss of heterosexual relationships. It did not appear to be a major problem of adjustment since within the prison they were not exposed to, nor did they react in their life outside to, visual erotic stimuli. There were few, if any, pin-ups or treasured photographs, and indeed only one case of pornography was known to the staff. The majority made an easy adjustment by the mere fact of the absence of women, although outside they had exclusively heterosexual relationships. In effect problems of adjustment were assisted by nocturnal emission, rather than by masturbation. A few succeeded in obtaining women during the course of outside work. The majority could understand but not tolerate homosexuality in others, and they constantly referred to the practice in admonitory terms, often trying to report physical acts to the warders.

He adopted an human behaviour of playing homosexual intercourse with the younger convicts. This made him to be disliked nearly by every convict. His life in the prison became tougher and could not associate with anybody with understanding. There are rumours of his evil doings.

A few made quasi-normal adjustments by adopting homo-sexual practices while in prison in order to get material advantages in the form of extra food or tobacco for consumption or trade. A further group entered the prison with homosexual traits already in existence and provided a service for the previous group; they were mainly Arabs or Somalis. They were not usually identifiable by ways of dressing or mannerisms. The majority of all fights were over what prisoners call their 'wives'.

He uses much ingenuity to steal the extra food or to make the necessary secret tradings with the cooks to get out extras. He eats this extra food with a certain young man who he has established as his wife. The others who sleep in the same dormitory cell say that he tells the young man that he will have no troubles during his sentence while the old man is there.

He doesn't like to work with his hands. He likes to sit and get his work task done by another. He likes to be clean. He doesn't like to talk to anyone else except the man who does his work for him. This man's body has changed to look like a woman's. He likes very much sweet things and that other man brings him sugar from his monthly canteen purchase even though he could buy it from his own money. He is like a small child as even a woman makes an effort to work with her hands. These are his habits only in prison. All the time he uses his eyes to glance about like a woman and even his voice has gone high to sound like a woman.

The convicts had lost their personal autonomy but they perhaps considered that its exercise outside the prison was more of a dis-advantage than an asset: the changing world had hurt them. The prison provided a social service which was parallel to their con-ception of a satisfactory family life outside.

There is a big difference between authority outside and inside the prison. Inside authority looks after you as a mother cares for her child, whereas outside it is as the child looked after by his parents.

Obviously, the convict's life is dominated by rules which he is ostensibly powerless to change, but the majority did not find this a difficult situation. They did not deny either the right of the state to punish them or that the prison authorities, as part of this power, might do it in this way or that, according to their wishes. Statements of convicts, juvenile delinquents and school children, both Moslem and Christian, on the characteristics of a good person, repetitively stressed, to the exclusion of almost any other point, that obedience to parents, teachers and government was all that was required. This has the corollary that the staff should obey the rules as well; they were willing to obey an order which had formal backing but not those which were felt by them to be personal and local variations without higher authority.

> Here in the prison I must obey the orders of the officer in charge as I am under his authority and if I do not I will be heavily punished in just the same way as when I disobeyed my father.

Those who did not fit into this pattern were those who had been longest away from their tribal environment and who had changed to a more individual response to authority, while perhaps receiving the least satisfaction from the change. They were out of place and could not manipulate an environment approximating to the tribal one from which they had moved away. They found the triviality of most of the staff's control irritating, particularly as the majority of the warders had only received primary education.

> I could see nobody of my equal apart from the commotion of poorly dressed chaps who still are my fellow inmates. I could read even far much better than the receiving warders. My situations were aggravated by the under-rational I was met with even from people I didn't and still don't trust that they were of any value to any class of society on the globe. The convict doesn't acquire even the least degree of rehabilitation; this is simply because the warders under whose observation he is kept are not better than an uncultured scrub completely nude of outside world evolution.

Within this atmosphere of passive acceptance, the staff did not demand compliance but rather took for granted the habit of accepting it, which they characterized as co-operation. This compliance came easily to the majority of the convicts; government has the power, therefore it has the authority; and this authority, within their own experience of the tribe or community, must have been approved, to exist in the first place. But at the same time there existed in the system a socially recognized system of manipulating those in authority not so markedly different from the methods and ideology with which they would have approached an outside authority. The convicts did and said what authority wanted and expected of them until they were out of sight. In addition, the authorities were as neutral to them as they were to authority— neither really wanted trouble in the prison and the convict was reluctant to do anything which predictably would cause him further inconvenience in the form of loss of remission or other penalties. Both geographically and socially, the staff and the convicts lived together, and it was only by the exercise of considerable mutual tolerance or self-interest that life for either party could be reasonably tolerable.

This was not a state of childlike dependency but a state of dependency on the prison community, in which they experienced no loss of identity and little trouble in adjustment. The prison, just like the outside world from which they had come, was largely illiterate, so that status inside as well as out came from a combination of age and brain enough to use the tongue to influence and control others. The social practices of the literate and illiterate groups were different and, in the prison, the latter predominated.

Developing from the background of tribal dependency, the colonial government and its extension into independence has given them an experience which may well appear to be even more authoritarian than what went before.

> The man must obey his parents; if he does not obey his parents will not succeed in life even a little. He will end up a bad man in the eyes of the world. After obeying his parents he must obey God, and after that he must obey the orders of Government, without obeying Government he can never be content.

Government in its modern form has never appeared to be under or even subject to their control, or, indeed, anything else but inexplicable. Many crimes such as game-poaching, unlicensed brewing of beer and cattle theft from another tribe are not thought by

304

the majority to be crimes at all, and the conflicting orders and periodic inefficiencies of the prison staff in general and the haphazard and periodic cursing of the warders, no more than part of the same pattern.

Outside, the convict as a citizen may have obtained no reward for his acceptance of dependency on the tribe, community or government; from childhood he has been taught to obey and, obtaining no return, he commits crime. Once inside, he is faced with a situation in which there is a straightforward relationship between the food, shelter and clothing he receives and the requirement of obedience.

> It is necessary to obey all leader of whom the bigest is government. Particularly to obey policemen and warders so that they may get their salary and the dignity due to their office. Government sees that I obey all rules and helps me when I am in trouble. We are all inside Government.

Although the prison administration appears to reduce men to mere numbers and locations without individuality, the convict may well be dealing with a situation of which he has had previous experience. He may feel that he has not had any individuality taken away and that he may, in fact, be able to gain something through socially prescribed and tolerated methods of opposition. Any bureaucracy has its failings and one run by clerks of limited education and experience for a community of illiterates cannot be expected to be, and was not, efficient; the convicts were able to get at least part of their satisfaction from the successful fiddling of goods and services.

> He obeys prison orders and copes all right with other convicts as well as warders. He talks to the convicts in a good manner, makes friends with askaris so as to get him something from outside. He makes friends with cooks so as to get him extra food. He has been very clever in passing food to other convicts and exchanging for hemp.

Only the warders had any continuous personal relationships with the convicts but this was not in the direction of reform or the development in the convicts of a greater sense of social responsibility. It was more in the way of tribal association or accommodation on the basis of mutual interests. Some warders wanted the rations and clothing issued to the convicts as well as their services in and around the workshop, while the convicts wanted the tobacco, cash and hemp for smoking which some warders had to offer.

Helped by a few trusted convicts, the bureaucratic machine was largely run by warder clerks and warders who were as much concerned in asserting their authority as in preventing convict fiddling, in which a small proportion of them were involved. They were controlled by a senior staff whose responsibilities for running complicated administrative machinery in accordance with the law, the necessity to keep the prison running and to protect themselves from false accusations, prevented them getting to know more than a few convicts personally.

The convicts did not form a uniform group and although they were united in theory in their opposition to authority they were not, in fact, united in practice. There was, in colonial times, the bond of African unity against European prison authority, but this no longer existed. There did not appear to be a code of convict behaviour which defined the convict's relationship with authority. They did not take much action against those who were thought to be informers, or indeed against those who stole from their fellows. There was nothing in their code which prevented them from getting to know a warder. The only rule which appeared to be generally known and acted upon was the avoidance of quarrels between convicts—such friction was universally condemned. Most cells had quasi-formal arrangements for the settling of quarrels, the organization of duties and the enforcement of penalties for misbehaviour such as committing homosexual acts in public or fouling the latrines. The convicts with the longer sentences were named judges and policemen, and gave out punishments such as walking on the knees twenty times round the cell, or carrying a bucket of water.

Most convicts did not appear to have friends. There were groupings rather than comradeship in which mutual interest in the guarding of possessions supplied the motivation. Many of them did express very strongly and repeatedly that they were not criminals and they objected to associating with real criminals. These ten-

306

dencies appeared to separate rather than unite groups. There was much personal selfishness. The convict with malaria might get no food; clothes and blankets were stolen so that guards had to be set up, and small personal possessions had always to be carried or hidden privately.

The prison community may represent the extended family in that it provides the basic necessities of life and companionship without the need to make any decisions, but in the absence of kin with definite roles, no one feels a more personalized obligation to another and, without this, there can be no reciprocity based on an emotional, as much as a kin, connection.

Continuing friendships would in fact have been difficult. Convicts came in and went out and were transferred to other prisons; they moved up in stage (the progressive granting of privileges), which involved moving to another cell block. The cell dormitories also encouraged these larger groupings, and tests of association seemed to show that their size was not more than four or five individuals associating continuously in a group. It would be possible for them to associate with people outside their own cell blocks, since the opportunity to move about the prison could be manipulated by most convicts wishing to do so, but it seemed that friendship without any economic backing did not provide sufficient incentive for the effort to be made.

The small cells containing one to three prisoners were given to the troublemakers, the mentally disturbed, some escapees and some convict leaders. Most convicts accepted the other members of their dormitory, which are called 'clubs', as they came and attempted no changes. Within a cell block, it was largely fortuitous in which dormitory a convict slept, and the authorities did not in fact know where each man slept, without having to go and inquire.

IV Reactions to Imprisonment[5]

Some prisoners recognized the legitimate right of the government, both before and after independence, to imprison them if it so wished. In a large number of cases they did not accept that they had done wrong or that they should have been sentenced to imprisonment for a particular offence, although only a small minority failed to admit that they had committed the offence as charged. They tended to shrug their shoulders, suggesting that this was the way that government always behaved, so that they accepted the prison because it existed.

> The man who never argues. He does just as he is told, no matter whether there is a warder nearby or not. Always cheerful to his fellow prisoners. Although there are some tricky prison rules that a prisoner can likely break and get punished, this man has been without any slightest report against him for the last three years.
>
> Even if the time for work is over, he will do something extra for the warders without arguing. He stays quiet when others made loud comments about the warders. He has no secrets and answers any questions put to him. He is a strong-minded person and tolerates the badness around him.

They recognized that conformity to the custodial regime was the best way of passing the time, while seeing the sentence as a period lost from life; they were usually cheerful, polite enough and worked just enough to get by. They never considered that there were any advantages in being in prison but much of the prison regime conformed to patterns of behaviour, which were already a part of the experience of most of them outside. This conformity thwarted the avowed purpose of the prison to punish and reform, and a number of staff felt embarrassed that the prison did not have the desired effect. There was thus individual conformity by the majority to the norms of prison authority, while at the same time no solidarity among the inmates.

2 INNOVATION

Very few convicts indeed made any specific criticisms of the prison regime—their observations were generalized. Those who are chosen by the convicts to supervise food issues, and to make such improvements as they can, are almost immediately corrupted.

> They are actually elected by the other prisoners to represent them in the food committee which in fact does not exist. So soon as they get to the kitchen they forget that they were to represent the people and become self seekers. They are the good pretenders. They are very proud type of people. Even outside they are the type who tries to be what they will never be. Underground type of people. Makes friends only when he have got something to gain from such friendship.

The more educated convicts stressed that there was nothing in the prison system which would assist in their rehabilitation. Many had ideas in relation to types of crimes as to how the judicial system should work for the benefit of the country; essentially in regard to crimes other than their own, they insisted that longer sentences and harsher treatment would deter. Rehabilitation appeared to occupy a very small part of their consideration.

3 RITUALISM

A further group of prisoners largely rejected the socially approved goals of the prison community of accepting authority and manipulating it to their own advantage and fell back upon a punctilious conformity to prison rules.

Within this group there were two types. Firstly, the ritualists who identified. Their attitudes were ambivalent; they occupied staff places, clerks, storemen and other special jobs. They were long-term prisoners who earned special privileges, and all of whom earned the tolerance, if not the respect, of the staff. From these positions, they regarded the majority of their fellow prisoners as criminals with whom they unfortunately had to associate. Typically, outside they were schoolmasters and clerks.

In jail everyone seems equal to the other no lower or big class. This believer is the sole cause why some prisoners forgets that they are prisoners and starts ordering the others. Mainly this comes when one wants to be the ruler and cannot win a majority by telling them how big he was as everybody says he was a big shot once in his life. They become prison dictators—the authorities does not encourage nor discourages. If they were encouraged they could use fiscal force. So they are always shouting giving orders which only fools obey. Masters of none and jackals of all.

Secondly, there were the dependent ritualists, who had gradually lost all initiative. In the outside world they had been unable to adjust to the demands of detribalization and town life and had failed equally to succeed even as petty criminals. They felt secure only when they were in prison, where they regained the comforting dependency which detribalization may have disturbed.

4 WITHDRAWAL

It has already been stated that there does not appear to be any development of an institutional neurosis in any type of convict which could be identified as mental decay. There were, however, three types of prisonized withdrawal which were not associated with fantasy.

Owing to the fact that the majority were illiterate, stimulus to retain contact with the social world had to come from conversation, which was not always available in a particular dialect or in a satisfying form. Large numbers withdrew into sleep, possibly putting in an average of more than twelve hours' sleep per day and literally, outside the hours of work required by the authorities and the need to eat, slept their sentences away.

If they find their fellow prisoners arguing, they never take interest. None of them will dare to tell you why they were convicted. When they are not sleeping, you will always find them in secluded corners just keeping quite like dolls. Always they look scared and out of place. We cannot tell for sure whether it is the length of their sentences or it is the boaring prison life which makes them to be good victims of sleep or it is their habit that they have become professional sleepers.

There is bitterness in his souls. He has no happiness. He gives no trouble and he receives no trouble. Just silence.

The second group was composed of social inadequates who read voraciously in books which were often beyond their comprehension—carrying books about the prison as amulets against their troubles in the outside world.

Lastly there are those who physically withdrew from the prison situation by escape. Very few were under any psychological compulsion to escape in order to attempt the solution of an outside problem, as family troubles did not appear to create this individual burden. There was no evidence of planned escapes or of any planning involving ingenuity; indeed, this was not necessary, as the opportunities to escape from both inside and outside were numerous. Escapes which did take place were usually last-second decisions to bolt from police custody prior to imprisonment and not in fact compulsive withdrawals from intolerable situations. Escapes averaged no more than one per thousand prisoners per year and attempts, which may have other objectives such as to gain access to a homosexual in the escape block, were about as common.

5 REBELLION

Despite the prevailing norm of conforming to an accepted authority, there were a few prisoners prepared to pit themselves against authority. They were both defiant, in situations which did not justify a struggle, and irrational, with the result that they got increasingly heavy prison punishment which the authorities often recognized as virtually useless in deterring other similar offences.

Since there appeared to be an identity of norms between outside and inside the prison, there was no appreciation of such a prisoner's virtues in attacking authority and no automatic support for his activities. Although these rebels were considered by many of the staff to be at the back of most of the supposedly organized troubles in the prison, they were, in fact, unpopular. They spoilt the even

311

continuance of irregular activity involving both the convicts themselves and their social relationships with the warder staff.

> The type of person who will not stand a duel in challenge. They are hypocritics and have a hot temper. They do not consider other opinions. They always think they are enjals, that what they ever say, do or else is the only right way.

> He neither gives nor receives respect. The trouble he sees around him is that which he creates himself.

Their activities were very spasmodic and probably formed a cycle of rebellion with which to jockey into a position of authority either accepted by their fellow convicts or in some way recognized by the staff. This developed into a stage of corruption, itself giving rise to a protest from which evolved the opportunity for another individual to stage his rebellion, which, to be successful, was often in the form of a challenge to authority over their alleged failure to give the prisoners their rights.

6 MANIPULATION

This group contained the brains of the prison community who sought their own ends of power and material benefit by contriving to outwit authority without coming into any conflict with it. Essentially they were men acting on their own to gain comfort rather than status by the manipulation of money and goods. A manipulator was not the leader of a gang and did not use force or fear. He was not regarded as a source of trouble by his fellow convicts. He did not act in order to gain status for his return to the outside world. He was very knowledgeable about prison routine and the ways in which it could be utilized to the prisoners' advantage. More than this knowledge of routine, he had a very clear understanding of how other humans—convicts, warders and senior staff—could be manipulated. Membership of this group was not related to recidivism, education or long sentences.

> They are always alert. Looks suspicious. Have many friend, few enemies. They are very obedient. Smiles always to hide their suspicious eyes. They never boast about their normal life. They are not accustomed to begging. Very secretive.

A further small group of the same type were those who sought to ameliorate the system as far as it concerned them by catching the ear of outside authority through smuggled letters or by informing inside in an attempt to change conditions without personally antagonizing authority.

> They are very friendly with new admissions. You can never call this class of prisoners as informers in the normal life because an informer does his duty for money or for another benefit like promotion or employment, but this class of prisoner do their for nothing, because the prison authorities do not reward them under any circumstances. What I have discovered about them is that the only gain to them is that they get a good chance to further their dirty business within the jail. In fact what they report is what they are the victim of. If you hear them reporting that there is a convict with hemp, they have already hidden theirs. The type which want a monopoly, hypocritics, the best double crossers which wants to please everybody.

Although the authorities were apprehensive about such outside allegations and laid down a formal procedure for dealing with complaints, their standing orders stated that no action would be taken on anonymous letters. Informers were used by the lower grades of staff but not by senior staff, who stated that their use undermined authority. Convicts who were thought to be informers were not assaulted or otherwise treated in a special way by their fellows.

V The Individual Experience

Although prison is obviously a group experience which fits in with many outside social norms and in which authority considers that it is dealing with an undifferentiated mass of largely bovine prisoners, it is nevertheless a very individual experience.

Convicts talk at length about their prison lives, stressing their isolation, not because they are unusually selfish, but because friendship is very rare, at least in the sense of more or less disinterested sharing and pleasure in one another's company. It is never sharing but the exchange of services for mutual advantage and protection. In sickness and health, a prisoner is alone and unlikely to receive or give help unless it is to someone's advantage to do so or because the authorities are potentially involved. On the one hand he may draw some strength from tribal identity and what he can create of clan and lineage groupings, while on the other hand he may be unable to develop these relationships, as would have been the case outside, by a full range of reciprocal goods and services.

For the convict who has not come from, and does not intend to return to, a tribal environment, his whole experience of prison is often mitigated by an inadequate perception of what his own true position will be when he returns to the outside world. He may not realize fully that he will find it very difficult to get employment and that he has been imprisoned by his own government, who regard him as a criminal. For these men, there continues the delusion of political martyrdom inherent in the colonial situation and carried through into independence. Nor does he realize that, in a situation of fast political change, his status will also have been lowered on getting outside by not being able to regain socially the momentum which he has lost by being absent in prison. For the majority of convicts, their improvement in health and increased weight resulting from regular diet and freedom from parasites, which they may not previously have experienced, may give them an optimistic frame of mind.

Almost every prisoner sees prison as unpleasant because it cuts him off from his own life. The physical conditions, which they accept as reasonable, are not a part of their assessment of their prison experience. To them prison is a deterrent by the fact of imprisonment—harsh or easy conditions would not appear to vary this opinion to any marked degree.

It does seem to be true that African convicts fit more easily into prison life than convicts in European countries. There is not very much difference between prison life and the life of a contract labourer on an estate or in a mining complex. Further, in a society that is mainly illiterate, imprisonment does not result in the loss of many literate activities, while retaining outside values. They find no difficulty in accepting authority reasonably applied and they certainly feel no instinctive need to challenge or personally resent its activities.

African convicts do not feel themselves, when in prison, to be in a criminal environment. The numbers in prison in proportion to population is much higher than in Britain, while those imprisoned for 'real' crimes form only a small proportion of the convicts present. Those imprisoned for game, liquor, licensing, stock theft, vagrancy, hemp smoking, immigration and tax offences do not see themselves as criminals. Lastly, as their loyalties are still mainly to the wider groupings of lineage, clan and tribe, they do not suffer the personality tensions from attachment to individuals and nuclear family groups.

The fact that prison and outside life have many parallels which make prison life easier to experience, does not make the convict into the stereotype of one who likes prison or is stupid. In so far as he is capable, the convict has assessed his own position very accurately: conformity brings no further trouble and shortens the sentence.

NOTES

1. Prison Ordinance to provide for prisons and prison officers' powers; Prison Rules to provide for the administration of prisons; Prison Commissioner's Directives and standing orders published in the Service's Monthly Orders; standing orders for the officer in charge of a prison relating to the particular administration of his own prison.
2. The balance of the population was convicted of stock theft: 4·8 per cent; sex offences: 1·3 per cent; liquor licensing offences: 9·2 per cent; game laws contraventions: 2·2 per cent; receiving: 3·2 per cent; manufacture and possession of drugs: 9·1 per cent; motor vehicle offences: 3·4 per cent; false pretences: 0·8 per cent; forgery: 1·2 per cent; others (tax, escape, immigration, etc.): 10·1 per cent.

3. | Prisoners | Total months in prison | No. letters received | No. letters written | Visits received |
|---|---|---|---|---|
| 42 literates | 482 | 75 | 149 | 37 |
| 57 illiterates | 614 | 92 | 103 | 36 |

4. 100 cents = 1 shilling; 20 shillings = 1 E.A. or sterling pound.
5. The typology of individual adaptation in Merton, *Social Theory and Social Structure*, rev. ed., 139–157 (1957), has been used with modifications and one additional classification.

12
Psychiatry and the Criminal Offender in Africa

ALAN MILNER and
TOLANI ASUNI

I Introduction

It is easy to understand why psychiatry was a relatively late-comer to the medical scene in sub-Saharan Africa. The emphasis of colonial medical services was naturally and properly on providing the qualified personnel and facilities to fight tropical disease, reduce needless mortality and increase life expectancy. For many decades now, resources have been expended on basic remedial work, so much so, in fact, that even adequate preventive programmes have had to await the prior provision of doctors, hospitals, nurses, and medical supplies, and public health specialists are still in short supply. And if the sheer size of the problems—in terms of the numbers of patients, the difficulties of travel and the diversity of language—were not enough, they have been multiplied by the resistance to change produced by superstition and ignorance.[1]

Throughout the colonial period, too, it must be remembered that even in Europe psychiatry was only slowly feeling its way forward towards acceptance. Basic ideas of the discipline were still evolving; facilities and personnel were only gradually becoming available as the barriers of European superstition and ignorance began to be broken down. With psychiatrists in short supply in Europe, few could be made available for service in the colonies. There was, too—sometimes articulated but often not—a tendency towards assuming that mental disorder was more the problem of the economically advanced, urbanized and overtly stressful nations. By contrast, the life situation of the less 'inhibited' African was seen as not so much fraught with possibilities of disturbance. Only the manifestly deranged needed isolation when they created a public nuisance, and for the rest the extended family was frequently seen to act as a general social welfare agency.

II Modern Psychiatry in Africa

In consequence, the psychiatric facilities of Africa today are not impressive. A survey south of the Sahara (excluding the Republic of South Africa[2]) in 1963 revealed that some countries, such as Bechuanaland, Swaziland and the Gambia, had no psychiatrists at all. Cameroun, Gabon, Congo (Brazzaville) had one psychiatrist each, who was not indigenous. The Niger Republic and Sierra Leone also had one each, who was indigenous. Zambia and Tanzania had two expatriate psychiatrists each; Kenya had three expatriates. Senegal had one indigenous and three expatriates; and Nigeria had the largest number of ten, only three of whom were from overseas.[3]

The lack of trained personnel is crucial to the understanding of the problems facing psychiatry in Africa. Just as happened with general medicine, the scale of the problems confronting the psychiatrist as the tropical countries of Africa began to be developed was such that his time was wholly taken up with his clinical and administrative work. The systematization of the basic groundwork of knowledge therefore suffered, and crucial basic work was perforce neglected. To this day, satisfactory studies of most areas of normal psychology are lacking; the impact of nursing, weaning and later child-rearing practices on developmental psychology is largely unexplored;[4] and the entire family situation in polygamous and masculine-dominated communities remains unexamined by comprehensive study as a factor in personality development.

The psychotherapeutic effectiveness of traditional measures taken by native healers has still to be properly assessed. Mental illnesses are often recognized as such in the customary African community and variously treated by the local equivalents of suggestion, manipulation of the environment, abreaction and group therapy.[5] The recognition and use of these culturally oriented agencies as part of the mental health programmes of developing countries in Africa has actually taken place in Nigeria[6] and been

320

urged elsewhere.[7] But whatever empirical studies have been undertaken, it is too extravagant to say, as one commentator has, that the traditional measures 'are as effective and as scientifically sound as any . . . practised in Europe'.[8]

Against this background of lack of scientific information, it is easy for the transient observer to give a generalized and wholly misleading—often an unfortunately ethnocentrically prejudiced—picture of African psychology and psychiatry. It is not many years ago, for example, that the psychiatric world was reliably informed that 'normal African mentality closely resembles the mentality of a section of the European population which is entitled psychopathic or sociopathic', and that 'for the most part Bantu Africans are very happy-go-lucky and inaggressive and would fall into the category of psychopaths called "inadequate".'[9]

By the same token, incidence studies both in general terms and in relation to specific psychiatric categories have been shallow and misleading. Depressive illnesses have been said to be rare, neurotic conditions seldom encountered and psychosomatic disorders typically non-African.

It is now clear that many of these misconceptions about African mental illness are the result of too hasty a survey of the local scene and too uncritical an application of psychiatric concepts across cultural boundaries. Psychiatric workers now accept that

> Both anthropologists and psychiatrists face the astonishingly difficult task of evaluating behaviour in terms of a series of factors, including its relation to accepted norms of behaviour for a given culture and the adequacy of behaviour in its social setting. A principal danger comes from mistaking the culturally defined norms of behaviour in Western culture to be ideal standards.[10]

The recognition of symptoms and the diagnosis of illness will therefore depend not only upon the psychiatrist's ability to overcome the language barrier but even more so on his ability to understand the cultural background in which he is working. The interpretation of behaviour or the identifying of delusions, for instance, will be impossible unless he has some familiarity with cultural norms and is able to take them into proper account when reaching his conclusions. Such matters as local peculiarities of family patterns, cultural conceptions of causation[11] and the widespread but varying beliefs in the immediate physical and mental consequences of supernatural action, will form an essential background to the understanding of abnormality. And even then a psychiatrist, working within a culture which is his own, may experience difficulty in delineating confidently where normal cultural beliefs cease and mental illness begins.[12]

With caution, however, one may say that the patterns of psychiatric disorder among Africans are closely akin to the known patterns already familiar in Euro-American cultures. There are, of course, demonstrated qualitative differences but, despite doubts which have been expressed,[13] it seems that in most cases these are susceptible to interpretation within the framework of the socio-cultural setting. Schizophrenia, for instance, particularly in its simple and hebephrenic forms, is commonly reported as the most prevalent psychosis.[14] Episodic confusion and hysteria-like symptoms characterize the illness more than in Europe and although the manic picture is easily recognized by its exhilaration of mood and thought, the depressive syndrome is less frequently manifested and more difficult to identify by mood criterion alone. Organically-based or predisposed conditions are regularly found, associated with trypanosomiasis, malaria, venereal infection and nutritional deficiencies.[15] It has been generally found that neurotic conditions are more likely to take culturally tolerable forms in African contexts and therefore less frequently find their way to mental hospitals.[16] It is equally clear, nonetheless, that strong cultural emphasis on sexual potency in the male and fertility in the female, and intensive belief in witchcraft and supernatural powers, are powerful anxiety-inducing agents. As the scope of psychiatric investigation has widened to surveying hospital out-patients, and those attending native healers and shrines, a greater range of neurosis has been disclosed.[17] In the whole range of clinical reports from African countries, only one distinctively African syndrome has been noted which, it is claimed, cannot be understood in terms of traditional diagnostic categories and it is still uncertain how far this can be regarded as a separate disease entity.[18]

It is important to stress again that it is only with the more careful modern studies that the above picture of the incidence of African mental illness has been built up. Past studies had concentrated their attention too narrowly on mental institutions. In developed countries this would be misleading enough; in Africa it proved to be infinitely worse. The solitary mental hospitals have all too often become havens for 'criminal lunatics, homicidal lunatics and lunatics without known domicile', as one older study expressed it,[19] and even today one of their primary functions is not so much the treatment of the ill as the protection of the public from the dangerous.[20] With the present differential in culture development within African countries, it has become clear as well that urban areas present atypical samples of mental illness. As Field reported, following her work in rural areas of Southern Ghana,

> A depressed patient is not considered mentally ill, for she is correctly orientated, accessible, and says nothing which is—in the ideological setting—irrational. . . . The depressive personality is, in sickness and health, self-effacing and is seldom a disturbing nuisance. She is therefore the last type of patient who would even find her way to any kind of European hospital unless she had some concurrent and conspicuous physical trouble. . . . It is not surprising therefore that psychiatrists and other doctors who see patients only in hospitals and clinics should have the idea that depression in Africa hardly exists.[21]

Potentially one of the most powerful forces affecting the incidence of mental illness in African countries today is the rapid rate of culture change. It has long been pointed out that

> . . . mental health problems grow in direct relation to the disturbing of traditional bonds that hold families and communities together. It is suggested that individuals socialized under such well-knit family conditions may suffer when they are estranged from traditional systems of security arrangements previously rooted in the family.[22]

It is only fair to say that much of the evidence to support this statement is of necessity highly impressionistic. Few field-workers have been able to deal with the problem in depth with adequate clinical and psychological facilities and with precise controls.

Tooth was able to discern in Ghana no apparent statistical relationship between psychosis and Europeanization, taking literacy as the criterion of the latter.[23] Carothers's inquiries were no more conclusive.[24] Lambo observed that both the prevalence and symptom pattern of disorders differed as between literate and non-literate groups.[25] In Algeria, De Vos and Miner reported evidence from Rorschach protocols that 'attenuation of traditional beliefs in the urbanized Arabs is related to increasing intra-psychic tensions ...', though by adhering to traditional social and religious beliefs they were not forced into patterns of dramatic cultural adaptation.[26]

The most significant study in this area is that undertaken by the Cornell-Aro Mental Health Research Project in Western Nigeria.[27] Based on a primary group of twenty-five villages in the same area and eight parts of a town, the Project was able to obtain an appreciable range with regard to size of community, traditional patterns, modernization and degree of socio-cultural integration. Taking such factors as poverty, ineffective leadership, broken homes and breakdown in lineage solidarity, as indicative of community disintegration, it was discovered that one and a half times as many people in the disintegrated villages as in integrated places (22%: 14%) were potential psychiatric 'cases'. Less than half as many (18%:42%) were 'well'. The relationship was particularly pronounced for women. In the integrated places there were ten times as many rated 'well' as were rated 'cases' (60%:6%), while in the disintegrated villages there were one and a half times as many women who were 'cases' as were 'well' (26%:15%). Socio-cultural disintegration certainly appears from this study to be directly associated with psychiatric disorder, though it was not indicated whether it preceded or followed it. The assumption must be the latter. At the same time, the role and effects of simple cultural change remain unexplored in detail, though it may perhaps be assumed with some confidence that the rapid cultural changes being experienced in the economic and political development of modern Africa will continue to bring socio-cultural disintegration in their train and thereby predispose to psychiatric disorder those who are enveloped in the changes.

III Pyschiatry and the Penal System

Very few African penal institutions, if any at all, are fortunate enough to have full-time medical officers, as basic medical facilities are so poor in the general community. It can easily be assumed that the psychiatric situation is much worse. Although there is good reason for supposing that a greater proportion of deviant and defective personalities will be found in the prison community than in the population at large, there are hardly any specialized prison psychiatric services in the continent.

The absence of these facilities, coupled with the usual lack of development of the general psychiatric facilities in any given community, has two important consequences. Firstly, the residential treatment facilities which generally are available in the community—be they in the form of a mental hospital (normally only one) or of asylums (normally several)—will be undifferentiating in their reception of patients. Civil committals, both voluntary and on certification, will be accommodated side by side with criminal committals, and the less seriously disturbed together with the chronically or acutely disturbed. The same strict security measures will be taken in respect of all patients and each will receive as much, or as little, treatment as any other, irrespective of condition. Occasionally, some countries do not allow the mixing of civil and criminal patients and apply security measures only to the criminal classification: these may be kept in individual cells or a few in a cell, as in Gabon, or isolated on an island, as on Fotoba Island in the Republic of Guinea.

Secondly, even though facilities may be labelled 'criminal' and 'non-criminal', such is the general lack of development of both that the distinction may not be easily recognized. Given that the capacity of properly equipped mental hospitals, where they exist, is strictly limited, the criminal defendant who is found to be irresponsible or unfit to stand trial may find himself committed either to prison or to an asylum physically adjacent to and under common supervision with it.[28] Once there, occasional sedation may be the extent of the treatment received and sometimes even this may be more than can be expected. Enahoro's grisly picture of the conditions of 'lunatics' in prison in Nigeria twenty years ago may not be far from the truth in many parts of Africa today:

> I saw more brutality to those unfortunate wretches in one year than I have seen in all the rest of my life. Considered fair game for baton practice by any warder, they slept on the bare floors, often denied blankets, their meals were irregular, they were frequently refused buckets for their natural needs, and some of them might never step out of their cells for weeks. . . . No one seemed to care, except on the rare occasions of the Visiting Committee's inspections when, after a general cleaning, the normal odour was masked by bucketfuls of disinfectant.[29]

If the 'lunatic' is incapacitated, he may be found sitting under a convenient shade tree in the prison yard; if he is violent, he may be chained.[30] Provision for the transfer to hospital of prisoners who are in need of treatment exists in all prisons legislation but for obvious reasons the procedure is not extensively used.[31]

In the former British colonies, the utter inadequacy and inhumanity of this situation has constantly been reiterated.[32] But only slowly, as other facilities have become available, have the mentally ill been moved out of the prison systems. In Nigeria, generally regarded as having better facilities than most independent African countries, the Prison Reports from 1950 to 1960 show that at the end of each year there were more than 400 mentally abnormal prisoners in the population of the Federal prison system alone (i.e. not including the local authority systems in Western and Northern Nigeria). On average, 250 of this number each year were civilly committed.[33]

The situation is distressing enough on its own account. It is perhaps more distressing when considered together with its implications for legal adjudication of responsibility. To this problem we now turn.

IV Psychiatry and the Courts[34]

How far psychiatric experience can be utilized by the courts will obviously be governed by the availability or otherwise of the facilities already discussed. Provisions referring to its use—in pretrial examinations, in trial determinations of responsibility, and in various post-sentence procedures—are not designed to reflect the regular availability of medical or psychiatric services in Africa but rather to give official idealized recognition to their role and lay the ground-work of machinery which may become more of a reality in future.

The realities of medical practice at the present time are such that the minute number of psychiatrists, burdened with heavy hospital and administrative duties, cannot give much part of their time to forensic psychiatry, no matter how anxious they may be to do so. In general, where there are psychiatrists in an African country, they will provide services only for the courts in the immediate vicinity, usually only in criminal cases, seldom in non-capital or at least non-violent cases, and irregularly with respect to capital crimes and offences of serious violence. It is probably true to say that a psychiatric opinion can be obtained in the majority of capital cases—usually murder cases[35]—in which it is requested, though sometimes the sheer physical difficulties involved in getting to see patients make it impracticable.[36] And usually, of course, no more than one expert opinion will be available, making the conflict between expert and witnesses in psychiatric matters an uncommon experience in African courts.

1 THE ACCUSED'S FITNESS TO MAKE HIS DEFENCE

If an accused person is not so manifestly deranged that he is removed to safe custody before his trial, the first occasion on which his sanity will come under consideration will be when he is brought to trial. At that stage, the issue will not be whether he was of unsound mind at the time of the offence, or even whether he is now of unsound mind, but rather whether he is fit to stand trial. No psychiatric standard is set here: the Anglophonic African jurisdic-

327

tions have followed the English pattern and established simple functional tests which can be applied by the courts without expert assistance.

An accused person is unfit to be tried if he can neither understand the charge against him, nor follow or appreciate the proceedings in court, nor instruct his advisers so that his defence may be properly prepared.[37] Incapacity in any one of these respects will render him unfit to be tried and the mere fact that in lucid moments he appreciates what is being said against him will not make him fit.[38] Similarly, if the accused satisfies all three tests but cannot make a positive defence for some other reason—for example, amnesia caused by supervening psychosis[39] or head injury[40]—he will not be deemed unfit for trial.

There are no African Briggs Laws and few mandatory procedures for calling medical evidence in any type of case. Most of the provisions simply instruct the courts to inquire into the accused's fitness without specifying how it shall be done[41] but it is common practice to fulfil the obligation by remanding for medical observation and report.[42] Ghana [43] and Nigeria[44] have both made medical evidence a prerequisite of a finding of unfitness—one assumes that this will be psychiatric evidence only in a small proportion of cases —but elsewhere there is no obligation to call such evidence, even if it is available.[45] The courts too have not been slow to emphasize that the question of fitness should not be determined solely on the basis of expert evidence when it is called.[46] Experience suggests that in this context there is considerable likelihood that psychiatric evidence will assume a minor role compared with the power of the court to ask questions of the accused, hear his answers and observe his demeanour.

A finding of unfitness to be tried will result in the suspension of further proceedings and either the detention of the accused[47] or in some countries his conditional release if the offence charged is bailable, if he is not dangerous and can safely be given into the custody of relatives or friends.[48] When he is reported to be recovered, the trial may be resumed and though in practice it will not normally be resumed if the delay has been of several months, it is clear from the reported authorities that the length of delay permissible cannot be the subject of complete generalization.[49]

Several countries have been troubled by the problem of securing the proper disposition of the deaf mute. The complicating factors peculiar to Africa are, once again, the shortage of psychiatric facilities to assist diagnosis—particularly valuable where the disability has existed since birth—the considerable likelihood that the accused will be illiterate and therefore unable to respond to written information and questioning, and his frequent isolation from his family or friends who will have established means of communicating with him. It is clear that if contact and comprehension can be established at all, the courts have a duty to inquire fully into the ways by which they can be established[50] and, if they are established, to proceed with the trial if the criteria for fitness to plead are satisfied. What will happen if he cannot be tried will depend on the particular jurisdiction.

The English-inspired Criminal Procedure Codes are often of little specific help, since the English precedents only provided for the disposal of the mentally disturbed offender whose fitness to plead was questioned and the English courts were therefore forced into the bizarre position of classifying the deaf mute as mentally disordered.[51] The South African Criminal Procedure Act and its variants in the other countries of southern Africa have adopted the same procedure.[52] Extensive criticism of it,[53] however, has led the courts of Southern Rhodesia to the point of refusing to commit an apparently sane person to psychiatric custody[54] and the current South African solution appears to be to hold that their legislation gives them sufficient leeway to commit such a person to prison pending the President's instructions.[55]

The codes which follow the early Colonial Office pattern[56] either provide specifically for the sane but unfit accused to 'be treated in like manner as a person incapable of making his defence by reason of unsoundness of mind . . .' or allow him to be treated in this way in default of specific provision. It obviates the difficulties of the situation, however, by providing for his discharge to the custody of friends or relatives if he can be properly cared for and is not dangerous to himself or others.

Only the East African countries have legislated a special procedure for this type of case. Provided that there is a finding that the accused committed the act alleged, he will be detained in prison pending a further order.[57] This power appears to be used sympathetically, to attempt to handle the social situation in its entirety, so far as it is possible to do so with limited resources. It has been used, for instance, to ensure the safe custody of an accused while arrangements were made for his future welfare—in terms of employment, guidance and supervision—when he had no home and no one to care for him.[58]

2 THE DEFENCE OF MENTAL DISORDER

The common law jurisdictions of Africa are haunted by the ghost of Daniel McNaghten. They, or the British Colonial Office before them, have put the McNaghten Rules—more or less—into statutory form in their criminal codes. Even where it has been less rather than more, the English-trained, McNaghten-orientated judges have often slipped into the familiar habit of reading the codes as if they simply restated English law.[59] At various times the McNaghten formulation has been read into statutes in which it never actually appeared,[60] has been used to give a gratuitous display of the bench's comparative knowledge,[61] and still lingers in the minds of some lower court judges (who are fortunately now being more regularly reversed) as a standard of decision preferable to the statutory formulae actually in force.[62]

In fact, the McNaghten Rules only appear in their original pristine inadequacy in one African country, Sierra Leone, which has adopted English criminal law in a piecemeal, uncodified form.[63] Elsewhere, the several different permutations on the original Rules fall simply into the categories of those which have taken approximately the McNaghten tests and those which have modified them.

Before dealing with these, however, we may conveniently discuss here the preliminary question of how far the actual description of mental disorder itself has been modified in the African codes. The McNaghten Rules themselves spoke in terms of a 'defect of reason' caused by 'disease of the mind' as the mental condition on which the defence was to be based. The principal hazard in this terminology was its vagueness and the resulting uncertainty about the place of subnormality, neurosis, psychopathy, neurological disorders and organic disorders of the brain under the Rules. Over a century of amplification in the English courts led to the inclusion of subnormality within the defence as a matter of practice,[64] the inclusion of neurological and other organic conditions as a matter of law,[65] and the probable exclusion of neurosis and psychopathy.[66]

Even before these developments had crystallized, the British government had become sufficiently aware of the deficiencies of the McNaghten formulation to make some changes in the codes given to the Empire. The Indian Penal Code, the original draft of which in fact ante-dated McNaghten,[67] provided the all-inclusive phrase 'unsoundness of mind',[68] which was later adopted by Northern Nigeria;[69] it is rivalled in completeness only by the Sudanese 'permanent or temporary insanity or mental infirmity'.[70] Slightly less comprehensive is Southern Nigeria's 'state of mental disease or natural mental infirmity'[71] and more explicit—but probably for that very reason unsatisfactory—are Ghana's 'idiocy, imbecility, or any mental derangement or disease affecting the mind'[72] and Liberia's 'idiot, imbecile, lunatic or insane person'.[73] The latter two, presumably, limit the defence to the low-grade defectives specified, and by omission exclude the higher-grade defectives who might otherwise take advantage of it.

The East and Central African codes, together with the Roman-Dutch laws of southern Africa, have retained the 'disease' concept. The Colonial Office used as its East and Central African model the English draft code of 1879, in which Sir James Stephen had formalized the McNaghten Rules.[74] The only easing of the confusion about the significance of 'disease' has come through the decision of the Eastern Africa Court of Appeal granting subnormality the legal, if not the medical or logical, status of a disease for these purposes.[75] South Africa has adopted the conceptions of what its leading criminal law textbook calls 'disease of the mind or mental defect',[76] yet although the same authority states categorically that

for legal purposes no distinction is to be drawn between idiocy, lunacy, mania, paranoia, melancholia, hypochondria, dementia, or any other species into which the various forms of mental aberration or defect may be classified by medical scientists,[77]

331

the Appellate Division has at least denied to a psychopathic condition the status of a mental disorder.[78] Organic conditions have been included within the scope of the defence.[79]

The adoption of the English draft code in the East and Central African jurisdictions has resulted too in the enactment of another of Sir James Stephen's emendations. Aware of the controversies which had surrounded the McNaghten Rules as to whether the judges were trying in 1843 to define insanity as a whole or merely to define that area of mental illness which would exculpate from crime, he stated his interpretation for the avoidance of further doubt. Appended to each statement of the responsibility rule, therefore, is the following:

> But a person may be criminally responsible for an act or omission, although his mind is affected by disease, if such disease does not in fact produce upon his mind one or other of the effects above-mentioned [i.e. ignorance of what he is doing] in reference to that act or omission.[80]

(a) Approximate McNaghten

The original McNaghten Rules were expressed in four answers to five questions. They posed two separate responsibility tests: the cognitive tests applicable in the case of a person who sets up the defence of insanity when suffering from a disease of the mind ('insane delusion respecting one or more particular subjects or persons' in the language of the original question); and a distinct test for a person suffering only from a 'partial delusion' ('an insane delusion as to existing facts'). Following the Stephen formulation, eight countries have adopted the cognitive tests as their only basis for decision. Eleven others have incorporated them into their statutory schemes in some form or other, though not as the exclusive criteria. Only Ghana[81] and the Sudan[82] have modified them by leaving out all reference to the accused's knowledge of the wrongfulness of the actions.

No reference to delusions, therefore, appears in the legislation of eight countries, primarily those of East and Central Africa. The cognitive tests are expressed in these terms:

> A person is not criminally responsible for an act or omission if at the time of doing the act or making the omission he is

through any disease affecting his mind incapable of understanding what he is doing, or of knowing that he ought not to do the act or make the omission.[83]

The question to be asked for survey purposes is how far the absence of provisions incorporating the delusion test narrows the defence. One must assume that an interpretation which reads the delusion test into the legislation when it has been omitted is not legitimate.[84]

Stephen certainly did not think that by leaving out all reference to partial delusions he was narrowing the defence. Unlike the great majority of his contemporaries on the English bench, he was not content with the idea that a man could be free from mental disorder and yet still suffer delusions limited to particular matters.[85] His own opinion was that delusions were relevant to the issue of mental illness, not merely with respect to the content of the delusion,[86] but either as evidence of the illness or as evidence that the accused's cognitive faculties were impaired.[87]

Today, whenever there is any expert testimony available, it seems unlikely that the courts will resort to the partial delusion test even where it is present in the legislation. In Nigeria, for example, where it is specifically included in the Criminal Code, insanity defences will commonly be based on the cognitive tests where the facts indicate paranoid or other delusion.[88] And under the Stephen-inspired codes it has been held to be perfectly appropriate for a deluded person to be dealt with under the cognitive tests.[89]

(b) McNaghten modified

Of the three principal modifications which have been made in the McNaghten formula in Africa, the first is basic to the scope of the cognitive tests.

Although the original Rules suggested that inability to know either the unlawfulness or the general wrongfulness of the action would support the defence, the modern English interpretation is in the direction of allowing a finding of irresponsibility only if the accused does not know that his act is unlawful.[90] In reliance on the modern English authority and overlooking East African authority in favour of the older view,[91] the East and Central African courts have held the same.[92] And this despite the intention of the original draftsman to keep the broader interpretation.[93]

Only South Africa appears to have kept the broader interpretation as a result of judicial decision,[94] but Northern Nigeria has again followed the Indian model and granted the exemption to one who is 'incapable of knowing . . . that he is doing what is either wrong or contrary to law'.[95] To say, though, that the defence is broadened is to use a very relative term. Since we are dealing here with a minute percentage of those who are mentally abnormal, any broadening of the rule which is expressed only in terms of cognition will extend it only slightly. Nonetheless, it is clear that some fact situations will fall within the defence which would not be allowed to form the basis of the narrower defence. In *Muswi s/o Musele v. R.*,[96] for example, the accused killed his wife believing that she was bewitching him, knowing that it was illegal to do so but being confused as to the morality of the act. The East African Court of Appeal held that on these facts the accused did not satisfy the narrower formulation of the test—but it seems fairly clear that his confusion as to the rightness or wrongness of what he was doing would afford him a defence had he been tried in Northern Nigeria or South Africa.

The second modification is one which in Africa—it was copied from West Indian codes—is peculiar to Ghana. As we have seen, Ghana has adopted a description of mental disorder which is full in some respects but perilously limited in respect of subnormal conditions, and has abandoned the knowledge of wrongfulness as a criterion for decision. It has taken further its policy of broadening the defence by adding, as apparently a complete alternative, a test based on a functional appreciation of the significance of delusions. The defence of insanity will be available to an accused person

> . . . if he did the act in respect of which he is accused under the influence of an insane delusion of such a nature as to render him, in the opinion of the jury or of the Court, an unfit subject for punishment of any kind in respect of such an act.[97]

This appears to mean that where the accused's mental condition makes punishment futile—presumably because he cannot be deterred and because he would not have committed the act if he had not been deluded—he should be exempted from it. This interpretation, suggested in an editorial note in the West African Law Reports in 1957,[98] was later adopted by the Ghana Court of Appeal in 1959.[99] It was reversed in 1960[100] in favour of a McNaghten-inclined interpretation that the delusion should be such that, if the imagined facts were true, they would provide justification for the action taken.

This interpretation is clearly possible. The judge or jury are given a discretion to exempt whomsoever they feel is unfit to be be punished and are entitled to set up guide-lines for the exercise of their discretion. At the same time, bearing in mind that the guide-lines chosen are those of the McNaghten formulation, it would appear a little strange that if they were intended they were not specified as such in the legislation. A later Court of Appeal has now held that the broad phrasing of the section is intended to confer a broad discretion which is to be exercised not in terms of the nature of the delusion but in accordance with the judge's or jury's assessment of the seriousness of the accused's illness.[101]

Finally, half a dozen countries have taken the first conservative step toward undermining the hold of McNaghten on African criminal law. South Africa and the neighbouring countries of southern Africa[102] have recognized the 'dangerous doctrine' of irresistible impulse as an overlay upon the McNaghten Rules, despite the persistent opposition to the extension by the English courts.[103] Nigeria and the Sudan[104] have specifically legislated in favour of the offender who is deprived by his mental illness of the capacity to control his actions, thus avoiding the implication of sudden impulsiveness of action but still carrying the overtones of total deprivation of will-power which will only be found, on an honest view of the facts, in a few cases. Nonetheless, although the form of the development has been criticized in recent years, it represented at the time of its first enactment a considerable step forward in the handling of the mentally abnormal offender and still, in the African context, offers greater freedom to defendants in these few jurisdictions than to those in the rest of the continent.[105]

3 EVIDENCE OF MENTAL DISORDER: THE PROCEDURAL PROBLEMS

Establishing mental disorder of such a sort that will bring a defendant within the exempting provisions of the law will lead to a finding of 'guilty but insane' and the placing of the accused at the disposal of the state.[106] He cannot, if his offence is capital, be executed, nor, in theory, can he be made subject to the normal punitive processes of imprisonment. He must be detained as a mentally abnormal offender, given periodic medical examination[107] and only considered for release when it is certified that he is no longer suffering from disorder, though even then discharge will not follow automatically.[108] In ideal circumstances, he would always be detained for treatment in a mental hospital: in reality, as we have seen, he may receive considerably less than ideal treatment.

Whatever the state's interest in bringing penal consequences to bear only on the responsible, and securing treatment for those deemed to need it, in adversary terms we are here considering a defence to a criminal charge. In the ordinary course of events, counsel for the accused will determine whether or not the defence should be raised at all—and with the prospect of indeterminate detention following a successful defence, it will normally be raised to avoid the possibility of the death penalty—and will introduce testimony to substantiate it. Indeed, since there is in each jurisdiction only one codified defence based on mental disorder—unlike in England, for example, where defences based on McNaghten and 'diminished responsibility' are alternatives in murder cases and the prosecution may rebut either defence by producing evidence that the accused is within the other[109]—the courts incline to the view that only the accused can properly produce evidence of disorder.[110] To hold otherwise, it is said, would be to produce the result that no party to the proceedings would be asking for a verdict of guilty, since either both prosecution and defence would concur in seeking a verdict of insanity, or the prosecution alone would seek it and the defence ask for acquittal.[111]

Such a purist's view of the assigned roles in adversary proceedings seems to be both unnecessarily dogmatic and out of tune with the actual conditions of Africa. Of greater significance are the cases which have faced up to the problems of the shortage of expert psychiatric testimony, the unlikelihood of the defence having access to a psychiatrist who is not a government-employed medical officer and the illiteracy and lack of sophistication of many defendants.

It has already been noted that in every jurisdiction, at least in a murder case, there is a good chance of psychiatric evidence being made available. In many cases, if there is any reason to suspect that the accused is not mentally normal, he will be examined by a psychiatrist while in prison awaiting trial—but at the instance of the state rather than of the accused or his advisers.[112] It seems to be established practice in most countries, following the English pattern, for the prosecution to provide the defence with a copy of the psychiatrist's or prison doctor's statement on the subject, and make him available as a witness to the defence if necessary.[113] This is clearly an essential practice to ensure fairness where most, if not all, medical practitioners will be government employees.

Whether the defendant in a capital case will be legally represented will depend upon the state of the legal profession, the practice of assigning counsel to indigent defendants and the nature of the court. There may not be an adequate number of lawyers to ensure representation in all cases, the courts may not be in a position to assign counsel, or—even in capital cases in some jurisdictions—the trial may be in a native court in which legal representation is not allowed. If, therefore, the uneducated defendant finds himself without representation, it is abundantly clear that he will not be able to make the best use of any expert testimony made available to him. If, as should then happen, the court undertakes to guide him in presenting his defence, a number of alternative solutions are possible.

It could be held, as in South Africa, that the prosecution should produce the evidence of insanity and ask for a verdict based on it, even though the defendant objects.[114] Kenya cases suggest that that country is moving in the same direction,[115] but it remains to be seen whether the Tanganyika suggestion[116] that the prosecution should not do this will have any impact in Kenya. Malawi has adopted a procedure which appears the most satisfactory. The

337

strategic decisions are left in the hands of the court, which should explain to the accused the implications of raising an insanity defence and only allow the evidence to be called if he then indicates that he is willing to face the consequences of a possible successful defence.[117]

It is commonly accepted that when the burden of proof is on the defence, it can be satisfied by the production of evidence which establishes the probability that the defendant was suffering from mental disorder within the statutory formulation.[118] The only formal exception is in the case of Liberia, which, though a common law jurisdiction, has not inherited the English procedures following a period of colonial rule. Section 15 of its Penal Law provides that once it has been established that the accused has previously suffered from mental disorder, the burden of proving that he committed the offence during a lucid interval then passes to the prosecution. No decisions have been reported on the questions of the burden and standard of proof when (as posited in the previous paragraphs) the defence does not call the evidence of mental disorder. It would be paradoxical if, just because the accused was undefended and the evidence was produced by the prosecution, his mental condition had to be established by the higher standard of proof normally applicable to the prosecution. There would seem to be no reason why the standard of proof should not be deemed attached to the issue, whichever side raises it: the defendant's insanity is to be established and whoever establishes it should only have to establish its probability.[119]

4 EVIDENCE OF MENTAL DISORDER: THE NATURE OF THE EVIDENCE

With the shortage of psychiatric experts, it is hardly surprising that virtually all the courts have accepted that the defence of insanity can properly be established without expert evidence. Only in Liberia has the Supreme Court insisted that there can be no determination of insanity without medical evidence,[120] though one is compelled to wonder how far this insistence is strictly followed in the absence of extensive medical facilities.

Elsewhere, when medical evidence is not available, the courts or

338

juries have to rely on the inferences they can draw from the surrounding circumstances and the proved acts or admitted states of mind of the accused. The inferences will be directed towards establishing the two separate aspects of the defence: the existence of the mental disorder (however it may be legislatively described) and the accused's knowledge, capacity to control, or whatever exempting feature may be specified.

The sophistication of the courts faced with a claim of mental illness has generally grown since the day when a trial judge could be reported as saying that he believed after observing the prisoner in court that he was not a mentally normal person.[121] Demeanour at the trial is now given little weight except to give visual confirmation to other evidence of disorder.[122] Yet there is still to be found the judge who confesses that

> ... in the absence of any evidence of treatment between the offence and the trial when it is alleged that the accused was insane when the offence was committed, one feels bound to look for some explanation of the fact that at the trial the accused is sufficiently sane to understand the nature of the proceedings. ...[123]

Fortunately, the variable nature of mental illnesses and their frequent episodic characteristics appear to be familiar conceptions in the minds of most judges.[124]

The crucial feature here is that the courts, so often relying on inference without medical help in assessing the significance of the inference, are in effect deciding for themselves the symptomatology of mental illness. That they approach this task carefully is beyond question; the accuracy of their diagnosis is another matter.

In their favour on both of these points is the fact that the courts have generally looked not at particular acts or aspects of the accused's life but rather at the totality of his situation. Diagnosis is not normally to be made on the strength of one or two aberrant actions but on the basis of an appreciation of as wide a range of factors as possible. If an accused has had pains in his head since childhood, frequently visited native doctors for this reason and taken their medicine,[125] laughed maniacally, thrown his food away, gone out half-dressed and babbled meaninglessly to his relatives, a court may naturally feel that he was not entirely normal.[126] Even a less bizarre history could justifiably lead to the same conclusion.

The difficulties that the courts have got themselves into through lack of expertise appear to be twofold. First, in examining a broad range of factors which they feel may have causative significance in mental illness, they have at times been too uncritical; second, and more important, they have laid down legal propositions that certain symptoms are not to be given weight.

They have, for example, accepted evidence of mental instability and behaviour disorder in an accused's relatives without any consideration of whether the type of disorder from which he is suffering is transmissible.[127] In other cases, of course, little critical ability may have been needed. Evidence of delusions, for many years in the 19th century considered essential to the existence of mental illness,[128] will almost always lead to a finding of disorder. An accused's description of paranoid beliefs—that strangers were coming to his house to steal his wife or commit adultery with her,[129] surrounding him with guns, matchets and sticks and trying to kill him,[130] or abusing him and calling him names[131]—is testimony that the non-medical mind can readily appreciate.

The findings of law which exclude or deny significance to facts capable of amounting to symptoms of mental illness, however, represent the less-informed side of the non-medical mind. The courts' treatment of belief in witchcraft and supernatural powers is a good illustration. Just as in other fields they have discounted such beliefs and refused to allow them to affect the issue of responsibility for crime although they may have crucially altered an accused's perception of what he was doing,[132] so in this field they have generally disregarded them as factors associated with mental illness.[133] Only one reported case can be found to have given weight to them: the trial judge in R. v. *Magata s/o Kachehakana*[134] expressed the opinion:

> . . . that an African living far away in the bush may become so obsessed with the idea that he is being bewitched that the balance of his mind may be disturbed to such an extent that it may be described as disease of the mind.

Magata had murdered his father, believing him to be Satan and to have bewitched Magata's family. One wife, two sons and some goats had died; another wife, the accused himself and his cow were sick—all the accused alleged, as a result of the deceased's activities.

It is clear that this is a particularly delicate area in which the greatest care must be taken. Belief in the immediacy of supernatural activity is widespread and is not statistically abnormal. Modern psychiatric studies suggest, however, that morbid fear of bewitchment and its consequences is closely associated with acute anxiety states, either as a cause or as a manifestation of the conditions.[135] Although differentiation of pathological from culturally normal beliefs in witchcraft and the supernatural may itself be exceedingly difficult even for the psychiatrist,[136] it is unfortunate that the courts should put themselves in the position of flatly rejecting the beliefs without further inquiry.

Similarly, lack of apparent motive for committing a brutal murder has been stigmatized by some courts as an unreliable guide to mental disorder, though psychiatrically it may be considered of some importance.[137] The Zambian court, in R. v. Tembo,[138] agreed that a savage, apparently motiveless killing could be consistent with mental illness but suggested that it might also show

> ... the mere indulgence of a savage but reasoning instinct ... a brutal but perfectly sane desire to cause bloodshed ... a foolish and reckless, but still not insane craving for notoriety— and ... possibly one or more or several other rational and culpable states of mind.

One legal writer has cautioned, too, that when dealing with the mental condition of 'persons who, for no apparent reason, run about making violent attacks upon everyone they meet', one should bear in mind 'that cruelty is a natural human instinct'.[139]

In West Africa, the courts have taken a less rigid view. Although they have held that motiveless behaviour cannot *by itself* be used to support a finding of insanity, it may nonetheless give secondary support to make evidence of another sort more convincing.[140] It is therefore particularly easy to use this inference where the accused has committed offences against near and beloved relatives[141] or simply run amuck and behaved in a wild and uncontrolled manner.[142] It is difficult to think of any other verdict than one of

341

irresponsibility when, for example, a man wanders into a completely strange village, sets fire to a hut, stabs an old man who tries to put the fire out, attacks and kills another man with a spear and a knife, sets fire to two more huts and finally wounds at least two other men before he is overpowered.[143]

It is in these cases of running amuck that the courts can most easily operate within the framework of the cognitive and control tests. They can infer with confidence from the accused's behaviour —whether he actually tells them so or not—that he did not know what he was doing. It is where the disorder takes a less dramatic and phrenetic form that the determination of his capacity for knowledge or control will be more troublesome. The accused's own description of his state of mind may or may not be helpful and may or may not be believed. And the facts from which inference can be drawn may be ambiguous—such as the accused's running away from the crowd at the scene of the crime, washing the murder weapon and apologizing for his behaviour[144] or immediately admitting the murder and surrendering to the police 'to be killed'.[145] Clearly even such an apparently unambiguous set of circumstances as buying a knife and stabbing with it a man against whom the accused has a grievance may take on a different complexion against a background of mental disorder.[146]

Expert evidence on this crucial issue of cognition or control at the time of the offence, where it is available, will need to be specific and detailed. The courts are unlikely to challenge any psychiatric assertion that an accused was suffering from a mental disorder at the time of the offence, though since there must be a finding of fact on this issue based on all the evidence they are entitled to do so. The divergence from medical opinion, if there is divergence at all, will come on the issue of cognition or control. The observations of the Chief Justice of Malawi indicate the basis for disagreement:

> In most cases the best evidence is that of those witnesses who can speak to the accused's actions and demeanour at and immediately before or immediately after the incident in question, and the experts can really reach their opinions only by inference from those facts supported by their expert knowledge of the subject and a somewhat belated examination of the ac-

cused. It is no wonder, therefore, that juries sometimes think that they can form just as good an opinion from the evidence as can an expert who has never seen the accused until some time after the moment at which he is alleged to have been insane.[147]

Without wishing to disagree with the Chief Justice's appreciation of the attitude of juries (which one feels can justifiably be extended to include many judges), much will surely turn on the psychiatrist's 'expert knowledge'. It is this knowledge which allows the psychiatrist to make an educated retrospective assessment of the accused's mental condition and state of knowledge in the light of the psychiatric diagnosis. The court obviously should not accept as adequate proof a categorical statement as to an accused's state of mind which is unsupported by facts and reasoning.[148] Nonetheless, by insisting too possessively on their right (or the jury's right) to be the final arbiters of fact, the courts often run the risk of undermining the significance of psychiatric testimony, reducing 'expert knowledge' to the status of simple opinion, and injecting their rational appreciation of events into an inherently irrational situation.

V Conclusion

The vital question is how far these tests and procedures are suited to Africa, given the conditions and facilities of Africa. They are not tests and procedures which were originally evolved in Africa but ones which have been fashioned by colonial or independent legislatures in the image of foreign models. The Imperial government approved them not because they were culturally sensitive but because they both embodied familiar common law formulae and, if adopted on a broad enough basis, could offer colonial uniformity. African governments which during the past few years have been engaged in codifying their criminal law have either copied the legislation of other African states (as Bechuanaland copied that of

Zambia in 1963), adopted well-tried overseas models (as Northern Nigeria modelled her law on that of India in 1959) or simply re-enacted their own earlier provisions (Ghana, 1892–1960). And in Africa, as anywhere else, merely retaining a code provision without alterations has not necessarily signified acceptance—especially, as is true of Africa, when the new governments have been pre-occupied with basic tasks of national development and are anyway content to leave their legal affairs in the hands of English or Eng-lish-trained lawyers.

Are these provisions the right ones for African countries today? When one considers the state of community knowledge of mental illness, the nature of the indigenous forms of treatment and the general inadequacy of modern medical facilities, one is tempted to draw a parallel with Europe and the United States in the late 18th and early 19th centuries. The tests for the recognition of mental illness and the criteria of criminal responsibility which were adopted were culturally viable in those times and places, whatever we may feel today about their inadequacy.[149] Is it possible, per-haps, assuming the equation of Africa today with Europe and the United States 150 years ago, to make use of the methodology developed then?

The suggestion must be firmly rejected: firstly, on the general grounds of scientific development and of international responsi-bility to assist in the spread of informed attitudes. We should no more think of reverting to a pre-psychiatric test of responsibility than we would of advocating a wholesale return to blood-letting, blistering and purging as measures of medical treatment. Although individual communities in Africa may be effectively isolated from the main currents of modern medical thought, the nations of which these communities form part are not. Their facilities may be poor but they are not themselves wholly unaware of this; to suggest that they isolate themselves even further from scientific development would be neither ethical nor humane nor politically feasible.

Secondly, there is certainly nothing to suggest that the variety of responsibility tests which were in common use in England or the United States before the formulation of the McNaghten Rules were capable of making a satisfactory distinction between the responsible and the irresponsible, or even between the dangerous

344

and the non-dangerous. From the 'wild beast' test of *Arnold's* case[150] through the various forms of cognitive test devised before the McNaghten Rules,[151] the result was uniformly the same: only the manifestly disturbed were identified. Since at the time, however, medical opinion leaned heavily in the direction of recognizing delusion and hallucination, together with inappropriate behaviour, as the principal symptoms of any mental disorder worthy of the name, the artificiality of the criminal responsibility tests simply ensured the detention of the grossly disordered together with the grossly disordered who had been civilly committed.[152]

Today we therefore say that the tests based upon an old-fashioned, pre-psychiatric view of mental illness are unsatisfactory. In the developed, scientific-age cultures of Europe and the United States we criticize the McNaghten Rules: they are based on a discredited view of the compartmentalization of the human mind; they focus unrealistically on the cognitive factor in mental disorder; they misleadingly rely on the concepts of delusion and partial and total insanity; they impede the giving of meaningful psychiatric testimony; they were devised under conditions of political pressure and probably narrowed the previously understood law; and they are workable only by reason of their regular breach. The result has been that the transatlantic jurisdictions have steadily moved away from the McNaghten position. Should Africa, torn between the 19th and the 20th centuries in terms of its psychiatric facilities, do the same?

The preliminary answer is that some parts of Africa, as we have seen, have done so already. There is only one carbon copy of the McNaghten Rules still in force and most of the significant developments are in the direction of expanding the responsibility tests to cover an accused's inability to control his behaviour. Nonetheless, most of the jurisdictions retain impaired cognition and moral-legal judgment as essential criteria in their responsibility formulations.

Moreover, it is generally true that in theory a defence based on the McNaghten right/wrong test will be broader than it will be in England or the United States. This is the inevitable result of the diversity of the African communities and their differential contact with the formal laws and community standards of their nation. There is for any African who is not wholly integrated into a westernized urban environment some difficulty in appreciating the state of the laws enacted by a remote central government. With the diversity of African and westernized cultures and the constant conflict/modification process of social evolution, there will be a similar difficulty in obtaining awareness of any single moral norm with which to accord one's behaviour. When, as we have seen, it is these very facts of culture conflict and change which are at the root of much mental disorder in Africa, the conclusion follows that the NcNaghten defence will probably be more widely available in Africa than in any more homogeneous culture.

But there is a stronger argument in favour of retaining the present position: the difficulty involved in implementing a change. Psychiatric facilities—psychiatrists to examine, diagnose, treat and testify, hospitals to accommodate, drugs and equipment as diagnostic aids and for specialized therapies—are only irregularly available. Most African countries have some facilities, few have none, none have all. Without any question, all that exists is being put to maximal use. If the number of patients to be diagnosed and treated were to increase without any corresponding increase in the facilities, either diagnosis and treatment would become unprofessionally meagre, or the system would break down. Neither is a palatable alternative. Yet either could be the consequence of broadening the present responsibility tests or of requiring pre-trial psychiatric examination on a wider footing.

If the present position does not change, on the other hand, an unsatisfactory system will be perpetuated. Most African countries, for example, have a mandatory death sentence for murder. The Roman-Dutch-based laws of southern Africa and the Indian-based code of Sudan recognize extenuating circumstances which may reduce the sentence to one of imprisonment. The mentally-disordered murderer who does not fall within the responsibility exemption will therefore either face the death penalty with the prospect of executive clemency, or hope for a judicial exercise of discretion in his favour.[153] But he may still be executed.[154]

Even conceding that he will not usually be executed, the result will be that the commuted sentence—or the judicial sentence in the case of a non-capital offence—will be served in prison. The consequences of this we have already examined:[155] they are likely to be strictly non-therapeutic and the possibilities of transfer to some more therapeutic regime are not exactly well-marked.

The practical realities of the situation are that no change will be made in African legislation and practices in this field in the foreseeable future. Legislatively and economically, the treatment of the mentally ill is a long way down the list of development priorities. Change must nonetheless be built into the fabric of social and legal attitudes so that the implementation of more progressive policies will be less painful when development has reached the stage of allowing it.

(1) Although legislation exists, which makes possible pre-trial medical examination of criminal defendants, more can now be done to provide diagnostic and information-supplying services to the courts. They are particularly deficient at the present time as a result of the continent-wide shortage of trained probation officers. Most countries have had legal provision for probation services for decades but the slowness with which the provisions have been implemented has been uniformly discouraging. Too much weight cannot be attached to the valuable auxiliary task performed by probation officers in presenting relevant background information to the courts and in assisting with the work of screening defendants for mental illness. As more light is thrown upon personality characteristics and the circumstances in which offences are committed, the greater is the aid given to the courts in deciding upon appropriate correctional measures.

(2) Something should be done to heighten the judges' awareness of psychiatric concepts, on a 'better late than never' basis. Although the supply of psychiatrists is slowly increasing, it will take many years before expert assistance is available in every case in which it is desirable. In the meantime, the judges will continue to instruct themselves, assessors or juries, as the individual case may be, on what constitutes mental illness. At the moment, there is only the inadequacy of an English legal education, and whatever personal insights and sympathies they have, to guide them. The answer may be a broader-based education at the new African law schools,[156] the interchange of information between psychiatrists and judges, or even the straightforward supplying of information about the symptomatology of common mental illnesses.[157] Amateur diagnosis

347

is obviously dangerous; but I take it for granted that amateur diagnosis that is sympathetic and partially informed is an improvement upon that which is neither. In due course, professional judgment involving clinical skill and experience would become available to supplant this makeshift expertise.

(3) Were change possible, the responsibility tests should be remodelled. Quite apart from any criticism of unreality which may be directed against the cognitive McNaghten-type formulation, an effort could be made to simplify the issues. What amounted to mental illness would always have to be determined somewhat imperfectly by the individual parts of the judge–assessors–jury trio, and no doubt this would continue to lead to the identification of only the manifestly disturbed offenders. The level of awareness of the latter two parts of the trio[158] might well be somewhat limited, but the hope would be that, with assistance and guidance from the judge, they would be able to function with rather more accuracy than at present.

If the basic postulate of mental illness, upon which the whole defence is to be based, can be described in the most general terms, the courts will be relieved of some of the embarrassment of trying to fit psychiatric categories into legislative language. A description such as 'unsoundness of mind' would give sufficient flexibility for the courts to fit their various conceptions of mental illness into the statutory formula. There would inevitably be doubt as to the inclusion of some psychiatric categories within this or any other description—'psychopathy' or 'sociopathy' in particular will probably defy classification (or even recognition) in the absence of psychiatric assistance—but simplification of the general terminology would make this no more difficult a task than under existing statutory formulae.

It is tempting to suggest that some guide-lines might be laid down as matter of law to help the courts in their determination of mental illness. Probably too many factors weigh against it. The existing findings of law which dictate the weight to be given to particular symptoms are good illustrations of the dangerous tendency such rules have to occlude certain areas of testimony which could otherwise be significant. Judgment must be exercised by the trier of fact but prejudgment may do an injustice to the issue.

348

Moreover, simplification of the responsibility issue could be arranged so as to have the effect of reducing the number of issues upon which a psychiatrically unaided decision was needed. The determination of the issue whether mental illness exists cannot be avoided, for it is the *sine qua non* of the whole topic. But whether the morality of African peoples, their governments or their legal advisers would require the continuation of additional tests which call for the differentiation of different classes of the mentally ill, be they in terms of cognition or control, is another matter. Responsibility tests which called for exculpation simply on the showing of cause and effect between the illness and the offence would be neither inappropriate nor impossible to operate.[159]

(4) It should not be impossible to make major improvements in correctional facilities without going so far as the wholesale revamping of the system of psychiatric institutional care. It is misleading to suggest, as one observer has suggested,[160] that the contribution of psychiatry to the solution of penal problems in Africa is necessarily measured by the presence or absence of psychiatric hospitals. Indeed, psychiatric hospitals of the conventional type have not adapted themselves easily to African conditions, and doubt may genuinely be cast on how much of a role they have to play in developed African penal systems.

Secure conditions of treatment are obviously going to be and remain a vital consideration in the case of some proportion of the mentally ill who find themselves caught up in the processes of the criminal law. But it must be remembered that at the present time committal to African mental hospitals through these processes is not so much a function of the dangerousness of the patient-defendant's condition but of the lack of availability of other facilities. Were probation machinery to develop further, it would become feasible to make more regular use of the insertion of psychiatric treatment conditions into probation orders. In this way, the increasing availability of psychiatrists could be put to maximal use without at the same time calling for an impossible extension of institutional facilities.

Greater use could also, perhaps, be made of other forms of minimum security treatment, either by using the probation device or by direct committal on finding of irresponsibility. Mental health work carried out in the context of Nigerian villages, for example, has demonstrated that a therapeutically organized community can give adequate care and minimize impairment and chronicity. The cost has been found to be low and the community attitudes favourable and helpful.[161] And if by the extension of legal activity into these areas the emphasis commonly placed on the link between capital charges and mental treatment can be reduced, considerable impetus will be given to the orderly development of further co-operation between law and psychiatry.

(5) Finally, the long-term plan must be to make psychiatric services available to a wider range of convicted criminals. How far they will be able to make a significant impact on the problems of criminality will naturally depend on the access the psychiatrist has to the offenders and in particular the means through which they are referred to him. Non-African studies may indicate the nature of the problem here. In the United States, for example, studies conducted at various times between 1935 and 1955 indicated that approximately 20 per cent of groups of either convicted offenders or prison inmates were in need of psychiatric treatment and that 2 per cent of these displayed severe psychosis.[162] A modern survey of over 500 successive routine admissions to a prison in the United Kingdom revealed that 24 per cent merited further examination for indications of subnormality and 32 per cent showed symptoms of other psychiatric disorder.[163] As soon as it becomes possible to adopt an effective treatment policy in association with penal objectives, the desirability of adequate psychiatric screening facilities is clearly indicated.

It may well prove helpful, too, for the prison community to have a psychiatrist resident within it. The articulated objective of most prison systems may be rehabilitation, but little or nothing has yet been done to implement this goal. Drastic adjustments will need to be made in attitudes within the systems, and in a broad sense the psychiatrist's role will be to make his special knowledge part of the professional commonsense of the personnel working in the institution. The task of reducing the punitive elements in penal institutions remains to be tackled—a task in which the psychiatrist can play a vital part if his ideas and objectives are not misunderstood. Opportunities must be allowed for individual inmates to express themselves freely to members of staff who are not wholly identified with the custodial regime—a role which can be played by the psychiatrist just as much as the social welfare worker or chaplain. But these are distant objectives, even in the more developed Western nations: in African prison systems, the under-education of prison personnel and the widespread lack of conception of the prison as a constructive agency mean that the objective is not even clearly seen and the means to reach it remain largely unconsidered.

Moreover, the psychiatrist has an important administrative advisory function within the present prison structure which may well be developed in the future. At the moment, it tends to be limited to advising the authorities whether or not a man convicted of a capital offence is of sound mind so that the sentence of death may be carried out. There are, however, opportunities even now for the authorities to seek advice about the release of convicts—for example, when considering the release of an offender who has been sentenced to life imprisonment. Advice is generally not sought from a psychiatrist but there are strong arguments in favour of making this a prescribed part of the pre-release system, should parole systems or indeterminate sentences find favour in Africa. Until predictive techniques are introduced and refined, psychiatric insights will provide valuable contributions to the development of reasonable and workable criteria for determining dangerousness.

In the long run, we may see the development of small-scale psychiatric units within prisons or larger-scale psychiatric institutions operating within the penal system. Such institutions as Herstedvester in Denmark, the Van der Hoeven Clinic in the Netherlands, Grendon Underwood in the United Kingdom, or the Patuxent Institute in the United States, provide varying models for such developments. But the outlay of capital on buildings, equipment and personnel which they call for, and the relatively sophisticated attitudes towards correctional treatment which they presume, make them unlikely developments for the next generation of psychiatry in Africa.

NOTES

1. For a modern synopsis of problems and progress, see Kimble, *Tropical Africa*, vol. ii, chap. 17 (1960). It must be remembered, of course, that not all superstition impeded the development of modern medical

facilities: see, e.g., Ajose, 'Preventive Medicine and Superstition in Nigeria, 27 *Africa*, 268 (1957).

2. Where there are 12 mental hospitals and 80 psychiatrists. The facilities are available at the rates of 3 beds/1000 white population and 1 bed/1000 non-white. All the psychiatrists are white. See Walton, 'Psychiatric Practice in a Multiracial Society', 3 *Comprehensive Psychiatry*, 255 (1962).

3. The division into indigenous and expatriate is not fanciful. Quite apart from problems of language, it may well be that social stresses in any given culture may make inter-racial communication more difficult in the doctor–patient relationship: see, e.g., the account given by Walton, *op. cit.* Dawson, 'Urbanization and Mental Health in a West African Community', in Kiev, ed., *Magic, Faith and Healing*, 341 (1964), reports that in Sierra Leone patients are often removed from the mental hospital and taken to traditional healers 'that have complete understanding of the social complications involved'.

4. See, however, Albino and Thompson, 'The effects of sudden weaning on Zulu children', 29 *British Journal of Medical Psychology*, 177 (1956).

5. These are dealt with in detail in the Yoruba context by Prince, 'Indigenous Yoruba Psychiatry', in Kiev, *op. cit.*, 84 (1965). See also Gelfand, 'Psychiatric Disorders as Recognized by the Shona', *ibid.*, 156; 'An Ndembu Doctor in Practice', *ibid.*, 230; Messing, 'Group Therapy and Social Status in the Zar Cult of Ethiopia', in Opler, ed., *Culture and Mental Health*, 319 (1959); Field, *Search for Security, passim* (1960).

6. The Aro, Abeokuta scheme, described by Lambo, 'Neuropsychiatric Observations in the Western Region of Nigeria', 1956 (ii), *British Medical Journal*, 1388; 'Patterns of Psychiatric Care in Developing African Countries', in Kiev, *op. cit.*, 443, 447–51; Randal, 'Witch Doctors and Psychiatry', *Harpers Magazine*, December 1965.

7. Jahoda, 'Traditional Healers and Other Institutions Concerned with Mental Illness in Ghana', 7 *International Journal of Social Psychiatry*, 245 (1961). The integration proposal is contained in most of the contributions to Kiev, *op. cit.* Opposition to integration appears to be based on a narrow commitment to Western psychiatry and over-simplification of the problem of supply and demand in Africa: see Margetts, 'The Future of Psychiatry in East Africa', 37 *East African Medical Journal*, 448 (1960).

8. Lambo, *art. cit.*, 1956 (ii) *British Medical Journal*, 1388, 1389.

9. Carothers, 'Frontal Lobe Function of the African', 97 *Journal of Mental Science*, 112 (1951).

10. Wittkower and Fried, 'Some Problems of Transcultural Psychiatry', in Opler, *op. cit.*, 489, at 492. Cf. Leighton, Lambo and others, *Psychiatric Disorder among the Yoruba*, esp. chap. vi (1963) ('The Problem of Cultural Distortion').

11. In particular, idea systems which rely heavily on belief in supernatural causation have profound implications for analysis, diagnosis and treatment. Leighton, Lambo and others, *op. cit.*, 113–14, report that the

Yoruba ascribe causative power in mental illness to such factors as malignant influences, superhuman and human, drugs and medicines, heredity, contagion, violation of one's own destiny, fate, cosmic forces and physical or psychological traumata.

12. E.g. Lambo, 'The Role of Cultural Factors in Paranoid Psychosis among the Yoruba Tribe', 101 *Journal of Mental Science*, 239, 247 (1955), speaking of the differentiation of normal cultural beliefs in supernatural powers and paranoid psychosis.

13. E.g. by Tooth, *Studies in Mental Illness in the Gold Coast*, 41 (1950).

14. Carothers, *The African Mind in Health and Disease*, 139 (1953), and studies cited there; Benedict and Jacke, 'Mental Illness in Primitive Societies', 17 *Psychiatry*, 377 (1954); Loudon, 'Psychogenic Disorder and Social Conflict among the Zulu', in Opler, *op. cit.*, 363; Lambo, 'Further Neuropsychiatric Observations in Nigeria', 1960 (ii) *British Medical Journal*, 1696, 1697 (noting no predominance of any sub-variety); Walton, *art. cit.*, 262.

15. Carothers, *op. cit.*, chap. 9; Loudon, *art. cit.*, 363; Wittkower and Fried, *art. cit.*, 493.

16. Carothers, *op. cit.*, 148–52; Loudon, *art. cit.*, 364–5.

17. Lambo, *art. cit.*, 1700–2 (out-patients and patients at native treatment centres); Field, *op. cit.*, 149 (1960), reported that depression was the most common mental illness encountered among rural Akan (Ghana) women 'and nearly all such patients come to the shrines with spontaneous self-accusations of witchcraft'; Walton, *art. cit.*, 262 (out-patients).

18. See Lambo, 'Malignant Anxiety: A Syndrome Associated with Criminal Conduct in Africans', 108 *Journal of Mental Science*, 256 (1962). One suspect that like the 'frenzied anxiety' reported by Carothers, *op. cit.*, Lambo's 'malignant anxiety' is only of pathoplastic significance in schizophrenia and not a disease *sui generis*.

19. Shelley and Watson, 'An Investigation Concerning Mental Disorder in the Nyasaland Native', 82 *Journal of Mental Science*, 701, 703 (1936)—of the Central Lunatic Asylum, Zomba, Nyasaland (now Malawi).

20. Cf. Tooth, *op. cit.*, 24—of the Colonial Mental Hospital, Accra, Gold Coast (now Ghana); and Dawson, *art. cit.*—Kissy Mental Hospital, Sierra Leone. It is interesting to note that in South Africa, where the psychiatric facilities for non-whites are limited (see note 2 above), the rate of admission of non-whites to mental hospitals following criminal charges is extremely high. The remainder of non-white admissions were all classified as emergencies: see Walton, *art. cit.*, esp. Table 2.

21. Field, *op. cit.*, 149.

22. Wittkower and Fried, *art. cit.*, 495.

23. Tooth, *op. cit.*, 61–2. He also noted, however (52), that delusional content in psychosis was determined by cultural factors and that the content in the cases of literate psychotics therefore differed from that of the illiterate; cf. Wittkower and Fried, *art. cit.*, 494.

24. Carothers, *op. cit.*, 130–3.
25. Lambo, *art. cit.*, 247.
26. De Vos and Miner, 'Oasis and Casbah—A Study in Acculturative Stress', in Opler, *op. cit.*, chap. 14. The quotation is from p. 345.
27. Published as Leighton, Lambo and others, *Psychiatric Disorder among the Yoruba* (1963).
28. Procedural legislation frequently provides for committal to 'a mental hospital, prison or other suitable place of safe custody': see, e.g., Sierra Leone Criminal Procedure Act, s. 64 (4); cf. Nigeria Criminal Procedure Act, s. 222; Ghana Criminal Procedure Code, s. 133 (5); Uganda Criminal Procedure Code, s. 162 (5); Zanzibar Criminal Procedure Decree, s. 156 (5). Where the medical facilities are inadequate, the legislation may simply call for committal to prison: e.g. Bechuanaland Criminal Procedure and Evidence Proclamation, s. 169 (1) and (2).
    The order made by the Nyasaland High Court in R. *v. Alidia*, 1959 (1) R. & N. 221, 224, is typical: 'It is hereby ordered that the Accused person be kept in custody as a criminal lunatic in the Mental Hospital at Zomba, or if suitable accommodation is not available at the Mental Hospital at Zomba, then in the Central Prison at Zomba, until such time as the wishes of the Governor are made known.'
29. Enahoro, *Fugitive Offender*, 92–3 (1965). The use of chains and other restraints, frequently without reason and without the keeping of proper records, was the subject of official report in Nigeria at this time: see Paterson, *A Report to His Excellency the Governor of Nigeria on Crime and Its Treatment in the Colony and Protectorate*, para. 12 (1944).
30. The barbarism is not necessarily colonially inspired. Prince has pointed out that traditional healers frequently resort to chaining their patients to prevent injury: Prince, in Kiev., *op. cit.*, 117.
31. E.g. Bechuanaland Prisons Regulations, reg. 17; Kenya Prisons Ordinance, 1963, s. 39; Nigeria Prisons Act, 1960, ss. 19, 21; Rhodesia and Nyasaland Prisons Act, 1955, ss. 72, 73 (now in force in Southern Rhodesia and Malawi); Liberia Criminal Procedure Law, s. 737; South Africa Mental Disorders Act, ss. 32–5; Zambia Prisons Act, 1965, ss. 70, 71. The Uganda Prisons Act, s. 58, provides that persons of unsound mind shall only be kept in prison long enough to effect certification, then transferred to a mental hospital.
32. See, e.g., *Memorandum on the Treatment of Offenders*, Advisory Committee on the Treatment of Offenders in the Colonies, para. 49 (1954). The recommendations of the Colonial Secretary's Consultant Psychiatrist for the reorganization of the Nigerian system are referred to in that country's *Annual Report on the Treatment of Offenders for 1956–57*. Not a great deal has since been done to implement them.
33. The 1960–1 Report (the first year of independence) is the last to be published. See *Annual Reports on the Treatment of Offenders*, 1950–7; *Annual Reports of the Federal Prisons Department*, 1958–61.

34. Unless it is otherwise stated, this section relates only to those English-speaking countries about which information is available to us.

35. The death penalty is commonly mandatory for murder. One consequence of this is that defendants are commonly advised to plead insanity only in defence to murder charges; in other cases, ordinary imprisonment or any lesser sentence may well be preferable to inadequate and indefinite treatment for mental illness.

36. We personally know of the refusal of an African psychiatrist's request to see all charged murderers, on the grounds that distances were too large and security arrangements too tenuous for the authorities to be able to agree. A judge warned the same psychiatrist that he would kill himself with work if he tried to carry out any such project.

37. R. v. Podola, [1960] 1 Q.B. 325, [1959] 3 All E.R. 418; R. v. Muyanda Mudia (1954), 5 N.R.L.R. 302 (Northern Rhodesia); Kaplotwa s/o Tarino v. R., [1957] E.A. 553 (Kenya).

38. Kaplotwa s/o Tarino v. R.

39. R. v. Njiri, 1959 (2) R. & N. 241 (Southern Rhodesia).

40. R. v. Phiri, 1958 R. & N. 1008 (Northern Rhodesia).

41. E.g., Sierra Leone Criminal Code, s. 64 (1): Kenya and Uganda Criminal Procedure Codes, s. 162 (1); Zanzibar Criminal Procedure Decree, s. 156 (1).

42. See, e.g., R. v. Nyasulu, 1956 R. & N. 633 (Nyasaland), setting out the practice for that country.

43. Criminal Procedure Code, s. 133 (1).

44. Nigeria Criminal Procedure Act, s. 223 (3); Northern Nigeria Criminal Procedure Code, s. 320 (3).

45. Sohan Singh s/o Lakha Singh v. R., [1958] E.A. 28 (Kenya)—but if the defence fails to call it, knowing that it is available, it will not then be allowed to claim that there was insufficient inquiry into the accused's mental condition. The position in Liberia is uncertain; it appears that in theory there must be medical evidence before a finding of mental illness for any purpose; see p. 338 below.

46. See, e.g., The Queen v. Madugha (1958), 3 F.S.C. 1 (Nigeria); R. v. Mandala, 1957 R. & N. 251 (Nyasaland).

47. For the place of detention, see note 29 above.

48. E.g., Sierra Leone Criminal Procedure Code, s. 64 (3); Ghana Criminal Procedure Code, s. 133 (3); Kenya and Uganda Criminal Procedure Codes, s. 162 (3); Nigeria Criminal Procedure Act, s. 225 (1); Northern Nigeria Criminal Procedure Code, s. 322; South Africa Mental Disorders Act, s. 40; Zanzibar Criminal Procedure Decree, s. 156 (3). The statement in R. v. Sepetsi, 1927 O.P.D. 312 (South Africa), that a finding of mental disorder under s. 28 of the Mental Disorders Act absolves the accused from all further proceedings, appears to be based on the misinterpretation of the section, which applies to those initially unfit to stand trial and

not to those raising insanity as a substantive defence. S. 36 allows the resumption of the trial following recovery.

49. E.g. *Sudan Government v. Abdel A'l Mahmud Khalid* (1962) S.L.J.R. 115 (Sudan)—2½ years.

50. The duty and the procedure to be followed are set out in R. *v. Katete and others*, (1948) 6 U.L.R. 200 (Uganda); *Leseroi v. R.*, [1964] E.A. 111 (Kenya).

51. R. *v. Governor of Stafford Prison, ex p. Emery*, [1909] 2 K.B. 81, on the interpretation of the Criminal Lunatics Act, 1800; cf. Archbold, *Pleading, Evidence & Practice in Criminal Cases*, 35th ed., ss. 464–5 (1962). Modern legislative reform does not appear to have changed the position, for the Criminal Procedure (Insanity) Act, 1964, although referring to the case of an accused under a 'disability' preventing trial (s. 4 (1)), then provides that the court shall order such a person to be 'admitted to such hospital as may be specified by the Secretary of State' (s. 5 (1)). Discharge will then be in the discretion of the Secretary of State.

52. South Africa Criminal Procedure Act, 1955, s. 164 and Mental Disorders Act, 1916, s. 28; R. *v. Mamykla*, 1913 T.P.D. 464 (South Africa); Southern Rhodesia Mental Disorders Act, 1936, s. 30; Bechuanaland Criminal Procedure and Evidence Proclamation, ss. 163, 169.

53. E.g., in Gardiner and Lansdown, *South African Criminal Law and Procedure*, 6th ed., vol. 1, 91–2 (1957) and see the authorities in notes 54 and 55 below.

54. *In re Pupu*, 1959 (1) R. & N. 377 (Southern Rhodesia), in which the Attorney-General finally did not oppose the discharge from mental hospital, committal to prison and later discharge. It does not appear that the trial judge's call for amending legislation has yet been acted upon.

55. *State v. Maxamba*, 1964 (1) S.A. 645 (South Africa). Section 28 of the Mental Disorders Act, 1916, the machinery of which section is incorporated into s. 164 of the Criminal Procedure Act, 1955, refers to committal to 'a gaol or institution'; cf. the English legislation, note 51 above.

56. E.g. Nigerian Criminal Procedure Act, ss. 225–35 (in force in the southern areas of the country); Sierra Leone Criminal Procedure Act, ss. 64–9; Northern Nigeria Criminal Procedure Code, s. 261; *Zaria Native Authority v. Aishatu yar Dauda Bakori*, 1964 N.N.L.R. 25.

57. Uganda, Kenya and Malawi Criminal Procedure Codes, s. 167; Zanzibar Criminal Procedure Act, s. 161; R. *v. Tselize*, 1956 R. & N. 232 (Nyasaland); *Leseroi v. R.*, [1964] E.A. 111 (Kenya).

58. R. *v. Tselize*, note 57 above.

59. The familiar habit is too common to be documented. Recent illustrations of its effect in African criminal statutory interpretation are given in Okonkwo and Naish, *Criminal Law in Nigeria*, 72–95 (1964) (*mens rea*); Naish, 'A Redefinition of Provocation under the Criminal Code', 1 *Nigerian Law Journal*, 10 (1964) (provocation); Seidman, 'Note—Intent and the Law of Murder', 1 *University of Ghana Law Journal*, 73 (1964) (*mens rea*); Seidman, 'Witch-Murder and *Mens Rea*: A Problem of Society

Under Radical Social Change', 28 *Modern Law Review*, 46 (1963) (*mens rea*).

60. E.g. R. *v. Ross* (1932), 14 K.L.R. 148 (Kenya); R. *v. Kibiegon arap Bargutwa* (1939), 6 E.A.C.A. 142 (Kenya); R. *v. Gerevasi s/o Lutabingwa* (1942), 9 E.A.C.A. 57 (Tanganyika); *Nyinge s/o Suwatu v. R.*, [1959] E.A. 974 (Kenya).

61. E.g. *Sudan Government v. Mousa Adam Ishag* (1958), S.L.J.R. 1 (Sudan); R. *v. Nasamu* (1940), 6 W.A.C.A. 74 (Nigeria); R. *v. Omoni* (1949), 12 W.A.C.A. 511 (Nigeria).

62. E.g. R. *v. Frafra*, [1959] G.L.R. 442 (Ghana); R. *v. Tembo*, 1961 R. & N. 858 (Northern Rhodesia).

63. See Elias, *Ghana and Sierra Leone*, 304 (1962).

64. *Report of the Royal Commission on Capital Punishment*, Cmd. 8922, para. 344 (1953).

65. *Ibid.*, paras. 386–92 (epilepsy); *Bratty v. Attorney-General for Northern Ireland*, [1963] A.C. 386, [1961] 3 All E.R. 523 (psychomotor epilepsy); R. *v. Kemp*, [1957] 1 Q.B. 399, [1956] 3 All E.R. 249 (cerebral arteriosclerosis).

66. E.g. *Report of the Royal Commission on Capital Punishment* (1953), paras. 212 (definition of 'mental disease'), 393–402 (psychopathy). In *Attorney-General for Northern Ireland v. Gallagher*, [1963] A.C. 349, [1961] 3 All E.R. 299, however, at least two of the Lords of Appeal appear to have contemplated the possibility that a psychopathic condition could come within the scope of the McNaghten defence.

67. The draft was originally submitted in 1837 and then underwent revision before being put before the Legislative Council and passed in 1860: Ratanlal and Thakore, *The Law of Crimes*, 19th ed., 1 (1956).

68. Indian Penal Code, s. 84.

69. Penal Code, s. 51.

70. Penal Code, s. 50.

71. Criminal Code, s. 28. 'Natural mental infirmity' refers to subnormality: R. *v. Omoni*; *The Queen v. Tabigen* (1960), 5 F.S.C. 8 (Nigeria).

72. Criminal Code, s. 27. At the time the Code was first promulgated in 1892 the only official categorization of mental defectives was that into 'idiots' and 'imbeciles' by the Idiots Act, 1886. Within a few years, a Royal Commission undertook the first full inquiry into mental deficiency and its management, and the 1913 English legislation recognized four categories of defectives: idiots, imbeciles, feeble-minded, and moral defectives. Although, therefore, the original intention in 1892 may have been for the Ghanaian provision to cover all classes of defectives, by the time the code was re-enacted in 1960, it is clear that its terminology did not.

73. Penal Law, s. 15. With the exception of one sentence, this was based on the New York provision (now Penal Law, §1120). The New York history appears to resemble that given for England in the previous note. In the early 19th century (at the time the Liberian law was being developed),

'idiocy' was recognized by the New York courts as a distinct classification and 'imbecility' was a blanket term covering all other weakness of intellect: see, e.g., *Odell v. Buck*, 21 Wend. 141 (N.Y., 1839); *Stewart's Executor v. Lispenard*, 26 Wend. 253 (N.Y., 1841); *Blanchard v. Nestle*, 3 Den. 37 (N.Y., 1846). By the beginning of this century, its was recognized that there were mental defectives who were not 'imbeciles' and who could therefore not have the benefit of the defence under the Penal Law (see, e.g., *People v. Farmer*, 87 N.E. 457, 194 N.Y. 251 (1909); *People v. Moran*, 163 N.E. 553, 249 N.Y. 179 (1928)). Following the adoption of mental deficiency legislation, the courts recognized at least three categories of defectives: idiots, imbeciles, and morons (*People v. Hoffmann*, 8 N.Y.S. 2d pro 83 (1938)). Were the Liberian courts to adopt the New York authorities, s. 15 of the Liberian Penal Law would not therefore give a defence to all classes of defectives.

74. See also his *Digest of the Criminal Law*, 6th ed., Art. 28 (1904) and *A History of the Criminal Law of England*, vol. ii, 149 (1883).

75. *Tadeo Oyee s/o Duru v. R.*, [1959] E.A. 407 (Uganda).

76. Gardiner and Lansdown, *South African Criminal Law and Procedure*, 6th ed., vol. 1, 87 (1957).

77. *Ibid.*, 89.

78. *R. v. Kennedy*, 1951 (4) S.A. 431 (South Africa).

79. E.g. *R. v. Anderson*, 1928 C.P.D. 195 (South Africa) (*encephalitis lethargica*).

80. E.g. Kenya Penal Code, s. 13; Uganda Penal Code, s. 12; Zambia Penal Code, s. 13; Zanzibar Penal Decree, s. 13.

81. Criminal Code, s. 27: the offender will be excused if he either does not know the nature or consequences of the act or is so deluded as to make him an unfit subject for punishment. Seidman, 'Insanity as a Defence under the Criminal Code, 1960 (Ghana)', 1 *University of Ghana Law Journal*, 42, 46–7 (1964) suggests that the use of the word 'consequences' in the text has the effect of bringing into issue the defendant's capacity to control his conduct. It is hard to agree: the scope of the cognitive test is admittedly expanded but still remains at no more than a cognitive level.

82. Penal Code, s. 50: the offender will be excused if he does not possess the power of appreciating the nature of his acts or of controlling them.

83. See references in note 80.

84. As was done in *R. v. Kibiegon arap Bargutwa*, and *R. v. Gerevasi s/o Lutabingwa*.

85. *A History of the Criminal Law of England*, vol. ii, 160 *et seq.* (1883).

86. Under the McNaghten formulation the accused 'would be considered in the same situation as to responsibility as if the facts with respect to which the delusions exist were real', *ibid.*, 156.

87. See note 85.

88. E.g. *R. v. Inyang* (1946), 12 W.A.C.A. 5 (Nigeria); *R. v. Omoni; Echem v. The Queen* (1952), 14 W.A.C.A. 158 (Nigeria).

89. E.g. R. *v. Tembo*; R. *v. Magata s/o Kachehakana*, [1957] E.A. 330 (Uganda).
90. R. *v. Codere* (1916), 12 Cr. App. R. 21; R. *v. Windle*, [1952] 2 Q.B. 826, [1952] 2 All E.R. 1. The pre- and post-McNaghten authorities adopting the broader view are reviewed in *Stapleton v. The Queen*, 86 C.L.R. 358 (1952) in which the High Court of Australia refused to follow the *Windle* decision. See also Morris, ' "Wrong" in the McNaghten Rules', 16 *Modern Law Review*, 433 (1953).
91. E.g. R. *v. Kamau s/o Njeroge* (1939), 6 E.A.C.A. 133 (Kenya).
92. *Muswi s/o Musele v. R.* (1956), 23 E.A.C.A. 622 (Kenya); *Golowa v. R.*, 1964 R. & N. 17 (Northern Rhodesia).
93. Stephen, *A History of the Criminal Law of England*, vol. ii, 167 (1883).
94. Gardiner and Lansdown, *op. cit.*, 90.
95. Penal Code, s. 51.
96. Note 92 above.
97. Criminal Code, s. 27 (2).
98. R. *v. Grumah* (1957), 2 W.A.L.R. 255 (Ghana); the question of interpretation was not raised at all in the actual report.
99. R. *v. Moshie*, [1959] G.L.R. 343 (Ghana).
100. *Kwame Degarti v. R.*, (1960) July–December Cyclostyled Judgments (Criminal), 120 (Ghana).
101. *Sergeant Bodie* (1964), Crim. App. No. 31/63 (Ghana); *Mohamadu Akpawey* (1965), Crim. App. No. 159/65 (Ghana). I am indebted to Professor R. B. Seidman of the University of Ghana for the last citation. See generally on the Ghana provisions, Seidman, 'Insanity as a Defence under the Criminal Code, 1960 (Ghana)', 1 *University of Ghana Law Journal*, 42 (1964).
102. R. *v. Hay* (1899), 16 S.C. 290 (South Africa); R. *v. Koortz*, 1953 (3) S.A. 303 (South Africa); R. *v. Sprighton*, 1939 S. R. 34 (Southern Rhodesia).
103. From R. *v. Haynes* (1859), 1 F. & F. 666 to R. *v. Kopsch* (1925), 19 Cr. App. R. 50 and *Sodeman v. R.*, [1936] 2 All E.R. 1133 to *Attorney-General for South Australia v. Brown*, [1960] A.C. 432, [1960] 1 All E.R. 734, the English courts and the Privy Council have vigorously opposed the 'dangerous doctrine' and 'fantastic', 'subversive' theory. Section 2 of the Homicide Act, 1957, now effectively allows a defence in the case of most manifestations of inability to control behaviour.
104. Nigerian Criminal Code, s. 28; Sudan Penal Code, s. 50.
105. Despite Stephen's hope that uncontrollable behaviour would be covered by the cognitive tests (*A History of the Criminal Law of England*, vol. ii, 167 *et seq.* (1883)), the East and Central African courts have uniformly held that it is not: R. *v. Ebrahim Weraga s/o Wamala* (1943), 10 E.A.C.A. 48 (Uganda); R. *v. Shekanga s/o Ndeka* (1948), 15 E.A.C.A. 158 (Tanganyika); R. *v. Wolomosi Phiri (No. 1)* (1954), 5 N.R.L.R. 186 (Northern Rhodesia).
106. E.g. Bechuanaland Criminal Procedure and Evidence Proclamation, s. 169 (2); Ghana Criminal Procedure Code, s. 137 (1), (2); Kenya Criminal Procedure Code, s. 166 (1); South Africa Mental Disorders Act, s. 29;

Uganda Criminal Procedure Code, s. 166 (1); Zanzibar Criminal Procedure Decree, s. 160 (1), (2). Nigeria uses the terminology of 'acquittal' on the ground of mental disorder but there is still a mandatory committal if the court finds that the accused actually did the act alleged: Nigeria Criminal Procedure Act, ss. 229–30; Northern Nigeria Criminal Procedure Code, ss. 326–7.

107. E.g. the South African Mental Disorders Act, ss. 25, 38, have the most complete obligatory report procedure, requiring annual reports during the first three years and reports in the fifth and every succeeding fifth year; the Kenya and Uganda Criminal Procedure Codes, s. 166 (2), call for a report on mental condition to be made to the execution three years after committal and every two years thereafter; the Nigerian codes require medical officers to report whenever requested by the executive: Nigeria Criminal Procedure Act, s. 231; Northern Nigeria Criminal Procedure Code, s. 328.

108. The discharge procedures are usually the same as those following the recovery of a person originally found unfit to make his defence: see pp. 328–30 above. In some jurisdictions, the judical authority may impose limitations on release at the time of original committal: see, e.g., *Sudan Government v. Adam Musa Abu Hamad*, (1961) S.L.J.R. 232 (Sudan)—never to be released without reference back to the court.

109. *R. v. Bastian*, [1958] 1 All E.R. 568; *R. v. Nott* (1960), 43 Cr. App. R. 8; *Bratty v. Att.-Gen. for N. Ireland*, [1961] 3 All E.R. 523, per Lord Denning. *Contra, R. v. Price*, [1962] 3 All E.R. 957. The practice is now approved by the Criminal Procedure (Insanity) Act, 1964, s. 6.

110. *Republic v. Mandi s/o Ngoda*, [1963] E.A. 153 (Tanganyika).

111. Although the verdict would be 'guilty but insane', it has been held that this amounts not to a guilty verdict but to an acquittal: *Felstead v. R.*, [1914] A.C. 534.

112. See, e.g., Northern Nigeria Capital Cases Procedure, Part A (1960). The procedure calls for the obtaining of information about antecedents ('with special reference to his mental condition') by the police: rule 2; and observation and report by a medical officer while the accused is in custody awaiting trial: rules 5–11. If the accused is detained in a town which has no medical officer, he must be transferred to one which has: rule 12. In Kenya, in addition to other investigatory procedures, the magistrate must automatically inquire of the local mental hospital whether an accused has any record there at the time of committing him for trial on a capital charge: *Circular to Magistrates*, No. 2 of 1937, 17 (2) K.L.R. 130.

113. *R. v. Emi*, 1957 R. & N. 201 (Nyasaland); *Nyinge s/o Suwatu v. R.*, note 60 above.

114. *R. v. Holliday*, 1924 A.D. 250 (South Africa).

115. *Muswi s/o Musele v. R.*, note 92 above; *Nyinge s/o Suwatu v. R.*, note 60 above. The Kenya courts have lent support to their position here by

taking the view in addition that the prosecution must establish the accused's fitness to stand trial if the court questions it: *Kaplotwa s/o Tarino v. R.*, note 37 above.

116. *Republic v. Mandi*, note 110 above.

117. *R. v. Emi*, note 113 above; *R. v. Mandala*, note 46 above.

118. *R. v. Smit*, 1950 (4) S.A. 165 (South Africa); *R. v. Sprighton*, note 102 above; *R. v. Kachinga* (1946), 13 E.A.C.A. 135 (Nyasaland); *R. v. Kabande s/o Kilugwe* (1948), 15 E.A.C.A. 135 (Uganda); *Republic v. Saidi Kabila Kinuga*, [1963] E.A. 1 (Tanganyika); *R. v. Mwose s/o Mwiba* (1948), 15 E.A.C.A. 161 (Kenya); *R. v. Yaro Biu*, 1964 N.N.L.R. 45 (N. Nigeria); *R. v. Ashigifuwo* (1948), 12 W.A.C.A. 389 (Nigeria); *R. v. Wangara* (1944), 10 W.A.C.A. 236 (Gold Coast).

119. The mental disorder bringing a woman within the offence of infanticide is deemed to give rise to a different situation from the straightforward insanity defence: the burden of proving normality therefore rests on the prosecution and a reasonable doubt that the woman is abnormal will be sufficient to establish the defence: *Yowanina Namayaja v. R.* (1953), 20 E.A.C.A. 204 (Uganda). *Sed quaere.*

120. *Scott v. Liberia* (1904), 1 L.L.R. 430 (Liberia); *Carew v. Jessenah* (1958), 13 L.L.R. 168 (Liberia).

121. *R. v. Anuku* (1940), 6 W.A.C.A. 91 (Nigeria).

122. *R. v. Tembo*, note 62 above; *R. v. Ashigifuwo*, note 118 above—in court the accused said he knew nothing about the charge or the offence; at times his answers were reasonable, at other times not; throughout he was listless and apathetic.

123. *R. v. Mandala*, note 46 above.

124. See, e.g., *R. v. Grumah*, [1959] G.L.R. 307 (Ghana).

125. ". . . not expert evidence of insanity but it is evidence of some abnormality of conduct': *R. v. Ashigifuwo*, per Verity, C.J., note 118 above; cf. *Sudan Government v. Gabra Angello Dafaalla* (1961), S.L.J.R. 32; *Sudan Government v. Ahmed el Obeid Saghayroun* (1961), S.L.J.R. 123; *R. v. Yeboah*, [1959] G.L.R. 434; *R. v. Grumah*, note 124 above.

126. These were the characteristics adduced in evidence in *R. v. Inyang*, note 88 above.

127. *Ibid.* This kind of evidence appears to have been given little weight in England: see Pitt-Lewis, Smith and Hawke, *The Insane and the Law*, 34, 232 (1895), and *R. v. Smith* (1910), 5 Cr. App. R. 123.

128. All the questions framed in the McNaghten case were, of course, expressed in terms of total and partial delusions. For 19th-century authorities which treated delusions as symptoms *sine qua non*, see Martin, B., in *R. v. Townley* (1863), F. & F. 839 and Parke, B., in *R. v. Barton* (1848), 3 Cox C.C. 275. The early stress on delusions in Anglo-American psychiatry is emphasized in Dain, *Concepts of Insanity in the United States, 1789–1865*, 6 (1964).

129. *R. v. Inyang*, note 88 above.

130. *Echem v. The Queen*, note 88 above; *Sudan Government v. Gabra Angello Dafaalla*, note 125 above; *Nyinge s/o Suwatu v. R.*, note 60 above.
131. *Sudan Government v. Mousa Adam Ishag*, note 61 above.
132. E.g., self-defence based on a supposed attack by witchcraft has commonly been rejected: *Konkomba v. R.* (1952), 14 W.A.C.A. 236 (Gold Coast); *Gadam v. The Queen* (1954), 14 W.A.C.A. 442 (Nigeria); *Attorney-General for Nyasaland v. Jackson*, 1957 R. & N. 443 (Nyasaland). Such a belief has, however, been taken into consideration in East Africa in determining whether provocation existed in law: see, e.g., *R. v. Fabiano* (1941), 8 E.A.C.A. 96 (Uganda); *R. v. Kajuna s/o Mbake* (1945), 12 E.A.C.A. 104 (Tanganyika); *R. v. Akope and others* (1947), 14 E.A.C.A. 105 (Kenya) and Malawi Penal Code, s. 199. The accused's belief that he was killing a spirit and not a human being has been held to exculpate in some jurisdictions (e.g., *Sudan Government v. Abdullah Mukhtar Nur* (1959), S.L.J.R. 1 (Sudan)) but not in others (e.g., *R. v. Mbombela*, 1933 A.D. 269 (South Africa). The authorities are critically reviewed in Seidman, 'Witch-Murder and *Mens Rea*', note 59 above.
133. E.g., *Muswi s/o Musele v. R.*, note 92 above; *The Queen v. Tabigen*, note 71 above; *R. v. Radebe*, 1915 A. D. 96 (South Africa) *R. v. Molehane*, 1942 G.W.L. 64 (South Africa).
134. Note 89 above.
135. See, e.g., Lambo, note 12 above; Field, note 5 above, *passim*. The Cornell-Aro study (note 10 above) found a high correlation between belief in supernatural forces and mental disorder. Their tabulation (from pp. 146–7) relates beliefs to mental disorder along an A–D scale on which A indicates positive disorder and D normality:

Beliefs in:	A	B	C	D
	56	48	92	66
Witches	55%	46%	26%	5%
Juju	25%	19%	12%	2%
Supernatural forces	14%	10%	2%	2%
Spirits	38%	12%	11%	2%

136. E.g. Lambo, note 12 above.
137. E.g. Whitlock, *Criminal Responsibility and Mental Illness*, 27 (1963).
138. Note 62 above.
139. Gledhill, *The Penal Codes of Northern Nigeria and the Sudan*, 92 (1963).
140. *R. v. Inyang*, note 88 above; *R. v. Ashigifuwo*, note 118 above; *R. v. Yayiye*, 1957 N.R.N.L.R. 207 (Northern Nigeria); *Salako v. Attorney-General for Western Nigeria*, 1965 N.M.L.R. 107 (Western Nigeria).
141. E.g., *R. v. Ashigifuwo*, note 118 above (woman 'like a mother to him'); *Echem v. The Queen*, note 88 above (friend); *R. v. Yeboah*, note 125 above (mother); *Muswi s/o Musele v. R.*, note 133 above (wife); *R. v. Magata s/o Kachehakana*, note 89 above (father); *Sudan Government v. Nafisa Dafalla Mohamed* (1961), S.L.J.R. 199 (Sudan) (husband); *Sudan Govern-*

ment v. Ahmed el Obeid Saghayroun, note 125 above (stepfather). It must be remembered, however, that in Africa, as elsewhere, even in the absence of mental disorder, murder is most likely to take place within the family group, however that may be defined: see Bohannan, ed., *African Homicide and Suicide*, chap. 9 (1960).

142. E.g. *R. v. Yayiye*, note 140 above; *R. v. Grumah*, note 124 above; *R. v. Moshie*, note 99 above; *Sudan Government v. Gabra Angello Dafaalla*, note 125 above.

143. The facts of *Sudan Government v. Mousa Adam Ishag*, note 61 above.

144. *Echem v. The Queen*, note 88 above. Echem was clearly schizophrenic with paranoid delusions.

145. *Nyinge s/o Suwatu v. R.*, note 60 above. Cf. Whitlock, *op. cit.*, 87—'It is in the setting of flatness or incongruity of mood that a schizophrenic patient can be overcome by an irresistible impulse to kill. . . . [It] is not unusual for such a crime to be followed by the minimum of attempt to cover up its traces, or the murderer may even go to the police to confess.' Nyinge was held to be outside the McNaghten defence on the ground that his immediate surrender and confession to the police established that he knew, at the time he killed, that he was doing wrong.

146. *Sudan Government v. Abdel Wahab Abdel Sakhi* (1961), S.L.J.R. 110 (Sudan): The accused had twice been under psychiatric treatment—once apparently suffering from a remarkable 'illness of false pretence'—and was found on examination the day after the offence to be mentally disordered. The court would not accept that the psychiatric history *per se* was enough evidence to base the defence on, and dismissed the medical testimony on the ground that it was uncorroborated and that it was 'known that most crimes are the result of temptation or impulses that are not resisted'.

147. *R. v. Mandala*, note 46 above.

148. *Ibid.*; *Sudan Government v. Abdel Wahab Abdel Sakhi*, note 146 above.

149. We have relied for our information about the historical appreciation of mental illness on Jones, *Lunacy, Law and Conscience, 1744–1845* (1955) and Dain, *Concepts of Insanity in the United States, 1789–1865* (1964).

150. (1724), 16 St. Tr. 695.

151. The more important authorities are collected in Jones, *op. cit.*, Appendix 1. It should be remembered, of course, that even apart from the 'wild beast' of *Arnold's* case, the pre-McNaghten tests were not uniformly cognitive. In *R. v. Oxford* (1840), 9 C. & P. 525, only three years before McNaghten, Lord Denman, C.J., was directing a jury that 'if some contributory disease was in truth the acting power within him which he could not resist, he would not be responsible'.

152. See Dain, *op. cit.*, 6.

153. E.g., *R. v. Biyana*, 1938 E.D.L. 310 (South Africa); *R. v. Lloyd*, 1941 C.P.D. 162 (South Africa); *R. v. Roberts*, 1957 (4) S.A. 265 (South Africa); *Sudan Government v. Nafisa Dafalla Mohamed*, note 141 above.

154. E.g., *State v. Harris*, Transvaal Provincial Division 1965, unreported: Harris was executed for causing the death of an elderly white woman by the explosion of a bomb in the concourse of Johannesburg Railway Station. It was common ground between the psychiatrists on both sides that Harris was emotionally unstable and showed extensive personality immaturity (we are indebted to Mr D. Welsh of the University of Cape Town for this information); *Sudan Government v. Barakia Wajo* (1961), S.L.J.R. 114 (Sudan): 'The accused was not insane or weak minded, but he was emotionally unstable to an abnormal degree. In my view this should not be a reason for commutation of the death sentence.'

155. Above, pp. 325–26.

156. Although most of the criminal law teaching in the new law schools is sympathetic to inter-disciplinary understanding of these problems, there are, to the best of our knowledge, no courses presently given which explore the problems in legal and psychiatric depth.

157. Gledhill, *op. cit.*, 87–91, gives a summary of some of the characteristics of major types of mental disorder, expressly on the basis of the difficulties in obtaining medical evidence. It is unfortunately not expressed in a very helpful form and is of too limited a nature to be of much practical value.

158. It is difficult to generalize about any community's awareness of mental illness. Some evidence suggests that it may be very largely developed: see, e.g., Gelfand, *art. cit.*; Leighton, Lambo and others, *op. cit.*, 113–14.

159. We are thinking here mainly of formulations in terms of the *Durham* test or the diminished responsibility test of the English Homicide Act.

160. Clifford, 'The evaluation and methods used for the prevention and treatment of juvenile delinquency in Africa south of the Sahara', *International Review of Criminal Policy*, No. 21, 17 at 25 (1963).

161. See note 6 above.

162. See Overholser, 'The Briggs Law of Massachusetts—A Review and An Appraisal', 25 *Journal of Criminal Law, Criminology and Police Science*, 859 (1935); Bromberg and Thompson, 'Relations of Psychosis, Mental Defect and Personality to Crime', 28 *Journal of Criminal Law, Criminology and Police Science*, 70 (1937); Poindexter, 'Mental Illness in a State Penitentiary', 45 *Journal of Criminal Law, Criminology and Police Science*, 559 (1955).

163. Robinson, Patten and Kerr, 'A Psychiatric Assessment of Criminal Offenders', 5 *Medical Science and Law*, 140 (1965).

13
Penal Policy and Under-Development in French Africa

JACQUELINE COSTA

I Introduction

The leaders of the new African nations have never been able to separate their struggle for political independence from their attempts to solve their economic problems. Their efforts to secure freedom have inevitably been followed by the mobilization of all their available national resources to 'break the vicious circle of poverty'.[1] It is an urgent task, the scope and complexity of which call for the co-operation of all disciplines in the search for a solution. The law must command a vital position amongst them, in so far as it alone can create an institutional framework without which purely economic measures must be ineffective. And the criminal law, which alone amongst legal techniques has the power of official compulsion behind it, must occupy a prominent position in the African attempts to revolutionize their ideas and motivations.

The role accorded to criminal law in relation to national development is as significant in jurisprudential terms as it is to the economic policies of the African governments. That different branches of the law should act in concert for the purpose of bringing about changes exclusively concerned with economic growth is in itself an innovation which strikes at the common conception of law as a discipline cut off from the social sciences. Yet perhaps even more novel is the use which is being made of penal sanctions. Whereas in European law the application of a sanction is merely the normal consequence of failure to follow a prescribed norm—and is recognized as such—in modern African law it is seen more as the expression of command the enforcement of which is carried out by the threat of penal action. In Africa, criminal law is not the codified expression of the values of an established social order. It is a tool to be used in the

367

very creation of such an order. It is at the same time part of that 'confused phenomenon which does not fit into the categories of the armchair theorists'. Like the struggle for economic independence itself, 'it has at the same time aspects which are both constructive and destructive'.[2]

The effective operation of a development economy presupposes in the first place that human and social obstacles will have been surmounted. The very first steps, in the words of President Touré, 'must be taken with the conscious participation of the people', since 'no profound changes can take place without popular support and complete spiritual identification with them'.[3] To meet the needs of the situation, African legislatures have chosen to act within the framework of existing penal codes, rather than fashion economic regulations which would of necessity be fragmentary and lacking in solid moral foundation.

The systematic penalizing of anti-economic actions in the recent codes and other legislation offers a striking example of a policy attempting to promote development by encouraging changes in individual motivations. Two forms of behaviour in particular have been comprehensively punished: firstly, the continuation of traditional practices which are actively hostile to a developing economy; and secondly, the unheeding submission to patterns of behaviour which are linked to a subsistence economy. Both have been the subject of legislation penalizing them to the extent that they seem likely to interfere with the future growth of the African nations. The solutions adopted share a superficial similarity with the French model, but it is probably the result not so much of a wish to imitate as of a desire to provide in a familiar garb answers to problems which are fundamentally dissimilar.

II The Criminal Law and Practices Hostile to Development

Custom does not merit respect. It is the fault of custom that African societies have remained at an extremely low level and it is the cause of under-development in all its forms. It is by these consequences that custom must be judged and it is by these consequences that it deserves to be condemned.[4]

Although much criticized, these remarks of Professor David have been echoed in the economic policies of modern Africa. Some customary practices have been stigmatized not merely as anachronisms but as actual dangers to the economic development of the new nations. Two in particular have been marked out for suppression: stock theft and the practices associated with bridewealth.

I STOCK THEFT

To certain pastoral tribes, stock theft is not so much the wrongful appropriation of the property of others as an exploit bringing to its perpetrator considerable prestige in the eyes of his fellow men. Be that as it may, it is still a genuinely disturbing practice which results in the considerable diminution of many privately-owned herds. In an attempt to impose some limitation on its scope, the governments of two large stock-rearing countries, Malagasy and Niger, and more recently that of Guinea, have resorted to remarkably severe penal sanctions.

(a) Malagasy and Niger[5]

In these two countries stock theft has been the subject of severe penalties for many years. Successive extensions of the scope of the offence and increases in the penalties leave no doubt as to the official desire to eradicate the practice.

(i) *The scope of the offence.* The actual definition of the offence can

369

only be expressed in greater detail by enumerating the kinds of animals which can be stolen. Adopting this principle, the Niger code has distinguished between smaller livestock (*menu bétail*— Penal Code, article 323) and *gros bétail*—camels, oxen and all animals of this nature (Penal Code, article 231), whilst in contrast the Malagasy law penalizes only the theft of oxen. But the effectiveness of the law as a means of restricting this particular kind of criminal activity derives not so much from the extension and elaboration of the list of animals which can be the subject of the offence, but from the very broad articulation of complicity which accompanies it.

The Codes penalize three kinds of complicity:

Firstly, furnishing the means for committing the offence, or giving aid and assistance to the offender with a view to facilitating preparations for the offence or its actual commission (Malagasy ordinance 60-106, article 8). The Niger Penal Code penalizes complicity to the same extent by the application of the general provisions of article 49, rather than by a specific provision in the chapter dealing with stock theft.

Secondly, furnishing means, sustenance or accommodation to the offender after the offence has been committed for the purpose of facilitating escape (Malagasy ordinance 60-106, article 8; Niger Penal Code, article 328). The Niger code in addition considers as an accomplice one who conceals or attempts to conceal the stolen animals, whilst the Malagasy ordinance punishes a receiver with the same severity as the principal offender (article 15), suggesting that receiving is to be considered not as a distinct offence, but simply as a specialized aspect of complicity.

Finally, in the Niger law 'the heads of the tribe, clan or village who, having knowledge of the stock theft, do not at once notify the administrative or judicial authorities, are equally liable as accomplices to the theft' (Penal Code, article 329). The Malagasy law for its part recognizes the responsibility of the *fokon'olona*—the village societies—though only to the extent of civil liability. Their collective responsibility is limited to the 'restitution of the stolen animals or the payment of compensation equivalent to their cash value' (ordinance 60-106, article 15).

Beyond these extensions of liability, the Niger code also establishes two presumptions of guilt: one, that any person found in

370

possession of a stolen animal is the thief (article 326 (1)); the other, that any person commercially involved in the sale of such an animal is an accomplice (article 327). These presumptions are extremely hard to rebut, since the only way of doing so is that prescribed by articles 326 (2) and 327—namely 'to furnish to the authorities information leading to the complete and precise identification of the person from whom the animal was obtained'.

It must be finally noted that, although failure to report a known theft or to divulge the whereabouts of a thief are not within the scope of the broad complicity provisions, both jurisdictions punish them as separate offences (Malagasy ordinance 60-106, article 12; Niger Penal Code, article 330). The counterpart of these provisions is included in the Malagasy law—namely, that false accusations of theft or receiving are punishable by sanctions as severe as those for the offences themselves. The principle underlying this provision is that the community must be encouraged to take an interest in the suppression of crime, but not to the extent of succumbing to the ever-present danger of making false accusations in situations of clan or tribal rivalry.

(*ii*) *The penalties.* The penalties which can be imposed for these offences are very severe. Through the use of the device of a wide range of aggravating circumstances, the offender may become liable to the capital penalty (Malagasy ordinance 60-106, articles 5–6; Niger Penal Code, articles 321–3). Although all the penalties are severe, the Niger Code allows an offender the benefits of the administrative reduction of sentence or the consideration of extenuating circumstances, where sentences of life imprisonment or death may be ordered. The Malagasy law has adopted the same solution by applying to this field the penal provisions of ordinance 60-029 of May 14th, 1960,[6] which was explicitly enacted to facilitate the control of certain types of criminal behaviour. And yet rigorous suppression *per se* is not the only motive for this attitude; the governments are, above all, concerned to ensure that an offender is not put in a position in which he can frustrate modern official policy simply by invoking the excuse of a customary obligation.

The Niger and Malagasy draftsmen have in these ways proceeded against the stock thieves themselves. Malagasy has gone further, however, in 'associating' the community with the measures leading to the detection and prosecution of the offenders. Extensive powers authorizing 'the taking of steps necessary for the discovery and arrest of the culprits' are conferred on the *fokon'olona* up to the level of the preliminary inquiry (Malagasy ordinance 60-106, articles 17–21). At the same time special criminal courts have been established to judge cases of stock theft; each one comprises a panel of four assessors drawn from a list of eighteen persons for each case, at least half of whom must be cattle farmers (ordinance 60-106, articles 41–50, as amended by ordinance 61-030).[7]

The principal measures taken for the eradication of the practice of stock theft rely in both countries simply on the classic processes of the criminal law. Are they appropriate to the difficulties encountered and do they produce the results required? One may think that the giving of an active role to the organs of the community at the level of prosecution and adjudication, or its involvement in the wide net cast for accomplices and receivers, offer the best guarantees against the continued prevalence of the practices. It is unfortunate that the contrary appears to be true; there is a reluctance to impose penalties which are believed to be too severe, and so their very severity creates a risk that the law may not achieve its objective. Thus in Malagasy it became necessary to pass the ordinance of July 10th, 1962,[8] prescribing measures of administrative supervision of stock thieves, in consequence of 'the strength of the feeling in the rural communities against known thieves going unpunished. The authorities agree that specific instances of acquittal or release justify these complaints.' This partial failure perhaps explains why the Guinean legislature has attempted to find an alternative solution.

(b) Guinea

The law of January 2nd, 1964,[9] springs from a revolutionary idea, combining the notions of economic crime and derogation from public welfare. Stock theft is assimilated with 'theft or the appropriation of public funds' and the confiscation of 'all the goods of the offender, his accomplices and receiver' is called for (Guinean Penal Code, article 332 (2)).[10]

The theft of animals which are the property of others is therefore seen as an offence against the *corpus* of the nation's stock, and the offender is obliged to make reparation from his own possessions for the damage caused to it. This idea completely cuts across the traditionally accepted idea of theft as 'interference with private property' but is in full accord with the socialist philosophy which has, for example, already led the Guinean legislature to prescribe that in all real estate matters it is a fundamental principle that the ownership of all open ground is vested in the state as landlord.[11]

The variety of penal solutions which have been devised to deal with theft points up the difficulties encountered by the governments concerned to change practices linked firmly to the traditional cultures. The desire for social advancement can be readily appreciated, but rapid change forced upon cultures from the outside—especially by the use of the wrong sort, or the wrong severity, of penal sanctioning—often gives rise to unfortunate social consequences. The same delicate issues can be seen in the modern interference with the customary giving of bridewealth, to which we now turn.

2 BRIDEWEALTH

Unlike stock theft, the customary practice of the giving of bridewealth is to be found throughout Africa. Although, in origin, bridewealth appears to have been merely a means of evidencing and guaranteeing marriage, it has more recently taken on definite commercial aspects. It is on a small scale a part of the larger mercenary development which has led to the depopulation of the rural areas, has impeded the growth of a scale of values for personal property and has thrown social injustices into sharp relief. The few states, however, which have legislated on the subject, have done so in different ways: either bridewealth has been regulated by fixing a maximum amount which can be paid and prohibiting only the fraudulent practices associated with it, or it has simply been banned.

The two types of measure had apparently contradictory ends in view: prohibition pure and simple leads to the abolition of the practice; but the suppression of the abuses alone strikes not at the practice itself but at the deviations from it, in effect reaffirming official support for the practice itself. Deprived of commercial significance, bridewealth simply reassumes its customary significance as a symbol. One suspects that, in any community whose future economic development is to be into the cash sector, the giving of merely symbolic weight to this procedure is really the more satisfactory solution.

(a) *Regulation of bridewealth*

Mali has opted for the solution of simply regulating bridewealth, as can be seen from the Jacquinot decree of September 14th, 1951, which is its basic legislation. Bridewealth is not forbidden, but a maximum amount is specified. It is law 62-17 of February 3rd, 1962,[12] which punishes, as for fraud, 'whoever obtains or attempts to obtain in consideration of marriage, gifts and bridewealth in excess of 20,000 francs for a girl, and 10,000 francs for a woman' (the penalties are those of the Mali Penal Code, article 185: 3 months to 2 years and fine). The sanction is directed only against obtaining, and it is only the person who receives the bridewealth who can be prosecuted. The same principle has been adopted by the Guinean law of April 14th, 1962, 'relating to the necessary conditions for contracting marriage'.[13] The payment of bridewealth for the benefit of the woman is required for the marriage to be valid (article 3) but it is further stated that 'bridewealth has only symbolic significance. Its amount is fixed by law' (article 4).

The Mali law, however, does not stop at levying sanctions against the non-observance of the specified maximum amount. It punishes as fraud practices which amount to using bridewealth as 'a means of either persuasion or bribery ... in ... obtaining or attempting to obtain the hand of a woman or girl already promised to another (Penal Code, article 185 (17)).[14] 'Anyone, including a parent, who knowingly incites, aids or assists the offender' (article 185 (3)) and 'those who are guilty of the barter of women, and their accomplices' (article 185 (4)) are dealt with in the same way.

Without going so far as to regulate the institution of bridewealth, the codes of Niger[15] and the Central African Federation[16] each penalize as fraudulent 'whosoever, in the case of a marriage to be celebrated according to custom, gives or promises in marriage any girl of whom he is not or is no longer entitled to dispose, having obtained or attempted to obtain all or part of the bridewealth fixed by custom' (Niger Penal Code, article 334; Central African Federa-

374

tion Penal Code, article 241 (3)). This last solution shows the way to a further prohibition.

(b) Prohibition of bridewealth

Only the governments of Gabon and the Ivory Coast have gone so far as to decree the abolition of 'the practice known under customary law as bridewealth, which consists of the giving of sums of money or articles of value in consideration of marriage by the future husband to the family of the bride' (Gabon law of May 31st, 1963, article 1).[17] The Gabon National Assembly passed the measure unanimously, prescribing a penalty of three months' to one year's imprisonment and a fine of 36,000–360,000 francs for 'whoever obtains or accepts, gives or receives gifts in money or in kind' (article 3 (1)), the furnishing of services being equated with gifts in kind (article 3 (2)). At the same time 'all mention of bridewealth in public or private deeds in future is prohibited' (article 2 (1)). A complete embargo is thus set upon the continuation of the practice. It is rounded out by a decree of July 24th, 1963, which prescribes, in the case of the proposed dissolution of a marriage, the method of repayment of bridewealth paid before the coming into force of the law of May 31st, 1963. No other payments of bridewealth can be recovered.

The example of Gabon has been followed in the Ivory Coast law of October 17th, 1964.[18] The penalties prescribed are particularly severe: imprisonment from 6 months to 2 years and a fine 'double the value of the sum agreed or the property received or demanded, provided that the fine shall not be less than 50,000 francs' (law 64-381, article 21). Moreover, the penalties are to be applied, whether or not the marriage has actually taken place, against 'whosoever, either directly or through an intermediary, (1) solicits or agrees to offers or promises of bridewealth, or solicits or receives bridewealth; (2) makes use of offers or promises of bridewealth or yields to solicitations, resulting in the payment of bridewealth'. Finally, rticle 22 prescribes that any person who acts as an 'intermediary' or who simply 'participates in bringing about a prohibited transaction' is liable to the same penalties. The Ivorian law thus appears to be the final stage in a process of evolution which is only just beginning in most other African countries.

375

The suppression of stock theft and the prohibition of bride-wealth are significant illustrations of the willingness of the African states to break with their customary past when it leads to stagnation. Yet they are nonetheless isolated examples: other practices which impede economic development call no less for sanctions. It is perhaps strange that the legislation of Niger should have proscribed tithes and other financial charges for the benefit of customary or religious authorities[19] but failed to specify any sanction. And certain traditional beliefs which have positively disastrous economic consequences are not penalized at all; for example, in certain districts the misappropriation of considerable sums of money derived from the sale of precious stones is not believed to require any penalty, since money arising in this way is thought to be under an evil spell.

A government's hesitation in condemning these anti-economic attitudes can often be explained by its natural fear of creating unnecessary tensions in the traditional milieu. Development brings about a revolution in the hierarchy of values and in moral or political ideas: 'One can never emphasize enough the courage and strength of purpose needed by the *élite* of an under-developed country to ensure its progress.'[20] Moreover, to positive resistance to change is allied the inertia associated with traditional practices firmly bound to the under-developed economy—practices whose strength is often harder to undermine.

III The Criminal Law and the Folkways of Under-development

'Slavery makes one servile; liberty makes one free', runs a Malagasy proverb. By the same token, under-development produces the kinds of behaviour which are peculiarly associated with under-development—vagabondage and begging, the use of drugs, the abuse of alcohol, usurious practices and so on. This creation of a tramp mentality (*clochardisation*)[21] must be counteracted, but this can only be done by persistent communal effort. 'Independence should be before all else the occasion for a nation to create itself anew, to reconstitute itself, allowing free play to the forces of initiative and full expression to those of its ideals which have been newly awakened and stimulated.'[22]

Two forms of behaviour can be seen to be particularly harmful to economic growth: idleness, which leads to unauthorized absence from work and chronic under-employment; and usury, which accentuates the economic imbalance existing between the poverty of large sections of the population and the considerable wealth of a few.

I IDLENESS

The existence of large unemployed or under-employed groups in the population is characteristic of the under-developed country. To counteract its economic backwardness, such a country must of necessity stress measures which promote the full and proper use of available manpower. A strong labour force is a basic element in productivity for, in the words of Perroux, 'growth is a work of collective creation'. The people must be exhorted to work—'to conscientious work, to ever better work, for the quantity of new products increases at the same time as their quality improves . . .'.[23] But before this can be done effectively, steps must be taken against those practices which are traditionally bound up with idleness—in particular vagabondage and begging and the use of intoxicants. Some countries have even gone so far as to penalize unemployment itself, thus stepping completely outside the framework of the older European-inspired legislation.

(a) *Vagabondage and begging*

New African legislation has made use of penal sanctions to combat these two forms of anti-social behaviour but has treated them not so much as dangerous conditions with criminal potentialities, which is the French approach,[24] but rather as implying attitudes impeding the development of the national economy.

Only the Ethiopian (article 471),[25] Malagasy (articles 269–82, as amended by ordinance 62-031 of August 10th, 1962),[26] Moroccan (articles 326–33)[27] and Senegalese (articles 241–7) Penal Codes have adopted with some modification the French conception of 'a crime against public order'. In this legislation, vagabondage and begging are put in the category of 'offences tending, or being of such a nature as, to provoke the commission of crimes'.[28]

The remaining African codes, on the other hand, see these two offences in an economic context. The completely new conception of a development law is expressed in the concise terminology of article 145 of the Mali Penal Code: 'Work is a duty for every Malian. In consequence, vagabondage is a crime.' The same idea of imposing a penalty in order to emphasize the 'obligation' of working has led to the Niger legislation making a specific exception for those who cannot be compelled to work: 'no penalty . . . shall be imposed upon a person who is more than sixty years of age or who is disabled' (article 180 concerning begging). The Central African (article 166) and Gabon (articles 196–7) Codes similarly specify that the term 'vagabond' can only be applied to persons who are 'able-bodied'. Lastly the Guinean Code, although coming very close to the classic conception of a crime against public order, preserves the exception of the man who finds it 'impossible to obtain work as a result of his age, state of health, or a condition of general unemployment' (article 224).

In the new economic context of these offences, it has become necessary to reshape their scope and the penalties attaching to them, so that they may fit more precisely into the outline of the overall criminal policy.

The definitions of vagabondage and begging have often been simplified, sometimes extended. The codes of Niger, Gabon and Central Africa—the latter only envisages the crime of vagabondage —have condensed into a single brief section the definitions of the offence and the penalty applicable. The innumerable varieties of circumstances in which vagabondage or begging can facilitate the commission of other offences (the carrying of weapons, threats, entering a dwelling house, the simulation of wounds or disabilities,

378

etc.)[29] have not been set out at length; this is, in fact, unnecessary, since it is the idea of idleness, in the sense of a lack of employment, that is at the basis of the offence, which is seen purely and simply as offending against the national labour policy. The Niger Code has extended the scope of begging to include organized bodies of beggars[30] who cause social and economic disorder and who are each liable to a maximum of two years' imprisonment (article 182). The same country has in another connection introduced into its Penal Code the provisions of Book II, article 62 of the French Labour Code on the use of juveniles for begging (article 181). The Moroccan Penal Code has adopted the same idea (article 328) and has in addition incorporated into its article 330 the French article 61 dealing with the employment of juveniles, though setting the applicable age limit at 13 and not at 16 years.

The inclusion in these penal codes of provisions drawn from French labour legislation is in itself a good illustration of the willingness of the African rulers to promote economic viability by the use of penal sanctions. At the same time, some countries have found that the simplification or extension of the offences has not gone far enough to meet the needs of the economic situation; they have instead found it more effective to remodel the penal sanctions themselves.

The majority of the African penal codes specify the maximum penalty of six months' imprisonment, which the French Penal Code, as applied overseas, already specified for simple vagabondage and begging. Only the Central African Republic, with a maximum of one year (article 166 (2), as amended by law 61-280 of January 15th, 1962) has adopted a heavier penalty. But, in addition, the wish to create a national working community is marked by the use of a measure unknown to French law, known as 'educational labour' in Tunisia[31] and 'obligatory labour with restricted liberty' in Ethiopia. This penalty, found in article 103 of the Ethiopian Penal Code, can be used in the case of offences other than vagabondage and begging, and figures in the general part of the 'principal sanctions' section of the Code. On the other hand, the 'educative labour' of Tunisian law, which involves 'employment for a fixed period on public works' (order-in-council 62-17, article 1) is envisaged as applying only to certain persons and offences: 'Every male person able to

379

work who, despite a previous warning, continues to live in idleness upon the earnings of his spouse or a minor of whom he has custody' (article 2 (1)); and 'Every male person who wilfully refuses to work and who has been twice previously convicted of crime, whether for vagabondage or not . . .' (article 2 (2)). Thus, again, it is primarily against the refusal to work that the law is directed. Vagabondage and begging, like all forms of idleness, are to be suppressed less because they are criminogenic states than because they basically represent anti-economic attitudes.

In the original Tunisian measure against idleness, the proscription of the use or the possession of narcotics is to be found side by side with that of vagabondage (order-in-council 62-17, article 2 (2)). This is in effect a separate problem in the same general area, and it is convenient to treat it as such here.

(b) Narcotics

The condition of physical and mental lethargy which is too often to be found in some African communities is in large part the result of chronic malnutrition. Africa is fully familiar with the *sequelae* of hunger: the search for alternative foods and for stimulants. It is an age-old problem[32] but it has been aggravated since European colonization by the development of a trading economy and the introduction of new drugs. Today, narcotics addicts and alcoholics[33] supply a considerable proportion of the ranks of the idle, who by sheer weight of their numbers impose a heavy burden on economies which are already weak.

The deeply-rooted causes of such a situation cannot be eradicated by a single piece of repressive legislation, but the availability of stern penalties gives the government an effective weapon against those who traffic in narcotics and their associates. The hope is that by taking energetic measures to suppress illicit traffic, the use of drugs may progressively diminish, perhaps even more quickly if the very use of drugs is considered and penalized in the same way. Action has been taken in two ways: on the international front, by the adoption of the 1961 International Convention on narcotics, and at the national level, by the African states' development of specific criminal policies.

The domestic developments have taken the form of the promulgation of new laws and the creation of specialized bodies for dealing with the problem. Thus Chad, the Ivory Coast, Gabon and Dahomey have successively established their own 'National Narcotics Bureaux',[34] whilst Togo has instituted a 'Central Bureau . . . charged with centralizing all information relevant to research into and the prevention of the illicit traffic in narcotics and co-ordinating all operations concerned with the suppression of this traffic'. Yet these are bodies essentially concerned with investigation and co-ordination, leaving the problem of actual suppression to be tackled, once all the documentation and collection of evidence has been completed. The solutions variously adopted are clearly geared to the local peculiarities of the problem in each country. The contribution of each legislature is, once again, distinguished by the differing scope of the offence and the greater or lesser severity of the sanctions prescribed.

So far as the scope of the offence is concerned, the definition of the object of the crime, of the criminal act and of the nature of the crime, is not identical in all the legislation. The enumeration of the toxic substances and of the means employed for obtaining them or making use of them is basically the same.

A majority of African states prohibit traffic in, or the use of, Indian hemp, under the names of 'rongony',[35] 'hashish',[36] 'yamba',[37] 'kif', 'chira' or 'takrouri'.[38] Only the codes of Ethiopia (article 510) and Gabon (article 208) relate to traffic in toxic products, drugs and narcotics in general. The Gabon statute specifies opium, hashish and their derivatives but merely as instances of 'substances officially classified as narcotics' (article 208). It even envisages a separate offence relating to 'poisonous substances not classified as narcotics' (article 207). In fact, the apparently restrictive character of other legislation does not present any major difficulty. The drugs used in Africa are almost exclusively Indian hemp and its derivatives, since they are much less expensive than opium and consequently much more widely available to Africans. The precise terminology of the statute is thus not as restrictive as it may at first appear, but is rather a simplification which makes the statute more meaningful in the African context.

By bringing a wide range of associated activity within the scope of the criminal law, the control of trafficking is made more complete. The cultivation, possession, shipment and trade in narcotics is punished by all the codes. But only the Gabon Code (article 208 (2) (i)), the Malagasy ordinance (ordinance 60-073, article 2), the Senegal law (law 63-18, article 1) and the Tunisian law (article 1) equate the use or consumption of narcotics with traffic in them. Gabon further envisages an original method of committing the offence, consisting of procuring one of the prohibited substances by means of fraudulent or forged prescriptions (article 208 (2) (ii)) or knowingly delivering one of the prohibited substances on the presentation of such a prescription (article 208 (2) (iii)). Article 3 (2) of the Senegal law and article 209 of the Gabon Code specify that an attempt is punishable with the same severity as the consummated crime, but the latter code goes further in providing that 'the prescribed penalties can be imposed even though the several acts constituting the offence are committed in different countries' (article 209 (2)).

Complicity is only specifically provided for by the laws of Malagasy, Senegal and Tunisia, which penalize 'any person who facilitates the commission of an offence by furnishing, either gratuitously or for reward, a vehicle or premises, or by any other means' (Malagasy ordinance 60-073, article 4 (i); Senegal law 63-061, article 4; Tunisian ordinance 60-073, article 8 (i)). The Ethiopian Code covers only the supplying of premises (article 510 (2)) but like the Gabon Code (article 209 (1)) and the Senegalese (article 3 (3)) and the Tunisian law (article 8), it punishes a conspiracy to commit the offence in the same way as the offence itself (article 510 (3) (a)).

The only consideration given to the nature of the victim of a narcotics offence (if, indeed, there be one) is in the Ethiopian Code (article 510 (3) (b)) and the laws of Senegal (article 5) and Tunisia (article 9 (1)), which deal specifically with the situation where narcotics are made available to minors.[39] But the consequences which follow—in terms of the penalty which can be imposed in these special circumstances—differ widely. Ethiopian law regards it as an aggravation of the simple offence punishable with five years' imprisonment; Tunisian law as an offence for which the maximum penalty is ordinary imprisonment; while the Senegalese law requires the suspension of the offender's civil rights.

The diversity of approaches to be found in specifying the scope of offences involving drugs is echoed at the sanctioning level, more especially as a wide range of additional penalties is available. The sternest jurisdictions are undoubtedly Malagasy, Senegal and Tunisia, which prescribe long terms of imprisonment (a maximum of five years) and fines of up to 1,000,000 francs or 10,000 Tunisian dinars (law 64-47, article 4). The Ethiopian penalty of five years' imprisonment is only applicable to the aggravated case discussed above. The codes of Niger, the Central African Republic and Gabon are much more lenient, limiting imprisonment to a maximum of two years, though in Gabon the pecuniary sanction may be as high as 1,000,000 francs.

To the principal sanctions of imprisonment and fine there have been added sometimes discretionary, sometimes mandatory, additional penalties. Drug traffic is, in fact, one of those forms of crime which can more effectively be prevented by the use of these additional penalties. All the codes require the confiscation and destruction of the articles seized, though in Senegal destruction may be forgone if the Minister of Health authorizes the use of the drugs (law of February 5th, 1963, article 6). In Malagasy and Senegal, the confiscation of the means of transport can be ordered (Senegal law 23-16, article 7 (7); Malagasy ordinance 60-073, article 4 (2)), whilst a highly original Senegalese provision envisages the additional forfeiture of 'moneys arising from the prohibited transactions' (article 1 (1)), which are then paid into the Treasury to the account of the specialist treatment centres (article 7). Lastly, the closure of the establishment in which the crime was committed may be ordered (Ethiopian Penal Code, article 717 (e); Gabon Penal Code, article 209 (4); Morocco Penal Code, article 90; Malagasy ordinance 60-073, article 4 (2); Senegal law 60-073, article 4) and the offender's movements restricted (Malagasy ordinance 60-073, article 4; Senegal law 63-16, article 4; Tunisian law 74-47, article 13).

In addition to making available these familiar penalties, the Senegal government has thought fit to give judges power to order additional security measures. 'Every person charged with or convicted of crime who is found after expert medical examination to be an habitual user of Indian hemp may be required by order of the examining tribunal or trial court to submit to a cure for addiction' (law 63-16, article 8). This provision is similar in its terms to article

135 of the Ethiopian Code and articles 80 *et seq.* of the Moroccan Code, which envisage 'admission to a therapeutic establishment . . . when it appears that the criminal conduct of the offender is the consequence of or otherwise associated with his addiction'. These three provisions are inspired by article 628 of the French Public Health Code (law of December 24th, 1953) but are less restrictive, since the French Code applies only to convicts. Their structure is, in fact, much closer to articles 335 *et seq.* of the French Code (as amended) concerning alcoholism; and, indeed, the Ethiopian and Moroccan Codes include both forms of intoxication within the bounds of the same offence. Considerable importance is attached to the therapeutic order, especially in the Moroccan Code, which devotes five sections to it (articles 80–3 and 91 (2)) and specifies that where more than one order is made upon conviction, that relating to therapy must always be the first to be put into effect (article 91 (2)).

Bearing in mind the wide range of legislation dealing with the traffic in and use of narcotics, the inadequacy and the fragmentary character of that concerning alcoholism is remarkable. Only the Codes of Ethiopia (articles 514, 773–5) and Niger (articles 301–5) and a Malagasy law of December 13th, 1961,[40] offer effective sanctions against public drunkenness and the protection of juveniles, and a recent law of the Ivory Coast (August 1st, 1964) appears highly original in calling for the severe punishment in the recidivist drunkard. But no systematic policy can be seen in the law's efforts to cope with what Dumont has labelled 'one of the major hazards of Africa'.[41]

Penal legislation against drunkenness probably has little chance of success in the face of the difficulties which confront it. If economic development is to be encouraged and the various forms of incapacity which prevent work are to be limited, it is against unemployment itself—whatever its causes—that restrictive measures must be taken. Some African states have taken the initiative in creating this category of offence, which remains unknown in Western law.

(c) Unemployment

The Ethiopian Code of 1957 considered an 'habitual inclination to idleness' as justifying the detention of recidivists (article 138), but one had to wait until 1962 before two ordinances, passed within a few days of each other in Gabon[42] and Malagasy,[43] aimed criminal sanctions directly at idleness itself. The official reasons given for the legislation in Malagasy[44] are revealing: 'The control of idleness does not concern merely that which is traditionally to be found in the towns. In the rural areas too there are unfortunately to be found those who dislike exertion of any kind and who live by relying on their families or on the generosity of others. . . . It is not our concern to compel these idlers to undertake forced labour. It is our concern simply to oblige them to cultivate their own land . . . in accordance with local requirements and the national development plan.' And the suppression of idleness finds its counterpart in the affirmation of the duty to work. 'Work is a duty for every citizen who is not prevented from working by age or physical incapacity' (Malagasy ordinance 62-062, article 1). 'Every citizen of Gabon who is more than eighteen years of age must be able to establish that he has an occupation, unless he is physically unfit or can produce evidence of enrolment as a student' (Gabon ordinance 50-62 of September 21st, 1962, article 1).

Although their basic principle is the same, there is at least one essential difference between the legislation of these two countries. Whereas in Malagasy an unemployed person is 'deemed' to be idle, in Gabon he must register as unemployed either at the labour office, an employment bureau or at the local prefecture, and a written acknowledgment evidencing such registration must be given on request (ordinance 50-62, article 2). Gabon thus gives effective administrative control to the public authorities, whilst this is lacking in Malagasy.

The same distinction is to be found in the sanctions enforcing the obligation to work. In Gabon, the authorities charged with issuing the acknowledgment will indicate available work (article 3); in Malagasy, the idle person will be compelled to undertake agricultural labour, though 'on his own account and on land belonging to him or on public land which can be made available for this purpose' (article 2). The sanction for failure to carry out this work is in Gabon the same as for vagabondage; in Malagasy it is a maximum of three months' imprisonment. In the latter country, therefore, in so far as it is treated as a separate crime, idleness is punishable less severely than in the traditional criminogenic context of vagabondage and begging. In another respect too Malagasy has extended the scope of its activity against idleness to take account of one of its more disruptive aspects, namely that of a 'rebellion' against work. 'Those who, by actions or words, written threats or activities of whatsoever nature, incite idle persons not to carry out their prescribed work' are brought within the ambit of the criminal law (article 4). Incitement of this sort is not covered by the Gabon ordinance.

To these two ordinances of 1962 must be added the Tunisian order-in-council of August 15th, 1962.[45] Amongst the several offences punishable with 'educative labour' is to be found (article 2 (i)) that involving the individual 'able to work [but] who, despite a previous warning, continues to live in idleness upon the earnings of his spouse or a minor of whom he has custody'. The controlling idea is thus the same, though without the affirmation of the duty to work as a legal principle. The principle has, however, found application in recent legislation in the Central African Republic:[46] 'All persons of both sexes between the ages of 18 and 55 years, and not suffering from physical incapacity duly certified, must establish either that they normally carry on some activity capable of maintaining them or that they are pursuing a course of study in a University or other educational institution.' They are otherwise considered as idle and liable to punishment with imprisonment of between three months' and one year's duration and a fine of from 50,000 to 100,000 francs, at least in the case of refusal to participate in activities of general interest 'designed to enable them to be reabsorbed into the ranks of active and useful citizens'.

2 USURY

The introduction of an economy based on the value of work, in place of one in which a premium is placed on getting something for nothing, not only strikes at a past filled with traditions and habits of idleness but throws into sharp relief any refusal to give way to the dictates of modern economic life. The well-being of the whole community, however, offers little in the way of attraction to those who make a living from the speculations of money-lending. For them, the extreme poverty of the peasant classes, the inadequacy of the arrangements for marketing their produce, and the lack of organization of credit facilities are essentials. Even if the regulation of loans were considered a 'necessary curb', its effectiveness would be limited by the ample opportunity for deception and 'the active complicity between lender and borrower which is commonly to be found'.[47] Although they can by no means totally solve the problem, the provisions of the criminal law raise a considerable obstacle to the future growth of the gap between the profits of the money-lenders and the impoverishment of their victims. As President Tsiranana deplored in the *Journées du développement malgache* on April 25th, 1962: 'All investment and development policy will be inhibited as long as usury is not controlled.'[48]

The lending of money at exorbitant rates is common in many African societies and especially in Malagasy. It does not solely take the classic form of the lending of money repayable in cash, but more commonly that of the lending of money or produce repayable in kind at future harvest-times. The figures cited by Dumont,[49] Gendarme[50] and Guth[51] give some idea of the extent of this practice in the island. Other African countries are, however, equally affected and the penal measures have had to be enacted there as well as in Malagasy.

The legislation in force before independence was the French order-in-council of October 8th, 1935,[52] which reformulates the crime of usury but without making special provision for habitual offenders and without defining the offence in terms solely of exceeding lawful interest rates, as the old law of December 19th, 1850, had done. Usury was established when a normal loan was made 'at a rate of interest exceeding by more than half the mean rate required in the same circumstances by lenders in good faith'. The 1935 order-in-council was applied to the majority of the overseas territories by the decree of September 21st, 1935,[53] in Algeria by the order-in-council of October 30th, 1935,[54] and in Tunisia by the Bey's decree of February 3rd, 1937.[55] In Malagasy a decree of September 22nd, 1935 [56] introduced a special form of control, based on the two measures which had been successively adopted in France: the law of 1850 and the order-in-council of 1935. Yet the truth of the matter was that all this legislation was largely ineffectual because it was not adapted to deal with the peculiarities of the African context.

The same problem confronted the Belgian legislature in respect of the Congo and two decrees of August 29th, 1959 were passed for 'the suppression of usury and criminal proceedings against the usurer'.[57] In the former French territories, however, it was only after independence that the new provision was devised.[58] They are all closer to the French model than, for instance, the Ethiopian solution of 1957 (articles 667 and 670), but all share in common a desire to extend and strengthen the laws against usury.

The Codes of Niger and the Central African Republic define the crime in the same way as the 1935 order-in-council. The Ethiopian Code and the Malagasy ordinance refer, in contrast, to the exceeding of lawful rates of interest,[59] following the lines of the 1850 law. The latter ordinance provides more specifically that the normal rates of interest shall not exceed 12 per cent per annum in the case of an ordinary civil loan, or be more than a quarter greater than the mean rate offered in good faith in commercial cases (articles 2–3). The Ethiopian Code goes behind these straightforward juristic criteria to put the offence in its psycho-sociological context. The usurer is one who 'exploits a state of financial embarrassment or dependence, material difficulties, or the hastiness, inexperience, weakness of character or of mind of any person' (article 667 (1)). In consequence, he is grouped together with one who 'promises or grants . . . in consideration of a loan, whether pecuniary or otherwise, inheritance benefits obviously out of proportion to the loan' (article 667 (1) (b)) and one who 'with the same objective in view, assigns a usurious debt to another or sets it off against a lawful liability' (article 667 (2)). In this way the Ethiopian Code, more than the Malagasy law or even the Niger and Central African provisions, leaves to the judge the greatest scope in defining the offence of usury.

What must also be considered an innovation upon the French system adopted in 1935 is the distinction to be found in Ethiopian law and Malagasy law between simple usury and usury which is aggravated as a result of being habitual. Ethiopia (article 670 (a)) makes reference to the person who 'carries on a trade in such activities', and Malagasy to 'those who, without being recidivists in a legal sense, are acknowledged to be guilty of habitual usury' (article 5 (2)). The Ethiopian Code recognizes further aggravated forms of usury, which are dependent upon the characteristics of the offender, or the victim, or upon the surrounding circumstances (article 670 (a), (b) and (c)). This subjectivization of the offence has perhaps been carried too far, but one must regret that the other African states have not been stimulated by this example, and have not emulated the Ethiopian Code at all. Circumstances notably calling for legislation are those in which there is 'abuse of profession, office or calling which he [the usurer] has been officially licensed to carry on' (Ethiopian Penal Code, article 670 (a)).

It is probably in the stiffening of the penalties against usury that the new African legislatures have made their distinctive mark. French law only prescribed fines for simple offences of this nature and imprisonment only in cases of recidivism. In contrast, the African countries which have taken action against usurers all impose imprisonment even upon first offenders.

The Codes of Niger and the Central African Republic have adopted a maximum of six months' imprisonment, which was that provided for recidivists under the 1935 order-in-council, but which is now equally applicable to first offenders. Provision is also made for the levy of a fine and whilst in Niger it must not exceed 200,000 francs, in the Central African Republic it can be as much as 2,000,000 francs and can be imposed concurrently with imprisonment. The latter solution is perhaps that best adapted to dealing with the usurer: a pecuniary sanction of some severity is likely to be an effective deterrent to those whose motives are dominated by that of financial gain. The Malagasy ordinance proceeds on the same basis, by prescribing a heavy fine of between 100,000 and 1,000,000 francs, which can be increased where necessary to equal the total amount of money lent (ordinance 62-016, article 5 (i)). The imprisonment provisions of the Malagasy law are equally severe, for a maximum of two years can be ordered 'without any reduction for extenuating circumstances in the case of those with previous convictions or those convicted in respect of habitual usury' (article 5 (1) and (2)). In the latter country too there can be no executive pardon or remission of sentence (article 5 (2)). The

389

Ethiopian Code lays down a maximum of five years' imprisonment for simple usury (article 667 (1)) and ten years for the aggravated version of the offence as envisaged in article 670, with the possibility of a fine up to 10,000 dollars.

Going beyond financial penalties and the deprivation of liberty, Malagasy law makes available the penalties of the prohibition of residence and expulsion (article 5 (3)) for those convicted more than once or in cases of professional usury. It also makes detailed provision that the effective rate of interest of the loan must be calculated by taking account of the apparent rate agreed and of all sums 'which do not constitute payment for a distinct service in connection with the loan or for credit granted' (article 8), and that the period of limitation for the crime of usury is to be calculated 'from the date of the last payment or the handing over of whatever is the subject of the transaction' (article 9).

The new Malagasy law and the Ethiopian Code thus represent the strongest measures which have been taken against usury. The ordinance of August 10th, 1962, is a partial fulfilment of the hopes of Guth:[60] the penalizing of the continued crime, the use of the sanction of imprisonment, the possibility of recognizing aggravating circumstances and the use of supplementary penalties. It is perhaps regrettable, however, that his suggestion of giving special publicity to convictions for usury has not been implemented, just as the abuse of public authority, as described above, still remains outside the scope of the law in all countries except Ethiopia.

The creation of a modern society freed from an archaic past and the bonds of recent colonialism is a long-term project. A government which has this responsibility must not hesitate to take action against attitudes and practices which impede development. The governments of Africa have made use of the criminal law in an attempt to eliminate those customs and habits which are geared to a gratuitous subsistence economy and to turn the minds of their people towards a monetary economy. Out of a law purely concerned with the negative aspect of sanctioning, they have begun to make a positive, constructive force and an instrument of economic action.

This basic transformation in legal technique has not led, however, to any radical changes in the sanctioning machinery. There have certainly been some innovations, such as 'educative labour', and supplementary penalties—notably those which affect an offender's property—have been brought into force, but the basic method of the legislator has been that of increasing the severity of the traditional penalties of fine and imprisonment.

This rediscovery of the primordial functions of the criminal law is perhaps the most important aspect of the modern developments in African law. In an era when penal sanctions are frequently becoming less rigorous and more re-educative, the severity of some of the recent African codes is perhaps a reminder to all that the criminal law is essentially based on coercion and that the threat of penal action is one of the best deterrents and preventives yet devised.

NOTES

1. Barre, 'Le développement économique—Analyse politique', 66 *Cahiers de l'Institut de Sciences Economiques Appliqués*, 18 (1958).
2. Fischer, 'La signification de l'expérience guinéenne', *Présence Africaine*, Dec. 1959–Jan. 1960, 53.
3. Touré, 'L'expérience guinéenne', *Présence Africaine*, 1959, 220.
4. Cf. Forster, 'La place de la coutume indigène dans le droit moderne de la République du Sénégal', *Revue Internationale de Criminologie et de la Police Technique*, 1963, 163–81, quoting the comments of David.
5. Malagasy: Law 59-22 of February 17, 1959 (J.O. February 21st, 1959) and law 59-55 of June 9th, 1959 (J.O. June 13th, 1959) repealed; ordinance 60-106 of September 27th, 1960 (J.O. October 1st, 1960, p. 1949); law 61-030 of October 18th, 1961 (J.O. October 21st, 1961, p. 1818) and ordinance 62-090 of October 1st, 1962 (J.O. October 19th, 1962, p. 2371). Niger: ordinance 59-061 of April 17th, 1959 (J.O. May 1st, 1959, p. 240) re-enacted in articles 321-331 of the Penal Code of July 15th, 1961 (J.O. November 15th, 1961).
6. J.O. May 21st, 1960, p. 867.
7. Cf. article 11 (2) of ordinance 60-106, as amended by ordinance 60-030 of October 18th, 1961 (J.O. October 21st, 1961, p. 1818).
8. Ordinance 62-001 and its objects and reasons, J.O. July 14th, 1962, p. 1288.
9. Law 11-64 of January 2nd, 1964, applying to stock thieves, their accomplices and receivers the provisions of article 1 of Law 75-62 of November 23rd, 1962 (J.O. February 15th, 1964, p. 67); brought into force January 15th, 1964 (J.O. March 1st, 1964, p. 83).
10. Law 43-65 of September 21st, 1965, brought into force November 30th, 1965.

11. Decree No. 25 of January 10th, 1962 (J.O. February 1st, 1962, p. 32).
12. Brought into force by decree 17-PG of February 26th, 1962 (J.O. February 27th, 1962, p. 1).
13. Law 54-62 of April 14th, 1962 (J.O. July 1st, 1962, p. 209).
14. Law no. 99 of August 3rd, 1961, amending the Penal Code (J.O. September 4th, 1961).
15. Law 61-27 of July 15th, 1961, amending the Penal Code (J.O. November 15th, 1961).
16. Law 61-239 of July 18th, 1961, amending the Penal Code (J.O. August 15th, 1961).
17. Law 20-63 of May 31st, 1963 (J.O. July 1st, 1963, p. 649).
18. Laws 64-375, relating to marriage, and 64-381 (articles 20–2) of October 7th, 1964 (J.O. October 27th, 1964, p. 1463).
19. Law 60-29 of May 25th, 1960 (brought into force by decree 60-107 of May 31st, 1960; J.O. July 1st, 1960, p. 373).
20. Barre, *op. cit.*, 57.
21. Term used by Germaine Tillion in *L'Algérie en 1957*.
22. Rabemananjara, 'Variations sur un thème guinéen', *Présence Africaine*, Dec. 1959–Jan. 1960, 83.
23. Touré, *art. cit.*, 146.
24. Cf. Rousselet, Patin and Goyet, *Traité de droit pénal spécial*, 7th ed., 154 (1958).
25. Penal Code of July 23rd, 1957.
26. Ord. 62-013 of August 10th, 1962 (J.O. August 18th, 1962, p. 1819).
27. Dahir 1-59-413, 28 joumada II. 1382 (November 26th, 1962; J.O. June 5th, 1963).
28. The titles of chapter I and section I of Title VI of the Ethiopian Penal Code.
29. Cf. articles 275–81 of the French Penal Code, reproduced in more or less identical terms in the Codes of Ethiopia, Mali, Malagasy, Morocco and Senegal.
30. Cf. the associations of beggars and begging 'en réunion' envisaged by article 276 of the French Penal Code, reproduced in the aforementioned African codes which follow the French model.
31. Order-in-Council 62-17, 15 rabia I. 1382 (August 15th, 1962) (J.O. August 17th, 1962).
32. *Pierre de la Faim*, discovered close to the first cataract of the Nile is, according to Josué de Castro, one of the earliest documents on the history of famine: see *Géopolitique de la Faim*, 297 (1962).
33. See Dumont, *L'Afrique noire est mal partie*, 34–6 (1962).
34. Chad: decree 91 of May 3rd, 1961 (J.O. June 1st, 1961, p. 229); Ivory Coast: decree 60 of May 3rd, 1961 (J.O. August 3rd, 1961, p. 1101); Gabon: decree 181 of July 20th, 1961 (J.O. August 15th, 1961, p. 534). Dahomey: decree 323 of October 21st, 1961 (J.O. November 15th, 1961, p. 88).

35. Malagasy: ord. 60-073 of July 28th, 1960 (J.O. August 6th, 1960, p. 1372).
36. Central African Republic: Penal Code, article 285.
37. Senegal: law 63-16 of February 5th, 1963 (J.O. March 18th, 1963, p. 390).
38. Tunisia: law 64-47 of 29 joumada II. 1384 (November 3rd, 1964) (J.O. November 3rd, 1964, p. 1275).
39. The Ethiopian Code equally makes provision in respect of 'the person suffering from mental deficiency or who habitually misuses drugs' (article 510 (3) (b)).
40. Law 61-053 of December 13th, 1961 (J.O. December 23rd, 1961, p. 2261).
41. Dumont, *op. cit.*, 34.
42. Ordinance 50-62 of September 21st, 1962 (J.O. November 1st, 1962, p. 757).
43. Ordinance 62-062 of September 25th, 1962 (J.O. October 12th, 1962, p. 2223).
44. Objects and reasons (J.O. October 12th, 1962, p. 2223).
45. Order-in-council 62-17 of 15 rabia I. 1382 (August 15th, 1962) (J.O. August 17th, 1962).
46. Ordinance 4 of January 8th, 1966 (J.O. January 15th, 1966, p. 21).
47. Malagasy: objects and reasons, and ordinance 62-016 of August 10th, 1962 (J.O. September 1st, 1962, p. 1709).
48. See *Information Economique, Financière, Juridique*, 1962, no. 1, 20.
49. Dumont, *op. cit.*, 115 *et seq.*
50. Gendarme, *L'Economie de Madagascar*, 125 (1960).
51. Guth, 'Aspects humains et juridiques du délit d'usure à Madagascar', 691 *Recueil générale de jurisprudence, de doctrine et de legislation coloniale*, 249–60; 694 *Recueil générale de jurisprudence, de doctrine et de legislation coloniale*, 689–705 (1962).
52. *Recueil périodique et critique Dalloz*, 1935, iv, 225.
53. J.O. September 24th, 1935.
54. *Bulletin législatif algérien*, 1935, 920.
55. J.O. February 5th, 1937.
56. J.O. October 26th, 1935, p. 1079.
57. B.O. Belgian Congo, September 15th, 1959, with the Report of the legislative council of July 11th, 1959.
58. Niger: Penal Code, article 364; Central African Republic: Penal Code, article 287; Malagasy: ordinance 62-016 of August 10th, 1962 (J.O. September 1st, 1962, p. 1709).
59. Malagasy: ordinance 62-016, article 1—5% civil loans, 6% commercial.
60. *Op. cit.*, 694 *Recueil générale de jurisprudence, de doctrine et de legislation coloniale.*

14
Capital Punishment in South Africa

DAVID WELSH

In the Americas, Australasia and Western Europe, capital punishment has increasingly come under criticism and in many instances has been abolished. In contrast to these penological trends elsewhere, the government of South Africa has set its face against abolition or even diminution in the use of the death penalty. The number of persons executed has dramatically increased over the last two decades, and the range of offences for which the death penalty may be imposed has been widened.

The purpose of this chapter is to examine the institution of capital punishment in South Africa and to attempt to relate it to a structural consideration of South African society.

I The Legal Background

I MURDER

Section 338 (1) of the Criminal Procedure and Evidence Act of 1917 (Act 31 of 1917) laid down that the death sentence was to be mandatory for the crime of murder, and permissive for the crimes of rape and treason. It was also to be permissive where a woman had been convicted of murdering her new-born child, or where the person convicted of murder was under the age of 16 years. In 1959 the age-limit was raised to 18.

In 1935 the mandatory death sentence for murder was modified by the introduction of the doctrine of extenuating circumstances. The law was amended to provide that if in any murder case extenuating circumstances were found to be present, the court would have the discretionary power to impose 'any sentence other than the death sentence' if it so chose. [1]

The introduction of the concept of extenuating circumstances was an attempt to remove some of the rigidity of sentencing inherent in any system of mandatory penalties. During the eleven years preceding the 1935 amendment, 663 (or 76·4 per cent) of the 868 persons sentenced to death for murder had been reprieved, and this 'entailed unnecessary suffering for the condemned person and much labour for the authorities', who were charged with the task of thoroughly investigating the case of each condemned person. [2]

Murder in South African law is defined as the unlawful killing of a human being where intent to kill is present. Where such intent is absent the offence is one of culpable homicide. The definition of murder includes those killings where death resulted from acts which an accused knew might result in death of the victim. In a 1945 case, the Appellate Division of the Supreme Court held that

> ... the crime of murder will at all events have been committed if it be proved, by necessary inference from all the circumstances, that the accused killed the deceased by an act which they must have known to be of such a dangerous character that death would be likely to result therefrom, and were reckless whether it did so or not. [3]

This extended definition of the intent to kill was more precisely stated shortly after:

> The general principle is that the Crown has to prove the intention to kill, but this expression has an extended or legal meaning. It covers not only a striving to achieve the actual death of the deceased but knowledge that the act being done is so dangerous as to be *likely* to cause death, coupled with recklessness as to whether death results or not. [4]

The circumstances which were to be regarded as extenuating were deliberately left undefined in the statute. The measure of elasticity accorded to the judiciary has allowed the creation of a body of judge-made law. An early definition was given by Lansdown, J.P., in R. *v. Biyana*: [5]

> In our view an extenuating circumstance in this connection is a fact associated with the crime which serves in the minds of

398

reasonable men to diminish morally, albeit not legally, the degree of the prisoner's guilt.

What circumstances have been deemed extenuating? An exhaustive analysis is beyond the scope of this essay. In his evidence to the 1949–53 Royal Commission on Capital Punishment, Dr C. W. H. Lansdown, Q.C., a distinguished South African jurist and co-author of a standard text-book on the criminal law of South Africa, summarized what might be viewed as extenuating circumstances:[6]

(i) immaturity of mind, as might be seen in youth or persons of retarded mental development;

(ii) degeneracy of mind, as might be seen in extreme old age or in neuropathic persons who are not definitely insane;

(iii) undue influence of a person in authority, though not amounting in law to coercion;

(iv) reason or judgment clouded, e.g. by drink or drugs, though not to the extent that would have direct legal effect: another example of this kind of circumstance is infanticide by a mother still suffering from physical strain with consequent mental disturbance arising from birth or lactation;

(v) distraction of mind not amounting in law to provocation, e.g. the killing of a brutal and unfaithful husband by his wife;

(vi) a wrong, but not entirely unreasonable, belief that a fatal attack was to be made;

(vii) minor degree of participation in the crime, e.g. where incomplete knowledge of common purpose existed or where the part played in carrying the crime into effect was a minor one;

(viii) diminished heinousness, e.g. 'mercy killings'.

Where a custom peculiar to some group in the country has given rise to a killing, the courts have allowed this to constitute an extenuating circumstance. A Bushman who killed his wife because she had committed adultery was found guilty of murder with extenuating circumstances, because it was found that such killing was a Bushman custom.[7]

In a recent case where extenuation was found to be present, thirteen Africans had killed a woman whom they believed had bewitched them. Belief in witchcraft survives among many Africans, and the court felt bound to take cognizance of the fact. The accused

399

were given sentences of imprisonment and a stern lecture by the judge on the foolishness of such beliefs. [8]

Conflicting decisions have occurred in relation to whether intoxication can be an extenuating circumstance. In several cases it has been held to be such. [9] In one case, however, the judge observed that he was

> not prepared to admit the principle that a man may dull his senses to a certain extent by drinking liquor and may in consequence become enraged all of a sudden and then stab and kill his victim and ask the Court to hold that there were extenuating circumstances. [10]

It has been stated that the concept of extenuating circumstances admits flexibility into sentencing policy. Only rarely does a court impose the death sentence on a person found guilty of murder with extenuating circumstances. The two best-known such cases involve accused persons whose mental states were found to provide extenuation. In *R. v. von Zell*[11] the Appellate Division directed that the case be sent back to the trial judge (who had originally passed sentence of death on the accused for murder), to pass sentence afresh on the basis that the jury had found extenuating circumstances which it proceeded to enumerate. The trial judge, however, exercised his discretionary right and reimposed the death sentence, and the accused was subsequently executed after a period of some nine months in the condemned cell.

In *R. v. Roberts*,[12] the court upheld the trial judge's decision to impose the death sentence even though the jury had found extenuating circumstances to be present. Passing sentence, the trial judge, van Wyk, J., had stated:

> My duty is to protect the public against the accused and other would-be killers. The accused belongs to a class of person whose conscience is gravely impaired. They are deterred only by fear of detection and punishment. I believe the fear of the death sentence is still the strongest single deterring factor with this type of person. I have a strong feeling that if the accused were set free again, this desire to rape and do violence to women under the influence of liquor may well manifest itself again. As I see it, anybody who should give the accused his liberty again

will be risking somebody else's life. The accused committed a horrible murder, a typical sex murder, and may strike again if given the opportunity.

Such cases, however, are exceptional, most judges being content to impose lengthy periods of imprisonment instead of the death sentence. The very flexibility of the concept and the fact that it involves in each case what is in essence a moral judgment inevitably leads to considerable variation in practice. It is well known that some judges impose the death penalty more readily than others. Some judges are more willing to find extenuating circumstances than others, and therefore a personal element may determine whether or not a man is sentenced to death. Subsequent executive investigation of the case provides only a partial remedy for this inconsistency, as the executive is to a large part guided in its findings by the judge's report on the case.

Further, the dividing line between murder and culpable homicide is in many instances exceedingly hard to draw, particularly in view of the extended definition of intent to kill described above. The writer's impression is that in certain cases the racial factor may have a significant bearing on whether the accused is found guilty of murder or culpable homicide.[13]

2 RAPE

Rape is defined as an unlawful carnal knowledge of a female without her consent by a male of 14 years or over. One also commits the crime of rape by assisting another in committing such an act.

In 1913 an official commission was appointed to inquire into assaults on women. Sexual assaults by non-white men upon white women had become more frequent by that time than at the turn of the century. The Commission condemned the idea of compulsory capital punishment for rape because experience in Natal, where the practice had been introduced, had shown that juries were frequently reluctant to convict in such circumstances. It also rejected emasculation as a punishment and concluded that the permissive death penalty be retained. This is the present position.[14]

In passing sentence for the crime of rape the courts may take into consideration the following factors: age and social status of the complainant; the degree of permanent injury to the complainant.[15] The race of the complainant and the accused is often a crucial factor in determining whether or not the death sentence is passed.[16]

3 TREASON

Treason is committed by those who, with a hostile intention to disturb, impair or endanger the safety of the state, either attempt or actively prepare to do so. The court has a discretionary power to sentence to death a person convicted of treason.

4 ROBBERY; HOUSEBREAKING WITH INTENT TO COMMIT VARIOUS OFFENCES

In 1958, the Criminal Procedure Act was amended to give the courts the power to impose the death sentence where 'aggravating circumstances' were found to have been present in the commission of the offences of robbery and attempted robbery, and also the offence of housebreaking or attempted housebreaking with intent to commit an offence.[17]

'Aggravating circumstances', in relation to housebreaking or attempted housebreaking with intent to commit an offence, were defined as 'the possession of a dangerous weapon or the commission of or any threat to commit an assault, by the offender or an accomplice on the occasion when the offence is committed, whether before, during or after the commission thereof'.

'Aggravating circumstances', in relation to robbery or an attempt to commit robbery, were defined as 'the infliction of grievous bodily harm or any threat to inflict such harm by the offender or an accomplice on the occasion when the offence is committed, whether before, during or after the commission thereof'.[18]

Why was the death penalty introduced for such offences? The then Minister of Justice, Mr C. R. Swart, used a compound of deterrent and retributivistic arguments to defend the proposed amendment in Parliament. He claimed that

the public is concerned about the number of robberies, particularly those concerning large sums of money, which have been taking place lately especially on the Witwatersrand. These incidents [the Minister continued] are quite clearly the work of well organized, reckless and murderous gangs who will not scruple to kill or seriously injure their victims.

Only the death penalty would have the desired deterrent effect.

If a person is sent to prison he lives reasonably comfortably for a number of years and eventually he is released, but the death sentence is final and they are afraid of it. It will certainly be deterrent. . . . Just as one feels that people who cold-bloodedly murder other people should rather be put out of this world, so it is better that many of these people who do these terrible things should leave this world.[19]

The Opposition argued that the possibility of receiving the death penalty would make criminals of this type even more dangerous because they would reason that if they were going to receive the death penalty in any event, they might as well kill those who attempted to apprehend them and thereby reduce the chances of subsequent identification and conviction. This argument was rejected by Parliament.

5 SABOTAGE

Faced with a mounting wave of sabotage and other subversive underground activity, the Republican government made dramatic amendments to the criminal law by means of the General Law Amendment Act of 1962. The terms of this statute, commonly known as the Sabotage Act, which define the crime of sabotage, are so comprehensive as to merit being set out in full:

21.(1) Subject to the provisions of sub-section (2), any person who commits any wrongful or wilful act whereby he injures, damages, destroys, renders useless or unserviceable, puts out of action, obstructs, tampers with, pollutes, contaminates or endangers:
(a) the health or safety of the public;
(b) the maintainance of Law and Order;
(c) any water supply:
(d) the supply or distribution at any place of light, power,

fuel, foodstuffs or water, or of sanitary, medical or fire-extinguishing services;

(e) any postal, telephone or telegraph services or installations, or radio transmitting, broadcasting or receiving services or installations;

(f) the free movement of any traffic on land, at sea or in the air;

(g) any property, whether movable or immovable, of any person or of the State.

or who attempts to commit, or conspires with any other person to aid or procure the commission of or to commit, or incites, instigates, commands, aids, advises, encourages or procures any other person to commit any such act, or who in contravention of any law possesses any explosives, firearm or weapon or enters or is upon any land or building or part of a building, shall be guilty of the offence of sabotage and liable on conviction to the penalties provided for by law for the offence of treason: provided that, except where the death penalty is imposed, the imposition of sentence of imprisonment for a period of not less than five years shall be compulsory, whether or not any other penalty is imposed.

(2) No person shall be convicted of any offence under subsection (1) if he proves that the commission of the alleged offence, objectively regarded, was not calculated and that such offence was not committed with intent to produce any of the following effects, namely:

(a) to cause or promote general dislocation, disturbance or disorder;

(b) to cripple or seriously prejudice any industry or undertaking or industry or undertakings generally or the production or distribution of commodities or foodstuffs at any place;

(c) to seriously hamper or to deter any person assisting in the maintenance of Law and Order;

(d) to cause, encourage or further an insurrection or forcible resistance to the Government;

(e) to further or encourage the achievement of any political aim, including the bringing about of any social or economic change in the Republic;

(f) to cause serious bodily injury or to seriously endanger the safety of any person;

(g) to cause substantial financial loss to any person or to the State;

(h) to cause, encourage or further feelings of hostility between different sections of the population of the Republic;

(i) to seriously interrupt the supply or distribution at any place of light, power, fuel or water, or of sanitary, medical or fire-extinguishing services;

(j) to embarrass the administration of the affairs of the State.

6 CHILD-STEALING AND KIDNAPPING

Section 10 of the Criminal Procedure Amendment Act of 1965 gives the courts power to impose the death penalty at their discretion for the offence of child-stealing and kidnapping. The Minister of Justice gave no reason to Parliament for the amendment, saying merely that they were capital offences in Roman–Dutch Law.[20] It is understood, however, that members of certain underground political organizations had made threats involving commission of these offences. At the time of writing (October 1965) no person has been sentenced to death for either offence.

II The Mentally Abnormal Offender

One of the factors most commonly associated with defences raised to capital charges will be that of mental abnormality. An accused

405

person may be placed in an institution for observation and treatment if he falls within the categories of 'mentally disordered or defective persons' delineated in the Mental Disorders Act, 1916. If he is unfit to make his defence, he will be detained in a mental hospital or prison, as the judge directs. From the trial stage onwards, the relevance of mental abnormality lies in the facts that it may in certain circumstances afford a defence to a criminal charge; that it may amount to extenuating circumstances so as to justify reducing the sentence passed by the court; and that it may be taken into consideration by the executive as a factor justifying the commutation of the death sentence. These three stages will be considered briefly here.

1 THE DEFENCE OF INSANITY

The basic Roman–Dutch common law position is wider than the English defence of insanity based on the McNaghten Rules. Although the McNaghten terminology was incorporated into the Native Territories Penal Code in 1886 and extended to the rest of the Cape Colony by judicial decision in 1899[21] and to the Transvaal in 1907,[22] Chief Justice Villiers in R. v. Hay stressed that the English test was not exclusive. A defence will be allowed if, apart from an accused's inability to distinguish right from wrong, he has

> by reason of . . . mental disease, lost the power of will to control his conduct in reference to the particular act charged as an offence.

2 EXTENUATING CIRCUMSTANCES

Mental abnormality which is not of a nature to give the accused a defence under the rules outlined above may be held to amount to an extenuating circumstance. The court will then have a discretion to impose a sentence other than the death penalty.

Analysis of reported cases since 1935, the year in which the concept of extenuating circumstances was introduced, reveals a lack of uniformity in defining the degree of mental abnormality that constitutes an extenuating circumstance.

In one early case, extenuating circumstances were deemed to be present where the offender has 'a mind, which though not diseased so as to provide exclusion of insanity in the legal sense, may be subject to a delusion or some erroneous belief, or some defect, in circumstances which would make a crime committed under its influence less reprehensible or diabolical than it would be in the case of a mind of normal condition'.[23]

In considering whether there was such provocation as could reduce the crime from murder to culpable homicide, an accused person is not entitled to any special consideration on grounds of his being a psychopath. The test here would be whether a person of ordinary mentality in the position of the accused would have been deprived of his power of self-control.[24] Yet extenuating circumstances were held to be present in a case involving an accused who was subject to mental instability in a high degree with definite psychopathic tendencies. This condition diminished his power of self-control and resulted in his having a 'lower breaking point than is usually the case'.[25] And psychopathy has, in several cases, been regarded as an extenuating circumstance.[26]

3 THE POWER OF REPRIEVE

In 1947 the Lansdown Commission on Penal and Prison Reform recommended that

> wherever there is the slightest possibility of doubt or any question of mental aberration, whether or not the law might have been able to take cognizance of it, such a circumstance should operate for the extension of mercy to the condemned person, and the Royal Prerogative of Mercy should be exercised.[27]

There is evidence of a consistent pattern of executive clemency being exercised along these lines[28] but in view of the cases of *von Zell* and *Roberts*, already mentioned, and more recently that of *Harris*,[29] it does not appear to be an invariable rule.

III Reprieves and Executions

After a convicted person has been sentenced to death, reports on the case are sent to the Minister of Justice by prosecuting counsel, occasionally by defending counsel and by the Attorney-General of the Provincial Division in which the trial was held. The trial judge forwards a report through the Minister of Justice to the State President in which he may make a recommendation for mercy.

The report usually describes in full the entire case and explains any aspects of the case which raised difficulty at the trial. The legal advisers of the Department of Justice study the report and also read the court record of the trial. They comb the material for irregularities and possible mitigating factors. At this stage, representation may be made on behalf of the condemned person. In addition, the legal advisers may ask the police to investigate a specific point, or call in a psychiatrist to examine the mental condition of the accused. Having completed their report, the advisers draft a report of their own to the Minister of Justice, who considers it, and either calls for investigation or signs an approved report, a copy of which is submitted to each member of the Cabinet.

The advice of the Cabinet (in practice, of the Minister of Justice) is submitted to the President-in-Council who acts upon it.[30] If a reprieve is not granted, the Minister of Justice signs an authorization for the execution which is submitted to the Pretoria Supreme Court. It is left to the Deputy Sheriff to fix a date for the execution. Should the condemned person be permitted to appeal against the sentence, the procedure outlined above is suspended pending the outcome of the appeal.

The Lansdown Commission considered that 'with all the safeguards against error which are applied in law and practice both at and subsequent to trial where there is conviction of murder, there can . . . be little ground for the assertion that in the continuance of the death penalty there is a real risk of executing an innocent man'. In a minority report, Mrs A. W. Hoernlé was more sceptical, arguing that the safeguards seemed impressive 'until it is remembered that very largely it is the same set of documents that is being studied
408

each time'.[31] The Rev. H. Ph. Junod, who made a close study of the procedure governing the trial and execution of capital offenders in his capacities as Director of the Penal Reform League and prison chaplain, stated in his evidence to the Commission that he was 'not convinced that innocent men are not hanged in South Africa'.[32] In 1960, Junod wrote: 'Mistakes have been made to our own knowledge; of that we are perfectly sure.'[33] Certainly several cases have occurred where reprieves have been granted only at the last moment before the execution.

The data on reprieves can conveniently be divided into four periods. Records are available since 1923 and Table 1 covers the period from that time until 1934. This was the period before the doctrine of extenuating circumstances was introduced into the South African law of murder and when accordingly death sentences were mandatory in all cases of murder. This factor presumably accounts for the high proportion of reprieves during this period, since the courts' inability to temper the law with their appreciation of an accused's lack of moral guilt meant that a larger number of hard cases found their way to the notice of the executive.

TABLE 1. DISPOSAL OF OFFENDERS CONVICTED OF MURDER, 1923–34

	Whites		Non-whites[34]		Total
	Male	Female	Male	Female	
Executed	14	1	186	4	205
Commuted	15	4	579	63	661
Total convictions	29	5	765	67	866
Executed as percentage of total convictions/ death sentences	48·3%	20·0%	24·3%	5·9%	23·7%

Sources: Report of the Penal and Prison Reform Commission, Appendices N and O (1947); Hellman, ed., Handbook of Race Relations, 98 (1949).

Table 2 then covers the period from the introduction of the extenuating circumstances doctrine until the Lansdown Commission reported in 1947. The absolute number of cases in which extenuating circumstances were found can be seen to have had a massive effect on the total number of cases which came up for executive consideration. The proportion of those convicted who were actually executed dropped sharply compared with the previous period; the proportion of those convicted *without* extenuating circumstances who were actually executed rose significantly as fewer hard cases came before the executive.

TABLE 2. DISPOSAL OF OFFENDERS CONVICTED OF MURDER, 1935-46

	Whites		Non-whites[34]		
	Male	Female	Male	Female	Total
Executed	4	—	206	1	211
Commuted	15	—	306	17	338
Extenuating circumstances	17	5	914	61	997
Total convictions	36	5	1426	79	1546
Executed as percentage of total convictions	11·1%	—	14·4%	1·3%	13·6%
Executed as percentage of total death sentences	21·0%	—	40·2%	5·5%	38·3%

Sources: As for Table 1.

The period beginning in 1947, which is covered by Table 3, is the period immediately following the war. Initially, at any rate, a certain amount of personal and social disorganization followed and there was certainly an increase in the general volume of crime. The period is marked by a dramatic increase in the proportion of persons executed; the figures for rape, included in the available data for the first time, show an even greater proportion of executions than for murder.

TABLE 3. DISPOSAL OF OFFENDERS SENTENCED TO DEATH, 1947-56

	Murder		Rape		
	Whites	Non-whites[34]	Whites	Non-whites[34]	Total
Executed	19	422	—	47	488
Commuted	11	348	—	9	368
Total death sentences	30	770	—	56	856
Executed as percentage of death sentences	63·3%	55·0%	—	84·0%	57·0%

Source: Minister of Justice, *House of Assembly Debates*, 1957, cols. 8765-6.

The last period for which information is available is 1957-64 (Table 4).[35] In this period, the overall proportion of executions increased still further; executions for robbery and housebreaking were recorded for the first time;[36] and the annual number of executions for murder rose above a hundred persons for the first time.[37]

TABLE 4. DISPOSAL OF OFFENDERS SENTENCED TO DEATH, 1959-64

	Whites	Non-whites[34]	Total
Executed	16	502	518
Commuted	2	191	193
Total death sentences	18	693	711
Executed as percentage of death sentences	88·8%	72·4%	72·8%

Source: Minister of Justice, *House of Assembly Debates*, 1965, col. 5268.

IV Capital Punishment and Racial Policy

I CAPITAL PUNISHMENT AND THE SOCIAL STRUCTURE

In 1947, the Lansdown Commission concluded that public opinion in South Africa was not ripe for the abolition of capital punishment. It conceded, however, that in a matter of 'vital social reform, the reformer must be in advance of and educate public opinion'.[38]

The Commission argued that capital punishment ought to be retained. The main reason for reaching this conclusion turned on the fact that the bulk of the African section of the population 'has not yet emerged from a state of barbarism'.[39] The Commission believed that African regard for the sanctity of human life was less than that of the 'western civilized man'. While it was not prepared to commit itself on the deterrent value of the death penalty, it denied that the experience of countries which had abolished the institution could be used in support of the abolitionist cause in South Africa because of the 'difference of racial and consequently of social and economic conditions'.[40] One member of the Commission, Mrs A. W. Hoernlé, submitted a minority report in which she put forward the arguments for abolition.

The 1947 Commission is the only official body ever to have investigated capital punishment in South Africa and it did so only in the course of a far wider survey of the country's penal institutions and policy. It is submitted that its paragraphs dealing with capital punishment are perfunctory and superficial. How does one interpret the argument that a large majority of the African population is 'just emerging from barbarism'? If the purport is that crimes of violence were frequent in the tribal societies of pre-European times, it can be rejected as false. The evidence of the early observers suggests that homicide and rape were rare.[41]

It is suggested that the significance of the Commission's conclusion lies in its articulation of views which are commonly held by members of the dominant white group and are frequently employed to justify the retention of the death penalty. The penal system of a

412

society cannot be viewed in isolation from other elements of the social structure. It is an integral part of the social control mechanism of society and must be seen in the light of that society's values and the relationships between the groups which constitute the society.

The social structure of South Africa has many features resembling those of caste society. The whites are determined to maintain their position of supremacy and various 'techniques of domination'[42] are employed to maintain the system of social stratification. White domination manifests itself in various ways in the enforcement of the criminal law. In many respects the criminal law is inevitably framed with the interests of the property-owning group (consisting mainly of whites) in mind. Certain other laws to which criminal sanctions are attached are applicable to Africans only, for example the 'pass' laws which regulate and control the movement of Africans. Some laws, such as the various master and servant laws, are heavily weighted in favour of the employer class, to the disadvantage of the employee class, which is mainly non-white.

The law-enforcement agencies are controlled and directed by personnel drawn from the dominant group. Supreme Court judges, magistrates, prosecutors, jury-members, assessors, attorney-general, senior police and prison officers are all white. Attorneys and advocates are predominantly white.

Supreme Court judges are formally independent of the executive arm of government. They are drawn from among advocates appointed by the President-in-Council on the recommendation of the Minister of Justice, and can be removed from office only on an address from both Houses of Parliament praying for removal on grounds of misbehaviour or incapacity. In practice, the Minister of Justice consults with the Judge-President and other senior judges of the Provincial Division in which the appointment is to be made. In making judicial appointments, regard is had to the language of the appointee. The Minister of Justice stated in 1960:

... we should try as far as possible to keep the two language groups, the Afrikaans-speaking and the English-speaking, on an equal basis; in other words, you must be watchful so that the proportion is maintained, and I accuse the previous government that they did not keep that watch.[43]

413

In practice, this favours the Afrikaans-speaking advocate whose numbers are considerably smaller than those of his English-speaking colleagues.

No conclusive evidence can be found regarding the influence of the advocate's political convictions and general social outlook on the possibility of his elevation to the bench. It is, however, widely believed to be an important factor. Indeed, had the opposition United Party been in power it is unlikely that the present Chief Justice would have been on the bench at all, for, although a distinguished jurist, as a government law adviser he would not have been considered eligible for the appointment. Several distinguished advocates of liberal or radical views, on the other hand, have been overlooked. In the present climate of opinion, it is inconceivable that a non-white advocate would be appointed to the bench.

2 RACIAL DISCRIMINATION IN CAPITAL PUNISHMENT

Racial discrimination in the distribution of punishment by South African courts has frequently been noted by observers.[44] Only one study, however, has attempted to demonstrate it for capital punishment. In a study written in 1949 it was suggested that the executive is influenced by racial considerations when deciding whether or not to grant reprieves in murder cases. It was conclusively shown that there is a greater probability of conviction in murder trials when the victim is white; that it is rare for a white to be convicted of murder when the victim is non-white; and that whites were never executed for the rape or murder of non-whites. Non-whites convicted of raping or murdering whites were usually hanged. This pattern was attributed to the fact that less value is attached to the life of a non-white, while emphasis is placed on the sanctity of the life of a white.[45]

The investigator wishing to ascertain whether these assertions are valid is handicapped by a dearth of statistical material and reluctance on the part of the Minister of Justice and his officials to provide information. The annual reports of the Commissioner of Prisons provide statistics on the number of persons sentenced to death and executed, their race, sex and the offences for which they were sentenced; but the race of the victim is not stated. Figures for

414

murder and rape convictions given in Parliament at odd intervals have given the race of the victims but have not given the sentence imposed on those not sentenced to death.

It is interesting to learn, from a study of the annual Reports of the Commissioner of Police, that, for the size of the population, more whites are charged with cross-colour (i.e. where the victims and the convicted person are of different colour groups, i.e. white or non-white) murder and rape than non-whites. The following tables of prosecution statistics illustrate this:

TABLE 5. PERSONS PROSECUTED FOR MURDER, 1953–62

	1953	1954	1955	1956	1957	1958	1959	1960	1961	1962
Both accused and victim white	28	22	40	29	31	33	26	31	35	40
Accused non-white and victim white	23	7	23	31	27	21	29	19	24	43
Accused white and victim non-white	25	25	24	24	33	20	40	20	28	39
Both accused and victim non-white	1,441	1,461	1,580	1,856	2,275	2,068	2,313	2,356	2,662	3,335

TABLE 6. PERSONS PROSECUTED FOR RAPE, 1953–62

	1953	1954	1955	1956	1957	1958	1959	1960	1961	1962
Both accused and victim white	72	44	52	68	71	83	108	89	74	73
Accused non-white and victim white	23	33	32	37	40	28	28	38	34	38
Accused white and victim non-white	36	32	29	40	33	48	43	41	38	45
Both accused and victim non-white	2,087	2,230	2,358	2,548	2,762	3,407	3,420	3,547	3,862	3,786

Source: Annual Reports of the Commissioner of the South African Police. The population of South Africa in 1953 was 13,376,000, made up of 2,744,000 whites and 10,632,000 non-whites; in 1962 it was 16,664,000, made up of 3,182,000 whites and 13,482,000 non-whites: *Statistical Year Book 1964.*

415

Analysis of sentences imposed for cross-colour rape and murder over a recent period of three years for which information is available, 1957–59 inclusive, shows that no white was sentenced to death for the rape or murder of a non-white in that period, while at least 37 and 13 non-whites were executed for the crimes of murder and rape, respectively, against whites.[46]

Certain facts are clear over a longer period. No white has ever been executed for the rape of a non-white woman. Since 1960 two whites have been executed for rape: in both cases the victims were whites as well. Whites convicted of raping non-white women generally receive sentences of imprisonment which rarely exceed five years.[47] Execution of a non-white for the rape of a white woman is, however, the general rule. In 1955, the Minister of Justice, Mr C. R. Swart, announced that during his term of office 'not a single non-white who has been sentenced to death for raping a European woman has escaped the death penalty'.[48] Execution of a white for the murder of a non-white is rare: only six cases (possibly seven) have been recorded between 1910 and the present.[49]

The inference one draws is that violent crimes committed by non-whites on whites are viewed by the courts as extremely serious offences, while the same crime committed by a white against a non-white is viewed less seriously. Judges, as noted above, are drawn from the dominant racial group. It is submitted that many judges are able unconsciously to identify more easily with an accused white person than an accused non-white person. For example, most judges are likely to understand more clearly the psychological motivations, and appreciate the stresses to which he is subjected, of a white than those of a non-white. It is possible, therefore, that extenuating circumstances are more readily found in murder cases where the accused is white without there being any deliberate bias or partiality in favour of the white. For example, youth is often found to be an extenuating circumstance.[50] The writer has the impression that this occurs more frequently and readily where the accused is white. In 1956 two African girls *said* to be 18 were hanged for the murder of a white woman. African births are not registered and age had to be inferred from medical evidence.[51] In a converse racial situation, the immaturity of the accused could very well have been found to constitute an extenuating circumstance.

416

Judges are not isolated from the sanction of public opinion within the white group; sentencing a white to death for the rape or murder of a non-white would undoubtedly raise a far greater sense of shock than in the converse racial situation, where the death penalty is widely held by most whites to be the only fitting punishment. In addition, the sense of shock experienced by the judge himself in sentencing a white to death is likely to be considerably greater than in the case of a non-white.

Where non-whites are involved as both victims and accused in murder cases, it is apparent that the courts tend to be more lenient than where the victim is white. Frequently the charge is reduced to culpable homicide or extenuating circumstances are found.[52] Myrdal noted a similar phenomenon in his study of the Negro in America:

> It is part of the Southern tradition to assume that Negroes are disorderly and lack elementary morals, and to show great indulgence toward Negro violence and disorderliness 'when they are among themselves'. . . . As long as only Negroes are concerned and no whites are disturbed, great leniency will be shown in most cases.[53]

Racial discrimination in the distribution of capital punishment is causally related to the system of racial stratification. Non-whites are widely assumed by whites to be subject to a greater proclivity to violence than whites. The sanctity of the white life and the white body is emphasized by the imposition of the severest possible sentences on non-white violators.

3 PAYMENT OF DEFENDING COUNSEL

It is submitted furthermore that poverty among lower status groups operates directly towards causing racial selectivity in the distribution of capital punishment. In a high proportion of cases where capital offences are alleged, defending counsel is remunerated on a *pro deo* (i.e. charitable) basis because the accused persons are too poor to engage counsel in the ordinary way. There is no statutory provision for the appointment of counsel in *pro deo* cases, but in practice it is always provided in response to a request from the trial judge.[54] Usually, but not always, *pro deo* work is done by the younger and less experienced advocates. The Rev. H. Ph. Junod, former Director of the Penal Reform League of South Africa, noted that 'the fee (£5.5.0. for the first day and £3.3.0. for each subsequent day) is hardly sufficient to induce them to give of their maximum, and it not infrequently happens that, in order to avoid additional expenses, they only leave for the Circuit Court on the morning of the trial, meeting their client merely half-an-hour or so before the hearing begins, and this for the first time'.[55]

Junod also argued that the defending counsel were insufficiently acquainted with tribal law and customs and with African languages so as to be able to communicate satisfactorily with African clients.[56] They are further handicapped by not having the assistance of an attorney, and have great difficulty in finding independent experts, such as psychiatrists, to assist them when proper remuneration cannot be provided.

V Conclusion

South Africa has one of the highest execution rates in the world. How does one account for the marked increase in the use of the gallows over the past decade and a half? In theory, a thoroughgoing rehabilitative penal policy has been accepted,[57] and the increased resort to capital punishment must be therefore regarded as somewhat paradoxical.

As far as the writer has been able to ascertain, no one has made a study of the sociology of penal practices in South Africa. Certain tentative hypotheses are put forward in an attempt to relate the institution of capital punishment in South Africa to the social structure of the society.

I THE ACUTENESS OF INTER-GROUP CONFLICT IN SOUTH AFRICA

It is suggested that the more acute the conflict between the classes or castes that compose the society, the more likely it is that the penal code will be severe; the ultimate index of severity being the use of capital punishment. Most whites in South Africa see themselves as an isolated minority group, separated widely in culture and values from non-whites, particularly from Africans, who constitute numerically the largest group in the country. A severe penal code, embodying extensive resort to capital punishment, is seen as a vitally necessary source of protection for life and property, as well as a mechanism for helping to maintain the hierarchical structuring of society. A widespread feeling of insecurity among whites predisposes them to the view that the death penalty must be retained and used extensively.

An official of the influential Nederduits Gereformeerde Kerk (Dutch Reformed Church) has been reported as saying that it was 'desirable that punishments for some crimes should be extreme if certain groups were to be protected from the lawless and violent behaviour of other groups'.[58] One of the country's leading criminologists, in justifying the retention of capital punishment, claimed that 'certain sections of South Africa's population were not sufficiently advanced culturally to understand the motives behind its abolishment [*sic*] and would interpret its abolishment as weakness'.[59] Abolition, he argued, would be an encouragement to an increase in violence.

Similar views enjoy widespread support among influential groups, such as the judiciary and the police. Of the two major political parties the governing Nationalist Party is staunchly committed to retention. The opposition United Party has no policy on the death penalty and would allow its members a free vote if the issue were to be debated in Parliament. The majority of its members hold retentionist views.

Capital punishment has never been debated in Parliament. On the one occasion when the Minister of Justice was asked to appoint a Commission of Inquiry to examine the possibility of more humane methods of punishment, he declined to do so.[60]

And, just as the government refuses to contemplate changing its means of secondary control of crime, so too it has done little to reinforce the primary controls. Little has been done to remove the basic causes of crime among Africans, analysed by the 1942 Committee, and substantially accepted by the Lansdown Commission of 1947.[61] Disrupted family life, poverty, overcrowded slum conditions and lack of facilities for recreation and relaxation remain characteristics of African life, in the urban areas particularly. Frustrations resulting from the rigidity of the colour bar is a cause of crime the importance of which is incalculable. It has been noted that 'the deliberate and large-scale violation of the law by Africans and Coloured reveals an attitude of defiance towards the existing structure of society'.[62] Similar sentiments were expressed by the former head of a reformatory for African juveniles, who argued that the denial of opportunities inherent in the caste-like structure of society creates a situation in which '. . . an undue proportion of the best non-white brains is devoted to crime'.[63]

In 1942 an Interdepartmental Committee stated bluntly that the

> consequences of many years of indifference, half-measures or measures whose intellectual content never aspired to rise above the conception of more and larger prisons, more and more frequent floggings and more (or less) spare diet, have been to produce a native population of industrial serfs, called upon to perform the unskilled labour of civilisation under exacting conditions and at wages which keeps it chronically on the verge of destitution and produces, *inter alia*, the native criminal.[64]

The consequence is a modern crime-rate of immense and ever-increasing proportions. The number of murders, which at the end of the 1939–45 war was relatively constant around an annual mark of 1,000, has increased annually to the extent that the most recent figures (1963–64) show an annual total of over 3,000. Calculated in terms of the growth in population, the rate is double that of twenty years ago. Property crimes reported to the police have increased from an annual 300,000 to 500,000 at the present time, though this increase is proportionate to population growth.[65]

2 THE INFLUENCE OF CALVINISM ON SOUTH AFRICA'S PENAL PRACTICES

The large majority of the dominant Afrikaner group adhere to the fundamental tenets of Calvinism, as interpreted by the three Dutch Reformed Churches. Inherent in Calvinism is a stress on the moral justification of severe punishment, and an emphasis on Old Testament notions of retribution.

Elsewhere, fundamentalist forms of Christianity have often undergone a transformation under the impact of liberal, secular and humanist ideas, as, for example, with Calvinism in Scotland. It is suggested that the majority of Afrikaners in South Africa, and their religious, political and social ideas, have been relatively unaffected by the liberalizing influences of 19th-century secular humanism.

Traditionally, Calvinism emphasizes personal responsibility, discipline and asceticism among its followers.[66] The doctrine entails a built-in resistance to any theories of crime causation which might appear to undermine the notions of free will. A leading Afrikaner criminologist writes:

> In my opinion, the criminal has always been viewed either too much as a victim of his imperfect, biological and physical heredity-determined structure, or too much as a victim of his living conditions. In viewing the criminal in either of these lights, the criminologist denies him all responsibility, freedom, possibility of choice, value determination, and other human attributes which distinguish him as a human being created in the image of his fellow men and God. . . . punishment should be enforced in a manner that will impress on the criminal the fact that he personally is responsible for his crime.[67]

Such a view predisposes a penal system towards retribution and shifts the emphasis away from any theories of crime causation which smack to Calvinists of determinism because responsibility is partly or wholly transferred away from the criminal to his environment.

Where it is the religion of the dominant group, Calvinism reinforces authoritarian patterns of government and provides moral justification for severe measures against criminals who are viewed as threats to law and order and, therefore, enemies of the state.

3 CAPITAL PUNISHMENT AND THE POLITICAL OFFENDER, 1910–65

The 20th-century history of South Africa has been marked by several militant political protests against government policy. Until the last fifteen years, however, the political offender has been white; today he is usually non-white. With the shift in colour has come a shift in the government's attitude towards the reprieving of political offenders from the death sentence.

The 1914 rebellion in parts of the Transvaal and Orange Free State, headed by senior army officers, resulted in only one execution —that of Fourie, who 'had never resigned his commission and had fired to kill to the last'.[68] The 1922 general strike, motivated by white miners' desire to prevent modification of the Industrial Colour Bar, resulted in the loss of 230 lives as the result of fighting between the strikers and troops. Eighteen death sentences were passed and four persons executed but the fear of creating more bitter antipathy led the government to commute the remaining sentences.[69]

The response to sabotage and subversion during the Second World War is even more striking. The activities of the two pro-Nazi organizations, the *Ossewabrandwag* and the *Stormjaers*, resulted in convictions for treason and offences against wartime regulations. In one case, that of Leibbrandt, an Afrikaner who acted as a Nazi agent, the death sentence was passed but was commuted following an impassioned speech in Parliament by the leader of the Nationalist Party, Dr Malan, calling for his life to be spared.[70] In another case, the death sentences on two members of the *Ossewabrandwag* for sabotage were commuted following the Nationalist party's nation-wide appeal for mercy and the presentation to the government of a petition for reprieve, signed at the top by Dr Malan and containing thousands of other signatures.[71]

Shortly after it came to power in 1948 the Nationalist government released all the prisoners who had been convicted of political offences during the war. According to the Minister of Justice, the decision was taken 'as a result of the desire of the new Government to relieve the people of the Union from the strain of the war years

422

and to endeavour to end all the unpleasantness and rancour which flowed from it'.[72]

Since 1958, the implementation of unpopular forms of rural local government and an increasing frustration with non-violent methods of political opposition have led to considerable unrest, terrorism and sabotage. It is beyond the scope of this essay to detail all the incidents which have occurred in this period. Unrest occurred in the Transvaal African area of Sekhukhuneland in May 1958, as a result of the implementation of the Bantu Authorities Act (a form of local government having some similarity to the system of indirect rule). Finally, fourteen Africans were sentenced to death for murder. All the sentences were subsequently commuted to life imprisonment.[73]

During 1960 and 1961 widespread unrest occurred in the African area of the Transkei. Its causes were protest against the Bantu Authorities and land rehabilitation schemes. Special courts were set up to hear cases resulting from the disturbances. By December 1961, thirty Africans had been sentenced to death for murder, nine of whom subsequently lodged successful appeals.[74]

From the second half of 1961 onwards various sabotage groups with general political aims became active, notably the African-led *Umkonto Wesizwe* (Spear of the Nation) and the white-led African Resistance Movement. A terrorist organization called Poqo (apparently consisting of members of the Pan-African Congress, which, together with the African National Congress, was banned by the government in 1960) also emerged at this time. It has been tentatively calculated that by the end of 1964 some fifty-one death sentences had been imposed for murder and sabotage committed by these organizations,[75] though another estimate claims that fifty political offenders have been executed since 1963.[76] It is not possible to obtain precision from published figures, since the government does not accept the concept of a 'political offender' and political motivations are therefore concealed with all other motivations in data published. It can only be stated with certainty that political motivation has been refused the standing of an extenuating circumstance,[77] that there have been some executions following convictions for sabotage[78] and that only one white has been sentenced to death and executed in this recent period of violent opposition.[79]

Most white political offenders have not attempted to undermine the caste structure of society. Their activities may have been aimed at overthrowing the government; but the alternative government established would have been no less dedicated to the system of white domination. The episodes of 1914, 1922 and 1941–5 were all intra-caste conflicts.

The comparison with the post-1958 picture shows the relativist character of the political offence. Since that time, violence has been directed at the very structure of society, and therefore it is suggested that the penalties have been commensurately more severe, even when it is a white, such as Harris, who is involved. Where African political offences are concerned, the executive does not have the fear that it may alienate political support if it recommends execution. On the contrary, refusal to grant reprieves to saboteurs and terrorists sentenced to death is more likely to prove electorally popular, the death sentence being widely considered by whites to be the most appropriate form of punishment for this type of case.

NOTES

1. General Laws Amendment Act, 1935, s. 61 (a).
2. Evidence of Dr C. W. H. Lansdown, Q.C., to the (British) Royal Commission on Capital Punishment, 1949–53: see *Report*, Cmd. 8932 (1953).
3. R. *v. Valachia*, 1945 S.A. 826, 831 (A.D.).
4. R. *v. Thibani*, 1949 S.A. 720, 729 (A.D.); cf. R. *v. du Randt*, 1954 (1) S.A. 313, 316 (A.D.).
5. 1938 C.P.D. 310.
6. *Report*, Cmd. 8932, 482 (1953).
7. R. *v. Mutkisub*, 1938 S.W.A. 4.
8. *State v. Ntongo & 12 others*, 1965, C.P.D. unreported; cf. R. *v. Radebe*, 1915 A.D. 96; *State v. Dikgale*, 1965 (1) S.A. 209 (A.D.).
9. R. *v. Ngobese*, 1936 S.A. 296 (A.D.); R. *v. Hugo*, 1940 W.L.D. 285; *State v. Babada*, 1964 (1) A.D. 26.
10. R. *v. Cameron*, 1943 N.P.D. 344; cf. *State v. de Bruyn & others*, 1965 C.P.D., unreported.
11. 1953 (3) S.A. 303.
12. 1957 (4) S.A. 265 (A.D.).
13. For further discussion on this point, see below, p. 409.
14. *Report of the Commission appointed to enquire into assaults on women*, U.G. 39 (1913).
15. See R. *v. Ramanka*, 1949 (1) S.A. 417 (A.D.); R. *v. Sibande*, 1958 (3) S.A. 3 (A.D.).

16. See below, p. 414, for further discussion on this point.
17. Criminal Procedure Amendment Act, 1958, s. 4.
18. In R. v. Sisilane, 1959 (2) S.A. 448 (A.D.), the Appellate Division held that the trial court had exceeded its powers in sentencing to death an accomplice in a robbery case. The appellant in the case had been the driver of the lorry which the robbers had used, and he had not himself inflicted or threatened grievous bodily harm. To overcome the effect of this decision, the legislature amended the relevant section to make an accomplice to such a crime liable to the death sentence: Criminal Law Further Amendment Act, 1959, s. 3.
19. House of Assembly Debates, 1958, cols. 353 ff.
20. House of Assembly Debates, 1965, cols. 8138.
21. R. v. Hay (1899), 16 S.C. 290.
22. R. v. Smith, 1907 T.S. 783.
23. R. v. Biyana, 1938 E.D.L. 310.
24. R. v. Kennedy, 1951 (4) S.A. 431 (A.D.).
25. R. v. Lloyd, 1941 C.P.D. 162.
26. R. v. Hugo, 1940 W.L.D. 285; R. v. Roberts, 1957 (4) S.A. 265.
27. Report of the Penal and Prison Reform Commission, para. 476 (1947).
28. Bennett, Freedom—or the Gallows, 243 (1956).
29. State v. Harris, 1965 T.P.D., unreported. Psychiatric evidence for the defence suggested that Harris suffered from hypo-manic ecstasy which affected his personality. It was common ground between the psychiatrists for the State and the defence that Harris was emotionally unstable and showed considerable personality immaturity.
30. Criminal Law and Procedure Act, 1955, s. 372.
31. Report of the Penal and Prison Reform Commission, para. 10 of Mrs Hoernlé's Reservation on Capital Punishment (1947).
32. Ibid.
33. Penal Reform Newsletter, No. 51, 10 (1960).
34. The category of 'non-whites' is not broken down further except for actual executions. This breakdown is: 1923–46, Coloureds 33 (8·3%), Africans 351 (88·4%), Indians 13 (13·2%) (Report of the Prison and Penal Reform Commission, Appendix N (1947)); 1947–64, Coloureds 162 (14·8%), Africans 916 (84·0%), Indians 12 (1·1%) (Annual Reports of the Commissioner of Prisons).
35. Some reliance is placed here on the published figures. Those given in the statement by the Minister of Justice do not cover the period 1957–8.
36. 22 between 1959 and 1963: Annual Reports of the Commissioner of Prisons.
37. 106 in 1961–2; 104 in 1962–3: Annual Reports of the Commissioner of Prisons.
38. Report, para. 475.
39. Ibid., para. 457.
40. Ibid., para. 460.
41. McLean, A Compendium of Kafir Laws and Customs, 59 (1858); Cetewayo, Evidence to the Cape Commission on Native Laws and Customs, 516 (1883);

Bryant, *The Zulu People as they were before the White Man came*, 568 (1949); *Report of the Commission appointed to enquire into assaults on women*, U.G. 39—1913, para. 36 (1913).

42. Hoernlé, *South African Native Policy and the Liberal Spirit*, Lecture 1 (1945).

43. *House of Assembly Debates*, 1960, col. 1467.

44. See, e.g. Hoernlé, *op. cit.*, 36; Hellmann, ed., *Handbook on Race Relations in South Africa*, 98 ff. (1949); Marquand, *The Peoples and Policies of South Africa*, 133 (1963). Nothing in this chapter, however, is intended to impugn or reflect upon the integrity of the judiciary.

45. Hellmann, *op. cit.*, 99.

46. The figures given for 1957 were not complete, the fate of 8 non-whites condemned to death for cross-colour murder or rape being still pending the executive decision at the time the figures were released. This accounts for the qualification 'at least' in the previous sentence: *House of Assembly Debates*, 1958, col. 208; 1959, col. 346; 1960, col. 999.

47. In a recent example of this, four white men convicted of rape on an African woman after beating up her boy-friend, were sentenced to six strokes with a light cane (3) and six strokes with an adult cane (1), together with a year's imprisonment suspended for three years: *Cape Argus*, November 24th, 1965. In 1966, the death penalty was demanded by the prosecutor in a Cape Town rape charge against a white accused of raping a coloured. The longest recorded sentence of twenty years was passed: *State v. Swanepoel*, *Cape Argus*, June 9th, 1966.

48. *Rand Daily Mail*, September 16th, 1955, quoted by Ellison Kahn, 'Crime and Punishment in South Africa, 1910–1960', 1961 *Acta Juridica*, 203.

49. The writer's estimate differs from Professor Kahn's, *art. cit.*, 205.

50. Despite R. *v. Hugo*, 1940 W.L.D. 285.

51. *Cape Argus*, January 28th, 1956.

52. Cf. Hellmann, *op. cit.*, 99; Barker, *The Man Next to Me*, 157 (1962).

53. *An American Dilemma*, 551 (1944).

54. See statement by Minister of Justice, *House of Assembly Debates*, 1960, col. 1406.

55. 'The Preparation of the Case for the Defence of Bantu accused of Homicide', *Penal Reform Newsletter*, No. 51, 6 (1960).

56. *Ibid.*, 9.

57. See Director of Prisons, *Developments in the Prevention of Crime and the Treatment of Offenders*, 67 ff. (1958–9).

58. The Rev. D. F. B. de Beer, Public Morals Secretary, *Cape Argus*, November 4th, 1961.

59. Prof. Herman Venter, *ibid.*

60. *House of Assembly Debates*, 1961, col. 5045.

61. *Report*, para. 32.

62. Hellmann, *op. cit.*, 94.

63. Paton, 'The Control of Serious Crime', *Penal Reform Newsletter*, No. 42, 18 (1958).

64. *Report of the Committee appointed by the Hon. the Ministers of Justice and Native Affairs to investigate the position of crime on the Witwatersrand and Pretoria*, para. 13 (1942).
65. The figures are taken from the *Annual Reports of the Commissioner of the South African Police* and from the *Statistical Year Book, 1964*.
66. Tawney, *Religion and the Rise of Capitalism*, 103 ff. (Penguin Books, ed., 1938).
67. Van der Walt, *Die Mens in die Kriminologie*, 25 (1964).
68. Walker, *A History of Southern Africa*, 3rd ed., 563 (1957).
69. Roux, *Time Longer Than Rope*, 2nd ed., 147 (1963); Doxey, *The Industrial Colour Bar in South Africa*, 126 (1961).
70. For the reasons for commutation, see *Cape Times*, December 23rd, 1943.
71. Van Rensburg, *Their Paths Crossed Mine*, 215 ff. (1956).
72. *Cape Times*, June 12th, 1948.
73. *Survey of Race Relations in South Africa, 1959–60*, 49 (1961).
74. *Survey of Race Relations in South Africa, 1962*, 12 (1963).
75. *Survey of Race Relations in South Africa, 1963* and *1964*, 53 and 84 respectively.
76. A South African, *Prisoners of Apartheid*, 32–3 (1965).
77. *State v. Mkaba & others*, 1965 (1) S.A. 215 (A.D.).
78. Minister of Justice, *House of Assembly Debates*, 1964, col. 3990.
79. F. J. Harris, who placed a bomb in the concourse of Johannesburg Railway Station in July 1964. An elderly white woman died from injuries caused by the explosion.

15
The Ghana Prison System: an Historical Perspective

ROBERT B. SEIDMAN

The prison system is at the core of Ghana's penal organization. It stands as a monument to colonial rule, as a memorial to confused goals, conflicting objectives, policies evolved and abandoned, and sometimes no policy at all. Today, it searches for its true role, if indeed there is any single role for it to play. It is caught between the urgings of a preventive policy, which recognizes that prevention may work where cure cannot, the deterrent policy of the courts, whose judges remain convinced of the efficacy of punishment as a power in the hearts of men, and the rehabilitatory ideal of the western world of which Ghana is a part.

The actual history of the prisons and the story of the working out of these conflicts falls into four parts: to 1876; 1876–1907; 1907–20; and 1920 to the present.

I Indigenous Criminal Law

It is, of course, impossible to generalize meaningfully about indigenous Ghanaian society, which ran the gamut from the highly centralized and sophisticated Ashanti to the relatively simply organized groupings of the north. But, however great the difference between the tribes, the gulf between their law and that of the colonialists was an abyss.

Before the advent of imperialist rule, the basic mode of production in Ghana was subsistence agriculture, with its associated culture and institutions. In most such societies, the central value is the maintenance of equilibrium, both mystically with the gods, to assure the repetitive cycle of the harvest, and practically within the

431

community, to assure communal solidarity against a harsh environment.[1] Both of these objectives permeated the criminal law of the indigenous ethnic groups in Ghana.

Among the Tale of northern Ghana, for example, homicide was at once a sin against the earth and the ancestors, and against the corporate unity of the victim's lineage. Sacrifices were required to be offered by the culprit's family, to which the victim's family also contributed in an effort to achieve both mystical and earthly reconciliation.[2] Deterrence or reformation of the offender was apparently at most a by-product, not an articulated objective.

Among the Ashanti, a highly centralized tribe occupying the forest zone of central Ghana, the same dual objectives can be discerned in the criminal law.[3] Grave offences—murder, unintentional homicide, suicide, serious sexual offences, offences against the chief, treason and cowardice in war, and witchcraft—were *oman akyiwade*, offences so serious that they threatened the mystical communion between the community and the ancestors and tribal gods. The remedy was sacrifice: sometimes of the offender himself, as in murder, or in swearing the chief's great oath; of a sheep or other animal, in the case of lesser delicts. *Efisem*, or minor offences, did not involve a rupture of the mystical relationship with the gods, and hence were compromised by a ritual *impata* or conciliation—a fowl or a small amount of gold-dust if within the lineage, or compensation if the victim and the offender were of different lineages. Again, deterrence, restraint of the offender, or even reformation of the offender were not consciously purposes of punishment.

It is significant that theft was a relatively rare crime in indigenous society. Among the Konkomba of northern Ghana, bows and arrows are sacred objects and no one would steal them; and clothing, the principal other sort of personalty, is practically held in common.[4] Among the Fante, too, theft was rare; it was not considered theft for a starving man to take food. Sarbah comments that 'among a people accustomed to have all things in common, the sensibility of many persons to the criminality of theft is not so great as in Europe'.[5]

II The Importation of British Penal Institutions: to 1876

Upon these societies, accustomed to view the problem of crime in terms of the restoration of equilibrium, the British imposed a criminal law and penal institutions which embodied objectives different *toto coelo*. English criminal law of the 19th century, designed to meet the demands of the 'sound' men to 'keep the multitude in order' by way of exemplary deterrence,[6] seemed well-adapted to the analogous problem posed to the imperialists in their effort to impose an alien rule upon the Gold Coast. The common law of crimes, by at once embodying norms of public order and of 'civilized' conduct, met the twin demands of the Dual Mandate—an orderly society for the purposes of trade, and the 'enlightenment' of the Africans towards civilization *à l'anglaise*.[7] With respect to the criminal law, as so often elsewhere, the Dual Mandate was inherently contradictory. To impose order, the imperialist overlords saw in harsh, exemplary deterrence the central objective of the law. But the civilization function encapsulates the seeds of humanism.[8] 'Keeping the multitude in order' by way of exemplary deterrence and humanitarianism are inconsistent objectives. The history of criminal law and prisons on the Gold Coast can best be understood in terms of these two conflicting conceptions of punishment.

Penal law started on the Gold Coast in an altogether irregular manner. From 1828 to 1842, the governance of the Forts of the Coast was in the hands of a Committee of Merchants, whose President, George Maclean, without a whistle of formal authority, exercised criminal jurisdiction not only within the Forts, but frequently outside them, achieving compliance by the power of his personality and, when necessary, the strong red-coated right arm of his soldiery.[9] In 1841, ninety-one persons were incarcerated in Cape Coast Castle, some of whom had been in gaol for four years.[10] Since in only one case was there a definite period of imprisonment recorded, it would seem probable that most of the prisoners were in gaol for debt.

The ethical problem which was to plague Ghanaian criminal law until today arose very early. In 1834, the sister of the chief of Denkyira died. The chief, in Maclean's absence in Accra, proceeded with the traditional funeral custom, sacrificing eighty-five persons, including three children. On his return, Maclean fined the chief £200 and required him to post an additional £400 as surety for good behaviour.[11]

Maclean's persistent enemy on the Coast, a trader named Jackson, remonstrated with the Colonial Office. He urged that such a penalty would only drive the custom underground. He wrote:

> They know not that they are committing a crime. Their money is taken from them, and they are irritated at the circumstance; they believe the object sought is only their gold, for the attainment of which the other is a mere excuse. Milder measures should, in the first instance, be resorted to. You are dealing with a nation, not an individual. They should be reasoned with, which, aided by the assistance of their friends in endeavouring to convince them of their error, would in time succeed with these people as it has with others.[12]

The protest was unavailing, but the argument was prophetic. Was the path of the 'civilizing mission' to be accomplished by harsh imposition of exemplary punishment, or by reformation of the mores of the people?

The period to 1874, when the Colony of the Gold Coast was formally created, marked the gradual extension of criminal jurisdiction to the entire southern part of present-day Ghana. It also marked the development of the prisons from custodial institutions to the punitive instruments envisaged by the English Prisons Act, 1865.

The original Bond of 1844, entered into by the Fante chiefs and the British, acknowledged British jurisdiction *de facto* in the areas surrounding the Forts.[13] The original theory of the Bond was that criminals were to be delivered to the chiefs for punishment. This, in effect, provided the chiefs with victims for precisely those human sacrifices which the British were determined to eradicate. Hence, to protect against what were deemed to be 'barbarous punishments', the sentences gradually came to be carried out in the Forts.[14] Sometimes the chiefs were permitted to carry out the sentence, but under

434

British supervision 'to see that the execution took place in accordance with humanity and the practice of civilized nations'.[15]

The prisons of the early period were mainly custodial institutions. By 1850, there were prison cells in four forts, holding a maximum of 129 prisoners. The convicts worked at repairing public roads, and were permitted to earn a trifle by making straw hats for sale to the public.[16] Efforts had earlier been made from London to ameliorate their lot. Gladstone, the Colonial Secretary, insisted that the prisoners should not be kept in chains.[17] Governor Winnett at first demurred, on grounds of security from escape.[18] By 1847, however, he had been brought to heel,[19] and in the 1850 Blue Book it was reported that prisoners were ironed not as a mode of punishment, but only to prevent their escape while working on the public roads. This was evidently only dust thrown in the eyes of the Colonial Office, however; as late as 1857 one Ouacu was charged with burglary and sentenced to three years' hard labour 'in chains'.[20] How long punishment in chains actually lasted cannot now be determined.[21]

The caretaker function of the early prisons was stabilized in the Prisons Ordinance, 1860, a mere series of rules for the safe-keeping of prisoners embodying no discernible philosophy of punishment. The diet was generous enough: six pounds of kenkey[22] daily, with a pound of fish thrice weekly.

In order to make the prisons punitive institutions of great deterrent power, agitation started in England in 1863 to transform them into institutions for the refined and systematic torture of prisoners without the shedding of blood.[23] Its ripples reached the backwater of the Gold Coast at a propitious moment, for the spread of British jurisdiction was about to begin in earnest. After all, if one is to rule over savage races, what better method than the lash, physical torture and diminished diet?

The Colonial Office took the lead in a series of Circulars addressed to all the Colonial Governors, seeking to place the entire colonial prisons system on the same basis as that of England. This system had three principal pillars: the separate system, penal labour and a minimum diet. The separate system called for solitary confinement by night, and, where solitary confinement was not possible by day, absolute silence between convict prisoners. Penal labour was unremitting, exhausting and perfectly useless physical work.

The three approved forms were shot drill, crank drill—the useless turning of a braked windlass for thousands of turns per day[24]—and the treadmill. These were to be accompanied by the minimum diet consistent with maintenance of life.

The stream of circulars was seemingly unending.[25] Their thrust is exemplified by that of 1865: 'It is indeed', wrote Lord Granville, 'by severe suffering in the earlier portion of a sentence, rather than by suffering prolonged through a series of years that a deterrent effect is produced, for the class of persons by whom offences are generally committed do not look far forward, and they are governed by what is presently, and not distantly in their view.'[26] There were circulars reporting the opinions of the several Colonial Governors: solitary confinement would produce 'the same effect on a black as a white man', and was the only punishment that 'prisoners really fear'. Moreover, in New South Wales the prisoners complained, somewhat inconsistently, that imprisonment in association left them no time for their religious observances.[27]

The Colonial Office were not mere theoreticians but eminently practical. They supplied a dimensioned drawing of a regulation 'cat' (nine cord tails with three knots in each tail, each 33 inches long; a handle $19\frac{3}{4}$ inches long; the handle to weigh $6\frac{3}{4}$ ounces, and the tails $2\frac{1}{2}$ ounces).[28] In 1871, they forwarded diagrams of a working treadmill.[29] Meticulous investigations were made as to the advisability of cropping females' (as well as males') hair as a deterrent.[30]

The Secretary of State followed these up with a personal letter to Mr Ussher, the Administrator of the Gold Coast in 1869. He gave sound advice on how to avoid overcrowding without the expense of building additional cells:

It may be done by resorting to shorter and sharper punishments, by whipping in addition to shorter terms of imprisonment or in total substitution for any imprisonment . . . by substituting in the earlier stages of imprisonment strictly penal labour, and by lowering the diet to the minimum required for health. By these means the crowding of Prisons becomes less not only by shortening the duration of each Prisoner's term but also (as experience has shown) by lessening the number of Offenders.[31]

436

The Gold Coast officials were anxious to please. Mr Ussher wrote in 1869 to the Governor-in-Chief at Sierra Leone that, while punishments were still insufficiently severe, he had effected a considerable diminution in the diet.[32] His ultimate objectives, and those of the Colonial Office, were finally achieved in the Gold Coast in the Prisons Ordinance, 1876.

That Ordinance, whose dead hand still moulds the Prisons Regulations of Ghana, was modelled carefully upon the Prisons Act, 1865. It rested on the same foundation stones: the separate system, penal labour and a low diet. Prisoners were to be locked into separate cells at night 'so far as accommodation will allow'.[33] Convict prisoners were forbidden to speak or make any signs to any other prisoners;[34] to sing or whistle;[35] or even to make complaints to any but a senior prison officer or a Visitor.[36] Visits and letters were permitted only once in three months.[37] Penal labour was enforced. Every prisoner was required to do hard labour of the first class until he graduated to the less onerous labour of the second class, but for the first three months of sentence every male prisoner above 16 years of age had to do shot drill for three hours per day.[38] Finally, the diet was sharply reduced, continuing Mr Ussher's salutary reforms. In 1876, the diet was sparse enough, less than one-half that of 1860.[39]

III 1876-1907: the Trial and Failure of Penal Labour

The administration made strenuous efforts to accomplish the objectives of the new law, but were defeated by a variety of factors: the physical structures themselves, the lack of personnel and a sense of humanitarianism that was revolted by the cruelty of the system. It was finally given a casual *coup de grâce* in 1907 by the abolition of one of the three foundation stones, penal labour.

From 1876 and even a few years earlier, the prison authorities endeavoured manfully to torture the prisoners sufficiently to meet the demands of Whitehall. Shot drill was enforced wherever possible; by 1900 it was reported in force in all prisons.[40]

The nature of the shot drill enforced, however, seems to have been a joke until 1899. William Low, the Acting Governor, wrote that he found that shot drill—'one of the most effective modes of punishment'—was being performed with nine-pound shot 'in a manner which was ludicrous'.[41] He therefore amended the prison regulations[42] to conform with the shot drill regulations in force in The Gambia. It was to be performed for three hours a day (two hours a day for Europeans, and 'care shall be taken that they are not needlessly exposed to the sun'). There were to be four paces between each shot, which were to weigh 24 pounds, except that a 32-pound shot might be ordered for a breach of prison discipline. Six shot per minute were to be moved, being 'lifted so that the elbows and shot when raised are on a level with the hips', the shot not being allowed to touch the body, and without bending the knees. Presumably after the regulation the drill was properly deterrent, although as late as 1911 the Superintendent of Prisons complained that he had no regulation 'shot', but only some odd lots left from old cannon ammunition weighing from 17 to 25 pounds. He helpfully suggested importing regulation shot from England.[43]

Crank drill was in force only in Accra, and there in only four cells. The cranks were inoperative for at least a year in 1903 before they were repaired.[44] Diet was suitably low, although in 1898, following three deaths from dysentery, it was slightly increased on the recommendation of the medical officer.[45]

Conforming to the grand design of harsh punishment, no effort was made at education. The Blue Books from 1877, in response to a standard question concerning education, stated without change that 'no system has yet been devised, but such an establishment is provided for by the Prisons Ordinance of 1876'. In point of fact, there was no education other than vocational training until 1947.

But the grand design was fated to fail. The separate system, one of its cornerstones, was never enforced in the Gold Coast. The requirements of the Prisons Ordinance, 1876—and indeed, of successive ordinances and regulations since that time to the present day, which have all required the separate system—have literally never been in force for a single day. The responses in the Blue Books were necessarily apologetic. Prisons were not on the separate system because there were no separate cells. 'All prisoners, owing to want of necessary accommodations', states the *Annual Report* of 1897, 'work and sleep together in groups of 6 to 15 men'.

The authorities complained bitterly that as a result it was impossible to enforce 'discipline', or to make the prisons sufficiently distasteful to the prisoners, for it was impossible 'adequately to make felt the want of social intercourse which every prisoner should experience'.[46] Sekondi Prison, built in 1905, was designed for the separate system, but it was never enforced there because of overcrowding; the Blue Books from 1906 kept promising that 'although not at present complete it will be later'—a promise that was never fulfilled.

The second source of the failure of the punitive system lay in the lack of warders. The *Annual Report* for 1902 spelled out the problem:

> In many cases the conditions of life generally are better for the prisoners than for the Escort Warders, and the prisoners themselves in many instances are more intelligent and of superior class to the Warders; the consequence is that the prisoners, instead of being controlled by them, bully their warders. . . . On occasions the Escort Warders themselves work instead of forcing the convicts to do so, so as to avoid being punished for not having made their Gang do the prescribed amount of work. . . .

To rectify the situation, the authorities sought to employ European warders. But they were little better. As early as 1871 the Governor in Sierra Leone was complaining to the Secretary of State that such warders fell into bad habits on the Coast. One Murray, given a salary of £300 when he had been receiving only £80 per annum in England, 'literally drank himself to death in exactly 4 months from landing'. Another had to be sent home to England 'in a state of imbecility from habitual drinking'.[47] Governor Nathan in 1901 repeated the same theme: 'The European gaoler on the Gold Coast adopts as his motto, "Do Nothing".'[48]

The state of the prisons was graphically described by Acting Governor Low in 1899. On visiting Cape Coast, he wrote:

> I found the Gaoler's quarters as unsanitary as a pig stye; the Gaoler himself half undressed and sitting conversing with the prisoners, his office in disorder and no copy of the Rules available. . . .

He went on to describe Accra Prison:

> The present place used as a prison in Accra is in every way unfitted for this purpose. It is an old Fort, formerly used by the Merchants for trade purposes. Within its walls prisoners are crammed into unsuitable rooms, sometimes as many as 15 in one room. There is no accommodation for the various grades of prisoners. Debtors, political prisoners, prisoners awaiting trial, are all huddled into one room at night and penned like sheep during the day within a small concreted yard under a galvanized iron roof. . . .[49]

For many administrators, the solution was to tighten the screw even further—especially since the convicts were Africans. Acknowledging that the cells in Accra prison were damp and airless, the Governor-General quoted the Chief Medical Officer, a Dr McCarthy: ' "I have repeated over and over again . . . that air rendered impure by his repository impurities does not injure the lower class of native." '[50] Another medical officer stated: 'A native in ordinary health and physique would probably be improved by a course of shot drill.'[51] The Inspector of Prisons, Major Kitson, said that 'very short sentence prisoners do not feel their imprisonment, because they get out of prison before they get hungry. . . . All short sentence prisoners should be dieted as part of their punishment.'[52] At this time, very short sentence prisoners were receiving the same diet as prisoners on punishment diet. Kitson complained in 1903 that discipline was difficult to obtain 'with . . . the lightness of the present punishments inflicted on half-civilized prisoners'.[53]

Not all the 'sound men' of Victorian England could enforce the penal regime relentlessly. After long and meticulous investigation of the deterrent effect of cropping the hair of females, for example, the Secretary of State peremptorily forbade the practice. He was willing to acknowledge its efficacy, but 'I share the general feeling of

repugnance against the infliction of this punishment on women'.[54]
The Secretary of State also forbade a combination of low diet and
hard labour.[55] Governor Rodgers deprecated 'the tendency to consider flogging the only appropriate punishment for Native
Prisoners . . .'.[56]

The core of the difficulty was that nobody really knew whether
prisons achieved their stated ends, either in England or on the Gold
Coast, and certainly nobody had ever considered empirically
whether the English prisons system was adapted to West Africa.
Governor Nathan groped towards this issue when he wrote to
Joseph Chamberlain, the Secretary of State, in 1901, that the British
prison system as adopted in West Africa had failed as a deterrent
from crime. It had failed not because it was insufficiently cruel, but
because the large group of people 'with but faintly developed criminal instincts' (i.e. in terms of English criminal law) were not deterred by the social disgrace of prison, as they were in England. Moreover, the low standard of living obtaining in the society was
attained within the prison walls as well. He felt that the matter was
important for the future commercial and administrative development of West Africa, for it was impossible to have commerce or administration if African clerks and officials were not deterred from
fraud by the threat of prison sentences.[57]

Chamberlain answered in universalist terms. He said that he considered that 'while one race or another no doubt differs from another in feelings and habits, no one of any race or colour, especially
if badly disposed, can be indifferent to loss of liberty, constant and
enforced hard work, rigid though sufficient diet, and . . . solitary
confinement at night and for part of the sentence in the day also'. He
urged the employment of European warders to teach the African
warders their duties.[58] It is noteworthy that both of the eminent
gentlemen assumed that deterrence was the sole objective of the
prisons system.

The patent failure of the system clamoured insistently for change.
Reform was in the air in England as well. The report of the Gladstone Committee of 1895 urged deterrence *and* reformation as the
objectives of punishment, and swept the dual concepts of the separate system and penal labour into the dustbin of English penological history.[59]

Intriguingly, the Colonial Secretary, unlike his predecessors in 1865, did not feel called upon to reform the Colonial prisons systems to match the new English practice. It came to pass in the Gold Coast almost casually. Kitson forwarded a draft revision of the Regulations to Governor Rodgers, designed primarily to make more severe in-prison punishments.[60] Rodgers added a brief minute: 'I see that shot drill and crank are included under "Hard Labour"; but, as far as I am aware, unremunerative labour of this description is only authorized in modern prisons, for purposes of punishment.'[61] The Regulations were duly amended without further discussion.[62] The only comment was by the Colonial Secretary (Lyttelton). He wrote that he had 'observed with satisfaction that unremunerative labour is being kept for purposes of punishment only'.[63]

Thus was the *coup de grâce* given to the central theses of the Prisons Ordinance of 1876. The separate system had never been in force; and now strictly penal labour had vanished from the pantheon. The reform of 1907 ushered in a new period in which the Gold Coast prisons took on a never-never-land character. The next thirteen years, from 1907 to 1920, can only be described in Gilbert and Sullivan terms.

IV 1907-1920: a Gilbert-and-Sullivan Prison System

The 1920 Report which initiated the reform and modernization of the Gold Coast prisons tells of 'strange tales . . . told of the Gold Coast Prisons': of prison gates commonly opened by the prisoner clerk; of a prison warder caught stealing cassava while working outside the walls by his own prisoners, who tied him up and bundled him back to the prison in bonds; of a prisoner who, when being discharged, asked, 'What for you go sack me?'[64]

There were other 'strange tales'. In Ashanti in 1904 there were thirty-five escapes, but none at all from the prison in the North-Eastern District. The reason given by the authorities was that no restraint at all was placed upon the prisoners there—a fact which they enjoyed so much that nobody tried to escape.[65] In 1916, the Acting Superintendent reported that it was not uncommon to find a prisoner to be the 'brain' of a labour party, and the warder 'a more or less interested spectator'.[66] In 1917, he wrote:

> Opportunities for escape are numerous and by and by a prisoner takes one. . . . If the warder and the other prisoners cannot catch him as it is generally a case of hue and cry in nearly every Report on an escape the warder's statement contains the phrase 'me and the other prisoners gave chase'. . . .[67]

Lacking any clear philosophy of treatment, it was perhaps to be expected that the prisons would degenerate into mere caretaking institutions. In so far as there was any articulated philosophy of punishment, it remained the harsh deterrence of the Regulations. There were repeated complaints that without the separate system it was impossible to enforce 'discipline'. In 1918, the Governor called attention to the 'somewhat disquieting situation' that in many of the prisons sentences of hard labour could not be enforced.[68] One of the objectives for the reforms of 1920, which actually laid the basis for the transformation of the prisons system, was to remove the anomaly of punishment diet without hard labour.[69] The Inspector-General of Prisons commented that he was 'decidedly of the opinion that prisoners in this Colony generally have too easy a time'.[70]

But the philosophy of deterrence could not be effectuated with two of its three cornerstones undermined: the separate system had died at birth, and penal labour had been abolished in 1907. Without adequate warders, faced by fearful overcrowding, the Gold Coast prisons became inefficient caretaker institutions.

A sanctioning philosophy arose to justify the result. The prisons were a necessary adjunct to government, for the prisoners constituted a reserve pool of inexpensive labour for government. As early as 1908 the *Annual Report* was pointing with pride to a growth in the return from prison industries, from £413 19s. 6d. in

1904, to £2693 11s. 4d. in 1908. In 1910, the Governor directed that prison labour only be used for government departments.[71] When the abolition of 'bush' prisons[72] attached to the District Commissioner's quarters was recommended, the Colonial Secretary stated in a minute that the big problem was the loss of prison labour, but adds that the time was opportune 'in view of the fact that labour is plentiful'.[73] The report of the committee set up to consider the recommendations of the Inspector-General in 1921 expressed concern whether it was possible to run a bush station without prison labour.[74] The Inspector of Prisons in 1915 had expressed the same concern.[75]

A change was pending, however, the result of the very sanctioning philosophy which had arisen to justify the use of the prisons as caretaker institutions. A new philosophy of reform arose as a further justification for prison industry. In 1906 it was reported that orders from the general public for work by the prisoners were coming in faster than they could be executed, 'and if it were not for the interest the prisoners take in this class of work, the energy they displayed, and the rapidity they showed in turning it out', many of the orders would have to be refused.[76] In 1910, as we have seen, skilled labour for the general public, such as the making and repairing of clothes, boots, shoes and furniture, 'and other industries likely to compete with local trade' were discontinued pursuant to the Governor's instructions.[77] This was, however, changed, and by 1918 the public was again permitted to use prison labour (mainly for cobbling); a larger shed had to be built to accommodate the boot-making shop.[78]

The major effort of the prison system thus turned away from harsh punishment to teaching prisoners a trade, not from any clearly articulated concept of penology, but to explain what was being done in fact. In 1906 Major Kittson, who had visited the English prisons that year while on leave,[79] wrote that the prisoners 'took a delight' in learning a trade

> and with the present instruction many of them when discharged will be able to earn their living by their trade instead of returning to labour as carriers or barrel rollers.[80]

By 1917, a new grade of warder called 'mechanical instructors' was added.[81] By 1919, the philosophy was clearly articulated.

444

Prison industries serve a twofold purpose: service to the public and the instruction of the prisoners in a trade which will be useful to them on discharge. For the first time, a theory of reform was advanced:

In the latter respect a prison aims at being a reformative as well as a punitive establishment. Service to the public, though incidental to the principal aim, is the natural corollary to its proper development. [82]

By 1920, therefore, the prisons were ripe for change. Punishment as the central objective had never been abandoned; old myths die hard. But the prisons were in fact caretaking institutions, and their only justification was that they supplied necessary labour for government. In the course of that labour, however, the prisoners might learn a trade, and thus be reformed. The notion of reform as an objective of the prisons was to slip in, as it were, by the back door.

V From 1920 to Today: the Trial and Frustration of Reformation

The Regulations adopted in 1922 marked a watershed between the deterrent notions of the 1876 Regulations and the humane concepts of reformation which today are the expressed objectives of the Prisons Department. The history of the prisons since 1922 has been one of efforts to achieve this noble goal, defeated in large part by the legacy of the past.

Captain C. E. Cookson became Inspector-General of Prisons in 1919. He had had no previous training in prison administration,

445

having been promoted from Assistant Colonial Secretary of the Gold Coast. His appointment coincided with the appointment of Sir Gordon Guggisberg as Governor. Guggisberg was the very model of a Colonial Governor. He believed deeply in the Dual Mandate but—unlike many British administrators in tropical Africa—he was not prepared to sacrifice the civilizing function for commercial considerations. Many institutions of modern Ghana find their roots in his administration, notably the system of secondary and higher education which he initiated with the founding of Achimota College (at which many prominent Ghanaians have been educated), Korle Bu Hospital, the most advanced hospital of its day for Africans, and Takoradi, Ghana's first deep-water port, carved whole out of the inhospitable coast. It is not, perhaps, surprising that the conversion of the Gold Coast prisons to the objective of reform occurred during the administration of this unusual man.

The change came about, as it had in 1907, almost casually, in the course of a general amendment of the Regulations. Cookson had three chief objectives when he undertook to reorganize the Prisons Department in 1920: to abandon the 'bush' prisons in the interest of administrative efficiency; to increase the severity of punishment, both by making hard labour effective, and by reducing diet;[83] and the 'development of Prison Industries primarily for reformative purposes and secondarily for the good of the community'.[84]

He rewrote the Regulations completely. He added a number of new ones, of which regulation 173 was the most significant. That section enjoined all officers to treat prisoners with kindness and humanity, and laid it down that 'the great object of reclaiming the criminal should always be kept in view'. This provision, drawn from the British prison regulations, was not regarded by Cookson as important. In his Minute explaining the changes, he said only that this and some other regulations replaced older rules on other points, 'adding some other maxims, based on English Prison rules'.[85]

In the voluminous Minutes by various officials concerning the new Rules, there is no other mention of regulation 173, nor are the larger purposes of punishment discussed or even mentioned. The new Regulations were enacted by the Governor-in-Council in 1922, and became effective on January 1st, 1923.[86]

446

Governor Guggisberg, however, perceived the significance of the change. In his Report, *The Gold Coast : A Review of the Events of 1920–1926 and the Prospects of 1927–1928,* he stated:

> The chief object of the Gold Coast prisons today is reform rather than punishment; and although there have been great difficulties to overcome, progress on the whole has been excellent in the past seven years. The chief way in which it is hoped to secure the reform of prisoners is through trade training. [87]

In the Gold Coast Annual Report for 1928–29, the same sentiments were expressed. It describes the system as 'gradually emerging from a system of negative prevention to one of training and reformation'. The earlier objective was simply to keep the convict isolated from the community. Now, it

> is to provide such training during imprisonment as will give the prisoner both the means and the incentive to lead the life of a decent, law-abiding citizen on release. [88]

The objective today remains unchanged. Regulation 175 is still in force. [89] Government unqualifiedly supports its 'great object'. In the debate on the Prisons Bill, 1962, the usual remarks by laymen were made, that the prisons were too 'soft'. One Member stated that there were 'regular visitors'—recidivists—who, he said, 'should be so treated as to make prison life unbearable to them'. [90] Mr Boateng, the Minister of the Interior, winding up for the government, asserted a contrary position. The policy of the government with respect of prisoners 'is one of reform and not necessarily to wreak vengeance upon people who sometimes through their unfortunate background and circumstances have found themselves behind bars'. [91]

The effort to reform the prisoner must be seen against the background of the legacy of physical plant and tradition embodied in the Regulations. As of 1962, there were in Ghana six central prisons, with a rated capacity (at 360 cubic feet of air space per prisoner) of 1,955 persons; seventeen local male prisons, with a total rated capacity of 822 persons; one caretaker prison (for elderly or invalided convicts), with a rated capacity of 3 persons; two central female prisons, with a rated capacity of 29; two prison camps, with a rated capacity of 1,111; one Borstal Institution, with a rated capacity of

447

366; and one contagious disease prison, with a rated capacity of 91;[92] no significant new construction appears to have been undertaken since.

It will be seen that the core of the prisons system lies in the six central prisons and the two prison camps; between them, they have a rated capacity of 3,066, while the other twenty-two institutions have between them a rated capacity of less than one-half that number. Of the six central prisons, one, James Fort, in Accra, is so old that it is not now used to hold prisoners. Ussher Fort in Accra is also very old, some portions of it having been built two centuries and more ago. It is cramped, confined, dungeon-like, and lacks proper workshops and recreation spaces. Sekondi Central Prison was built in 1905, and follows the contemporary notions of a central prison: great crenellated walls, watchtowers, all the apparatus of a dungeon keep. Kumasi Prison, built in 1904,[93] is little better.

By 1949, overcrowding was already of crisis proportions.[94] From a population of 1,500 before the war, by 1951 the population had reached about 3,600 and showed no sign of decreasing. Except for Ankaful Prison Camp and James Camp (both 'open' prisons) no new prison had been built in the period. A Committee on Prisons was created, which reported to the 1951 Parliament.[95]

It recommended the construction of a new central prison at Nsawam. This was finally constructed and completed in 1961, with a rated capacity of 717 prisoners—and was immediately filled to far past its capacity. In 1962 it held a daily average of 1,672·53 prisoners. It has adequate workshops and recreational areas, farmland, and even built-in water-closets. The M'Carthy Committee had urged that it be built on high land, 'so that a view of the surrounding country may be had from the cells', a recommendation happily followed.

Nsawam was the first Ghana prison formally to abandon the separate system (although it has never actually been in force in Ghana). The Committee had strongly recommended dormitory accommodation instead of cellular construction. Where, as in the Gold Coast, the majority of the prison population is illiterate and unaccustomed to long periods of loneliness, it was believed that the single-cell system imposed 'too harsh a penalty' upon the prisoner.[96] As built, Nsawam has an average of 20 prisoners per cell.

But the promise of Nsawam has been negated by fearful overcrowding. Table 1 shows the relative overcrowding of the Ghana prisons in terms of percentage of prisoners compared with the number of places at a standard 360 cubic feet of air per prisoner.

TABLE I. RELATIVE OVERCROWDING: ALL PRISONS. SELECTED YEARS, 1953–54 TO 1964

Year	Daily average of population	Places @ 360 cu. feet per prisoner	% overcrowding
1953–54	3,523	2,797	125
1957	4,422·38	2,981	148
1961	5,567·06	4,438	125
1962	6,384·03	4,438	146
1963	7,216·41	4,438	163
1964	7,238·39	4,438	164

Source: To 1962, *Reports on the Treatment of Offenders*; 1963–64, figures supplied by the courtesy of the Prisons Department.

But this tells only part of the story. The critical shortage is in space at the Male Central Prisons, for it is here that the majority of male adult offenders are kept. Table 2 shows the relative overcrowding in these prisons.

TABLE 2. RELATIVE OVERCROWDING: MALE CENTRAL PRISONS. SELECTED YEARS, 1953–54 TO 1962

Year	Daily average of population	Places @ 360 cu. feet per prisoner	% overcrowding
1953–54	1,794·90	1,055	170
1957	2,053·27	1,055	195
1961	2,637·89	1,723[1]	153
1962	3,307·30	1,723	198

Source: To 1962, *Reports on the Treatment of Offenders*.

Note: James Fort, with 232 authorized places, is not used because of its decrepit condition.

Almost equally serious conditions of overcrowding exist in the local prisons. In 1962, 17 local male prisons with a rated capacity of

822 prisoners had a daily average of 1,476·26, an overcrowding of 180 per cent.

On the other hand, the prison camps and the female prisons are not seriously overcrowded. The two central female prisons, with a rated capacity of 64 prisoners, had a daily average in 1962 of only 49·92. Most important of all, the two prison camps, James Camp, near Accra, and Ankaful, near Cape Coast, with a rated capacity of 1,111, had a daily average of only 997·80.[97] As we shall see, it is the prison camps which are the brightest spots in the picture of Ghana's prisons, and the lack of overcrowding in these camps, carefully maintained by the Department, in no small measure contributes to their success.

There appear to be a number of reasons for the increase in overcrowding in recent years. There have been a vastly increased number of habitual offenders sentenced to very long sentences. The median length of long-term sentences has risen. Both the number of short-term sentences and of imprisonments in default of fine have risen sharply. Remand prisoners have increased—and some remand prisoners remain in prison for as long as six months awaiting trial.[98]

Brooding over the entire prisons system, moreover, is its confused and melancholy history. The stamp given by the Ordinance and the Regulations in 1876 has never been wholly erased. Prison labour is still divided in the Ordinance into hard labour of the first class and hard labour of the second class. The Regulations ordain the separate system.

The General Rules for the conduct of prisoners—requiring them to obey orders, not to be idle or negligent at work, not to swear or be guilty of disorderly conduct, not to sing, scream or whistle, not to damage prison property, not to enter any cell except their own without permission, and requiring that 'no criminal prisoner shall at any time speak or make signs to any other prisoner'—have not been changed since 1876. Whole sections of the Regulations—e.g. the rules concerning the conduct of gangs working outside the prison walls—have hardly been changed in their punctuation, let alone their content, since the earliest days. That these regulations are unobserved except in the breach means only a partial alleviation of their effect upon the prisoner.

The impact upon the convict admitted to the prisons must be the same as it was in 1876. He sees the same fortress-like structures. He meets conditions of almost animal overcrowding.[99] The Regulations are read to him, on their face imposing a severe, degrading, dehumanizing regime. He perceives a rigid discipline expressed in terms of peremptory commands in every aspect of his life. It is only to be expected that the prisoner enters prison stripped of self-respect, determined not to reform but to exist until released, antagonistic to the Department and the prison officials as the representatives of the society which has incarcerated him. The prisoner, by the mere fact of being sentenced and entering the prison, is thus removed as far as possible from successful rehabilitation. The conscious and articulated effort of the Prisons Department is, however, one of rehabilitation, as it has been since the early 1920s. The central means to achieve this objective has always been trade education, conceived as having the object 'of providing the prisoner with a means of livelihood on discharge'.[100]

The sorts of trades chosen for instruction have been, however, severely limited by four factors. The trade must be one for which there are local materials available; the tools must not be prohibitively expensive;[101] and the prison workshop may not compete with private industry. Today, all the work done is for government departments.[102] Finally, the sort of work selected must be kinds for which there is a demand by employers in the Gold Coast, such as carpentering, or which the individual could undertake in self-employment, such as cobbling or tailoring. As a result, the list of industries today is not very different from what it was in 1926: tailoring, carpentering, cabinet making, mat weaving, cane-chair weaving, basket making, drag-net weaving, animal husbandry and fishing, fish curing and a few others.

Prisoners who are able to engage in these trades receive considerable instruction. In 1927–28, there were two European technical instructors and sixteen trade instructors for a daily average of 1,706·25 prisoners.[103] By 1962, this had grown to a force of 102 trade instructors, a senior instructor of industries and three instructors of industries.[104]

By 1949 classes in the theory of the trade were well developed, two afternoons a week being devoted to them.[105] But this effort too has been swamped by the overcrowding, for lack of staff and lack of space has forced their discontinuance, although instructors try to teach some theory during working hours.[106]

How successful the training has been in fact is impossible to determine, for no empirical study has been made to discover what proportion of trained ex-convicts employ their prison-taught skills. One welfare officer reports having seen a cobbler's shop with the proud sign, 'Trained in Prison'. A number of ex-convicts annually obtain employment in their crafts through the efforts of the Department of Social Welfare.

Overcrowding has seriously reduced the percentage of prisoners who can be given trade training, for although the number of prisoners has increased, the size of the workshops has not. In 1937–38 all prisoners with terms of more than six months were given trade training.[107] By 1962 it was limited to prisoners serving more than eighteen months.[108] Today, only convicts sentenced to more than three years are admitted into the workshops.[109] Thus less than 10 per cent of the prisoners receive trade training—which the Department regards as its central instrument for reformation.

Whether the admission of shorter-sentence prisoners to trade training has ever been valuable, however, may be questioned. The 1954–55 Annual Report stated that about 70 per cent of the prisoners who received trade training were released before completion of training. There is no opportunity after release to continue trade training. Half-educated, however, the ex-prisoners frequently declined unskilled jobs. They thus tended to roam the streets until they found themselves in conflict with the law. There is even one pathetic story of

> a young man who became a recidivist in order to complete his knowledge of the trade he had partially mastered in Ussher Fort Prison. He eventually obtained employment with a Firm of Building Contractors and soon rose to the grade of Head Carpenter . . . he has not since been known to have reverted to crime.[110]

For the 10 per cent or less of Ghana's prisoners who receive trade training there is at least some prospect for reform, however slight. The core of the problem is the reformation of the remaining 90 per cent of Ghana's prisoners—the shorter-sentence prisoners, and the occasional long-sentence prisoner not adapted to trade training.

The principal solution in Ghana has long been to employ these prisoners in farming whenever possible, as in England the basic solution has been to employ them in sewing mailbags. A number of factors contributed to making farming the central form of unskilled labour. It began as a device to lower the cost of rations. Cookson reported that an experimental farm in Kumasi reduced the cost of rations per prisoner spectacularly from 9·60d. per head in April 1920 to 1·97d. per head in April 1921.[111] Moreover, humanitarian notions stopped the earlier 'sanitary' work which had been one of the chief occupations of prisoners.[112] Mr Eyison has written of the days when prisoners had to carry head-loads of night-soil, a filthy and degrading job which required purification upon return to civilian life.[113] Maintenance work upon the prisons could occupy only a certain amount of time.[114] The local prisons, having no industries attached, particularly needed some occupation for the prisoners; farming was an obvious solution. Finally, the 'government use' rule made it impossible to conceive of a variety of industrial labour which would not compete with private industry. Farming for the prisons system itself was the obvious solution. Among all these reasons for the solution, the one consideration never examined was whether farming was an occupation adapted to the reformation of the criminal.

But at most of the Central Prisons their situation has made farming extremely difficult. The prisons in Accra, Sekondi and Kumasi —save for the new prison at Nsawam, the core of the prisons system—occupy buildings many years old, all now situated in the heart of the city. In Accra, for example, the closest farming land is fifteen miles away. Thus in the largest of the prisons, there is no farming available for prisoners.

The lack of farmland, the general overcrowding and the increase in short-term sentences has resulted in a very sharp decrease over the years in the percentage of prisoners who have been set to work daily. Table 3 shows the ratio between the daily average population of the system and the daily average set to work, for selected years since 1953–54.

TABLE 3. DAILY AVERAGE OF PRISONERS PUT TO WORK AS A
PERCENTAGE OF THE DAILY AVERAGE OF CONVICTED PRI-
SONERS. SELECTED YEARS, 1953–54 TO 1963

Year	Convicted prisoners Daily average	Prisoners put to work Daily average	Percentage of employment
1953–54	3,326	3,479·95	a
1957	4,073	2,734·73	67
1961	4,843·58	3,095·39	69
1962	5,311·11	3,117·55	58
1963	5,583·79	4,226·24	75

Source: Annual Reports on the Treatment of Offenders.
a Apparently non-convicts (debtors and remand prisoners) were put to work
as well as convicts.

Not only has the total number daily put to work declined in relation to the number available to work—a disastrous decline, corrod-
ing the morale of both staff and prisoners—but the hours of work
have also declined. The M'Carthy Committee in 1951 found that the
evening lock-up was at between 3.30 and 4.00 p.m. The Committee
considered it important that the prisoners be locked in their cells for
the minimum possible period. They recommended a much later
lock-up, pointing out that in England lock-up time was 9.00 p.m.
As a result, lock-up time was postponed in the Ghana prisons to
8.00 p.m. The present overcrowding and the consequent shortage
of staff has compelled the Department to advance lock-up to
6.00 p.m.[115]

Work as a system of reformatory training for short-sentence
prisoners does not exist in the Ghanaian prisons in any realistic
sense. In addition to trade training, classification has been a major
instrument in the effort to attain rehabilitation of the prisoner.
The statutory classifications remain largely the same today as they
were in 1876: remand prisoners must be kept apart from convicts;
debtors, persons committed for contempt of court, and those who
have refused to enter into recognizances to give evidence, from
criminal prisoners; juveniles under 14 years, from adult prisoners.
All convicted criminal prisoners must be kept in a separate class (in
1876, these were further subdivided into felons and misdemeanants);
women are kept separate from men.[116]

More sophisticated classifications have been made administratively. In 1931–32 recidivists were given distinctive badges, and were housed and put to work together, although accommodation did not permit their being placed in single cells.[117] By 1947 Ussher Fort, in Accra, was used as a central prison for recidivists only.[118] The persistent overcrowding, however, has defeated this practice, so that the Department has reverted to the earlier practice of segregating them at night, but working them in mixed gangs during the day.[119]

The first separate institution built for a distinct class of offenders was the Boys' Home, originally constructed at Ada.[120] From this small institution, started in 1929, has grown the present system of juvenile institutions.

The next major step in administrative classification occurred in 1945 when the Industrial Institution (Borstal) and the open Prison Camp at Ankaful were built. The Borstal Institution today contains some 567 inmates, with a 6:1 warder–inmate ratio.[121] The Institution is completely open. Young Persons (16–20 years of age) are sent immediately to the Borstal Institution if their sentences so specify, or if they are sentenced to more than one month's imprisonment.[122] Where a short sentence must be served in an adult prison, they are segregated from the adult prisoners, and their only form of employment is cleaning their own rooms and yards, and other domestic services of the prison.[123]

There is a full-time teaching staff, including one certificated teacher, and classes are conducted leading to the School Leavers' Certificate. Illiterates must attend the school, and in practice most of the boys who have not received their Certificate do attend. Every lad is encouraged to learn a trade—pottery, carpentry, shoemaking, tailoring, blacksmithery, building construction, draughtsmanship, knitting and fitting among others. There is an incentive scheme by which it is possible for a Young Person to earn two or three shillings a month, half of which is saved and half used for small comforts.

Considerable effort is made to instil habits of self-discipline. An extensive system of captains, sub-captains and other positions of leadership requires a large proportion of the boys to assume responsibility not only for themselves, but for others as well. Everywhere one sees boys walking from one place to another without supervision, or engaged in work by themselves. In the tailor shops, the boys sit around a single machine, the most experienced operator demonstrating what is to be done.

Punishment for infringement of discipline is relatively light and infrequently invoked. Difficult cases are placed in punishment cells for substantial periods, but these are fortunately rare, and the cells are not solitary.[124]

Considerable effort is made to provide a well-rounded recreational programme. Games, athletics, a fife-and-drum corps, a choir and a cinema all flourish. At a recent demonstration, the tumbling and gymnastics group ended their performance with a human pyramid, unfolding at the top a fluttering banner labelled 'African Unity'.

As a matter of policy, no boy is detained in the Borstal to the end of his sentence. The inmate is invariably released on six months' licence, during which time he is supervised by an After-care Agent. Before his release, he is given a brief home leave to prepare for life outside.[125]

Escapes are relatively frequent, as might be expected from the almost total lack of security and the unselective mode of assignment. The Department, however, is of opinion that the number of escapes is amply compensated for by the absence of a 'prison' atmosphere. There are no available statistics on recidivism among Borstal graduates, but the staff believes that they are lower than the average of the prison population.

The second innovation in 1945 was the building of Ankaful Prison Camp, Ghana's first open prison; it was soon followed by James Camp, near Accra, also an open prison. Ankaful in 1962 held 562 prisoners, and James Camp 549 prisoners.[126] They receive only long-sentence first offenders and selected second offenders.[127] Both are completely open camps, surrounded by ample farm land.

Great effort is made in the camps to emphasize decision-making by the prisoners. It is regular practice to send small groups of prisoners to the far reaches of the farm under the leadership of a selected prisoner, without warders. The prisoners are regimented as little as possible. Modern farm machinery including tractors is used by the prisoners. Industrial training is emphasized.[128]

The success of the Camps cannot be doubted; they point the way for future improvement of the system.[129] In the first five years of the Camps there were no escapes,[130] and only a very few since then. Recidivism rates are believed to be considerably better among Camp graduates than among the prison population at large. The plans of the Department include expansion of the Prison Camp system. Sites for large prison farms have already been selected in the Northern, Ashanti and Western Regions, and a site for a Prison Camp in the Volta Region.[131] Only lack of funds blocks the programme.

But overcrowding threatens even these institutions. Formerly, offenders were not sent to the Prison Camps until they had been observed for at least six months in a Central Prison, to ensure that there was a reasonable prospect of success at the Camp. Now, for lack of facilities in the Central Prisons, they are sent to the Camps immediately.[132]

In addition to labour and classification, the Department has used education as an instrument of reform. It was slow in arriving. As late as 1934, there was no education, except that books were supplied to literate prisoners on request[133]—although the statute has since 1876 provided:

The Governor[134] may authorize the employment of fit and proper persons for affording prisoners religious[135] or secular instruction under the superintendence of the Chaplain.[136]

In 1946 Bible-reading classes, study circles, play-reading and lectures by outside persons were introduced for long- and medium-term prisoners.[137] By 1950 'schools were a popular feature' in every prison.[138] A high proportion of the admissions—87 per cent in 1950 —are illiterates, many of whom are taught to read and write. Mass education classes are conducted by the Department of Social Welfare. In 1962, 365 inmates were illiterate on committal, but literate in English on discharge; 155 in vernacular languages.[139] Classes are optional for adult prisoners.

But even education has been adversely affected by overcrowding. It has become impossible to conduct many of the classes in the central prisons. There is less education today in the prisons than there was only a few years ago.[140]

Women prisoners are given special training in domestic and

457

homemaking techniques. Knitting, sewing, oil manufacturing, soap making, crocheting, mat weaving, embroidery, gardening and the making of garri, a pounded meal food, are all taught. It is reported that the enthusiasm among the prisoners for these educational activities is very high.[141]

Faced by the physical limitations, however, and the built-in problems of traditions, reformative efforts have been unable to advance beyond industrial work, trade training, sophisticated classification, and general education. Already in 1949 the authorities felt that they had reached a dead end. 'The day of cautious approach has passed', they wrote, 'and we now advance with confidence on an enlightened stage of penal administration.' But, they added, 'at present we have reached the limit of the modern methods of penal reform that can be carried into effect in such old and antiquated buildings'.[142] Complaints about the seriousness of overcrowding permeate the reports since 1949, as they had perennially before that.

The staff has therefore devoted much of its energy to making the conditions of imprisonment as humane as possible, recognizing, in the words of the Report of the M'Carthy Committee, that 'only by improving conditions can corrective training have its full influence'. The regime of silence, despite the Regulations, is not imposed. Instead, warders have discretion to permit conversation between prisoners, subject only to ordinary standards of orderly behaviour. Visitors are permitted once a month as a matter of course, but permission is readily granted for more frequent visits from relatives and friends. Letters too are permitted once a month, but more frequent letters are permitted readily by way of special dispensation. The schoolteachers and literate fellow-prisoners write letters for illiterates. When possible, long-term prisoners are transferred to local prisons near their homes for short periods to facilitate visits from their friends and relatives who might be unable to visit them in a central prison.[143]

So far as is possible in the difficult circumstances of most of Ghana's antique prisons, the physical conditions of life are ameliorated. Sanitary buckets are emptied twice and sometimes three times daily if necessary. Bathing facilities permit baths daily—sometimes twice a day. The prison uniform is a simple suit, and no longer carries with it the broad arrow of disrespect. Lack of money, however, is a serious problem. The Department, although it would like to do so, cannot even supply sandals to prisoners who are used to wearing them.[144] Since 1958, even male prisoners have not been cropped on admittance.[145]

Diet has been improved since 1951. The usual diet calls for two different menus: one five days a week and one twice a week. The protein content is, for Ghana, reasonably high: $1\frac{1}{2}$ oz. of beef a day five days a week, and $4\frac{1}{2}$ oz. of fish twice a week. Fruit—'one orange or a similar number of fruit'—is to be given each day. Six oz. of vegetables are to accompany each main meal. The former 'European Diet' has disappeared. Its place is taken by 'Ordinary Diet B', with a menu obviously designed for European tastes: tea, cocoa or coffee, bread, potatoes, tomatoes and fish, mutton, beef or mince for protein. One egg is required to be served daily. The Ordinary Diet B is to be served to any prisoner the Medical Officer directs.[146]

As might be expected, the harshness of in-prison punishment has been successively ameliorated, whilst the relative frequency of its imposition has dropped spectacularly. In 1901, for example, for a daily average of 482 prisoners, there were 3,231 punishments ordered—a rate of more than 6:1 — including 71 floggings, 1,416 at shot drill, 145 on crank drill,[147] and 339 by leg ironings.[148] In 1962, for a daily average of 6,484·03 prisoners of all classes, there were only 1,017 disciplinary cases. Of these, 96 were awarded close confinement, 549 forfeiture of remission, and 372 punishment of other sorts. There was only one case of corporal punishment (now caning, not flogging) awarded for gross personal violence to a prison officer.[149]

This remarkable reduction in the ratio of punishments imposed to the daily average is the end-result of a long development away from maintaining discipline by coercive sanction. The philosophy which viewed harsh exemplary punishment as the principal end of imprisonment was hard put to it to discover any method of further punishment for prisoners who, in the very midst of the regime of harshness, committed further offences. Flogging appeared to be the only option left; and it was used. In 1892, the Secretary of State found it necessary to censure a judge who had passed a sentence of 300 strokes upon the convict George for escape, characterizing the sentence as 'barbarous'.[150] Although the new Criminal Code of that year limited the number of strokes to thirty-six, it nevertheless retained flogging as the penalty for escape from prison, although the St Lucia Code, which formed its model, did not so provide. Mr Hutchinson, the Chief Justice, explained that he included flogging in this case since 'all officials in the Colony who have had to do with the charge of prisons hold it to be of great importance to retain this punishment'.[151]

One by one, these harsh punishments were dropped: irons, shot drill, flogging (corporal punishment by whipping remains, but is very little used). In their place there came a system of rewards and deprivations, of which the mark system and its successor, remission of sentences for good behaviour, and the payment of wages, have been the most important. The *Annual Report* for 1938–39 commented favourably upon the improved discipline:

> There is little doubt that the cause of this improvement is the newly-adopted policy of granting certain privileges for good behaviour. These privileges include the remission of marks, permission to play draughts or the native game of 'warri' in prisoners' cells, listening to wireless broadcasts, and freedom from direct supervision when working inside the prison. Such privileges are liable to be withdrawn if a satisfactory standard of conduct is not maintained. This method of dealing with prisoners has proved to be more effective than the use of repressive measures. The latter are only reverted to in dealing with hardened cases.

The principal reward for good behaviour has always been remission of sentence. The English mark system was urged by circular letter from the Secretary of State,[152] and was instituted in the Gold Coast in 1905.[153] As described in the Regulations, it was extremely complex, requiring the overseeing officer to record the marks earned by each prisoner each day. In time it became evident that practically every prisoner was in fact earning the maximum number of marks—i.e. that the whole routine of individual assessment of the individual prisoner's work had become a formality. The system was therefore changed to provide for an automatic remission of sentence, at first one-quarter. In 1951, the M'Carthy Committee recommended, as a device to relieve overcrowding, remission of one-third of sentence which was accomplished in the 1954 Regulations. Although not primarily a device designed for disciplinary purposes, the use of clemency—the release of long-sentence prisoners before the normal expiry of their term—plays a role. This was initiated as early as 1882, when the Secretary of State sent around a copy of the Ceylon prison rules providing for automatic review of life sentences by the Governor after fifteen years.[154] The Rules now require such a review with respect to all life sentences: there is no specific remission of sentence but the sentence is reviewed as soon as the prisoner shall have served 4, 8 and 12 years, 13 years and 4 months, 14 years and 20 years.[155] The decision is in fact made by the Minister upon the recommendation of the Director of Prisons. There are no statistics available to indicate how long the average life sentence prisoner in fact serves.

The second form of reward used is the earnings scheme. This was instituted in 1922, when a 'special class' of prisoners was created who, for good conduct, were permitted to earn one penny *per diem* for 'remunerative labour'.[156] A more complete earnings scheme was introduced in 1947, for prisoners on sentences of more than twelve months, by which each prisoner might earn three shillings per month.[157] The scheme worked well at first; by 1951 it was characterized as 'a great inducement to better discipline and greater industry'.[158] The amount has not, however, been increased since then, and the senior staff at present are of the opinion that the scheme is not as effective as it might be if the stipend were to be somewhat raised. One-half of the sum earned must be saved; the remainder is usually spent on sweets or other comforts.[159]

Recreational facilities are as good as circumstances permit. Films are shown fortnightly in the larger prisons. Radio diffusion boxes are available, sometimes in the cells themselves. Every cell has draughtboards painted on the floor, and dug into the floor are the twelve holes for playing warri, a popular Ghanaian game. Books are easily available for literates. Outdoor games—football is the most popular—are organized. Table tennis is available. In the larger prisons there is an inmate band which gives concerts for the other prisoners from time to time.[160]

Health and psychiatric care is on a reasonably high level. Prison medical officers attend the prisoners daily. There is no psychiatrist attached formally to the Prisons Department, but cases of mental illness are brought to Accra to be treated by the government psychiatrist. Lack of facilities has made it impossible, however, to pursue any regular course of psychiatric counselling or group therapy for any except the critically ill inmates.[161]

Suspected lunatics are still confined to prison for observation, a practice injurious to the lunatic and difficult for the prisons, which have neither accommodation for them nor experts to observe them. All that the Department can do is to try to have their medical examinations conducted speedily, so that they may be committed to an asylum or released.[162]

The staff, since 1962 entirely Ghanaian,[163] although woefully short in numbers to cope with the overcrowded conditions, has improved in quality over the decades. A minimum standard of education to Standard Seven is now required of all warders. Recruits attend a three-month training course, and a senior staff course of six months' duration is given as well, all taught by senior prison officers in Accra. At least one senior officer a year visits the United Kingdom, so that practically every senior officer has inspected the English prisons system. No member of the senior staff, however, has done university-level work in penology; and, as yet, no member of the senior staff has inspected the prisons systems of other countries than England.

The numbers of staff have reached a crisis state. The Department has a standard of one member of staff for every three prisoners. The ratio is now one to four and in many prisons one to five, a ratio which the senior staff considers to be dangerously low for both the safe custody and the welfare of the prisoners.

VI Conclusion

A number of consistent strains have influenced the Ghanaian prisons throughout their history. The system was originally a foreign import, whose central objective was alien to indigenous systems of public order. An occasional administrator, at his wit's end to explain a system which on its own premise was woefully insufficient, tried to rationalize its manifest failure in terms of its alien character, as did Governor Nathan in 1901. But it is remarkable that no modern administrator in Ghana has ever remarked that prisons were not abhorred by the population, or claimed that Ghanaians did not understand why they were imprisoned. The last recorded observation of that sort—Cookson's story of the prisoner who asked why he was being sacked—carried clear overtones of racial bias. Careful questioning of many Ghanaians has not revealed one who felt otherwise than that imprisonment was a deep disgrace.

But the prison system remains a foreign import. The original regulations, the regime of penal labour, the abandonment of shot drill in 1907, the adoption of 'the great object' in 1922, the mark system and its successor, the emphasis on trade training, and a host of details—all were borrowed, lock, stock and barrel, from the British system. So far as appears, nobody has ever examined carefully the penal problem in relation to its specifically Ghanaian environment.

Secondly, the system has been plagued throughout by a total absence of empirical information. Nobody knows whether trade training in fact has achieved any results in lowering the rate of recidivism; whether in-prison education aids in reform; whether more or less regulation of the prisoners' lives in prison is beneficial. Until such empirical studies are made, penology in Ghana must remain a hit-or-miss affair.

Thirdly, and perhaps most important, the system has suffered through the years from a regrettable contradiction between numbers and buildings: the numbers are too large and the buildings too small. Overcrowding has been endemic and more than any other single factor has frustrated the humanely motivated and strenuous efforts of the staff.

Fourthly, a strain of humane feeling plays persistently, albeit at first faintly, in the cacophony, and now is the principal theme. Punishment for its own sake has long since been abandoned; and, were it possible to accomplish, reform would be the principal objective.

But reform is impossible in the present circumstances. The Department has plans for the acquisition of additional land for prison farms and for more open prison camps, so that the benefit of Ankaful and James Camps may be made available to many more prisoners. But it cannot achieve them without money; and so far money has not been available.

As a result, the prisons have become caretaking institutions. The government made this the more inevitable when in 1965 it increased the penalty for a prison officer assisting an escape, even involuntarily. New legislation imposing high minimum sentences for many offences has contributed to the situation by long sentences for prisoners who do not need sentences nearly so long if reformation were indeed the objective. The courts have also sharply intensified the problem by the number of short-term prisoners they commit; there is precious little reform that can be accomplished in three months. The work programme has declined precipitously, so that a majority of the prisoners have nothing constructive with which to occupy their time.

It is not, therefore, to be wondered at that the Prisons Department has resiled from the bright prospect of reform as its central objective. Its 1962 *Report* states it more modestly, and no doubt more realistically:

The policy of seeking the welfare and education of the lawbreakers in custody continued to be the main objective of the Department.[164]

Thus has 'the great object of reclaiming the criminal' been shrivelled by insufficient funds, and by courts which have no understanding of the penological problem.

NOTES

1. Analogous values seem to have permeated the religion of Ashtarte and Baal of Biblical times, as well as many other African societies: Mould,

Essentials of Bible History, rev. ed., 177 ff. (1951); Fortes and Evans-Pritchard, eds., *African Political Systems, passim* (1940).

2. Fortes, 'The Political System of the Tallensi of the Northern Territories of the Gold Coast,' in Fortes and Evans-Pritchard, *op. cit.*

3. See Busia, *The Position of the Chief in the Modern Political System of Ashanti*, 64–78 (1951).

4. Tait, in Goody, ed., *The Konkomba of Northern Ghana*, 68–9 (1961).

5. Sarbah, *Fante National Constitution*, 30 (1906).

6. Smith, S., in the *Edinburgh Review* of the 1830s, quoted in Radzinowicz and Turner, eds., *The Modern Approach to Criminal Law*, 39 (1945).

7. 'We develop new territory as Trustees for Civilisation, for the Commerce of the World.' Joseph Chamberlain, quoted in Lugard, *The Dual Mandate in British Tropical Africa*, 5th ed., p. vi. (1965).

8. 'I am profoundly convinced that there can be no question but that British rule has promoted the happiness and welfare of the primitive races': *ibid.*, 618.

9. As late as 1865 King Aggery complained to Governor Pine of Maclean's methods: 'A white face, a red jacket was . . . a terror on the Gold Coast.' Quoted in Kimble, *A Political History of Ghana: The Rise of Gold Coast Nationalism, 1850–1928*, 204 (1963).

10. *Report of Her Majesty's Commissioner of Inquiry on the state of the British Settlements on the Gold Coast, at Sierra Leone and the Gambia, 1841*, Parl. Papers, Session 1842, vol. 12, p. 15.

11. Metcalfe, *Maclean of the Gold Coast*, 151 (1962).

12. Quoted in Sarbah, *op. cit.*, 185.

13. Thus calling into play the Foreign Jurisdication Act, 1843, which purported to grant to the Crown full jurisdiction over any area over which it had *de facto* exercised jurisdiction. It is doubtful that the Fante chiefs were advised of the consequences of the Bond under English law: see Kimble, *op. cit.*, 194–5, 204.

14. Sarbah, *op. cit.*, 99.

15. Fitzpatrick [Judicial Assessor] to Secretary of State, June 11th, 1849, ADM 1/450. ADM references are to the National Archives, Accra.

16. *Blue Book*, 1850.

17. Despatch No. 2, December 30th, 1845, Secretary of State to Governor, ADM 1/4.

18. Despatch No. 22, May 16th, 1846, Governor to Secretary of State, ADM 1/449.

19. Despatch No. 3, January 16th, 1847, Governor to Secretary of State, ADM 1/449.

20. *Civil Record Book*, I, April 9th, 1857. In 1852 Koey Djommedu was sentenced to 'three months in the Chain with hard labour' for 'defaming plaintiff's character in court': *ibid.*, January 26th, 1852; in 1859 Tatta Lackie was sentenced to 'chains with perpetual hard labour': *ibid.*, June 14th, 1859. Stocks were apparently in use in Accra until about 1860: *ibid.*,

December 28th, 1858 (stocks three times a week during an imprisonment of three months). In 1860 George Quigley Carr, found guilty of larceny, was sentenced to 12 months' imprisonment 'and should the stocks be repaired during that period he will be out in them at any time that the Commandant thinks proper': *ibid.*, November 13th, 1860.

21. As late as 1876 the Secretary of State had to write to the Governor deprecating the use of chains: Despatch No. 17, June 20th, 1876, Secretary of State to Governor, ADM 1/520.

22. Ground, boiled maize: a staple of Fante diet.

23. See, generally, Elkin, *The English Penal System*, 116 *et seq.* (1957).

24. In 1907, crank drill on the Gold Coast required 5,000 turns in twenty-four hours, or the prisoner was placed on half-rations: Minute of October 5th, 1907, in MP 1267/05. MP references are to original files of minute papers in the National Archives, Accra.

25. See Circulars, June 28th, 1869, ADM 1/389; June 3rd, 1869, ADM 1/389; January 21st, 1865, ADM 1/387; January 18th, 1867, ADM 1/388; January 23rd, 1871, ADM 1/390; February 24th, 1871, ADM 1/390; April 15th, 1871, ADM 1/390.

26. Circular, January 21st, 1865, ADM 1/387. In 1870 the Earl of Granville (then Colonial Secretary) wrote a despatch to the Governor, Sierra Leone, complaining that the Administrator of the Gambia had taken it upon himself to abolish strictly penal labour there because there was such a demand for prison labour in useful work on roads and other public works. Such a course, he wrote, detracts from the object of imprisonment, which is 'to deter from crime': Despatch No. 130, The Gambia, June 18th, 1870, Secretary of State to Governor, Sierra Leone, ADM 1/389.

27. Circular, January 23rd, 1871, ADM 1/390.

28. *Ibid.*

29. Circular, January 18th, 1867, ADM 1/388.

30. Circular, June 7th, 1871, ADM 1/391. The Inspector-General of Prisons minuted that he had no doubt that cutting females' hair would have a 'decidedly deterrent effect': Minute of January 10th, 1872, in ADM 1/391. The Secretary of State ultimately left the matter to the discretion of the colonial governors: Circular, September 12th, 1872, ADM 1/391.

31. Despatch No. 95, November 19th, 1869, Secretary of State to Administrator, Gold Coast, ADM 1/27.

32. Enclosure to Despatch No. 136, Administrator, Gold Coast, to Governor, Sierra Leone, September 21st, 1870, ADM 1/690. Penal labour was apparently introduced administratively in 1872 without a formal change in the Ordinance: Blue Book, 1872. See also Despatch No. 110, December 17th, 1872, Governor, Sierra Leone to Secretary of State, ADM 1/463 (penal diet and shot drill in force at Cape Coast Prison).

33. Regulations, 1876, reg. 14. The Regulations were a Schedule to the Prisons Ordinance.

34. Regulations, 1872, reg. 59.

35. *Ibid.*, reg. 58.
36. *Ibid.*, reg. 60.
37. *Ibid.*, reg. 51.
38. *Ibid.*, reg. 36. If the sentence was for less than three months, the period of shot drill was reduced to two months for a sentence of two to three months, and to one month, if the sentence was less than two months. The Governor-in-Council later added crank drill and treadmill as permissible alternatives: Order-in-Council, March 26th, 1885. No treadmill, however, was ever constructed on the Gold Coast.
39. First-class prisoners received daily 1½ lb kenkey and ¼ lb of fish; second-class prisoners, 2½ lb kenkey and ½ lb of fish. Punishment diet was 1 lb of kenkey daily. Prisoners awaiting trial received second-class diet; women and children, first-class diet: *Blue Book*, 1872. The diet in 1876 was the same, except that a diet for white persons was added: ½ lb of bread, meat or fowl thrice a week, and 1 lb of fish a day four times a week; two eggs a day; ½ lb of rice daily; and tea and sugar: *Blue Book*, 1876.
40. *Blue Book*, 1900.
41. Despatch No. 119, March 28th, 1899, Acting Governor to Secretary of State, ADM 1/498.
42. Enclosure to Despatch No. 147, May 9th, 1899, Acting Governor to Secretary of State, ADM 1/498.
43. Minutes of September 7th, 1911, in MP 1803/1911.
44. *Annual Report, Prisons Department*, 1903. [Hereinafter *Departmental Report*].
45. Despatch No. 117, March 18th, 1898, Governor to Secretary of State, ADM 1/497.
46. *Departmental Report*, 1897; see also *Departmental Report*, 1901 ('impossible to ensure the severity of punishment which is necessary'); *Departmental Reports*, 1902, 1903; *Blue Books*, 1878, 1879, 1894, 1900, 1901, 1902, 1903, 1904, 1905, 1906.
47. Despatch No. 62, June 2nd, 1841, Governor, Sierra Leone, to Secretary of State, ADM 1/442.
48. Despatch No. 408, August 25th, 1901, Governor to Secretary of State, ADM 1/50.
49. Despatch No. 239, June 22nd, 1899, Acting Governor to Secretary of State, ADM 1/48.
50. Quoted in Despatch No. 385, September 13th, 1898, Governor to Secretary of State, ADM 1/498.
51. Minute of June 15th, 1905, in MP 1267/05.
52. Minute of July 3rd, 1906, in MP 1267/05.
53. *Departmental Report*, 1903.
54. Circular, April 22nd, 1876, ADM 1/393. Handwritten on the circular is a minute: 'The hair of female prisoners [on the Gold Coast] is never cut unless especially ordered.' In 1908 the Secretary of State ordered that, while it was permissible to shave the head of Moslem male prisoners, it was for-

bidden to shave his beard, for religious reasons: Despatch No. 232, Secretary of State to Governor, August 25th, 1908, in MP 1267/05.

55. Despatch No. 181, April 25th, 1898, Secretary of State to Governor, ADM 1/126.
56. Despatch No. 212, May 3rd, 1904, Governor to Secretary of State, ADM 1/152.
57. Despatch No. 408, August 25th, 1901, Governor to Secretary of State, ADM 1/501.
58. Despatch No. 204, April 8th, 1902, Secretary of State to Governor,ADM 1/146.
59. Elkin, *op. cit.*, 117.
60. The original draft appears in MP 1267/05.
61. Minute of April 25th, 1905, initialled J[ohn] R[odgers] (the Governor).
62. Prisons (Amendment) Bill, 1907. The Statement of Reasons appended to the Bill read: '. . . to remove from the ordinary form of labour involved in a sentence of hard labour and to retain solely for punitive purposes in connexion with prisons offences, shot drill, crank, [etc.] . . .'
63. Despatch No. 424, October 10th, 1905, Secretary of State to Governor, ADM 1/162.
64. Sessional Paper VIII, Legislative Council, 1919–20, ADM 14/15.
65. *Annual Report, Ashanti,* 1904.
66. *Departmental Report,* 1916.
67. *Departmental Report,* 1917.
68. Despatch No. 734, October 9th, 1918, Governor to Secretary of State ADM 1/558.
69. Sessional Paper VIII, Legislative Council, 1919–20, Appendix, ADM 14/15.
70. *Ibid.,* para. 48.
71. *Departmental Report,* 1910.
72. These were small prisons attached to D.C. headquarters at which were kept short-sentence prisoners. There were constant complaints about them: they were distant from Accra, and hard to inspect (*Departmental Report,* 1898); and warders seemed to rot away when assigned to them.
73. Minute annexed to enclosure to Despatch No. 1043, September 27th, 1921, Governor-General to Secretary of State, ADM 1/587.
74. Sessional Paper XII, Legislative Council, 1920–1, ADM 14/16.
75. Minute of November 2nd, 1915, MP 4925/15.
76. *Departmental Report,* 1906.
77. *Departmental Report,* 1910.
78. *Departmental Report,* 1918.
79. Despatch No. 100, March 7th, 1904, Governor to Secretary of State, ADM 1/506 (requesting that arrangements be made for Kittson to inspect English prisons while on leave). His deputy, Capt. Watson, inspected English prisons before coming to the Coast in 1905: Despatch No. 403, August 16th, 1904, Governor to Secretary of State, ADM 1/507. Kittson

acknowledged that Watson's experience in English prison administration 'while at home on leave' was of great assistance in formulating the proposed changes in the Regulations: Minute of February 27th, 1905, in MP 126/05.

80. *Departmental Report*, 1906.

81. *Departmental Report*, 1917.

82. *Departmental Report*, 1919; see also Despatch No. 426, May 26th, 1920, Governor to Secretary of State, ADM 1/578; MP 8750/20.

83. One of Cookson's objectives was to increase the powers of punishment of the Inspector-General of Prisons. The Attorney-General, however, vetoed this on the ground that 'the legal provision whereby prisoners can only be subjected to serious punishment by an *independent outside authority* is of fundamental importance for the protection of the prisoner. It is the rule in English prisons and should be retained here': Minute of May 23rd, 1921, in MP 15459/21.

84. Sessional Paper VIII, Legislative Council, 1919–20, ADM 14/15; Sessional Paper XII, Legislative Council, 1920–1, ADM 14/16; and see MP 1043/22.

85. Minute (undated) in MP 427/22.

86. Regulation 29 of 1922, December 9th, 1922.

87. P. 310.

88. Para. 145.

89. Now reg. 165.

90. 27 *Parliamentary Debates* 7.

91. 27 *Parliamentary Debates* 18.

92. *Annual Report*, 1962.

93. Extensively reconstructed in 1926.

94. *Annual Report*, 1949–50.

95. Sessional Paper III, 1951 (*Report of the Committee on Prisons*, 1951; hereinafter, the *M'Carthy Report*).

96. *Ibid.*, para. 17.

97. *Annual Report*, 1962.

98. Information supplied by the Prisons Department.

99. In 1869, when the Secretary of State was most vigorous in urging severe punishment, he wrote that Accra Prison, where six men were crowded into 1,200 cubic feet of space, suffered from 'animal overcrowding'. In 1962, the average cubic space per prisoner in the central prisons was about 180 cubic feet of space—less than the amount of space per person which led to the Secretary of State's harsh epithet almost a century before: Despatch No. 95, November 19th, 1869, Secretary of State to Administrator, Gold Coast, ADM 1/27.

100. *Departmental Report*, 1933–4.

101. *Ibid.*

102. *Annual Report*, 1962. Some cobbling is nevertheless still done for private persons.

103. *Departmental Report*, 1927–8.
104. *Annual Report*, 1962.
105. *Annual Report*, 1949–50.
106. Information supplied by the Prisons Department.
107. *Departmental Report*, 1937–8; see also 1933–4.
108. *Annual Report*, 1962.
109. Information supplied by the Prisons Department.
110. *Annual Report*, 1954–55.
111. Despatch No. 583, June 10th, 1921, Governor to Secretary of State, ADM 1/585. Governor Guggisberg suggested an audit of the April 1920 accounts; the results seemed too good! See also *Departmental Report*, 1923–4.
112. Objections had earlier been raised that persons under compulsion should not be put to degrading labour, and Cookson agreed. Sessional Paper VIII, Legislative Council, 1919–20, ADM 14/15, para. 48.
113. In Drake and Omari, eds., *Social Work in West Africa*, 79 (1962). Mr Eyison was writing about events within his own memory, so that despite the earlier decision to stop requiring such labour from prisoners, it must have continued to fairly recent times.
114. As early as 1911, the *Departmental Report* complained that it was difficult to find sufficient work for the prisoners intramurally.
115. Information supplied by the Prisons Department.
116. Regulations, 1958, reg. 18. The Regulations were observed only by chance until relatively recently.
117. *Departmental Report*, 1931–2.
118. *Departmental Report*, 1947–8.
119. Information supplied by the Prisons Department.
120. *Departmental Report*, 1928–9.
121. Information supplied by the Prisons Department.
122. Annual Report, 1951–2. The rule is still in force.
123. Annual Report, 1962.
124. Information supplied by the Prisons Department.
125. *Annual Report*, 1962.
126. *Ibid.*
127. Selected second offenders were originally added to relieve overcrowding elsewhere, and the experiment proved to be a success: *Annual Report*, 1954–5.
128. Information supplied by the Prisons Department.
129. The M'Carthy Committee in 1951 reached the same conclusion: *M'Carthy Report*, para. 11.
130. *Annual Report*, 1950–1.
131. *Annual Report*, 1962.
132. Information supplied by the Prisons Department.
133. *Blue Book*, 1934.
134. Now the Director of Prisons, with the approval of the Minister: Regs., 1958, reg. 52.

135. 'Religious' omitted in Regs., 1958, reg. 52.
136. Regs., 1876, reg. 45.
137. *Departmental Report*, 1946.
138. *Annual Report*, 1950–1.
139. *Annual Report*, 1962.
140. Information supplied by the Prisons Department.
141. *Annual Report*, 1962.
142. Information supplied by the Prisons Department.
143. *Annual Report*, 1948–9.
144. Information supplied by the Prisons Department.
145. Regs., 1958, reg. 8. On admission, hair is 'decently cut if it is considered necessary'.
146. Regs., 1958, First Schedule. Inquiry among inmates at the Borstal Institution at least suggests that the Schedules are adhered to reasonably well.
147. In 1902 the *Departmental Report* stated: 'The cranks being out of order, they should be repaired, as it is a form of punishment the prisoners object to.'
148. *Departmental Report*, 1901.
149. *Annual Report*, 1962.
150. Despatch No. 125, May 20th, 1892, Secretary of State to Governor, ADM 1/97.
151. Enclosure to Despatch No. 16, January 26th, 1892, Secretary of State to Governor, ADM 1/96.
152. Circular January 27th, 1892, ADM 1/406.
153. Regulation No. 7 of 1905.
154. Circular November 17th, 1872, ADM 1/396.
155. Regs., 1958, reg. 66 (1).
156. Regulation No. 29 of 1922, reg. 94; see MP 427/22.
157. *Annual Report*, 1947–8.
158. *Annual Report*, 1950–1.
159. Information supplied by the Prisons Department.
160. Information supplied by the Prisons Department.
161. Information supplied by the Prisons Department.
162. Information supplied by the Prisons Department.
163. African warders were employed from the earliest times. The standard at first was very low, especially for the (illiterate) Escort Warders. Acting Governor Low ascribed this to the haphazard hiring policies of the officers-in-charge, who were in the habit of employing 'the first man they met in the street', and clothing him 'in a uniform conspicuous for its brilliancy'. This 'peculiar arrangement', he wrote, did much 'to prevent the prisoners from realizing the fact that they are under sentence for their offences'—apparently despite penal labour, strict diet, and the silent system! Despatch No. 239, June 22nd, 1899, Governor to Secretary of State, ADM 1/48. In 1910, the Governor complained that African warders could not maintain discipline when dealing with their own countrymen:

Despatch No. 331, June 1st, 1910, Governor to Secretary of State, ADM 1/520. The introduction of recruit warder training courses did much to help, however, and there have been no complaints about the efficiency of the warders in any of the *Reports* over the past three decades. The last English Director of Prisons retired in 1962.

164. *Annual Report*, 1962.

Index

473